STUDIES IN CHRISTIAN HISTORY AND THOUGHT

Holiness:
The Soul of Quakerism

An Historical Analysis of the Theology of Holiness in the Quaker Tradition

STUDIES IN CHRISTIAN HISTORY AND THOUGHT

A full listing of all titles in this series
appears at the end of this book.

STUDIES IN CHRISTIAN HISTORY AND THOUGHT

Holiness:
The Soul of Quakerism

An Historical Analysis of the Theology of Holiness in the Quaker Tradition

Carole Dale Spencer

Foreword by Arthur O. Roberts

WIPF & STOCK · Eugene, Oregon

Wipf and Stock Publishers
199 W 8th Ave, Suite 3
Eugene, OR 97401

Holiness: The Soul of Quakerism
An Historical Analysis of the Theology of Holiness in the Quaker Tradition
By Spencer, Carole Dale
Copyright©2007 Paternoster
ISBN 13: 978-1-55635-809-8
ISBN 10: 1-55635-809-1
Publication date 1/15/2008

This Edition Published by Wipf and Stock Publishers by arrangement with Paternoster

Paternoster
9 Holdom Avenue
Bletchley
Milton Keyes, MK1 1QR
Great Britain

Series Preface

This series complements the specialist series of *Studies in Evangelical History and Thought* and *Studies in Baptist History and Thought* for which Paternoster is becoming increasingly well known by offering works that cover the wider field of Christian history and thought. It encompasses accounts of Christian witness at various periods, studies of individual Christians and movements, and works which concern the relations of church and society through history, and the history of Christian thought.

The series includes monographs, revised dissertations and theses, and collections of papers by individuals and groups. As well as 'free standing' volumes, works on particular running themes are being commissioned; authors will be engaged for these from around the world and from a variety of Christian traditions.

A high academic standard combined with lively writing will commend the volumes in this series both to scholars and to a wider readership.

Series Editors

Alan P.F. Sell, Visiting Professor at Acadia University Divinity College, Nova Scotia, Canada

David Bebbington, Professor of History, University of Stirling, Stirling, Scotland, UK

Clyde Bibfield, Professor Associate in History, University of Sheffield, UK

Gerald Bray, Anglican Professor of Divinity, Beeson Divinity School, Samford University, Birmingham, Alabama, USA

Grayson Carter, Associate Professor of Church History, Fuller Theological Seminary SW, Phoenix, Arizona, USA

CONTENTS

Foreword by Arthur O. Roberts	xi
Preface	xiii
Acknowledgements	xv
Abbreviations	xvii
Chapter 1 A New Perspective on Quaker History	1
1.1 Introduction	1
1.2 Defining Holiness	3
1.3 Methodology: Theology as Autobiography, Biography, and Hagiography	4
1.4 Holiness in Christian History	6
1.4.1 A Typology of Holiness	10
1.5 The Essential Elements of Holiness Quakerism	14
1.5.1 Scripture	15
1.5.2 Eschatology	17
1.5.3 Conversion	18
1.5.4 Evangelism	22
1.5.5 Charisma	23
1.5.6 Suffering	27
1.5.7 Mysticism	28
1.5.8 Perfection	32
1.5.9 Summary	33
1.6 The Essentially Orthodox Nature of Quaker Holiness	34
1.7 Theories of Quaker History	39
1.7.1 Jones, Nuttall, and Barbour: The Mystic vs. Puritan Debate	40
1.7.2 Melvin Endy: The Spiritualist Synthesis	43
1.7.3 Lewis Benson: Prophetic Quakerism	46
1.7.4 Douglas Gwyn: Apocalyptic Quakerism	48
1.7.5 Richard Bailey: Divinization	49
1.7.6 Arthur Roberts: Evangelical Holiness	54
1.7.7 John Punshon: Evangelical Holiness, Non-Mystical	55
1.7.8 Thomas Hamm: Holiness as Non-Quaker	55
1.7.9 Summary of Previous Theories	56
1.8 Chapter Summary	57

Chapter 2 Quaker Development – Holiness Interpreted   59
2.1 Mysticism, Perfection and Puritanism in the Seventeenth Century   59
2.2 George Fox   63
2.3 James Nayler   69
    2.3.1 Summary and Conclusions   73
2.4 Edward Burrough   75
2.5 Robert Barclay: Theology of Perfection   75
    2.5.1 Perfection, *Epektatis,* and Detachment   79
    2.5.2 Summary and Conclusions   81
2.6 Thomas Story: Holiness in the Transitional Period   83
    2.6.1 Conclusion: The Poetry of Perfection   87
2.7 Chapter Summary: Holiness in Post-Restoration Quakerism   89

Chapter 3 Holiness in the Golden Age of Quietism   91
3.1 Quietism and the Apophatic   91
3.2 Anthony Benezet and the First Quaker Reformation:
    Holiness Renewed   92
    3.2.1 The Spirit of Prayer: Quietist Spirituality   98
    3.2.2 Summary and Conclusions   103
3.3 Stephen Grellet: Evangelical Social Holiness   105
    3.3.1 Conversion   107
    3.3.2 Asceticism   114
    3.3.3 Summary and Conclusions   116
3.4 Chapter Summary   119

Chapter 4 The Breakdown of Holiness and Divergent Paths   121
4.1 Schism   121
    4.1.1 The Gnostic Theology of Elias Hicks   123
    4.1.2 The Theology of Job Scott   125
    4.1.3 Quietist Conversion Narratives   128
    4.1.4 Summary and Conclusions   133
4.2 Joseph John Gurney and Orthodoxy: Non-Mystical Holiness   135
    4.2.1 Conversion   138
    4.2.2 Perfection   142
    4.2.3 Mysticism   143
    4.2.4 Summary and Conclusions   146
4.3 John Wilbur: Radical Holiness   148
    4.3.1 Divine Indwelling   150
    4.3.2 Quaker Communion   153
    4.3.3 Summary and Conclusions   155
4.4 Chapter Summary   157

Contents

Chapter 5 Quakerism and the Holiness Revival — 161
5.1 The American Holiness Movement — 161
5.2 Reactions to Revivalism: Joel Bean — 164
    5.2.1 Anti-Revivalism — 168
    5.2.2 Summary and Conclusions — 172
5.3 British Reactions to Revivalism — 173
    5.3.1 Walter Robson — 175
    5.3.2 Robson's Experience of Revivalism — 177
    5.3.3 Summary and Conclusions — 182
5.4 Hannah Whitall Smith: Holiness Evangelist — 183
    5.4.1 Smith's Religious Experience — 186
    5.4.2 Summary and Conclusions — 190
5.5 Chapter Summary — 192

Chapter 6 Holiness and Quakerism in the Twentieth Century — 195
6.1 Holiness and Modernity — 195
    6.1.1 Jones and Mysticism — 196
    6.1.2 Jones and the New Quakerism — 198
    6.1.3 Jones and the Inner Light — 200
    6.1.4 Jones on Barclay and Calvin — 202
    6.1.5 Jones and Cambridge Platonism — 204
    6.1.6 Conclusions — 205
    6.1.7 Summary — 206
6.2 J. Rendel Harris: Modernist Holiness Mystic — 207
    6.2.1 Harris and the Holiness Movement — 209
    6.2.2 The Mysticism of J. Rendel Harris — 211
    6.2.3 Harris' Writings on Holiness — 213
    6.2.4 Quakerism, Modernism, and Holiness — 217
    6.2.5 Summary and Conclusions — 221
6.3 The Case of William Littleboy: Non-Mystical, Non-Holiness — 224
6.4 Thomas Kelly: Holiness via Liberalism — 228
6.5 Everett Lewis Cattell: Holiness via Evangelicalism — 232
    6.5.1 Summary and Conclusions — 234
6.6 Contemporary Trends: A Renewed Evangelical Mysticism — 234
6.7 Chapter Summary — 236

Chapter 7 Quaker Holiness: A New Lens — 239
7.1 Holiness and Worship: The Unimportance of Forms — 239
    7.1.1 Holiness and Silence — 241
7.2 Re-Mapping Quakerism — 243
7.3 Conclusions — 248
7.4 Summary — 250

Appendixes
A. Sources of Early Quaker Mysticism 255
    1. Augustinian Mysticism and Deification 255
    2. Bridal Mysticism and Love Mysticism 258
    3. Monastic Perfection 260
B. The Relationship between Quakers and other Seventeenth Century Holiness Movements 265
    1. Devotion to the Sacred Heart of Christ 265
    2. Barclay and Catholicism 266
    3. Jansenism 268
    4. Quietism 269
C. The Relationship between Quakers and Methodists in the Eighteenth Century 271
    1. Wesley and Quakers 271
    2. Wesley and Mysticism 277
    3. William Law and Quaker Quietism 280
    4. Law's Anti-Quaker Period 283
    5. Law Moves Toward Quakerism 285
    6. Law and Quaker Holiness 287
    7. Law and Wesley 291

Bibliography 293

Index 313

Foreword

"Be perfect," said Jesus, "as your Heavenly Father is perfect" (Matt 5: 48). Jesus' words challenge. They penetrate the vicarious comfort of gloriously flawed cultural heroes. Holiness haunts us! Deep within we hear its soundings. If we cover our ears the Divine voice trumpets. If we shroud our souls with darkness, the Light shines through cracks in the psyche.

A hunger and thirst for righteousness gnaws at us. We crave its ethical fruits if not its spiritual roots. The *good*, the *true*, and the *beautiful*-- like doves from the ark of God these ideals circle about searching for solid ground in a soggy world. Holiness summons body, mind, and spirit. Sometimes that call blares like a siren; at other times it wafts gentle as a breeze. If we hunger and thirst after righteousness, promised Jesus, we will be filled.

In this excellent book Carole Spencer elaborates how Quakers have responded to Jesus' compelling summons and appealing promise. She provides a careful analysis of Quaker holiness teaching and experience with its supportive biblical texts, and relates this witness to other Christian theologies.

Using, sociological models, historical description, logical analyses, and chapter summaries, Spencer provides a comprehensive interpretation of this Christian doctrine as taught and lived by one Christian group. After relating Quaker concepts of perfection to typologies of spirituality and theology, Spencer posits Quakerism as a "new type of holiness movement that combined elements from each of these models in a radical and innovative way." The text explicates distinct Quaker expressions of holiness doctrine and practice, the interface with Wesleyan theology, and historical development through the energies and insights of Quaker leaders throughout the centuries.

Her inclusion of suffering as an aspect of holiness is insightful. Friends recently or currently living amid civil violence or under religious persecution can resonate with first generation Quakers who experienced much suffering and who understood martyrdom "as the supreme form of witness to perfection."

With Spencer's work, historiography regains access to mystical aspects of normative Quaker perfectionism. Responding to Rufus Jones' focus upon mystical rather than Puritan antecedents, Geoffrey Nuttall, Hugh Barbour, and Arthur Roberts, among others, at mid-twentieth century had recovered Quakerism's neglected Puritan setting. Spencer, however, posits a biblically based *Christ-mysticism* as integral to Quaker holiness theology. As one of the Quaker scholars examined, I find her conclusions fair and discerning, leading me to accept the word *mystical* (now freed from Platonic overlays), as an apt characterization of my own evangelical views.

Carole Spencer's descriptions of holiness theology in recent times contributes greatly to an understanding of the contemporary scene. Her conclusion is well-stated: "This study requires all scholars of Quakerism to revisit their assumptions and research findings and look again at the central place holiness has had in the theological history of Quakerism."

Arthur O. Roberts
Newberg, Oregon

Preface

I was born and raised in Philadelphia, Pennsylvania, a city founded by the Quaker William Penn, as the capital of the Quaker colony known as "The Holy Experiment." Quaker institutions such as schools, meetinghouses, and colleges, and local Quaker history were part of my childhood landscape. Yet I was a complete outsider to the Quaker community, never attended a Quaker meeting, and had no direct connections to any Quakers or their institutions.

My real introduction to Quakers came in my mid '30s while enduring a long period of disenchantment with the evangelical tradition in which I was raised. A friend, sensing my spiritual malaise, loaned me a small book called *Testament of Devotion*, by the Quaker, Thomas Kelly. When I opened to the first page and read "Meister Eckhart wrote, 'As thou art in church or cell, that same frame of mind carry out into the world, into its turmoil and its fitfulness.' Deep within us all there is an amazing inner sanctuary of the soul, a holy place, a Divine Center, a speaking Voice, to which we may continually return. Eternity is at our hearts...." I read on entranced, and quickly devoured the book. I felt as if a door had opened for me into a spiritual reality where God could be known and felt in a way I had never experienced before. I suddenly realized that God was closer to me than I was to myself.

Little did I know then, that I had been given my first mystical glimpse into holiness as it was embedded within the Quaker tradition. Thus began my exploration into Quaker history and theology, a process that paralleled and eventually converged with my own spiritual journey. Quakerism provided a door for me to enter into the mystical dimension of the Christian faith I had long been searching for.

I will always remain in part an "outsider" to Friends, not having been born into the tradition. But by having no family history to revere or reject, nor a particular version or vision of Quakerism to defend or assail, I could explore Quakerism like a traveler in a wholly new country.

As my research deepened, my faith deepened. Despite the fact that this study of holiness was a product of the academic discipline of writing a doctoral dissertation, the process itself became a journey of spiritual discovery. God became present to me as I entered into the lives and absorbed the writings of men and women, largely unknown and mostly forgotten, who had experienced the love of God as mystical union, and who became my spiritual mentors.

Acknowledgements

Of the many friends, colleagues, and contemporary mentors who have encouraged, inspired, and stimulated my thinking during the course of this work, I will only mention a few: Marge Abbott, Josiek Jung, Doug Gwyn, John Punshon, Gay Pilgrim, Sherry Olsen, Vail Palmer, and Hugh Barbour. Of the many individuals with whom I discussed particular aspects of my research, Alessandro Falcetta, deserves special mention for his helpful correspondence. I would acknowledge my great debt to the Woodbrooke Quaker Study Center for providing not only the great wealth of research materials in their library and special collections, but also for the community network and support they offered me over four summers of residency. A special note of thanks goes to the librarian, Mary Jo Clogg (now retired) and staff, for their assistance during the course of my research. My sojourn with the vibrant, stimulating environment of the Woodbrooke community was a reward in itself for the many days and nights of hard work.

I would also like to acknowledge my colleagues at George Fox Evangelical Seminary, especially MaryKate Morse, who has encouraged me on the scholarly path and has been a spiritual guide to me for many years. I am especially grateful for the many students who listened and responded to bits and portions of my work incorporated into class lectures. Sara Cohoe, who proofread the draft, deserves a special word of appreciation for taking on that task so ably. Thanks too, must go to Sarah Hoggatt for her technical assistance on the final manuscript.

Two towering Quaker scholars whose assistance made this book possible are Arthur Roberts and Ben Pink Dandelion. Arthur Roberts was not only an advisor in the formal sense, giving direction and counsel, but also offered wisdom and inspiration beyond the purely academic. And as for my thesis advisor, Ben Pink Dandelion, I owe him more than I can express. He provided much needed structure, gave wise counsel, and helped spark many of the ideas and insights that made this book possible. I will always be indebted to him for the unfailing attentiveness he bestowed on my work, and the gentle rigor with which he prodded me in flagging times.

And finally, I want to thank all of the individuals from the Northwest Yearly Meeting of Friends who were brave enough to plough through the original manuscript in its dissertation form, and affirm to me that my perspective and analysis of Quakerism and holiness truly made sense to them. I also appreciate all those Friends who were willing to spend an entire weekend listening to me present the material in this book at Twin Rocks Seminar-by-the-Sea and engage in helpful dialogue and discussion. Special thanks goes to Ken Beebe, director of Twin Rocks Friends Camp and Conference Center for inviting me to do the Seminar, and for his genuine interest in my work.

ABBREVIATIONS

BF   *British Friend*

CQ   *Congregational Quarterly*

FQ   *Friends' Quarterly*

JFHS *Journal of the Friends Historical Society*

JR   *Journal of Religion*

NRSV *New Revised Standard Version*

MH   *Methodist History*

PG   *Patrologia Graeca*, J. P. Migne (ed.)

PL   *Patrologia Latina*, J. P. Migne (ed.)

QH   *Quaker History*

QRT *Quaker Religious Thought*

QT   *Quaker Theology*

TF   *The Friend (London)*

CHAPTER 1

A New Perspective on Quaker History

1.1 Introduction

The religious tradition known as Quakerism, which began in mid-seventeenth-century England, is called today by several names: Quakers, the Society of Friends, and the Friends Church. The beliefs, spiritual practices, and lifestyles within its various branches are widely divergent. Not only does Quakerism embrace a range of theological positions from fundamentalism to universalism, but also it includes a wide array of spiritualities from charismatic to New Age to post-Christian, and to the blending of other religions to create Buddhist-Quakers and Jewish-Quakers (Dandelion, 1996; Huber, 2001). Many religious denominations contain broad spectrums of religious beliefs, but Quakers today are arguably among the most diverse. For not only are they polarized ideologically between Christocentric[1] and Universalist,[2] but also they are uniquely divided by two forms of worship. Although Quakers are connected by a strong sense of history, having maintained a relatively unified vision for almost 200 years, links or commonalities between liberal[3] Quaker Meetings and Evangelical[4] Friends Churches today are barely visible even to the most discerning observer.

The purpose of this book is to determine what unifying themes or values exist in Quaker history and theology, traceable to its beginnings, that can be identified as a distinct Quaker spirituality. The possibility of finding a common link first came to my attention when I read "Quietism preserved the soul of Quakerism" (Punshon, 1984, 102). If an eighteenth-century Quaker tradition that seemed so radically different from the early period could preserve the soul of Quakerism, I wondered how the "soul of Quakerism" could be described. Silent worship and the Inward Light are the most common identifiers. As I examined subsequent movements, such as the nineteenth-century Holiness Revival and the modern Evangelical Friends Church, I found

---

[1] A Christocentric Quaker believes in the centrality of Christ in religious experience.

[2] A Universalist celebrates the universality of all religious experience.

[3] A liberal may be Christocentric or Universalist in orientation, allowing for a wide variety of personal religious experience with an emphasis on ethics rather than on beliefs and doctrines.

[4] An evangelical has an inward experience of conversion based on faith in Christ as Savior, accepts the authority of the Bible and traditional orthodox Christian doctrine, and is committed to spreading the faith through evangelism.

that their historians believed they, too, preserved the soul of Quakerism, yet silent worship and the Inward Light were rejected (Beebe, 1968; LaShana, 1969; Roberts, 1975; Williams, 1987).

Arthur Roberts, a prominent historian from the evangelical tradition, claims "Fox wove his doctrinal teachings around the concept of holiness" (1953, 147-8). My book argues that holiness is the paradigmatic theme of Quaker history and theology. It proposes to show that holiness is the key to unlocking the complex interpretative problems that revolve around the origin of Quakerism and its relationship to other spiritual movements, its place within the broader Christian tradition, and the relationship of later Quaker developments to its original insights and essence. This study establishes the nature and shape of Quaker holiness, traces themes and variations through Quaker history, and explores implications for remapping the standard diagram of the evolution of Quakerism.

For early Quakers, holiness began with a mystical experience of union with God. Holiness required an experience of encounter and illumination that went beyond the "faith alone" and "imputed righteousness" of the Protestant Reformation. Quakerism, rather than a Puritan culmination of Protestant radicalism taken to its ultimate conclusion as is generally received (Barbour, 1964; Nuttall, 1992; Punshon, 1984), was a radical holiness movement with greater continuity with medieval mysticism and monastic ideals than has been acknowledged in previous scholarship. Quaker holiness combined many historical types of holiness, including such non-Protestant types as asceticism, contemplative mysticism, and apophatic theology, and synthesized them into a new form of ethical and mystical perfection. Quaker holiness was innovative only in its emergence in an English puritan context, shaped by the political and social circumstances of its beginnings in Anglican soil. Although early Quakers were denounced and persecuted by mainstream puritans, Presbyterians, and establishment Anglicans, Quakerism did not depart in any significant way from orthodox Christian foundations and was rather more biblical and more incarnational than most of its seventeenth-century opponents.

Early Quaker holiness was closer to patristic concepts of deification than to Protestant Reformation soteriology. Although the concept of the "Inner Light" or, more correctly, the Inward Light, is claimed to be the unique contribution of Quakerism to religion and the concept that provides structure and definition to the movement, this study finds holiness to be the overarching theme, not replacing the Inward Light, but subsuming it within the way of holiness. Holiness, therefore, provides the ongoing thread that serves as the common denominator of normative Quakerism. This study is the first attempt to trace the theme of holiness and its interpretations through three centuries of Quaker history. Using the lens of holiness or perfection as the paradigmatic theme of Quaker theology changes the generally received mapping of Quaker history. In particular, the nineteenth-century revival movement and its vigorous descendent, the Evangelical Friends Church, shifts to a more central location in Quaker evolution and can be seen as a legitimate adaptation in continuity with historical Quakerism rather than as a radical departure. The first chapter explores the range of meanings for the terms *holiness*, *perfection*, and *mysticism* and sets the parameters for the way the terms are used in this study. It also demonstrates the need for the study and the methodology used. And lastly, chapter one surveys previous scholarship that has explored the sources and complex relationships between Quakerism and other spiritual traditions and evaluates its findings in relation to the holiness theory.

1.2 Defining Holiness

In attempting to define holiness, *The Oxford Companion to Christian Thought* suggests that it "embraces a range of concepts to do with the otherness of God and the character of a human life which is ordered so as to be consciously centered on [God] and [God's] service" (Davies, 2000, 302-3). The *Encyclopedia of Catholicism* defines holiness as "a spiritual quality derived from participation in the life of God who is the source of all holiness" (McBrien, 1995, 617). In the New Testament *hagios* is the Greek word translated as holiness. Holiness is characteristic of the saints, *hagioi*. Christians, as saints, are to "present their bodies as a living sacrifice, holy and acceptable to God (Rom. 12:1). Holiness is associated with the notion of suffering, death of self (Heb. 9), and rebirth through the Spirit into purity (freedom from "the body of sin," meaning "original sin") and wisdom (true *gnosis*, divine, not human). By the third century holiness became connected to ascetic ideals, such as virginity, poverty, solitude (especially monasticism), and the liturgical life of the church. Holiness became divided into a category of being and of acting, with the distinction between the active and the contemplative life.

In this study, holiness is defined as "a spiritual quality in which human life is ordered and lived out as to be consciously centered *in* God." For early Quakers holiness was centered *in* and *with* God as participation and union. Union with God, or union with Christ, or "Christ in me" for the Puritan was metaphorical and analogical—God and human could not really touch—but for the Quaker those phrases were not metaphors but reality, ultimate union, *unus spiritus*.

Quaker holiness is closer to the Roman Catholic understanding, but with a rigorous Puritan ethic of obedience.[5] In Catholicism, holiness is synonymous with perfection, and early Quakers often used the terms interchangeably. Perfection was the natural vocation of the sanctified Christian: growth in grace

---

[5] In the Roman Catholic understanding of holiness, response to God's presence results in virtuous acts performed with varying degrees of love, but the more they are performed in pure love, the more perfect the holiness, which, in turn, depends on the individual's openness to the love of God (McBrien, 1995, 617).

and love. Holiness, therefore, is inseparably linked with a doctrine of perfection. Perfection is the *telios* of *hagios*. New birth is the beginning of *hagios; telios* is the end (but paradoxically an end that never ends) to which *hagios* points and proceeds. To be reborn means to begin the process of perfection in love. Quaker holiness necessitates a concept of perfection. Holiness is paradoxically unending beginnings, dynamically spiraling, thus eternal, the infinite Light, "God as all in all" (Eph. 4:6). Perfection refers to the culmination or fullness of an ever-deepening relationship with Christ in God.

1.3 Methodology: Theology as Autobiography, Biography, and Hagiography

In early Quakerism theology was experiential and mystical (*cognitio Dei experimentalis*), therefore developed and formulated most effectively as autobiography.[6] Autobiography was supplemented by biography and then sanctified by hagiography. This study looks at Quakerism as holiness (*hagios*) by way of hagiography (lives of the saints), which encompasses the literature of personal religious experience of *hagioi*. Along with the Bible, hagiography and its related literature (rather than doctrinal treatises) have been the primary textual means by which the Christian faith has been transferred through generations. After the Bible, the lives of saints, their journals or spiritual diaries, and their devotional manuals have been the most formative influences in the teaching of holiness.[7]

To examine the concept of holiness and the Quaker understanding of it, I have first created a typology of holiness based on the macrocosm of Christian history and the microcosm of Quaker history within that larger framework. The typology of holiness provides a helpful method to measure and compare the different expressions of holiness and to identify the continuities of holiness in Quaker history. It also provides a constructive understanding of the breadth and depth of holiness spirituality from doctrinal to experiential to mystical to ethical. Second, I identify and isolate the eight essential characteristics of early Quaker theology and show the relationship between these defining elements and the concept of holiness. I show how these key elements have been changed,

---

[6] One significant exception is Barclay's *Apology* (1676), which is in part a scholastically constructed systematic theology, but is also in part a mystical theology in which Barclay at times inserts himself and his own experience. Mystical theology is defined as "theoretical treatments of the values and methods of mystical experience" (Ozment, 1973, 1).

[7] Of course, the Bible itself is essentially a record of the lives of the saints, those through whom God is revealed and whom the New Testament refers to as "so great a cloud of witnesses" (Heb. 12:1 NRSV).

eliminated, reduced, or heightened at different periods within different branches over time (see Figure 4, p. 323).

Third, I take a narrative approach, examining written texts, autobiographies, journals, biographies, and devotional and theological writings of key leaders to demonstrate how these influential figures described, interpreted, and appropriated holiness into their lives. More important than doctrinal formulation, and essential because Quakers were theoretically non-creedal, was the actual depiction of lives through which readers could be given the means to understand and measure themselves through the model of earlier saints. Holiness (other than Barclay's early formulations, see 2.5) was not emphasized so much as a doctrine, but rather as experience, modeled by the lives of Quaker saints.

The most common form of teaching and Quakers' main reading material were the journals of its saints, George Fox's *Journal* being the prototype (Wright, 1932). These journals were written to describe and define a life of holiness and to teach by example. This study uses a similar approach to understand holiness as it came to be expressed in different eras and in different contexts. It explores holiness as the lived lives of representative Quaker leaders and exemplars.

Sometimes these exemplars wrote about holiness in theological language; sometimes they wrote about holiness in mystical, poetic, metaphorical language. The varieties of expression were greatest among the first generation of Quakers, expressed in the following ways:

1. Ecstatic Rapture (example: George Fox's "openings," see 2.2)
2. Theology of Perfection (example: Naylor's early writings, see 2.3)
3. Testimony to the experience (example: Dewsbury's narrative, see 1.5.3)
4. Creed—Statement of belief—despite being technically non-creedal (example: Burrough, see 2.4)
5. Existentially as quality of life or "the spirit of holiness" (example: Naylor's last testament, see 2.3)
6. Doctrinal Proposition (example: Barclay's *Apology*, see 2.5)
7. Hymn or poem (example: Thomas Story's consecration hymn, see 2.6)
8. Literature of sufferings (example: Joseph Besse, *A Collection of Sufferings of the People called Quakers,* 2 vols., London, 1753, see 1.5.6)[8]

Often the most profound understanding of holiness comes at the end of the spiritual journey, at the *telios* of the Christian life. (Because of that belief, last words and testaments were considered highly significant and were often recorded.) Indeed, as Stanley Hauerwas describes so cogently, in words that

---

[8] Besse's writings were based on Foxe's *Acts and Monuments (Book of Martyrs)*. See also Knott, 1993, 218; Watkins, 1972, 183.

could easily be applied to Quakers, the goal [of holiness] is "not clearly known prior to the undertaking of the journey, but rather we learn better the nature of the end by being slowly transformed by the means necessary to pursue it" (1998, 128). In fact, as Hauerwas explains, it is often the case that we misunderstand the nature of perfection and the means necessary to pursue it, and thus we must learn by our suffering, our mistakes, and through tears and repentance (1998, 126, 128). Such was the case with James Naylor, who became convinced he was called to witness to perfection (Christ in him) through the actual imitation of Christ in the form of a dramatization of Jesus' entry into Jerusalem. The outcome of that event brought disgrace upon Quakers and charges of blasphemy upon Naylor, who was imprisoned and tortured. Yet, his recorded deathbed speech is perhaps the most profound and beautiful expression of holiness as *telios* learned via suffering though his own lived experience[9] (see 2.3). Stanley Hauerwas concludes: "We learn better the nature of the end [*telios*—perfection] by being slowly transformed by the means necessary to pursue it. Thus the only means to perceive rightly the end is by attending to the lives of those who have been and are on the way" (1998, 128). Holiness cannot finally be explained by a doctrine or definition or description of abstract stages.[10] It must in the end be modeled by a lived life. Chapters 2, 3, 4, and 5 examine the life and religious experiences of selected figures from Quaker history who represent different types of holiness across the spectrum of its evolving theology.

1.4 Holiness in Christian History

This study is concerned with the idea of holiness in Quakerism from its beginnings in the mid-seventeenth century to the twentieth century. But Quaker holiness cannot be understood without knowing its roots in earlier Christian traditions. Although Quakers claimed to be recovering the primitive church of the Apostolic age and declared the church from the post-apostolic to the seventeenth century to be in a state of apostasy, (Gwyn, 1986, 30), their dependence on a continuous tradition of interpretations of holiness is an important shaping influence. Quaker holiness did not simply appear *sui generis*. The Bible was the primary text for their idea of holiness, but how the

---

[9] This reality explains, for example, why John Wesley in the eighteenth century had a group known as the Penitents in his structures meant to promote holiness. The penitents were those who had "fallen" in one way or another, and after being "restored" had the ability to express and embody the greatest wisdom, maturity, and understanding of holiness (Watson, 1986).

[10] The classic pattern of spiritual growth throughout the Middle Ages was based on the three stages known as the "Triple Way" of purgation, illumination, and union (McGinn, 1991, 117).

holiness texts of scripture were exegeted through history influenced their reinterpretations of holiness.

Holiness and perfection are prominent themes in the New Testament and tend to be equated in the Gospel accounts. Jesus challenged his disciples with the vision "Be perfect therefore as your heavenly Father is perfect" (Matt. 5:48).[11] This injunction is often translated as "Be holy as your heavenly Father is holy." What this mandate of perfection entailed became interpreted in many ways, some mystical and some ethical. Holiness as a state of being "in Christ" is prominent in the Pauline letters. The phrase "in Christ" occurs 164 times in Pauline (and pseudo-Pauline) writings, for example, Gal. 3:27. The phrase "Christ in me" also occurs in Pauline writings (e.g., Gal 2:19-20, Phil. 1:21). The implication of being "in Christ" is freedom from sin: "if Christ be in you, the sinful body is dead" (Rom. 8:9). Holiness as perfection is also a common exhortation in the Johannine writings, in which the intimacy is extended to one of mutual indwelling: "Thou in me, and I in you" (John 14:20; 17:21) and metaphorically as "the vine and branches" (John 15:4-5).[12]

Perfection as a doctrine can be traced to the Apostolic Fathers. The Greek Fathers such as Irenaeus, Clement of Alexandria, Origen, and Gregory of Nyssa, and others to the end of the fifth century developed the concept of perfection into full-fledged doctrinal formulations, called *theosis,* or deification. In Eastern Orthodoxy the equivalent doctrinal term for perfection is *theosis,* the notion of the birth of the Word in the soul of the believer.[13] All Christians can enter the mystical life and can potentially be deified (McGinn, 1991, 268). Deification plays a central role in Eastern Orthodox theology and is inseparable from the doctrine of the incarnation, commonly stated in the expression "God became man so that man can become God"[14] (see 1.7.5).

---

[11] The parallel account in Luke reads, "Be merciful, just as your Father in heaven is merciful" (Luke 6:36).

[12] The Johannine concept of union as mutual indwelling is common to early Quaker writings; for example, Francis Howgill writes, "He that hath the Spirit of God, is in that which is equall, as God is equall, and his wayes equall; And he that is joined to the Lord is one spirit, there is unity, and the unity stands in equality it selfe. He that is born from above is the Sonne of God, and he said, 'I and my Father are one.' And when the Sonne is revealed, and speaks, the Father speaks in him, and dwells in him, and he in the Father" (sic) (1659, 22). See also, for example, Richard Farnworth (d. 1666), who published 49 tracts. In *A Bunch of Grapes and an Iron Rod*, Farnworth, one of the more poetic of the early preachers, used the closing, "Thine in the Vine, R. F." (1654a, 12).

[13] This is not the same thing as self-deification, which comes from hubris, or ego, nor does it mean absorption into God and the loss of distinction between the essence of God and the self. See Lossky, *The Mystical Theology of the Eastern Church,* 1976, especially pp. 9-10, 135-136, 154-155, for a detailed theological discussion of this Eastern Orthodox doctrine.

[14] See, for example, Irenaeus of Lyons (c. 130-200): "The Son of God became man that man might become son of God" (*Against Heresies*, III, 10, 2; III, 19, 1); Athanasius of

The Western Christian tradition is less comfortable with the term *deification*, (it is used primarily in the medieval mystical tradition). The Roman Catholic Church prefers instead the classic term "perfection" as the goal of holiness. In its definition of perfection, *The Harper Collins Encyclopedia of Catholicism* explains that in the Christian tradition "the goal of Christian life is union with God in love, and it recognizes love, expressed as virtuous life, as the means to this goal" (McBrien, 1995, 985). Perfection is the *sine qua non* of the Christian mystical tradition, the goal of the spiritual quest, the fruit of longing for God, the gift of the vision of God (*visio Dei*) or Divine union (*unio mystica*). In the mystical tradition, perfection is equated with the highest state of contemplative prayer, pure love, the prayer of the heart, love itself as knowing (*amor ipse intellectus est*).

Volumes of reflections and formulations on the nature of perfection as love are found in the treatises of Christian dogma, but in the popular mind perfection simply was, and is, equated with sinlessness. Numerous historical investigations have been written speculating on the source of this doctrine—is it biblical, Gnostic, pagan, or Eastern?[15] The Pauline epistles in particular easily support a doctrine of sinlessness here and now; thus, it is no surprise that early Quakers with their immersion in the Pauline epistles (see 1.6) would be drawn to a doctrine of perfection with claims of overcoming sin. But the ultimate source of the belief may not be in biblical texts or esoteric traditions, but in experience. As one historian has observed,

> Its origin was genuinely empirical. Sudden conversions, resulting in an apparently complete and effortless cessation, if not from *all* sins, at least from one or more besetting temptations, are perhaps a rarer phenomenon under the conditions of modern Western civilizations than in less sophisticated epochs or continents. But they do occur, as every student of religious psychology knows; and there have been times when they have occurred plentifully. There is no reason to suppose that the dawn of Christianity was not such a time; or that the contrast which S. Paul loves to draw between the present purity and the past infamy of his converts is based on anything less than fact. And if so, there was sufficient empirical ground for the doctrine that some Christians at least, under the influence of the Holy Spirit and the enthusiasm of conversion, passed through a change so sudden and so

---

Alexandria (c. 296-373): "The Word made himself 'bearer of the flesh' in order that human beings might become 'bearers of the Spirit'" (*On the Incarnation and Against the Arians*, 8); and Gregory of Nyssa (c.335-394): "The Word, in taking flesh, was mingled with humanity, and took our nature within himself, so that the human should be deified by this mingling with God: the stuff of our nature was entirely sanctified by Christ, the first fruits of creation" (*Against Apollinarius*, 2).

[15] See, for example, Bouyer, 1994.

far-reaching as to make them in effect, if perhaps only for a moment, new and sinless men. (Kirk, 1931, 233)

In Protestantism perfection is identified with sectarianism and is often viewed as a Gnostic heresy or sectarian obsession (Flew, 1934, xii). In Roman Catholicism perfection has been historically a special vocation, but it still lives as an ideal for all in Catholic spiritual theology. But in Eastern Orthodoxy perfection is the goal for all Christians and the very heart of Eastern Orthodox theology.

R. Newton Flew, who has written the only major, and now classic, historical study of the concept of perfection in Western Christian tradition from a Protestant (Methodist) perspective, concludes with a triumphal declaration that perfection is the mainstream of Christian theology:

The doctrine of Christian perfection—understood not as an assertion that a final attainment of the goal of the Christian life is possible in this world, but as a declaration that a supernatural destiny, a relative attainment of the goal which does not exclude growth, is the will of God for us in this world and is attainable – lies not merely upon the by-paths of Christian theology, but upon the high road. (1934, 397)

Yet, in Protestantism the doctrine of perfection has never become mainstream. How perfection might be applied to a life of faith was problematic for the Reformers, who eliminated special vocations to holiness and reduced the lofty, mystical speculations of union with God to faith alone. Thus, Luther had to conclude that Christians can never be more than *simul justus et peccator* (simultaneously justified and sinner). The doctrine of perfection in Reformation spirituality became a continuing source of controversy.[16] Perfection as the pursuit of holiness, whether culminating in a mystical vision of God or in an ecstatic heartfelt experience, has long been the central dynamic of spiritual renewal movements in Christian history. Spiritual reformers who challenge the Christian church to a higher standard of love, justice, and purity, as well as those who wish to inspire hope in the marginal, oppressed, and spiritually disillusioned, are invariably motivated by a vision of perfection attainable in real life. Hugh Barbour defined perfectionist movements as "movements that hungered for ethical purity for all true Christians, both as a call and as a possibility by the power of God" (1979, 2). Thus, in the Puritan context of

---

[16] Roman Catholicism has historically resolved the dilemma of perfection by offering a two-tier understanding: "command" for the religious, "counsel" (optional) for the layperson. In Protestantism the Anabaptist movement arose to reclaim the pure church, with high standards of holiness for all Christians, and spawned Puritanism in English Calvinism and Pietism in German Lutheranism.

seventeenth-century England, Quakerism emerged as a radical holiness movement recovering for Reformation Protestantism, the patristic and medieval mystical tradition of Christian perfection.

1.4.1   A Typology of Holiness

The concept of perfection in Christian history is closely related to the degree that union with God is deemed possible. A variety of terms reflecting different ways of expressing and experiencing that union are found in the literature of spirituality and theology. Some of the most common are: perfect love, union of wills, perfect obedience, union with Christ, contemplation, vision of God, deification, spiritual marriage, entire sanctification, and baptism of the Spirit. The metaphors or expressions used to convey holiness reflect the way that perfection is perceived, experienced and manifested in life, forming an institutional matrix or a distinct spiritual tradition. While typologies have the danger of oversimplification, they can also be helpful in mapping out complex patterns. Urban Holmes (1984, 3-5) has designed a typology that is widely used in the study and application of Christian spirituality (See Figure 1, p. 18). A circle with four quadrants of spirituality symbolizes this typology:

1. Kataphatic-Speculative
2. Kataphatic-Affective
3. Apophatic-Affective
4. Apophatic-Speculative[17]

This study adapts this model and expands upon it by using it as a matrix to represent four basic historical patterns or forms which holiness has taken in Christian tradition (see Figure 2, p. 19):

Quadrant 1: Sacramental/symbolic holiness
Quadrant 2: Experiential holiness
Quadrant 3: Contemplative holiness
Quadrant 4: Ascetical holiness

Hugh Barbour has distinguished six historical ideal types or models of perfection and identifies Quakerism as one type (1979, 2-3):

---

[17] Kataphatic means prayer or worship "with images"; apophatic, prayer or worship "without images" or beyond images, ideas, concepts, and intermediaries, often referred to as the *via negativa*. Affective refers to the feeling dimension, the heart or emotions; speculative, to the thinking dimension, illumination through the mind.

1. The "perfect obedience" or discipleship of the Anabaptists, Hussites, and Waldensians, and of the classic sects, which derived from them
2. The "perfectly surrendered will" of the radical Calvinists (Puritans)
3. The "perfect openness to guidance" of the Quakers
4. The "perfect love" or intention of the Wesleyan tradition
5. The "perfect humility" or self-kenosis of the monk, the Franciscan, and the Pietist
6. The "perfect inner stillness" of the Quietist or mystic[18]

For the purposes of this study Barbour's model will be applied synthetically. Barbour defines Quaker perfection as "perfect openness to guidance." This aspect is but one facet of the early Quaker understanding of holiness. This study will treat the Quaker model as a development and integration of earlier understandings of holiness, rather than a separate and distinct model focused primarily on divine guidance.[19]

By combining the basic structure of Urban Holmes' typology with an expansion of Barbour's types, this study proposes the following eight historical types as a way to construct and visualize a circle of holiness in Christianity up to the Quaker movement. (See Figure 3, p. 20):

1. Roman Catholic (real presence)
2. Lutheran (*sola fides*)
3. Puritan/Pietist (divine guidance)
4. Charismatic (Spirit-baptism)
5. Quietist (silence/passivity)
6. Mystical (*unio mystica*)
7. Monastic (obedience/renunciation)
8. Anabaptist (suffering/martyrdom)

Type 1 and 2 form the first quadrant, the Sacramental-Symbolic (Christ for us); Type 3 and 4 form the second quadrant, the Experiential (*unus spiritus*); Type 5 and 6 form the third quadrant, the Contemplative (union with God); and Type 7 and 8 form the fourth quadrant, the Ascetical (imitation of Christ) (see Figure 3).

This study argues that Quakerism emerged as a new type of holiness movement, which combined elements from each of these models in a radical and innovative way, forming a distinct Quaker expression of holiness. This holiness dispensed with the Catholic sacramental system, yet retained the real

---

[18] Barbour adds this type in a footnote as a derivation or subtype not relevant to his study because it leads beyond good and evil in ethics and "thus beyond all Awakenings except in the Buddhist sense" (1979, 3).

[19] Barbour admits that some persons or movements draw on more than one type (1979, 3).

presence of Christ in communion (Type 1) without the material elements. It incorporated the Lutheran notion of faith (Type 2), but added free will in a synergistic cooperation with grace. Emerging directly from a Puritan context, Quakers experienced rapturous love and divine leading (Type 3). The charismatic baptism of the Spirit brought empowerment and freedom from sin (Type 4). The passivity of Quietist prayer became incorporated in silent worship (Type 5). Union with God through Christ became the primary descriptor of the process of holiness (Type 6). The ascetical ideals of obedience and humility of monasticism were reframed for a lay movement (Type 7). And the ultimate imitation of Christ in his sufferings through persecution characterized Quaker holiness as a martyr spirituality in continuity with the earliest church and the sixteenth century Anabaptists (Type 8).

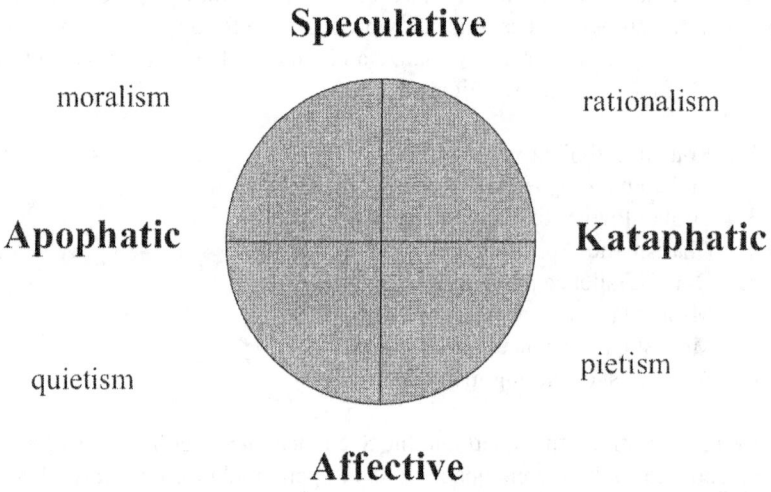

Figure 1: A Typology of Spirituality

Adapted from *A History of Christian Spirituality*
by Urban Holmes, 1980, 4.

A New Perspective on Quaker History

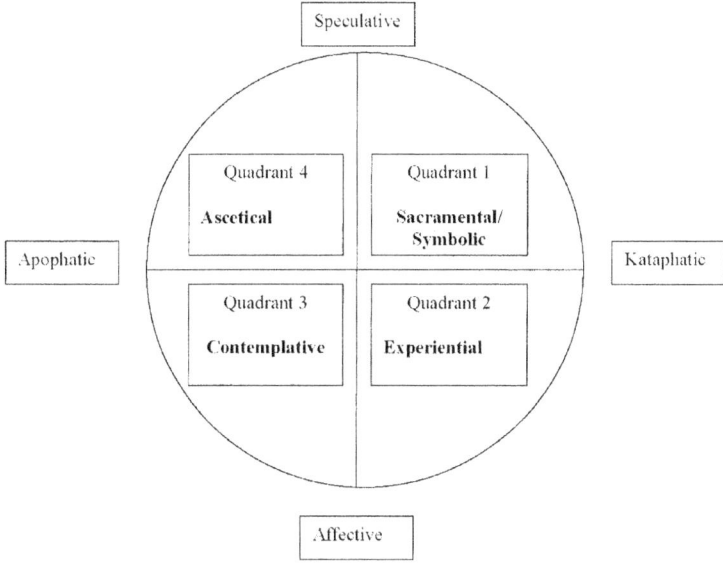

Figure 2: Four Types of Holiness

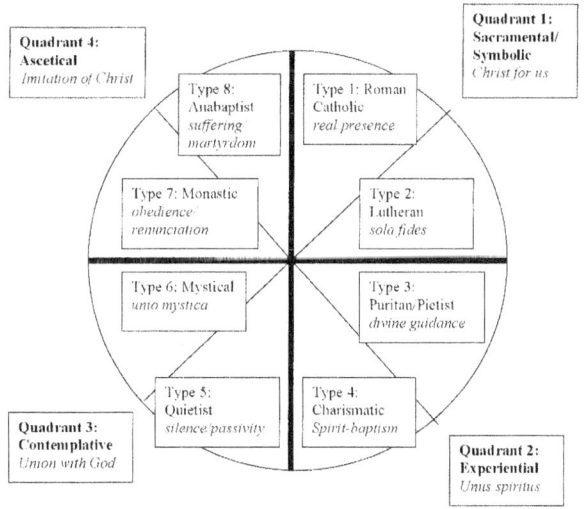

Figure 3: Eight Historical Traditions of Holiness

1.5 The Essential Elements of Holiness Quakerism

This study identifies eight essential elements of Holiness Quakerism, and argues that they represent basic early Christian beliefs and conform to the core values of Christian faith and experience. These eight elements characterize historical Quakerism in its first generation and can be found with differing emphases in the writings of all early Friends[20] (Moore, 2000).

1. Scripture—Quakers had a thoroughly biblical worldview and believed the Bible was authoritative, although the way they understood the Bible was closer to the spiritual interpretation of the early church than Reformation Biblicism.
2. Eschatology—Quakers initially anticipated the imminent second coming of Christ, but when it did not happen literally they recognized that Christ had come again spiritually, within each person.
3. Conversion—Quakers were born again – the old self died and a new self born; they shared the same soteriology as other Puritans.
4. Charisma—Quakers were enthusiasts, that is, they were Spirit-filled and led. Although they did not formulate an explicit pneumatology, the role and work of the Holy Spirit were prominent features in the early movement.
5. Evangelism—Quakers were evangelistic and prophetic, preaching good news to the poor and denouncing oppression, both spiritual and social.
6. Mysticism—Quakers were mystical. Knowledge of God came through direct experience and they incorporated the apophatic, an approach to God beyond images and words, into their spirituality.
7. Suffering—Quakers were persecuted and martyred, imitating Christ by joyfully bearing the cross.
8. Perfection—Quakers experienced union with God, the *telios* of holiness, the fully restored image of God and victory over sin.

These elements combined define the nature of Quaker holiness. Because Quakers blended elements from all of the previous holiness traditions, as explained in 1.4, none of these traits were unique; all can be found in earlier forms of spiritual life, and in many other radical groups of the time. But the constellation of all eight together form the uniqueness of Quaker holiness and

---

[20] A leading contemporary historian of early Quaker thought, Rosemary Moore, in her comprehensive study of the faith of the early Quakers through an analysis of themes in their pamphlet literature, corroborates the strong presence of all of these elements in their writings. However, she does not identify and isolate them in the same way as this study, nor link them to the overarching theme of holiness (2000).

differentiates the Quakers from other movements and subsequent holiness traditions.

1.5.1 Scripture

Quakers' sacred text was the Bible and their language and modes of expression were almost entirely biblical. They were especially dependent on the New Testament texts of the Pauline letters, the Gospel of John, Acts, Hebrews and Revelation. References to the synoptics were infrequent (Barbour, 1964, 157, n104) (Moore, 1993, 61). In the Old Testament the Prophets were primary texts for early Friends. They used the Bible as a liberationist text which pointed the way to freedom from sin, self, and the world. The Bible shaped their experiences and provided the framework for their beliefs and practices.[21] They were as drenched in Scripture as were all Puritans, but ultimately the Quaker view of the relationship between revelation and scripture separated them from the Puritans.

The difference between the two groups was not simply that Quakers claimed the Spirit was "above" scripture. Puritans would have agreed with Quakers that true understanding of scripture only comes through illumination of the Spirit (Nuttall, 1992, 33). But Puritans believed that the Holy Spirit did not operate *apart from Scripture* (in much the same way as the Roman Catholic Church said the Spirit did not operate *apart from the sacraments*). Quakers, on the other hand, did not confine the Holy Spirit to Scripture. Quakers believed in continuing inspiration as an additional source of authority, a belief which links this element with the charismatic. For early Quakers, revelation was not closed. The Bible was God's inspired revelation, but inspiration was not limited to Scripture, nor was the Holy Spirit confined to the reading of the Bible. But Scripture was the touchstone of truth; it would always be used to confirm all direct, continuing inspiration. Any inspiration or revelation contradictory to Scripture was false mysticism or ranterism. Thus the Bible was the safeguard for self-deception. While the Bible was never regarded as the Word of God (Christ was the Word) it was nevertheless the *words* of God, and therefore, authoritative.[22]

---

[21] See Jones, "The Bible: Its Authority and Dynamic in George Fox and Contemporary Quakerism," QRT, 4, 1962, 18-36; Damrosch, *The Sorrows of the Quaker Jesus*, 1996; Barbour, *Quakers in Puritan England*, New Haven, 1964, 157-159; and Ash, "Oh, No. It is Not the Scriptures!": The Bible and the Spirit in George Fox, *Q H.*, 63, 1974, 94-107.

[22] George Whitehead's declaration on Scripture summarizes the centrality of Scripture and its authority for early Friends:

The Bible was not an external authority ("a paper Pope") but an internalized authority. Quakers lived, breathed and were infused by the words of Scripture. It was foundational to all their theology and spirituality. Hugh Barbour claims that seventy percent of their writings were either quotes, paraphrases, or allusions to Scripture (1964, 157).[23] Their understanding and use of Scripture has stronger affinity with the spiritual interpretation practiced by the early Greek Fathers such as Origen and John Chrystostom than the Reformers had[24] (Schneiders, 1985, 1-20; Schneiders, 1999, 15-18). The Bible had a literal, historical meaning but also a deeper, spiritual meaning (sometimes called allegorical or typological), a mystical meaning that would be illumined by the Spirit for those who were truly converted.[25] Quakers were considered suspect for devaluing scripture by those who considered themselves the keepers of true Christian orthodoxy, though in practice it informed every aspect of their lives and undergirded all of their theology. George Fox explained this distinctive "mystical" view of scripture when he wrote:

> I had no slight esteem of the Holy Scriptures, but they were very precious to me, for I was in that spirit by which they were given forth, and what the Lord opened in me I afterwards found was agreeable to them. (Nickalls, 1952, 34)[26]

> The Scriptures...were given forth by the Spirit of God, and no whit altered by translations, they are a perfect Testimony of God. ...whatsoever is written ought to be believed and received for Truth. (Moore, 2000, 58)

[23] Rosemary Moore substantially confirms this in her more recent study of Quaker literature before 1660 (1993, 60).

[24] The only exception was the scholarly Samuel Fisher who approached the Bible with a more modern historical-critical perspective, but his approach was not normative among early Quakers. See Moore, 2000, 58.

[25] Karen Torjesen describes Origen's biblical hermeneutic as a process of the reader being placed within the text and its meaning written on the soul (1986, 39-41, 130-183). Quakers, in the tradition of the early Church, also saw "types" of Christ everywhere in the Old Testament. Moses and the prophets are foreshadowings of Christ. They reach through figures, types and shadows to Christ (McKay, 1994).

[26] A contemporary understanding of Scripture and revelation with striking similarities to the early Friends can be found in Keith Ward's description of the biblical views of Karl Barth and Emil Brunner: "Revelation is not propositional, but primarily lies in encounter with the living and active Word of God, a personal and dynamic reality. Scripture functions as a witness to the occurrence of such an encounter and as a means of seeking to evoke a similar encounter in the reader or hearer. Brunner speaks of 'the fatal equation of revelation with the inspiration of Scriptures'" (Ward, 1994, 221). For a recent discussion of the Quaker understanding of Scripture see Pyper, "Can There Be a Quaker Hermeneutic?" *QRT,* September 2001, vol. 30, no. 3, 63-69.

The "spiritual" meaning of Scripture became characteristic of the mystical Anabaptists a century before the beginnings of Quakerism. Hans Denck, for example, differentiated between the inward revelation of the Spirit and the external words in his writings in 1528:

> I hold Scriptures dear above all of man's treasures, but not so high as the Word of God, which is living, strong, eternal....Salvation is not bound to Scripture, even though Scripture may be conducive to salvation. The reason is this: Scripture cannot possibly change an evil heart even though it may make it more learned. (1975, 123-4)

This understanding of Scripture as above human knowledge, but subordinate to the living Christ, the Word of God, was adopted by early Quakers.

1.5.2 Eschatology

Quakers believed that the Kingdom of Christ had come and they were called to proclaim it, a belief referred to by later historians as a "realized eschatology" (Damiano, 1988, 96-7). A radical apocalyptic millennialism[27] prevailed in the beginnings of Quakerism similar to many Puritan radicals at the time, but was soon modified to a "realized eschatology," in which "through the power of Christ, people are transformed and can experience a paradise where all things are eternal" (Damiano, 1988, 97).[28]

James Naylor was among the first to articulate the change: "You have been seeking without, but it is within you, and there you must find it..." (1653, 1).[29] Early Quakers preached that Christ had come again, but inwardly, not with a body of flesh. Christ came (a second time) to those of the first generation of Christians. Christ also came a second time to that generation of Quakers. And he would come again in the future to those who had not yet received him (Underwood, 1970, 98).[30]

---

[27] Early Quakers did not anticipate a literal 1000 year reign of Christ on earth, so in a sense they were not true millennialists.

[28] During the English Civil War (1542-45) many Puritans believed that they (the saints) would bring the Kingdom of God to earth through political means, and the execution of Charles II and the new Puritan Parliament (the "rule of the saints") were viewed as the beginning of that process (Moore, 2000, 60). Some early Quakers initially carried such hopes of an outward, political kingdom that would redress social evils. (Moore, 2000, 61). But a shift began to occur by 1653, when the new Parliament disbanded, from hopes of an earthly political kingdom to a purely spiritual one.

[29] An allusion to Luke 17:21 where Jesus says, "the Kingdom of Heaven is within you."

[30] George Whitehead wrote in 1660: "The coming of Christ in the flesh...was one coming and his appearance in Spirit to save his people from sin, is another coming, which they that truly looked for him receive; and they that yet have his coming to look

Early Quakers did not deny a future bodily resurrection, but their opponents accused them of it, because they spoke of resurrection as deliverance from sin and emphasized the inward, spiritual resurrection. Resurrection, therefore, was understood as a present, embodied experience of God which would result in true righteousness, or perfection (Underwood, 1970, 101).

The *parousia,* another term understood by their contemporary religionists as referring to the second coming of Christ, became for early Quakers the real *presence* of Christ in the *present,* the experience of the immediate presence of Christ in them and through them. By means of conversion, the reborn (spiritual person) could live continually in the intimate, ongoing presence of God.

Early Quaker eschatology thus meant that perfection could be realized in this life, in the present age, by mystical union with Christ. Unlike many sectarian millennial groups, Quakers did not develop any detailed doctrine of eschatology or end times events, nor emphasize eternal rewards in heaven. (Barclay formulated no proposition related to eschatology.) Quakers lived with a heightened sense of the eternal present. Commentators on Fox's *Journal* have noted the mystical pattern of "transcendent moments, each complete in itself but otherwise unrelated to what goes before and after" and the sense that "life was itself a spiritual moment" (Olney, 1972, 177). George Fox is purported to have said on his deathbed, "All is well. The Seed of God reigns over all, and over death itself" (Nickalls, 1952, 760). The Kingdom of God *is* come.[31]

1.5.3 Conversion

Quaker conversion was a dramatic, intense, and life changing experience. "Born-again," "new man," "new creation," or "new birth"[32] were the terms most often employed. "I witness I am regenerate and born again of the immortal seed" (Dewsbury, 1655, 12-14). Francis Howgill, writing c.1656, graphically describes this process of personal transformation:

> ...I became a perfect fool, and knew nothing, as a man distracted; all was overturned, and I suffered loss of all. In all I ever did, I saw it was in the accursed nature. And something in me cried, "just and true is his

---

for, and wait for it, he shall so appear to their Salvation" (*The Authority of the True Ministry*, 1660, 2-3, qtd, in Underwood, 1970, 98).

[31] This sense of triumph and paradoxical optimism that transcends the harsh realities of life is common to the mystical sensibility, for example, Julian of Norwich's well-known phrase, "All will be well, all is well, and all shall be well."

[32] Fox, writing of his conversion, states, "...the Lord said unto me: 'Thy name is written in the Lamb's Book of Life...And as the Lord spake it, I believed, and saw it in the new birth" (Nickalls, 1952, 33).

judgment!" My mouth was stopped, I dared not make mention of his name, I knew not God. And as I bore the indignation of the Lord, something rejoiced, the serpent's head began to be bruised...and as I did give up all to the judgment, the captive came forth out of the prison and rejoiced, and my heart was filled with joy...Then I saw the cross of Christ and stood in it...And the new man was made. (Barbour and Roberts, 1973, 174)[33]

Fox summed up his dramatic encounter with Christ with the phrase, common among Quakers, "...this I knew experimentally" (Nickalls, 1952, 11). The seventeenth century word "experimental" is often equated with "experiential," but the modern term "transformative" may be a closer equivalent. When Quakers spoke of being "experienced" people, they meant radically transformed people. The Quaker term for conversion was "convincement," although it represented not so much a changing of the mind as a dramatic heart-change, more affective than cognitive.[34] Some authors say convincement is a six stage process of which conversion is the first element (Tousley, 2003, n39).

In one of the most thorough recent studies of the experiential element in religious movements of the seventeenth century, Ted Campbell coins the phrase "religion of the heart" to describe the early Quaker movement with its central mystical-experiential dimension of faith (1991, 11-12, 59).[35] Campbell contends that "religion of the heart" movements generally maintain traditional values but diverge from establishment traditions in several ways. Most distinctive is the way they understand "how the separation between the divine and the human is to be overcome" or in the way they approach the divine (1991, 2). This approach is through individual "heartfelt" experiences of conversion or more intense, sometimes mystical experiences of personal illumination. Quakerism, in its early enthusiasms and on into eighteenth century Quietism (though rarer and less dramatically), and again in the mid-nineteenth century in more dramatic expressions, is characterized by the "experiential" or the heartfelt encounter with Christ as the central point of

---

[33] Howgill, *The Inheritance of Jacob*, in *Works*, *The Dawnings of the Gospel Day*, 1676, qtd. in Barbour and Roberts, 1973.

[34] John Punshon suggests that convincement was closer to the Wesleyan "second blessing" or entire sanctification than initial conversion, since early Quakers were, from a modern perspective, already Christians, often devout (2001, 35).

[35] Campbell suggests that movements for a "religion of the heart" were part of a broad range of spiritual renewal movements that spread across Europe and religious traditions (Catholic, Protestant, Orthodox, and Jewish) during the 17th and 18th centuries (1991, 1-2). He classifies them as movements of devotional affection which were inter-related and mutually enriching. All of these movements he insists have in common the affective, personal religious experience, and are in different degrees "mystical" (though Campbell is somewhat reticent to use the term).

contact with Ultimate Reality or Truth. Campbell tentatively calls this kind of religious experience "mysticism" (1991, 3).

In English Puritanism of the seventeenth century we see the emergence of a "devotion of rapture" and the seeking of private mystical experience as a longing for assurance of election and validation of beliefs.[36] Inward experience of the heart also became an important source of authority and assurance for Quakers. However, what they meant by "experience" was not just any kind of felt presence of the divine, but an encounter with God through a direct revelation of Christ. Quaker conversion narratives followed a traditional pattern of approach to God which included many of the same elements found in other Puritan accounts (Barbour, 1964, 3, 109; Vann, 1969, 26). Conversion narratives, with slight individual variations, describe a pattern of intense seeking and struggle, a dramatic personal awakening to grace, recognition and sorrow for sins, inward struggle with darkness or emptiness, repentance, and finally a dramatic breakthrough that results in peace and fulfillment.[37] William Dewsbury's (1621-1688) convincement narrative is one example:

> Not withstanding all my strict walking in observation in which I was seeking the kingdom of God, I found it not, but the flaming sword cut me down and my sorrow increased...And after the Lord discovered to me that his love could not be attained in anything I could do...thither the flaming sword turned, which kept the way of the tree of life, and fenced me from it...crying in the depths of misery...waiting for the coming of Christ Jesus, who...purged away the filthy nature...so through the righteous law of life in Christ Jesus I was made free and clean from the body of sin and death, and my garment is washed, and made white in the blood of the lamb, who hath led me through the gates of Jerusalem...where my soul now feeds upon the tree of life which I had so long hungered and thirsted of... (1655, 12-14)[38]

---

[36] For a description of seventeenth century Puritan spirituality see Rupp, 1977; Hambrick-Stowe, 1986; and Nuttall, 1975.

[37] The pattern was an ancient one, called in antiquity the "Triple Way" (*via triplex*) of purgation, illumination, union. In terms of the classical stages of the spiritual journey, convincement or conversion represents this first stage of purification. For studies on conversion narratives in Quaker journals see Barbour and Frost, 1973, 151-241; Brinton, 1972, Vann, 1969, ch. 1; and Wright, 1932.

[38] Note also the use of the metaphorical language of the Garden of Eden. Salvation as a reversal of the expulsion from paradise and return to the unity (perfection) of creation differentiates Quakers from the Puritan mainstream understanding of salvation as a covenant made between God and humanity in the sense of a legal contract. Quakers also used covenant terminology, but differently; to be in the New Covenant meant the *via mystica* and the *unio mystica*, which they coined the "Covenant of Light." See Moore on salvation and paradise imagery (1993, 83) and Covenant of Light (1993, 86-87).

George Fox describes the culmination of his own seeking with a dramatic inbreaking of revelation through Christ in 1647. After a desperate search for a human spiritual guide led him only to the depths of despair, he finally exclaims with utter joy and absolute certainty:

> ....when all my hopes in them and in all men were gone, so that I had nothing outwardly to help me, nor could tell what to do, then, Oh then, I heard a voice which said, 'There is one, even Christ Jesus, that can speak to thy condition,' and when I heard it *my heart did leap for joy.* Then the Lord did let me see why there was none upon the earth that could speak to my condition, namely, that I might give him all the glory; for all are concluded under sin, and shut up in unbelief as I had been, that Jesus Christ might have the pre-eminence, who enlightens, and gives grace, and faith, and power. Thus, when God doth work who shall let [prevent] it? And this I knew experimentally. (Nickalls, 1952, 11)

One significant difference in Quaker and Puritan theology evident in conversion narratives is the Quaker sense of certitude and assurance, the capstone of which is their doctrine of perfection. This difference is especially evident in Fox's journal, which conveys a sense of triumph, peace and certainty, rather than the continuing struggle for assurance.[39] Although Fox experiences occasional post-conversion periods of darkness and even depression, these are a result of his often dire circumstances and the sins and hostility of others, not a struggle with his own sin, guilt, anxiety, and uncertainty, as is found in most Puritan journals. Luella Wright in her classic study of Quaker literature describes this significant difference:

> In the attainment of mystic peace lies the principal line of demarcation between the journal of George Fox and the recorded spiritual anguish of John Bunyan in *Grace Abounding to the Chief of Sinners*. The latter temporarily secured peace of mind, but never retained it for any length of time. Quite differently and with great uniformity, the confessions of the Friends indicate that the writers, ideally at least, after they had definitely accepted the inner Light as a guiding gleam, did not consume their energies with questions of future rewards or the fatalities connected with the unpardonable sin, but employed them

---

[39] See Tousley, "The Experience of Regeneration and Erosion of Certainty in the Theology of Second Generation Quakers," 2001, for a comparison of conversion experiences of first and second generation Quakers. Tousley argues for a rapid decline in the certainty of assurance in Quaker religious experience.

almost wholly with carrying out the commands of the Spirit. (1932, 199-200)

In addition, for the Quakers as distinct from other Puritans, conversion was a continuous process of deeper and deeper intimacy with God. Vann writes that most Quakers had already had a conversion experience, perhaps several before joining with Quakers. They sought a communion with God that would be ongoing, "so deep that it might be called 'continuous conversion'" (1969, 32).

1.5.4 Evangelism

Quakers were a missionary-oriented movement, adopting an itinerant, apostolic style of preaching (called "the Lamb's war"). Fox's life modeled the Apostle Paul in the book of Acts. Their desire to spread the Quaker Gospel and witness to all of England, as well as Ireland, Scotland, the continent, Turkey, the Middle East, the American colonies and the Caribbean made them a missionary movement on a grand scale. Quaker evangelism united the political and the spiritual in the same manner in which the Old Testament prophets denounced their kings for "grinding the faces of the poor." Quakerism arose as a response to religious oppression, both spiritual and social. A concern for equality of all persons and social justice were corollaries of their evangelism in so far as these principles emerged from early Quakers' religious beliefs. Evangelism and social witness were one and the same, not two separate entities. Early Friends' protest against tithing was both a religious and political protest. Religion and politics could not be separated in the seventeenth century (Nuttall, 1973, 145-164).

The response of early Quakers to repressive social conditions was significant, but the purpose of this study will not be to examine the sources and exact nature of their political and social grievances. Other studies have undertaken that task.[40] This study will focus rather on the underlying spiritual values that shaped their social program. The Quaker concept of holiness, to the modern mind, appears to be puritanical, moralistic rigorism of the highest kind. But to the early Quakers, holiness was a manifesto of freedom. It allowed the Quaker movement to release its followers from the darkness of religious, spiritual, and social oppression (Nuttall, 1973, 147-8).[41]

---

[40] Theories of Quaker origins that focus on their social radicalism can be found in Hill, *The World Turned Upside Down* (1972) and Reay, *The Quakers and the English Revolution* (1985).

[41] But as Moore and others have pointed out, Quakers were not as socially radical as some of the sectarian groups of the time (1993, 62-65). Quakers did not publicly advocate the abolition of private property, for example. Specific social reforms were not the most prominent themes in their pamphlets, but they were addressed generally in

The evangelistic fervor continued throughout the seventeenth century, but began to diminish in the Quietist period, although the itinerant, traveling ministry did not. Most Quietist ministry focused on visiting other Quaker communities with a particular "concern," although public, open-air meetings were still held. Evangelistic outreach began again with fervor in the late eighteenth century and became one of the distinguishing features of the Holiness Revival. Evangelism is the obvious manifestation that powerful experiences of conversion cannot be private affairs. The effect of the inward revolution is to be thrust out into the world to spread the message of liberation that has been personally experienced.

Beyond the necessity of individual rebirth, Quakers also placed the "rebirth of the true church at the center of their lives and from the beginning they displayed an extraordinary missionary fervor and the organizational genius to make the fervor effective" (Endy, 1973, 68). Fox was not simply concerned with individual salvation, but also "to bring people...off from their churches...to the church in God" (Nickalls, 1952, 35). If evangelicalism is defined in a broad sense as a "religion of the heart" based on an inward experience of conversion, through faith in Christ, and spread by the Gospel message, then early Quakers were "evangelicals" of their time (Campbell, 1991, 172-77).

Quakerism was the first great mission movement to come out of English Protestantism (inasmuch as Quakers can be labeled Protestants). Most Puritans with a belief in election did not evangelize. The Quaker belief in the universality of the Light of Christ (grace available to all, not just the elect) became the impetus and motivation for evangelism (Nuttall, 1992, 160).

1.5.5   Charisma

Early Quakers could arguably be called a grass-roots Pentecostal movement.[42] They saw their experience reflecting the pattern of the growth of the primitive church in the book of Acts (Knott, 1993, 234-5). The experience of being "in

---

a style similar to the Old Testament prophets whom they often quoted. Social reform was subsumed under church reform (Hill, 1972; Reay, 1985).

[42] The term Pentecostal is here used to refer to a primitivist movement that claims the experience of the first Christians at Pentecost as the norm for all true Christians, rather than an extraordinary period not to be repeated (Nuttall, 1992, 156). Braithwaite, 1912, describes a number of "strange excitements" in which individuals came under the influence of "the power" which, he acknowledges "justifies the nickname Quaker" (73) See, for example, his description of the "Pentecostal meetings at Malton (xi, 73-77) in which some phenomena he determines was "not altogether healthy" (77).

the power" is one of the most recurring phrases in Fox's Journal.[43] It referred to being "Spirit-filled" and included physical manifestations such as trembling, quaking, trances, fainting, and other ecstatic phenomena of that type, as well as "signs and wonders," prophecy, and miracles such as healings and exorcisms that are found in the book of Acts.[44] All of these charismatic manifestations were common in the early period, including "singing in the spirit" and possibly even speaking in tongues. There are some references to "incoherent" praying in the Spirit.[45] The more dramatic of these declined after the 1660s, or at least they were not so triumphantly proclaimed in the slightly less enthusiastic formative post-restoration period. But charismatic phenomena of a less ecstatic type were not uncommon throughout the Quietist period. Direct guidance of the Spirit, manifested by speaking spontaneously out of the silence when "in the power" in worship, became the most evident charismatic phenomena of later periods.[46]

The Holy Spirit could be found within (the Light of Christ) and could also come in an extra measure from without, as in the descent of the Spirit at Pentecost. Early Friends often used the term "poured down" to refer to whole meetings that were influenced by the "pouring down" of the Spirit and thus "in

---

[43] In a literary study of Fox's *Journal*, John R. Knott finds the same sense of charismatic power that historians and theological interpreters observe: "The expression, 'so the Lord's power came over all,' appears so frequently in the *Journal* as to make this power appear a vital force with a life of its own" (1993, p. 245).

[44] See Nuttall, *Studies in Christian Enthusiasm,* 1948, for a comprehensive analysis of the charismatic dimension of this period.

[45] See Henry Cadbury's *George Fox's Book of Miracles,* 1948, for a fascinating picture of the reality of the charismatic phenomena of this period with his careful reconstruction of the miraculous material omitted from later printed documents, but still available in the original manuscripts. On speaking in tongues, the evidence is inconclusive. Nuttall, 1992, finds its relative absence surprising. Thus early Quakers were not Pentecostal in the sense of the modern movement traced to Azusa Street where tongues-speaking was most characteristic. The physical phenomena which occurred among early Quakers was never considered exceptional or given special importance. The fruit of the Spirit and leading of the Spirit, rather than seeking after miraculous gifts of the Spirit, was always primary. In the 19th century Holiness Movement, the issue of tongues speaking divided Holiness advocates from the emerging Pentecostal movement (spawned by the Holiness Movement) (Jones, 1974). Pentecostals claimed tongues-speaking as evidence of the Baptism of the Spirit, a feature that Holiness Quakers did not embrace. Those that sought for the gift of tongues generally left Quakers. Thus Quakers are to be identified as Holiness, but not Pentecostal, in the modern, denominational sense. However, glossolalia referred to as "prayer language," is practiced by some Evangelical Quakers, but is considered a devotional practice and not a part of corporate worship.

[46] According to Isichei, Quietist ministers often claimed telepathic gifts, intuitive powers, and psychical experiences. They lived in a heightened spiritual atmosphere in which even the daily details of life were inspired (not unlike some modern Pentecostals and charismatics) (1970, 24).

the power." Edward Burrough's descriptions of a Quaker meeting reflecting the Pentecostal experience is typical:

> And while waiting upon the Lord in silence, as often we did for many hours together, with our mindes (*sic*) and hearts toward him, being stayed in the Light of Christ within us...and harkening to his word, we received often the pouring down of the spirit upon us, and the gift of God's holy eternal Spirit as in the dayes (*sic*) of old. (Fox, 3:1831, 13)

In the Quietist period the mystical-sounding phrase "celestial showers" became the common term for the pouring down of the Spirit (Wilbur, 1859, 127). The effects were described as "broken meetings" or "tender," meaning hearts were opened, touched, and moved by the presence and power of the Spirit of Christ (see 3.3).[47]

Several recent studies of Fox portray him as a healer (Bailey, 1992;[48] Ingle, 1994). Healing ministry is a major dimension of the Christian mystical tradition. Catholic saints must have performed at least two verifiable miracles to be canonized. Healing, and other signs and wonders, play a major role in all popular charismatic movements. That Fox as a charismatic leader would have healing gifts is not at all remarkable; it would be expected in the context of a "new age of the Spirit" that ushered in a grass-roots Pentecostal movement. A belief in a supernatural divine intervention in the form of miracles of healing and exorcisms was a part of the world-view of the period. The spiritual world was still as real as the physical in the medieval age. Quakerism arose in that unstable transitional period between the medieval and the modern. Fox remained firmly planted in the medieval world; he never stepped into the modern, as did William Penn and Thomas Ellwood (editor of Fox's *Journal*). That Ellwood and other second generation Friends would minimize miracles in the editing of Fox's *Journal* (Cadbury, 2000 [1948], 35-6) and other documents is perfectly consistent with the dawning of the age of reason and the Enlightenment when dramatic miracles, as well as physical manifestations, were downplayed in a quieter and more rational era. The minimizing of the miraculous is in keeping with the intellectualist and modernist philosophical "Inner Light mysticism" of twentieth century interpretations (see 6.1, especially 6.1.3). The holiness Quakers of the nineteenth century recaptured the charismatic spirit of healing. The belief in divine healing, "the faith cure," was

---

[47] Spirit as "poured down" is like Hebrew "rûah"; Spirit as Light is closer to Greek *logos*. Nuttall considers identifying *logos* with Spirit in later Quakerism an error. See Nuttall, "Towards a Theology of the Holy Spirit," *CQ,* Vol. xxii, Oct. 1944, 305-6.

[48] Richard Bailey argues that Fox's healing powers proves his doctrine of "celestial inhabitation" (see 1.7.5).

a major component of holiness belief (Dieter, 1996, 251).[49] Bailey's and Ingle's recovery of the importance of healing and miracles in the early Quaker movement is a significant contribution. Bailey concludes even more unequivocally, "early Quakerism was a fully Spirit-led, charismatic movement" (1992, 53). That earlier biographers such as A. N. Brayshaw (1933) downplay this aspect of Fox in spite of the substantial and irrefutable evidence is an example of modern liberal anti-mystical bias.[50]

Rosemary Moore's exhaustive study of early Quaker documents affirms this assessment: "The importance of these charismatic phenomena has been underestimated by most writers on early Quakerism, Winthrop Hudson and Barry Reay being exceptions" (1993, 94).[51] Moore asserts that "The coming of the 'power of the Lord' and the shaking of the minister and worshippers was one of the most notable features of early Quakerism" (1993, 27) and the phrase "'power of the Lord' unambiguously meant quaking" (1993, 94). When ecstatic phenomena reappeared in a similar fashion in the revival of holiness among Orthodox Friends in the nineteenth century, respectable Victorian Quakers were shocked and horrified (Isichei, 1970). The reaction to Quaker revivalism by Orthodox Friends can be compared in some ways to the seventeenth century Puritan censure of early Quakers, as well as the twentieth century separations between Pentecostals and modern evangelical Christians.[52]

---

[49] See also the example of Mary Thomas, a prominent Baltimore Quaker minister, and sister of Hannah Whitall Smith, as a fervent believer in the "faith cure" (Spencer, 1991).

[50] Charismatic phenomena and ecstatic experiences are not essential to or even reliable evidences of mysticism, but most mystics experience some forms of them. In the teachings of many mystics, and most notably in the Eastern Orthodox mystical tradition, ecstasy or rhapsodies are viewed as manifestations that occur primarily in the early stages of the contemplative life. Historically, in the beginning of charismatic movements, extensive physical, bodily phenomena are common and decrease as the movement matures. This is the pattern in Quakerism and the reasons for it are usually seen as accommodation to respectability, and increasing institutionalization and control. But just as ecstasies diminish in the maturing spiritual journey of the individual mystic (and Fox is a prime example here--his most dramatic mystical openings came earlier in his life), the same principle may apply in group spiritual development. Another theory may be related to the close connection between spirituality and sexuality, with sexual intensity decreasing with age, but this is a matter beyond the scope of this research.

[51] Moore does not cite Bailey's work (1992) here, but his findings would also support this claim, though his interpretation would differ from the meaning this study gives to charisma.

[52] See Taylor, *Quaking: A Study of the Phenomena of Quaking, Trembling, and Shaking in Early Quakerism*, MA thesis, University of Wales, 1992. Taylor claims, "The Quaker in the 17th century stood apart from his more orthodox Puritan brethren in the same way that the charismatic/pentecostal does from the evangelical contingent in today's church" (1).

1.5.6 Suffering

Quakers identified themselves as belonging to the long line of martyrs for God's truth and developed a literature of sufferings as a distinct form of writing (Knott, 1993, Braithwaite, 1919, 282; Barbour, 1964, 208-9; Wright, 1932, 87-96). The fullest bibliography of Quaker writings records 224 tracts, petitions, and autobiographical narratives composed before 1689 based on the theme of sufferings (Knott, 1993, 218).[53]

In 1753 Joseph Besse published *A Collection of the Sufferings of the People Called Quakers*. He patterned his book after Foxes' *Acts and Monuments*, commonly known as *Foxes Book of Martyrs*, thus becoming a Quaker version of Foxe (Knott, 1993, 218). Besse defined sufferings as "any harm inflicted because of belief or practice," ranging from the seizing of goods with their value noted, to an event of the magnitude of the death of Frances Howgill in prison (Knott, 1993, 219). Sufferings comprised fines, beatings, trials, imprisonment, and death. Sufferings arose from legal harassment by those who should have protected and defended them (kings and magistrates) and the brutality of mobs and hostile crowds (Knott, 1993, 219).

The experience of suffering developed into a theology of suffering which linked Quakers to the persecuted church of early Christianity, beginning in the book of Acts[54] (Moore, 2000). In the same way as the martyrs before them, Quakers could assert joy in suffering and even ask forgiveness for their persecutors (like Jesus, and Stephen in the book of Acts) (Knott, 1993, 220, 222). Suffering becomes redemptive because it is given meaning and purpose as identification with Christ and viewed positively for the sake of Christ. When Christ is truly incarnated in the individual, that individual bears the cross of Christ. Participation in God means participation in the cross and in the passion of Christ.[55]

Ellis Hook's *The Spirit of Christ* (1661) is one of the first publications to draw upon Foxe's *Acts and Monuments* to place Quakers in the tradition of a martyr church (Knott, 1993, 223). Thus begins the development of a theology of suffering as the way of holiness, and martyrdom as the supreme form of witness to perfection. Besides the many Quakers who died from mistreatment in prison, (243 from 1660-1689, according to Reay) four individuals executed in Boston by Puritans became undeniable martyrs: William Robinson and Marmaduke Stevenson, hung in 1659, Mary Dwyer in 1660, and William Leddra in 1661.

---

[53] See Smith, *A Descriptive Catalogue of Friends Books*, 1867.

[54] Children were introduced to suffering from infancy. Women who were imprisoned kept their babies with them in prison rather than leaving them to the care of others (Galgano, 1986, 129).

[55] James Naylor's entry into Bristol is an example of one way this theology became expressed literally (see 2.3).

The cross thus becomes a central symbol in Quaker theology, not only as the symbol of a historic event or a doctrine of atonement (they were accused of denying both), but a daily enacting of the suffering of Christ, a cross-mysticism. William Penn writes "the bearing of thy daily Cross is the only true testimony" (1682, 25).

This study suggests that after persecution ceased, self-denial and renunciation became evidence of holiness similar to the way "blood martyrdom" became the "white martyrdom" of monasticism in Constantinian Christianity (Knott, 1993, 224). Testimonies against unfair laws and social customs of domination were ways of continually testifying to one's faith and evidence of submission to God's will, "a continually enacted crucifixion to the world" (Knott, 1993, 224).[56] The belief that holiness involves suffering, even requires it, is much stronger in Quakers than other Puritan non-conformists. Even the Baptist separatist John Bunyan is willing to concede, "I am not for running myself into sufferings" (Knott, 1993, 224). Penn and early Quakers seem to embrace suffering more deliberately, and even invite it.[57] Such identification with suffering is also a characteristic trait of Christocentric mystics who experience union with Christ. (St. Francis of Assisi and John of the Cross are among the most notable.) A strong Quaker example would be James Naylor (see 2.3).

1.5.7   Mysticism

No scholar as yet has come up with a satisfactory definition or criteria of mystical experience and there is no consensus on the nature of mystical experience.[58] Rather than define the term (which he claims is utopian), Bernard

---

[56] Penn's *Primitive Christianity Revived*, 1686, also promotes the ideal of plainness with suffering. Penn idealizes the early church and later persecuted movements such as the Waldensians as "poor suffering Christians" in *No Cross, No Crown*, 1682, 292, 531, 528.

[57] In comparing Quakers to other nonconformists and radicals of the time, Moore asserts that "none showed the Quaker resistance to official persecution" and observes that "Ranters and Diggers were not martyrs" and "Baptists were full of self-doubt" (1993, 259n).

[58] For classic studies of mysticism see Inge, *Christian Mysticism*, 1899; William James, *The Varieties of Religious Experience*, 1902; Evelyn Underhill, *Mysticism*, 1911; Baron Von Hugel, *The Mystical Element in Religion as Studied in Saint Catherine of Genoa and her Friends*, 2 vols., 1908; Edward Cuthbert Butler, *Western Mysticism*, 1923; and Kenneth E. Kirk, *The Vision of God*, 1931. For more recent studies see Karl Rahner, *The Practice of Faith: The Handbook of Christian Spirituality*, 1983; Hans Urs von Balthasar, *The Glory of the Lord: A Theological Aesthetics*, 1982; Andrew Louth, *The Origins of the Christian Mystical Tradition: From Plato to Denys*, 1981. For philosophical approaches see Stephen Katz ed., *Mysticism and Philosophical Analysis*,

McGinn in his *Foundations of Mysticism*, explores it under three areas: "as a part or element of religion, as a process or way of life; and mysticism as an attempt to express a direct consciousness of the presence of God" (1991, xv-xvi). McGinn identifies "presence" as the central category of mysticism—a consciousness of the direct presence of God (1991, xvii). Quakers are mystics based on this definition.[59]

Although Quaker scholar Rufus Jones defined mysticism as an "unmediated, direct experience of God," most scholarship today questions the possibility of any kind of "unmediated" experience.[60] Andrew Louth offers a definition that reflects the conclusions of most recent scholarship (e.g., Katz), which argues for the contextuality of all mystical experience:

> ...[mysticism] can be characterized as a search for and experience of immediacy with God. The mystic is not content to know about God, he longs for union with God. 'Union with God' can mean different things, from literal identity, where the mystic loses all sense of himself and is absorbed into God, to the union that is experienced as the consummation of love, in which the lover and the beloved remain intensely aware both of themselves and of the other. How the mystics interpret the way and the goal of their quest depends on what they

---

1978 and *Mysticism and Religious Traditions*, 1983; Louis Dupré, *The Deeper Self: An Introduction to Christian Mysticism*, 1981. For comparative approaches see Rudolf Otto, *Mysticism East and West*, 1932 and R. C. Zaehner, *Mysticism Sacred and Profane*, 1957. For the most complete and thorough history and theology of mysticism, see the three volume series of Bernard McGinn, *The Foundations of Mysticism*, 1991, *The Growth of Mysticism*, 1994, *The Flowering of Mysticism*, 1998.

[59] Quakers would not have used the term "mystic" to describe themselves, nor termed their practices as "mysticism." They were rather "children of God" who worshiped in spirit and truth. They were aware, however, of the term being applied at that time to a sect of monks who practiced contemplative prayer and recognized this kind of prayer as "mystical" and the basis of true spiritual worship. (See Barclay, *Apology*, 354-5.) The term mysticism, as used in modern times as private experience, did not come into existence until the 17th century (first used in France, "la mystique"), coinciding with the beginnings of Quakerism (see McGinn, 1991, xvi, 266-7). Mysticism for early Quakers was thus spiritual, communal worship, a mystically feeding on Christ through group contemplation, but without the use of the Roman Catholic rites.

[60] Stephen Katz unequivocally asserts, "There are no pure (i.e., unmediated) experiences...All experience is processed through, organized by, and makes itself available to us in extremely complex epistemological ways" (1983, 4). And after giving strong support to this argument he concludes that "the ontological structure(s) of each major mystical tradition is different and this pre-experiential, inherited structure directly enters into the mystical experience itself" (1983, 40). Katz argues that all mystical experience is preconditioned and shaped by historical, linguistic, social, and theological contexts.

think about God, and that itself is influenced by what they experience: it is a mistake to try to make out that all mysticism is the same. (1981, xv)

Louth suggests that mystical experience is one of "immediacy," yet cannot be "unmediated." So in effect we have a paradoxical kind of "mediated immediacy." This study will use Louth's definition of a mystic as a person not content to know about God, but one who longs for and seeks union with God (1981, xv).

Mysticism takes two paradoxical paths in classical terminology, the *via negativa* and the *via positiva:* the language of negation (beyond words, sensations, and images) and the positive language of presence (the use of words, images, and senses). "The paradoxical necessity of both presence and absence is one of the most important of all verbal strategies by means of which mystical transformation has been symbolized" (McGinn, 1991, xviii). Early Quakerism manifested the paradox of both apophatic negation and kataphatic affirmation.

Early Quakers, it could be argued, had profound insight into the limits of language in expressing Reality (which they called Truth), and also insisted a Reality existed which was *not* relative to language, and which transcended it. This belief is reflected in their most distinctive practice of silent worship, a type of apophatic mysticism.[61] All Christian mysticism values the element of silence, the end of speech, but no Christian tradition, outside of monasticism, has elevated the use of silence on a regular, communal basis to the extent of the early Quakers (see 7.1.1 n3) (Bauman, 1983). Silence became an alternative symbol for their spiritual world, as opposed to the words and symbols of institutional religion. Liturgy, prayer-books, scholarly preaching, rituals and sacraments came to be seen as cultish idols preventing, rather than mediating, God's presence.

At the same time that language cannot convey union with God, those who experience divine union often feel compelled to speak, preach, and write with an overwhelming profusion and proliferation of words, hoping to bring others into that union which they have experienced as Reality. The care early Quakers took to record, preserve, and publish a vast body of literature shows

---

[61] Barclay explains that Quaker worship originated ("did naturally spring") from the principle of silence and surrender to God as together each person made it their work "to retire inwardly to the measure of Grace in themselves, not only being silent as to words but even abstaining from all of their own thoughts, imaginations, and desires" (2002, 297). Barclay also takes care to add that this worship "in one spirit" (*unus spiritus*) is mediated by Jesus "inwardly in one Spirit and in one name of Jesus, which is his Power and Virtue...thus his Name comes to be one in all..." (2002, 298). This description of apophatic communal mysticism would not describe the general practice of silent worship among Quakers today.

how highly they valued language as the means of expressing and conveying their mystical world in the particular and distinctive way they experienced it as Reality. They used language to convince and persuade, and developed a distinct biblical-mystical-symbolical language to spread their message of Truth.

The kataphatic is expressed most vividly in ecstatic experience. An example of the place of both apophatism and affirmation as ecstasy in Quakerism, can be found in the many descriptions of their communal worship, begun in the negation of deep silence, beyond words and thoughts, and ending in a luxuriant cascading of religious images in an attempt to witness to the experience. Edward Burrough provides one of the many descriptions of this consciousness of God, which begins in silence and negation:

> ...waiting upon the Lord in silence, as often we did for many hours together, with our minds and hearts towards him, being stayed in the light of Christ within us, from all thoughts, fleshly motions, and desires... (Fox, 1831, 3:13)

The hours of apophatic emptying eventually brings:

> ...the pouring down of the Spirit upon us, and the gift of God's holy eternal spirit, as in the days of old, and our hearts were made glad, and our tongues loosed, and our mouths opened, and we spake with new tongues, as the Lord gave us utterance, and as his Spirit led us, which was poured down upon us, on sons and daughters; and to us hereby was the deep things of God revealed, and things unutterable were known and made manifest, and the glory of the Father was revealed; and then begun we to sing praises to the Lord God Almighty, and to the lamb forever, who had redeemed us to God; and brought us out of the captivity and bondage of the world, and put an end to sin and death, and all this was by and through, and in the light of Christ within us; and much more might be declared here of that which could not be believed, if it were spoken... (Fox, 1831, 3:13)[62]

When early Quakers gathered in silent worship they were expressing an elevated and intense mystical consciousness and were all witnessing essentially the same "direct, knowledge of God," union with God mediated through Christ, a Christ-mysticism experienced as the consummation of love.

---

[62] This description of early Quaker worship was published in 1659 in the "Epistle to the Reader," which prefaces Fox's *The Great Mystery* (*Works* 1831:3). Barclay's 11th proposition on worship in the *Apology*, 1678, thoroughly supports this expression of the mysticism of Quaker worship, even to the extent of his inclusion of his own spiritual experience (2002, 298-301) (see also note 42).

Apophatism is also embodied in a process of detachment from the world, and a strict asceticism. In the words of Fox, "the Spirit draws off and weans you from all things that are created and external, (which fade and pass away) up to God, the fountain of life, and head of all things" (Fox, 1831, 3:26). Apophatism is also embodied in the annihilation of the self, the letting go of the ego, and is thus related to conversion, suffering and perfection (see 1.5.3, 1.5.6, and 1.5.8).

1.5.8 Perfection

Perfection was a key component of early Quaker soteriology.[63] Perfection was the culmination, the *telios* of the process of salvation, which begins with justification. The seventeenth century Quaker theologian Robert Barclay defined justification as "a holy, pure, and spiritual birth, bringing forth holiness, righteousness, purity, and all these other blessed fruits ..." The "holy birth" he defined as "Jesus Christ formed within us, and working his works in us" (2002, 167) and perfection as "this pure and holy birth...fully brought forth" (2002, 205). Perfection is thus the goal of spiritual formation ("Christ formed within us") and through this process of formation "....also comes that communication of the goods of Christ unto us, 'by which we come to be made partakers of the divine nature' as saith Peter, 2 Pet. 1:4, and are made one with him, as the branches with the vine" (2002, 175, 208). (See 2.5 for further discussion of Barclay's doctrine of perfection.)

Perfection is thus participation in God through Christ, or in classical mysticism, union with God. In those who experience divine union,

> the body of death and sin comes to be crucified and removed, and their hearts united and subjected to the truth; as not to obey any suggestions or temptations of the evil one, but to be free from actual sinning and transgressing of the law of God, and in that respect perfect. (2002, 205)

And yet Barclay adds, in order to make clear he is not speaking of sinless perfection, nor the perfection of God, "...doth this perfection still admit of a growth; and there remaineth always in some part a possibility of sinning, where

---

[63] In Newton Flew's classic study, *The Idea of Perfection*, he claims the Quaker doctrine is most closely aligned with the New Testament idea: "The Quaker doctrine [of perfection] has this distinction among all the types of teaching from the 3rd century to the 18th, that it returned wholeheartedly to the attitude of the New Testament" (1934, 282).

the mind doth not most diligently and watchfully attend unto the Lord" (2002, 205) (see 2.5.1).

The word for perfection in early Christianity was rendered in Greek as *theosis*, God-likeness, or deification. In seventeenth century England in the Puritan cradle where Quakerism was born, perfection was the equivalent theological term for the concept of *theosis*. *Theosis* was the goal and culmination of the spiritual life, and although the Greek term was not used by Quakers, they regularly employed its English equivalent, divine indwelling. For early Quakers, seeking perfection became the terminology of personal transformation.

Although the conversion experience generally happened individually and privately for each person, perfection, the process of ever deepening intimacy with God, took place within the church, the community of the convinced. As in the Greek concept of *theosis*, perfection has a parallel and essential communal aspect. (In Quakerism salvation might be found outside the church, but the measure of perfection could only be realized within the purified church.) Unlike other individualistic radical groups, who taught perfectionist doctrines, Quakers were concerned about both individual rebirth and the rebirth of the true church (Endy, 1973, 68). Thus, seeking for perfection as both a mystical process and an ordered way of life within the spiritual community became a distinguishing characteristic which set Quakers apart from Puritans and other radical religious movements of its day (Moore, 2000). The distinctive emphasis on perfection reappeared with renewed vigor in a slightly different form in the nineteenth century Holiness Movement (Barbour, 1964, 149) (see 5.1).

1.5.9 Summary

These eight elements – scripture, eschatology, charisma, conversion, evangelism, suffering, mysticism, and perfection – as a constellation form the continuity of experience which characterizes Quaker Holiness. These key elements have been changed, reduced, conflated or heightened at different periods within different branches over time; nevertheless, holiness is the *sine qua non* of what it means to be a Quaker.

1.6 The Essentially Orthodox Nature of Quaker Holiness[64]

Most historians would not seriously dispute these eight elements (Barbour, 1964; Punshon, 1984; Gwyn, 1986; Moore, 2000). The evidence for their characteristic presence in early Quakerism is reasonably clear. What will be disputed is the interpretation of their significance and their "essentialness." In particular, the emphasis upon mysticism as essential to early Quakerism (and the meaning of mysticism itself) is far from being generally held (see 1.7). The idea of perfection as union with God and divine indwelling would likewise be challenged. For example, Hugh Barbour assumed that:

> Friends were not 'Christ-mystics' anymore than they were seekers of mystical union with the Godhead. Their 'unity in the Eternal Being' was their bond with other Friends...the sense of a personal presence, of the inward fellowship of Christ's personality, was quite rare among early Friends. (1964, 110)[65]

In a later study, *Early Quaker Writings,* Barbour, along with Arthur Roberts, consistently maintained, "Friends did not experience mystical union" (1973, 25). And T. Canby Jones claims that "Fox's belief in perfection is not to be distinguished sharply from a simple faith in or obedience to Christ" (1955, 149).

---

[64] The term "orthodox" will be used in three distinct ways in this book:
 1. orthodoxy (with small "o") refers to the commonly held beliefs shared by almost all Christians in the "primitive" church, the inherited tradition of the first three centuries summarized in the Council of Nicea in A.D. 325. This classical Christian theology was expressed in the creeds (or "rule of faith") of the Christian Church as it developed through the first five centuries. Early Quakers opposed the recitation of creeds as an expression of belief (right "knowing," which may not reflect the immediacy of experience), but did not reject the core content of this theological tradition.
 2. Orthodoxy (with capital "O") refers to the Eastern Orthodox tradition of the Christian Church (mainly Christians in Eastern Europe, Egypt and Asia) which split from the Western (Catholic) Church in 1054. They accept the authority of "Christ and the seven Ecumenical Synods" (from Nicea I in 325, to Nicea II in 787), but not the authority of the Pope.
 3. Orthodox Quakerism (with capital "O") refers to the branch of Quakerism that developed out of the split with the Hicksites in 1827-28. Orthodox Quakers identified closely with traditional Christian orthodoxy, particularly in maintaining biblical revelation and the doctrine of incarnation and atonement. They are often equated with "evangelical." (Barbour, 1964, 252)

[65] Barbour also asserts that "Penington (one of the leading spiritual writers among early Friends) was a mystic, but most early Friends were not" (1964, 108).

This study argues for a Quaker holiness which *is* a form of Christ-mysticism and depends on an intimacy with God, beyond simply a "bond with other Friends." Quaker holiness also implies a sense of personal presence, which goes beyond "simple faith in Christ" into a transcendent knowing, and an ongoing process of perfection as union with God.

The concept of deification, *unio mystica*, a participation in God through Christ, is the foundational experience of all Christian mystics and has always existed within, and alongside, the dogmatic, liturgical and institutional faith. This mystical aspect of faith as divine union, biblically expressed as "partakers of the divine nature" (II Peter 1:4), was so central to the beginnings of Quakerism that one early leader, Richard Farnworth, actually made it into a ditty: "Written by one whom the world called a Quaker, but is of the divine nature a partaker" (1653, 2).[66]

This experience-based faith was anchored to (and indeed could not be understood apart from) the mystery of the Trinity. Fox cared nothing for the dogmatic formulations, but the experience of the three persons, God, Christ, and Spirit, and the ultimate unity in the diversity of persons was paramount.[67] This experience-based faith was also anchored in the doctrine of the incarnation, the Word becoming flesh, and the atonement, Christ's offering on the cross. The key biblical text for Quakers, John 1:9, "the true Light that enlightens everyone," could not be understood apart from the incarnation, because the true Light was the Word become flesh. And Fox, like the Greek Fathers, did not stop there, but recognized the inverse as well, that transfiguration was a two-way process. Since Word (God) became flesh, flesh could also become god-like (deified, perfect).

George Fox explains in his *Journal* what Christ meant when he said: "Be ye perfect even as my heavenly father is perfect":

> ...he who was perfect comes to make man and woman perfect again and bring them again to the state God made them in; so he is the maker up of the breach and the peace betwixt God and man.... But I

---

[66] Barclay uses II Peter 1:4 twice in his *Apology*, once in explaining justification: "By this also comes that communication of the goods of Christ unto us, *by which we come to be made partakers of the divine nature*, [his emphasis] as saith Peter, 2 Pet. 1:4, and are made one with him, as the branches with the vine..." (2002, 175). He uses it again in his explanation of perfection: "Wherefore if man must be always joined to sin, then God would always be at a distance from him ...whereas on the contrary, the *saints* are said to *partake*, even while here, *of the divine nature* (2 Pet. 1:4) and to be *one spirit with the Lord*, I Cor. 6:17" [his emphasis] (2002, 208). This text is the key scripture used in the Eastern Orthodox Church to support biblically the doctrine of deification.

[67] Debate regarding the Trinity abounds in contemporary Quaker literature, but reading the original sources has convinced me that Quakers were in practice, conceptually and doctrinally, Trinitarian, even though they refused to use the term Trinity because it was not found in Scripture (see 1.7.2, n81).

told them Christ was come freely, who hath perfected for ever by one offering all them that are sanctified, and renews them up in the image of God, as man and woman were in before they fell; and makes man and woman's house as perfect again as God had made them at first. (Nickalls, 1952, 367-8)

Fox understood perfection as the return to the original God-likeness in which humanity was created, which Christ had restored through his incarnation and atonement. This concept of perfection as restoration and earthly glorification, rather than a glorification only to be experienced in eternity, is common to Christian antiquity and continues to be the traditional understanding of holiness in the Eastern Orthodox Church.

However, the greatest area of contention will be disagreement over what is not on the list, in particular the notion of "the inward Light," or "Inner Light" as it later came to be called, which modern interpreters generally hold to be the unique contribution of Quakerism to religious thought.[68] In a recent study, however, Catherine Wilcox contends that the remarkably consistent, central message of early Quakers is the proclamation of Christ as the all-powerful Savior who redeems from sins and restores people to perfection, and whose felt presence is an inward source of guidance and teaching (1991, 30). This central proclamation corresponds to the Gospel message of the New Testament, as well as holiness movements throughout Christian history.

The longest ongoing debate between historians of Quakerism revolves around the question of the relationship of early Quakerism to core Christian doctrinal affirmations. Modern religious liberals, beginning in the 20th century, felt quite certain Quakers were teaching a radically new form of advanced Christianity, both Humanist and Universalist, although early Quakers themselves claimed they were not teaching any new gospel, but rather "primitive Christianity revived" (Penn, 1686). Barclay, in fact, was adamant that "We do firmly believe that there is no other gospel or doctrine to be preached, but that which was delivered by the apostles...So we distinguish betwixt a revelation of a new gospel, and new doctrines, and a new revelation of the good old gospel and doctrines; the last we plead for but the first we utterly deny" (2002, 82).[69]

---

[68] This will be taken up in Chapter 6, especially 6.1.3, but see, for example, Brinton 2002, 17, and Isichei, 1970, 7.

[69] Earlier writers such as Edward Burrough were equally clear: "Though our name is new, our religion is old" (1672, 322, qtd. in Wright, 1932, 56). Gwyn identifies both "primitives" and "progressives" in the English Seekers of the seventeenth century and calls them Type A and Type B Seekers. He concludes that early Quakerism provided a synthesis of both types. (Dandelion, Gwyn, Peat, 1998, 97-80). William Penn, perhaps, more than most early Quakers, represents a synthesization of the two types.

This study considers early Quakerism to be more a look backward (primitive Christianity revived) than forward. Early Friends found the idea of perfection primarily in the Bible, yet they also reflected the perfectionist teachings of the early Fathers of the Church with their emphasis on deification, as well as the medieval mystics who continued to maintain that tradition throughout the Middle Ages (see appendix A). Quakers were innovative in the way they appropriated the long history of holiness (which *is* the basis of Christian mysticism) into a new kind of radical (in the true sense of the word, *radix*, root) holiness movement in a puritan, post-Reformation, and politically revolutionary context. They combined elements of the various forms which holiness had taken within the boundaries (though sometimes on the knife-edge) circumscribed by Christian tradition. The boundaries of Christian orthodoxy and orthopraxis are much wider and more flexible than those of a particular established church of any historical period. Experiential Christianity is always in tension with Institutional Christianity, and even the great mystics who are now recognized as saints were often viewed with suspicion, suffering oppression and betrayal from the institutional church at some point in their lifetime.

One of the imminent Jewish scholars of mysticism, Gershom Scholem, asserts "All mysticism[70] has two contradictory or complementary aspects: the one conservative, the other revolutionary" (1965, 7). Scholem theorizes that mystical knowledge generally relates to foundational religious traditions and ultimately deepens tradition rather than revolutionizes it. He shows how the conservative side of mysticism is manifested when the mystic identifies the source of revelation with the original vision grounding the tradition, and thus serves to renew and deepen the tradition through an awakening of a new religious perception (1965, 7-9). This study suggests that early Quakerism is an expression of that kind of dynamic in its vision of holiness available for everyone through the Light of Christ. It also explains why Quakers, after the initial enthusiastic upsurge, established basically conservative beliefs and values, and settled into essentially conventional structures.

One of the strongest accusations of the Quakers' Puritan opponents was the charge that Quakers denied the historical Christ and the work of the atonement (see 1.7.2). Some historians today echo that same indictment (Moore, 2000; Endy, 1973). Moore argues that Quakers continued to "emphasize the divine eternal Christ at the expense of the human, and the contemporary accusation, that Quakers did not believe in a human Jesus, had much evidence to support it" (2000, 110). Though she admits "part of the problem was the nature of the debates, when Quakers, forced on to the defensive, had to concentrate on trying to define "the light" and its operation (Moore, 2000, 110).

---

[70] Scholem defines a mystic as someone "who has been favored with an immediate, and to him, real, experience of the divine, of ultimate reality" (1965, 5).

Hugh Barbour and J. William Frost take a moderating position: "The Society of Friends has always existed somewhat uneasily within the pale of orthodox Christianity" (Barbour, 1988, 79). They acknowledge, along with Moore, the continual tension for early Friends in explaining the relationship between the "Light within" and the historical Jesus. They suggest this tension might be exaggerated and conclude it was more a problem for their opponents than Quakers themselves, who found no tension between the Christ of history and the glorified Christ as Light. Quakers were emphasizing the new life Christ brought, rather than history, but it is quite clear they never denied the history or its essentialness (Barbour, 1988, 79). In fact, Robert Barclay states this even more explicitly by asserting, "We do not hereby intend any ways to lessen or derogate from the atonement and sacrifice of Jesus Christ; but on the contrary do magnify and exalt it" (1886, 99). Barclay shows how Quakers understood their message as deepening the tradition rather than undermining it.

Barclay, of course, is a post-Restoration writer, and his purpose in writing the *Apology* is different than for the earlier Quaker pamphleteers. This aspect provides another rather obvious reason for the early Quaker emphasis on Christ as the Light, rather than the historical Jesus, in that the earliest writings (those which Moore examines) arose out of the requirements of the first Quaker polemics. They were composed to express what the new emphasis (the Light) was and what the new movement stood for. The first documents, therefore, would highlight the differences with Puritanism, rather than the similarities. Thus, the earliest writings are differentiating Quakerism from Puritanism and all other "isms" of the time. Quakerism comes out of Puritanism, yet is anti-Puritan (Barbour, 1964; Nuttall, 1992; Gwyn, 1986) (see 1.7). It needs to differentiate itself from its parents, so to speak. Orthodoxy often depends on whom you are standing next to.

For early Quakers, Christ's overcoming of sin in the human soul is the primary focus, and it is in that framework, above all, that Quakers spoke of the Light (Wilcox, 1991, 41). The Light of Christ brings the soul to perfection. The Light is both saving and perfecting because it is the inward work of the Atonement. The Light is the ongoing power of the Atonement to transform the individual who responds to the Light. As Wilcox concludes, "Whatever doubts later Quakers many have had about the relevance of the figure of Jesus to salvation, these were not shared by the first Quakers" (1991, 42). The Light is always identified with Christ and presumes an orthodox soteriology and Christology (Jones, 1955; Wilcox, 1991; Davie, 1992; Dobbs, 1995; Roberts, 1961).

This study argues that holiness for early Quakers was the mystical process of the transformation of the personality by the Light (or grace). For early Quakers, the Light of Christ always meant "Christ-in-me" and a "being-in-Christ," a participation in God, the divine indwelling. The doctrine of perfection as a firmly held tenet of faith continued to be central in later periods, though its expressions became more formally prescribed.

1.7 Theories of Quaker History

This section reviews and evaluates the two main schools of previous scholarship: Rufus Jones on Quakers as essentially mystics, and Geoffrey Nuttall and Hugh Barbour on Quakers as Puritans. It then examines Melvin Endy's integration of these two main schools of thought, creating a third alternative, "Spiritualist." This section also evaluates Lewis Benson's prophetic model, Doug Gwyn's eschatological model, and Richard Bailey's divinization model. Of the current theories that examine holiness, Arthur Roberts' and John Punshon's evangelical models most closely resemble the Holiness model, though both minimize the place of mysticism in holiness. Thomas Hamm, who has done the most extensive research on nineteenth century Quaker Holiness, fails to see holiness as a continuation of Quakerism's seventeenth century roots.

Before examining the primary literature on theological interpretations of Quaker history, a brief mention of two major studies in the broader field of historical theology provides a larger context in which to examine Quakerism in Christian history more generally. Ted A. Campbell includes Quakers in his work as part of a broad spiritual movement of "affective devotion" that arose all over Europe as well as Russia and across cultures and religious traditions (1991). The framework in which he places the Quakers provides support for the contention of this study that Quakerism emerged as new kind of spiritual movement that retained at its core a mystical Christian orthodoxy, but in a new context. It borrowed, reshaped, and radically simplified the spirituality of an earlier Catholic mysticism and created a hybrid movement of popularized mysticism of Christian perfection for laypeople, which this study calls holiness, within a Post-Reformation Protestant Puritan cultural context.[71]

Louis Bouyer recognizes the affinity of early Quakerism with the Catholic mystical tradition:

---

[71] Since early Quakers believed they were a return to the earliest primitive church, they summarily dismissed 1500 years of Christian history and tradition as irrelevant, so that with few exceptions, such as the scholarly Robert Barclay and William Penn, the immense volumes of Quaker writing contain no references to other thinkers, scholars, writers, mystics or saints, other than the Bible and their contemporary opponents. Nor did they in their early publishing period reprint edited versions or extracts of other works which supported their own views. Studies of the libraries of early Friends, e.g. George Fox, reveals a collection of volumes containing many earlier mystical works by radical thinkers such as Sebastian Frank and Henry Nicholas, but even such a list does not prove that Fox read them or if he did, he agreed with them. Nevertheless, it seems reasonable to suppose that some of the mystical concepts found in these works would filter into his own thought world and shape his interpretations of his own experience. See Nickalls, "George Fox's Library, *JFHS*, 1931, vol. 28, 3-21.

It may seem surprising, but is not really so very odd, that Quakerism has provided the environment in the heart of Protestantism in which people have been most ready to give a warm and instinctive welcome to the highest teachings of the Catholic mystics, from St. Teresa of Avila and St. John of the Cross to such a man as Fenelon. The temptation to quietism in the movement has always been a lively one, but it has always been counter-balanced by evangelical charity. (1968, 163-164)

Bouyer views Quakerism as essentially Protestant, yet with an instinctive attraction to Catholic mysticism. He recognizes the balance within Quakerism of contemplative mysticism, interiority and quietism with evangelical activism. All of these characteristics converge in the ethos of holiness.

1.7.1   Jones, Nuttall, and Barbour: The Mystic vs. Puritan Debate

In 1912 Rufus M. Jones formulated the first theory of the origins and essence of Quakerism as fundamentally "mystical" in his introduction to William Braithwaite's history of Quakerism[72] (Braithwaite, 1912). In 1921, he emphatically reaffirmed his thesis: "No other large, organized, historically continuous body of Christians has yet existed which has been so fundamentally mystical, both in theory and practice, as the Society of Friends..." (Jones, 1901, xiii). For over 25 years, Jones' claim seemed too accurate to question. But in 1955 a major shift in Quaker studies occurred when Hugh L. Doncaster claimed that new scholarship viewed Quakerism in another light.[73]

The paradigm shift had been set in motion with the publication of Geoffrey F. Nuttall's work, *The Holy Spirit in Puritan Faith and Experience,* in 1946 (revised 1992). Nuttall, a non-Quaker historian, supplanted Jones' mystical theory with a new theory of Quakers as radical Puritans. According to Nuttall, George Fox and the Quakers,

> ...who in the exclusive sense are not puritans but the puritans' fiercest foes, ...repeat, extend, and fuse so much of what is held by the radical, Separatist party within Puritanism, that they cannot be denied the name or excluded from consideration. (1992, 13)

---

[72] Jones based his introduction on an earlier exploration of the history of Christian mysticism, *Studies in Mystical Religion*, one of a handful of pioneering works in that field in the early twentieth century (1909). A few years later he expanded his study with *Spiritual Reformers of the Sixteenth and Seventeenth Centuries* (1914).
[73] See L. Hugh Doncaster, "Forward to the Second Edition," in Wm. C. Braithwaite's *The Beginnings of Quakerism*, ed. Henry J. Cadbury (1955).

Ever since, scholars have been attempting to understand the relationship between Jones' theory of mysticism and the social context of Puritanism in the development of Quaker thought. This study will argue that both the Catholic mystical and the Puritan radical provided fertile soil for the emergence of the Quaker movement, primarily because Puritanism itself was deeply steeped in the medieval mystical tradition.

One of the most important modern histories of Quakerism is Hugh Barbour's *Quakers in Puritan England*, which built on Nuttall's study of Puritanism (1964). A new generation of scholars adopted his interpretation of Quakers as essentially Puritans:[74]

> Most of their insights in ethics and worship were in fact the same as those of the puritans. Even characteristically Quaker teachings were often puritan attitudes pushed to severe conclusions....Quakers shared ideas and language with the "spiritual Puritans" of the time. Their conflicts with puritan leaders had the loving desperation of a family feud. (1964, 2)

But the "mystical school" and the "puritan school" had been set in opposition by Jones. For Jones, Quakerism "broke with the theological systems of Protestantism as completely as Luther and Calvin had done with Catholicism" (1901, xiv). Puritanism for Jones (who wrote before major revisions of puritan history were undertaken) was decidedly not mystical, but rather "forensic," by which he meant based on logic and reason, and the infallibility of Scripture rather than "transforming personal experience" (1932, 19). Jones asserted that "puritanism and mysticism were antithetical. They cancelled each other out." However, he noted with a great sense of irony that mysticism in England came to birth in the "greatest nursery of Puritanism, Emmanuel College at Cambridge," and singled out a small group of Puritans who could be called genuine mystics, the Cambridge Platonists (1932, 115).[75] This small elite group of highly educated Puritan neo-Platonists were the only Puritans Jones considered true mystics and with whom he felt some affinity.

Ultimately for Jones, Quaker roots were not to be found in Puritanism, but in the sixteenth century spiritual Reformers of the continent, mystical Anabaptists of the Radical Reformation, such as Hans Denck, Sebastian Franck, Caspar Schwenckfeld, and the Lutheran mystic, Jacob Boehme (1909).

---

[74] See for example, the work of Henry J. Cadbury and Frederick Tolles.

[75] They were: Benjamin Whichcote (1609-83), John Smith (1618-52), Ralph Cudworth (1617-88), John Norris of Bremerton (1657-1711), Nathaniel Culverwell (1618?-51), Henry More (1614-87), Peter Sterry (d. 1672) and several others who were for a period of time Quakers: Francis Mercury van Helmont, Lady Anne Conway, and George Keith (Jones, 1932, 114 n1).

Jones also made it clear that Quakers were not heirs of the *via negativa* tradition of Catholic mysticism, but only of the type which he called affirmative mysticism.

In *Mysticism and Democracy* (1931) Jones explicitly differentiated Quaker mysticism from what he called the "classic Catholic Model," which he equated with the *via negativa*. This type, according to Jones, was characterized by the goal of ecstasy, a pattern of ascents, God as unknowable, "a flight of the alone to the alone," and a "super-mind" attainment (1931, 12-13). In contrast to this type, Jones claimed mysticism's "essential aspect is rather the *conviction of certainty* that the person's own soul has found its goal of reality in God" [his emphasis] (1931, 13). Jones defined mysticism as "an immediate, intuitive, experimental knowledge of God, or one may say it is consciousness of a Beyond, or of a transcendent Reality, or of Divine Presence" (1939, 251). As valuable as his lifelong and often profound research on mysticism has been for understanding Quaker spirituality, it is not without some major limitations. Jones failed to take into consideration the widespread "devotion of rapture" among the Puritans, with its own brand of affective mysticism, thus missing the real spiritual continuities with Quaker mysticism. More importantly he discounted almost entirely the pervasive influence of the apophatic (*via negativa*) mystical traditions, an ingredient in Quaker spirituality from its earliest beginnings, insisting instead that "Quietism" (the quintessential form of the *via negativa*) was a later distortion of a wholly "affirmative mysticism."

Barbour continued to develop the Puritan school of thought, chipping away at Jones' mystical school (1964). But he admitted Jones' theory was attractive and compelling for modern Quakers (1964, xi). Barbour, however, made one small concession to the possibility of mysticism as an element within seventeenth century Puritanism by noting that "in describing their faith Friends used many ideas and phrases shared with 'spiritual Puritans'" (1964, 2).[76]

The difficulty in identifying Quakers with radical Puritans stems from the fluidity and breadth of the seventeenth century Puritan movement and hence the impossibility of determining the outer limits of Puritanism and its overlapping with Quakerism. Indeed, as Puritan historians also admit, nailing down the essential nature of Puritanism is proving to be an elusive task in itself (Greaves, 1977, 257-8). Critics of Jones conclude that he erred in his underestimation of the experiential aspect of Puritan life (Endy, 1981, 11).[77] Barbour emphatically identified the pivotal experiential component when he

---

[76] Many of the "spiritual Puritans" Barbour identifies (1964, 27-28) are the same as those singled out by Jones in *Mysticism and Democracy*, 1932, 114; *New Studies in Mystical Religion*, 1927, 482-500; and *Spiritual Reformers*, 1914, 266-87.

[77] As Endy jibes, in critiquing Jones's work, "Whereas [H. L.] Mencken defined a Puritan as anyone burdened with an over-riding fear that someone, somewhere might be happy, Jones seemed to see the Puritan as marked above all by the dread thought that someone, somewhere might be having a religious experience" (1981, 11).

asserted "...for puritans, personal experience of conversion and sanctification became crucial as for no other Christian group" (1964, 3). More importantly for this study, Barbour pinpoints the essential difference between Puritan experience and the Quaker experience:

> The relation of Spirit and personality in Quaker thought came to its acute focus in the idea of perfectionism, the issue for which puritans took Quakers to task more often than any other...[Quakers] stressed the infallibility of the Spirit, because they would not recognize any sin or evil which the Spirit might not overcome. (1964, 149)

Barbour further observed, "Quaker perfectionism, like the 'Holiness' doctrine of modern American sects (which it only partly resembles), rested on personal religious experience" (1964, 149). Rosemary Moore's exhaustive research on Quaker writings up to 1660 provides the most extensive documentation of the paradigmatic Quaker religious experience to be a sense of real union with God through Christ the Light, a clear identification of early Quakers with mysticism (2000, 79). Although the way of union might be described differently – "static, mystical union" in Naylor or "dynamic take-over" in Fox – the idea of divine indwelling is paramount, and Moore is certain unity with God is central to early Friends (2000, 79). But all previous research, including Moore's, gropes for an understanding of mystical union, and thus the meaning of holiness for early Friends.[78] For modern historians, as well as the Quakers' opponents in the seventeenth century, mystical union remains for most an incomprehensible spirituality. Perhaps Quaker mysticism will always be in part an enigma to outside interpreters unless they have taken that step into the transcendent themselves. Because of the mysterious and ineffable dimension of Quaker holiness that cannot be easily explained, but only experienced, the conceptualization of holiness and the theological formulations about it have tended to focus on the more pragmatic "eradication of sin" rather than the mysterious union with God upon which holiness is rooted.

1.7.2 Melvin Endy: The Spiritualist Synthesis

Melvin Endy attempts to find a synthesis between Jones' "somewhat simplistic" mystical theories (preferred by Quaker liberals) and the Puritan theories (preferred by evangelicals and ecumenists). He affirms the enduring

---

[78] After quoting a seventeenth century opponent of Quakers who attempts to define the distinction between heretical claims to divine union and his own orthodox view, Moore can only respond that "Much of this section could have been written by a Quaker" and in the final analysis Moore confesses that "it is very difficult to pinpoint the distinction" (2000, 80).

value of Jones' interpretation, despite its blind spots and limitations (Endy, 1981, 12-13). Endy finds Nuttall's research affirms much of Jones' judgments, and that both views can be integrated on many points to give a more accurate picture of the complex relationship between the two movements. Endy proceeds to add his interpretation of early Quakers as essentially "spiritualist" (1981, 13).

In an earlier work, Endy explains what he means by "spiritualist" (1973). Their distinctive beliefs are based on four elements. The first two are related to dualism, one a belief in the radical disjunction between human and divine, the other on a duality between the physical and spiritual (Endy, 1973, 40-41). A third characteristic of spiritualist is a dehistoricizing of Christianity (Endy, 1973, 44). And fourthly, spiritualists were millennial (Endy, 1973, 45). Endy groups spiritualists together with orthodox Puritans who have spiritualizing tendencies along with more radical groups such as "Seekers," "Familists," and "Ranters" (1973, 48). Although Endy highlights important differences in Quaker teachings from other spiritualist groups, and admits they "do not fit neatly into the spiritualist categories," he finds this spiritualist alternative, rather than Jones' mystic or Barbour's Puritan, most satisfactory (Endy, 1973, 90).

This study argues that Quakers were not dualist in the same sense as Endy's definition of spiritualist, because Quaker perfection overcomes the twin dualisms of human and divine, and physical and spiritual. Dualism is dissolved in mystical union, though humans never become God in essence. Just as in the earliest Christian theology, humans through grace become what God is by nature. Union with God is a complete restoration of the image, and thus perfection.

Endy draws two significant and critical conclusions, based on his own work and that of Jones and Nuttall, on which all three find basic agreement. Firstly, Endy maintains along with Jones, (and finds support in Nuttall against Jones' other critics) that the "Puritan drive toward immediacy in the relationship between God and man and its impatience with the indirectness and ambiguity of sense knowledge was not tempered in Quakerism, as it was among the Puritans, by the Calvinist emphasis on the awful distance between the sovereign Lord of being and his lowly creatures" (1981, 13-14). The degree of immediacy and range of intimacy with God was far more profound among Quakers than even the mystical Puritans. And the difference rested in the restrictive effect of Calvinistic theology with its emphasis on the transcendence and sovereignty of God.

Endy affirms the basic agreement between Puritans and Quakers on original sin and total depravity. Endy even surprises by suggesting Quakers had a realistic appreciation for the reality of human depravity, "a healthier respect, they claimed, than that of the Puritans" (1981, 14). On this point Endy differs considerably from Jones who projects a positive view of human nature onto the first generation, and locates the shift to a negative view with Barclay and the second generation.[79] Quakers emphasized in particular the corruption of human reason. While the logic of holding a doctrine of divine immanence along with a doctrine of original sin may seem contradictory (at least in the Protestant tradition), the medieval mystical tradition combined both, as does the Eastern Orthodox Church.

As this study will demonstrate, the most significant contrast between Quakers and Puritans can be found in the greater affinity of Quakers to a pre-reformation medieval anthropology in which there is no precise differentiation between the natural and the supernatural in the soul. A corollary of this belief is that of an immanent capacity for God, a capacity for the divine not destroyed by the fall, which developed into the Quaker doctrine of the Inward Light of Christ and the potential for perfection in all persons. This study will show that Quaker theology held, in a balanced tension, the paradox of the transcendence and immanence of God. The divine without as well as within (a position which can be traced back to Augustine, despite his inherent dualism [see appendix A]), had far greater potential for divine union than could be realized in Reformation theology.

Secondly, Endy insists, along with Nuttall and Jones, that Quakers, unlike Puritans, "spiritualized" Christ to the extent that they ignored the incarnation and were reluctant to accept the doctrine of the Trinity (Endy, 1981, 16; Nuttall, 1992, 159; Jones, 1914, 337). This "spiritualization of Christ" to the neglect of the historical became a constant theme in Puritan attacks on Quakerism, and one which Quakers defended vigorously. Endy sides solidly with Jones, and the Quakers' opponents, such as Henry More, who were certain that Quaker heresy was found in their "excluding the external Christ from the business of Religion, and only admitting the internal Christ."[80] Endy suggests this might be an exaggeration "but it was on target" nonetheless (1981, 17). On the other hand, Endy admits that some Quakers emphasized the historical Christ more than others, among them two key leaders, George Fox and Robert Barclay (1981, 16). In fact, he admits that "Quakerism was conservative by instinct under Fox's leadership" (1981, 12-13). His conclusion conforms to recent research such as that of Katz, who contends mystics are both traditional and innovative at the same time, embodying some radical elements which challenge established traditions, yet conservative in nature (Katz, 1983, 3)[81] (see also 1.6).

---

[79] See Katheryn Damiano for a mediating view of Barclay on sin, *On Earth as it is in Heaven*, 1988, 107-111.

[80] Qtd. in Endy, 1981, 17, from Henry More, *Divine Dialogues* (2nd ed.), 1713, 565.

[81] Endy identifies scholars who hold to a view that Quakers did not devalue the incarnation, the Trinity or the atonement: Arthur Roberts; Hugh Barbour in some of his works (his collaboration with Roberts in *Early Quaker Writings*, 1973, 26, 245, 150), but who takes a somewhat different direction in *Quakers in Puritan England*,1964 and Tolles in *Atlantic Culture*, 1960, 109 (Endy notes this is atypical of Tolles) (1981, 17

The other basic agreement between Quakers and Puritans, according to Endy, is the insistence of both on the utter dependence on grace (1981, 14). This study demonstrates that Quaker perfection was, in fact, a concept that held in balance the relationship of grace and works in a pre-Reformation understanding called synergy, a working with grace, which can be traced back to the early Fathers. A doctrine of perfection necessarily implies a synergistic relationship between the human and the divine, in the Pauline sense of "pressing toward the mark of the high calling of God," or in short, "pressing" on to perfection. In the eighteenth century, Wesley's belief in Christian perfection also depended on the cooperation of grace and works, which led him back to a patristic understanding of synergy, and separated him from strict Calvinism (Maddox, 1994, 91-92).[82]

1.7.3   Lewis Benson: Prophetic Quakerism

The fiercely independent scholar, Lewis Benson, was one of the first to seriously challenge Jones' mystical views of Quaker essence and origins (1942). Benson interpreted Quakerism as a "prophetic" faith, meaning a mission-oriented, apostolic faith called to bring renewal and hope to the modern world, just as Fox did to the seventeenth century world. Benson gave an appreciative nod to Jones' writings for bringing hope to one generation of Quakers, but after his own painstaking study of the writings of George Fox he concluded that Jones' interpretations of Quakerism, as well as that of most modern scholars, bore no resemblance to the faith of the early Quakers (Benson, 1942) (Wallace, 1996). Benson sought to return Quakerism to its Christ-centered, Gospel-centered, mission-oriented roots. Benson maintained that Fox taught the "The Christ of history is the Christ of inward experience" (1942, 52). Benson was emphatic in asserting that the historical Christ is also the living Christ, and the same message Fox preached over 300 years ago is

---

n42). I would add Benson, in *Catholic Quakerism*, 1966; T. C. Jones, "The Nature and Function of the Light in the Thought of George Fox," *QRT*, Vol. 16, Winter, 1974-75, p. 53-71; and Cooper, in *A Living Faith*, 1990. Interestingly, Janet Scott, (also perhaps atypically, a liberal British Quaker) has moved to defending a Trinitarian basis for early Quakerism (Woodbrooke lecture, June, 2000). A non-Quaker scholar whose recent work on twentieth century British Quaker theology contrasts modernist and liberal British Quaker views with their earlier orthodoxy concludes that Quakers in England up until 1895 accepted the core of conviction of Christian beliefs and doctrines, including the incarnation and the Trinity (Davie, 1992, 40).

[82] Some Wesleyan scholars would not use the term "synergy" but rather "co-operant grace" or "responsible grace," but most would agree with Maddox's statement: "Wesley did indeed affirm a role for meaningful human participation in salvation....[but] this role was grounded in God's gracious empowering, not our inherent abilities" (1994, 92).

still relevant today and needs no reinterpretations to make it palatable to the modern mind.

Benson promoted a thorough and consistent Christocentric interpretation of Fox. True to Fox, Benson avoided all theological terminology, such as "incarnation" or "Trinity," though in essence his interpretation of Quakerism would fit into that core of conviction of Christian beliefs. Benson, however, did not view Quakerism in continuity with orthodox Christian tradition. Benson refused to label Quakerism as Protestant or Catholic, but rather following the Anabaptist tradition, saw it as a third way. He also insisted Quakerism had no connections to the Christian mystical tradition, which he maintained was derived solely from Greek Platonic thought. He took a decisive turn away from Jones' theory of mystical influences through the radical German reformers to a conception of Quakerism arising divinely out of the blue, much as George Fox claimed.

Neither did he acknowledge Quakerism to be rooted in Puritanism. Benson took a classically sectarian viewpoint, holding to a view that the Quaker movement arose as something entirely new by divine intervention and without historic causation. In *Catholic Quakerism* (a rather ironic designation for such a sectarian thinker), he claimed in the manner of the early Quaker preachers against all other Puritans that all modern forms of Quakerism, whether it be evangelical, mystical, ecumenical, humanistic, or liberal, had departed from the truth and compromised what was distinctive in true prophetic Quakerism (1968, 1-8).

When Benson referred to holiness, using Fox's favorite term, perfection, he claimed it meant "only that when God commands we can both hear and obey" (1968, 26). Benson, in his radical primitivism, disallowed any continuity or development within Quakerism. He reduced holiness to ethical obedience with a works-orientation which leaned in a strongly Pelagian direction, because he allowed a minimal place for grace, synergy, or the experience of the Holy Spirit. He claimed that the Holy Spirit was not central in Fox's thought (1968, 7). Benson found no resemblance in Quakerism to holiness in the Wesleyan movement, and was highly critical of holiness preaching.[83] His rational, neo-orthodox affinities combined with a radical sectarian mindset brought out fiercely anti-mystical leanings. However, his sectarian desire for a church of the pure has strong similarities to holiness preaching. Benson concluded that "righteousness and community are the central core of Fox's Christianity" (1968, 19).

But Benson's rationalism separates his message from the affective heart-religion of Quaker holiness. Benson claimed that holiness "is experienced through a master-disciple relationship to Christ" (1968, 19). He further

---

[83] For Benson's critique of holiness in the Wesleyan tradition see, "The Gospel preached by John Wesley" in *Recovering the Early Quaker Universal Mission and Message*, 1986.

explained that "we experience it as the sound of a voice that speaks to us in the tone of a command" (1968, 22). Unlike earlier Quakers, and Fox himself, Benson disclosed little about the manner of his own conversion or alluded to his own spiritual experiences in his writings.[84] (As dependent as Benson is on Fox alone, he does not explore Fox's more rapturous experiences such as being caught up in an "ocean of love," and what that might mean.) Benson's vision of early Quaker holiness as being prophetic stressed obedience and ethics to the neglect of the experience of divine indwelling which empowered it.

1.7.4   Douglas Gwyn: Apocalyptic Quakerism

Douglas Gwyn, following along the lines of Lewis Benson, provides a similar critique of Jones' mystical interpretation. Gwyn rightly observes that Jones' portrayal of Quaker and Puritan worldviews as "the chance collision of two different thought-worlds" is an imaginary one, and that the struggle was always within the same worldview (1986, xv). Gwyn is willing to concede that "Fox's approach may perhaps be accurately called mystical but not by the definition Jones gave to that word," but he does not explain what mystical might mean (1986, xvi).

Gwyn also challenges, as did Benson, the "Protestant" (i.e. Puritan) interpretation of early Quakerism. Gwyn agrees with Benson that Quakerism's radical theological shift was a "Copernican revolution" in the religious world (1986, xviii). (This is an exaggeration, since Quakerism was but one manifestation of a broad "religion of the heart" movement – see Appendix B). Gwyn, following Benson's lead, instinctively recognizes that Quakerism is not so thoroughly "Protestant" as is generally assumed, but also fails to recognize the mystical Catholic aspects which it incorporates in its central doctrine of Christian perfection. Gwyn's theory postulates eschatology as the central framework of the early Quaker movement. But he is careful to connect the apocalyptic, "Christ's return as a presently unfolding reality," with revelation as present experience, or "realized eschatology" (1986, xxii). The apocalyptic therefore becomes interiorized. The Quaker response to the "delay of the parousia" is to proclaim it has come into the heart, and is not simply a future hope. The battle between good and evil is fought within one's heart, and the evil is overcome by the good as one is brought into the light (restored into the

---

[84] A 1996 publication by the New Foundation Fellowship (the organization inspired by Benson) *None Were So Clear: Prophetic Quaker Faith and the Ministry of Lewis Benson*, edited by T.H.S. Wallace, includes some formerly unpublished autobiographical material in which Benson identifies with Fox's narrative in his *Journal* and describes his turning to Christ through his reading of Fox. "My Quest for a Faith that Overcomes the World," is in this Wallace publication, 142-148.

image of Christ). The Kingdom comes not on earth as a golden age, but reigns within each individual believer's heart. And consequently, the individual indwelling of Christ within each believer is magnified when Christ is incarnated corporately within the true worshipping community (1986, xxii). Gwyn does not describe this Kingdom of God within as mystical union with Christ. But his analysis of Fox's eschatology and Christology points to that as a possible meaning, as his concluding statements seem to infer when he quotes Albert Schweitzer in *The Mysticism of Paul the Apostle* (1931) which speaks of the potential of mystical holiness:

> Great has been the work as a reforming influence which Paul, by his doctrine of justification by faith alone, has accomplished in opposition to the spirit of work-righteousness in Christianity. Still greater will be the work which he will do when his mystical doctrine of being redeemed into the Kingdom of God, through union with Christ, begins to bring quietly to bear upon us the power which lies within it. (1986, 218)

Schweitzer's insight coincides with the Quaker understanding of salvation as beyond mere faith alone to mystical union with Christ, through the work of the Spirit that brings perfecting power (Gwyn, 1986, 218).

In more recent work Gwyn does allude to, though briefly, perfection as union with God, and the Quaker claim of mutual indwelling, quoting Francis Howgill, "there is equality in nature though not in stature" (Gwyn, 2000, 244). He also cites Fox's bold claim that "To have Christ within was to be of Christ's flesh and bone, eating it and becoming the same substance with it" (Fox, 1831, 398-99).[85] Gwyn does not link this idea to deification or develop it theologically as Quaker holiness, but employs his references to the concept of divine union as the basis for the Quaker egalitarian social ethic.

1.7.5 Richard Bailey: Divinization

The early Quaker concept of union with Christ, or more accurately the experience of "being-in-Christ" and "Christ-in-me" in the sense of a divine mutual indwelling, which is the essence of their mystical faith, continues to be an enigma to most modern interpreters. Their Puritan opponents either genuinely misunderstood, or strongly overreacted, to early Quakers' exuberant expressions of the indwelling Christ, and accused them of blasphemy for claiming to be equal to Christ. Later historians and contemporary interpreters

---

[85] This statement by Fox is cited by both Gwyn and Bailey (Gwyn, 2000, 242-3; Bailey, 1992, 78).

alike have found "union with God" language to be among the most baffling and at times embarrassing statements of early Quakers.

Lewis Benson, in his extensive research on Fox, rarely mentioned union with God but concluded that the phrase "Christ has come to teach his people himself" is key to Fox's message and his new discovery (1968, 21). Without doubting the epochal nature of this insight for Fox and early Quakers, Benson's interpretation of teaching as conveying information and knowledge does not fully capture the sense in which Fox felt himself to be possessed by the energies of God (see 1.7.3). As Rosemary Moore rightly observes in the most exhaustive research to date on early Quaker writings, for Fox it was more like a "dynamic take-over" (2000, 79). Moore's findings are highly significant in that she provides extensive evidence that "Belief in a real union with Christ, however expressed, remained the keystone of Fox's theology" (2000, 109).

Another recent interpreter, Richard Bailey, devotes an entire book to this issue, unearthing a few seemingly baffling passages in letters and other texts, deliberately ignored or overlooked, which express the union experience in its most startling forms (1992). He proposes one of the more novel theories to date as a way to explain this material, which he terms, "celestial inhabitation" (the notion that the saints became flesh and bone of Christ) (1993, 110).

Both Moore (2000) and Gwyn (2000) add their correctives to this view. But Moore agrees that Bailey's description of the early Quakers' union relationship is "as nearly accurate as it is possible to come" but objects to his using language of eastern religions to describe it (2000, 263-4 n9).

Since Bailey's work explores in exhaustive detail a central theme in the concept of perfection as union with God, this study will give particular attention to an examination of Bailey's theory. Bailey is aware that the experience of union with Christ was central to the spirituality of early Quakers, but he does not interpret it within a traditional Christian mystical framework. He insists Quakers are describing a concept which goes far beyond the boundaries of the any remotely orthodox mystical tradition. He contends that Quakers did indeed teach a "feeding on the glorified body of Christ" which he calls "celestial habitation" (1993, 111). Bailey interprets this in a most literal fashion, insisting that celestial habitation is a doctrine not conceived of by Puritans, mystics, or even Catholic sacramentalists: "...celestial inhabitation is an impossible paradox: the inhabiting of a mortal body with a spiritual 'stuff' like the glorified body of Christ as an actual substance" (1993, 113).

Admittedly, the Quaker language of union had it own peculiarities of expression, and did at times push the envelope of orthodoxy (as mystical language has the ability to do). But anyone who has immersed themselves for any length of time in the writings of the Christian mystical tradition, even the safely orthodox mystics, would not find their language so extraordinary. Rhapsodic, ecstatic, hyperbolic language is common discourse in the Christian mystical canon. The difficulty in distinguishing between essential union, union of likeness, and union of nature is a continual one in the mystical canon. The

Christian church took eight centuries to work out basic formulations of humanity and divinity of Christ and ideas of *theosis*, so it is hardly surprising that Quakers, unsophisticated as they were theologically, would have difficulties in expressing what is essentially the paradoxical "Christian mystery."

Bailey's interpretation of George Fox is original and creative. But all original theses, which claim "new light," need further light to refine and correct them. The scriptural passage on which Bailey's idea is based is Eph. 5:30-33, where the church is called the body of Christ, and the analogy of man and woman at creation being joined as "one flesh"[86] is used to describe the union between the body of Christ and the church. In the creation account of Gen. 2:23 this union is described as "bone of bone and flesh of flesh." Paul uses this analogy for the mystical union with Christ (vs. 32) of his church (in this passage), and to the believer and Christ in other instances. The phrase "my bone and my flesh" is a phrase used frequently in the Old Testament for acknowledging kinship.[87] Bailey claims Fox is casting himself as a new incarnation of Christ. Yet Christ indwelling each Christian, individually as well as corporately as the Body of Christ, is precisely the central message of Paul. It is the mystical doctrine of "being-in-Christ."

One critical aspect that Bailey does not explore seriously enough is the extent of the kind of rhapsodic language which was used in the broad sweep of experiential religion in the seventeenth century. The prevalence of the expression "bone of bone and flesh of flesh" to describe union with Christ, which Bailey seems to think is so unique to Fox and evidence of celestial habitation, is commonly found in Christocentric mysticism in that period. Puritanism has a vast body of mystical literature that is the Protestant inheritance of the medieval mystical tradition, and a major source of seventeenth century experiential religion (Hambrick-Stowe, 1986, 28).[88] (See Appendix A)

---

[86] In some versions of this verse, perhaps a version Fox used, the phrase "bone and flesh" is added to verse 30, so that it actually reads, in reference to Christ, that we are "members of his body of his flesh and of his bones"). See *Harper Collins Study Bible*, NRSV, Eph. 5:30 note.

[87] See *Harper Collins Study Bible*, NRSV, Gen. 29:14 note.

[88] Here is one example from the writings of Puritan Edward Polhill, in *Christus in corde: or the mystical union between Christ and believers* published in 1680: "The Deity is an Immense Ocean of mercy and goodness, but it flows out to us only in and through a Mediator; Jesus Christ is a Mediator of Alsufficient righteousness and merit; but he communicates himself only to those that are in union with him. . . . This mystical union... is very signally set forth in Scripture; There it is said, that Christ dwells in Believers, and they in him; which expressions point out a mutual inexistence of him and them. But, (because this mystery is very deep) the Holy Ghost, in condensation of our weakness, shadows out this weakness by many earthly patterns, [he lists biblical examples concluding with]... the intimate union and incorporation of the Food and the

The debate over divinization that Quakers resurrected in the seventeenth century is a long and complex one in the history of Christianity, much like the concept of perfection itself, which has always been suspect as teaching deification. Briefly, the deification of the believer, which is the spiritual purpose and end for all humans, is an established tenet of Eastern Orthodoxy, grounded in the writings of the early Greek Fathers.[89] Athanasius came to this position as a natural corollary to the doctrine of the incarnation:

> The word became flesh, that he might offer it on behalf of us all, and that we, partaking of his spirit, might be able to be deified; we could never have attained this if he had not put on our created body. (*Decr. Nic. Syn.*, 14)

Divinization as described in the theology of Gregory of Nazianzen sounds as shocking to modern ears as Fox's most radical statements:

> He took our flesh and our flesh became God, since it is united with God and forms a single entity with him. For the higher perfection dominated, resulting in my becoming God as fully as he became man. (*Third Theological Oratio*, PG 36, 537-8)

Western Christians feel uncomfortable with talk of holiness in terms of deification (Snelling, 1997, 133; Drewery, 1975). In Eastern Orthodoxy, deification, divinization, and *theosis* all mean perfection, growth in holiness through a process of assimilation to God short of complete identity. Quaker

---

Body.... The Bonds of this union are Faith and the Holy Spirit; Faith sees, comes to, receives, leans on, puts on, feeds upon Christ, as being the universal capacity to take in Christ into the Soul; the Holy Spirit is *primaria commissura,* the primary ligature, which knits us to Christ: That Spirit. . .brings us into union with Christ; that Spirit (which united the two natures in Christ) unites us to Christ: Hence we become mystical parts of him, of his flesh and of his bone; nay *hen pneuma,* one spirit with him (qtd. in Nuttall, 1975, 523). Nuttall implies that Polhill is not unique or eccentric among puritan writers but is "representative...in his evident evangelical purposes and ethical concern as well as his restrained manner" (1975, 524). The tone and expression is typically Puritan, and stated with more sophisticated nuance then is common to Fox, yet Polhill is attempting to convey a similar kind of understanding of union. But the critical difference between the language of Polhill and Fox may be only the more cautious and careful wording of a theologically trained minister, rather than a charismatic lay-preacher.

[89] The stance of the Western Church however, is more complex, and divinization is but one of many categories for union. Reformation Protestantism finds this doctrine a distortion of biblical faith and a turn toward Platonic pantheism, with a blurring of the distinction between the creature and the Creator. The Eastern Church, however, clearly understands *theosis* as a "union of energies" (which can be shared with God) but not of essence (which cannot be shared with God). See Lossky, 1998.

perfection was another way of describing the same process: union with God by attaining the measure of the full stature of Christ[90] (see 1.4 and 2.5.1). It would be surprising in a lay movement with such a powerful sense of Christ's indwelling that Messianic language and saint-like adulation for a leader such as Fox did not erupt at times in its formative stages. That the movement as it became more reflective, discerning and theologically mature would curb the inherent messianic tendencies of a spirituality of deification with its dangers of delusion is to their credit. This transpired not so much by editing and censorship as by taking the moral highroad and balancing a holiness of mystical experience with the *imitatio Christi* and the ethical ideals of the Sermon on the Mount, radical obedience, the *via negativa* of suffering and self-annihilation, and elevating humility as the highest virtue.[91]

Bailey rightly locates Fox's spirituality in his experience of Christ-in-me as divine union, but interprets it as a unique, extreme, and far too literal understanding than seems warranted by the data. What Bailey coins as "celestial habitation" is simply the doctrine of deification as it came to be expressed by Fox in the seventeenth century. Rather than understanding holiness as embodied in relationship, Bailey interprets it as literally embodied.[92]

---

[90] Although Wesley read and assimilated much of his concept of perfection from the early Fathers (particularly Clement of Alexandria) who used the term deification, he never adopted the term (for a more detailed account of perfection and deification in Western perspective see Snelling, 1997, 133).

[91] Next to the Light of Christ, the Cross of Christ may be the most prominent symbol in Quakerism. In 1668-9 William Penn while imprisoned in the Tower of London, wrote one of the classic Quaker books of devotion, *No Cross, No Crown: a Discourse Shewing the Nature and Discipline of the Holy Cross of Christ, and that the Denyal of Self, and daily Bearing of Christ's Cross, is alone Way to the Rest and Kingdom of God*. The title is a good summary of what continued to be a resounding theme in Quakerism and an integral aspect of holiness and the doctrine of perfection: self-denial, renunciation, and taking up the cross. Perfection cannot be merited through asceticism; it comes through grace, but the natural result of growth in grace will be renunciation and separation from the world. Penn is completely Protestant in his denunciation of the monastic life, yet in effect he has internalized the monastery so that it can now be carried as a cross into the world. This lifestyle has been called "intramundane asceticism," a worldly monasticism (Tolles, 1957, 45).

[92] For a related discussion of holiness and embodiment see Douglas J. Davies, "The Sociology of Holiness: The Power of Being Good," in *Holiness: Past and Present*, Stephen C. Barton (ed.), 2003.

1.7.6 Arthur Roberts: Evangelical Holiness

Arthur Roberts understands Quakerism as a holiness movement both evangelical and experiential.[93] His vision of Quakerism is most similar to the argument of this study. But because he was a part of the movement of young Quakers scholars in the 1950s who reacted against Rufus Jones' theory of mysticism with its close identification with liberal theology, Roberts rarely links mysticism to holiness. Yet in his descriptions of the experiential he often describes what this study defines as mystical. Roberts is more of a theologian of holiness than a historian of holiness, thus he does not develop an overall theory of Quaker origins and its evolution. He does not connect Quietism to holiness, but rather sees it as an aberration. However, he has written primarily on the theology and spirituality of twentieth century Evangelical Friends. He has written one of the many biographies of George Fox, *Through Flaming Sword*, in which Fox is viewed primarily through evangelical eyes. Roberts intentionally calls it a "spiritual biography," thus more devotional and popular (hagiographical) than academic. Though Roberts is a modern evangelical theologian, he identifies himself explicitly as a Quaker theologian rooted in the holiness tradition. He recognizes that holiness (which he equates with Christian perfection), is central to Quaker theology. He also differentiates Quaker holiness from Wesleyan holiness and the "neo-holiness" of the American Revival Movement. Quaker holiness predates Wesleyan holiness, but he sees that both have the same biblical and experiential roots. For Roberts, Quaker holiness balances the ethical and the experiential, which Wesleyan, Revival, and neo-holiness, often do not (1993, 154). Roberts also asserts, against other evangelical forms of holiness, that the peace testimony is an integral part of holiness (1993, 154).

Some of Roberts' clearest statements on Quaker holiness and its distinctiveness from Wesleyan forms (which were pervasive among Evangelical Friends of his generation) are found in his spiritual autobiography, *Drawn by the Light* (1993). A remarkable expression of kataphatic mysticism is found in his 1996 *Messengers of God: The Sensuous Side of Spirituality*, where he describes a spirituality shaped by an awakening of the senses to the creative world. Roberts offers a corrective to distorted notions of false asceticism in which the senses are repressed and viewed as barriers to holiness (1996, 5). His most developed work on holiness, given in a recent lecture series, provides

---

[93] See "Early Friends and the Work of Christ", *QRT*, vol. 3, 1; "Holiness and Christian Renewal," *QRT* Vol. 9, Spring 1967; "The Universalism of Christ in Early Quaker Understanding, *QRT*, Summer 1989, pp. 1-17; *Through Flaming Sword, A Spiritual Biography of George Fox*, 1959; "The Concepts of Perfection in the History of the Quaker Movement, B.D. thesis, Nazarene Theological Seminary, 1951; and *The Association of Evangelical Friends: A Story of Quaker Renewal in the Twentieth Century*, Barclay, 1975.

both a critique of holiness movements and testimony to the power of the holiness vision (2003). By the definition of mysticism used in this study, Roberts is a mystic, having a direct experience of God, a distinct conversion experience, a divine call, and living with a continual sense of God's presence. (See 6.6, contemporary trends)

1.7.7 John Punshon: Evangelical Holiness, Non-Mystical

John Punshon, a British Quaker, has written the most recent history of Evangelical Friends (2001). He includes a substantial chapter on holiness theology and identifies it as one of the main principles of the Friends Church (Ch. 8: Righteousness and Holiness). Punshon, however, also locates holiness in early Friends and identifies it as normative to Quakerism (2001, 259). He recognizes that holiness is not confined to Friends, and that Quaker holiness can be differentiated from Wesleyan and other forms of holiness (2001, 260). He admits holiness is not heard much among Evangelical Quakers today, and identifies only three Yearly Meetings as "avowedly Holiness" now (only one in the US), but these are more Wesleyan than Quaker in their theology. Punshon thoroughly analyzes holiness as a doctrine, but less so as an experience. He recognizes that entering the arena of holiness is a step across the ordinary into the extraordinary, into the transcendent (2001, 156). But though he identifies holiness as transcendent, he resists using the word mystical, and does not develop the experiential side of holiness as a relationship of intimate presence. Punshon provides clear biblical exposition and a sympathetic summary of the history of holiness from Wesley through the holiness movement and its impact on American Friends. Punshon's survey is broad and more general than Hamm's detailed historical analysis (see 1.7.8), but provides a positive counter to Hamm's more skeptical assessment. In the final analysis, Punshon writes that "Holiness is not the whole of evangelical Quakerism, but is an essential component of the faith" (2001, 285). This study will argue that for early Quakers, perfection was an essential component of the faith, and holiness was the whole of Quakerism.

1.7.8 Thomas Hamm: Holiness as Non-Quaker

Thomas Hamm is the sole Quaker historian to have explored in depth the Holiness revival movement and its impact on Quakerism in the nineteenth century. His *Transformation of American Quakerism* filled a huge gap in Quaker history (1988). His research is thorough and impeccable. But his conclusions regarding the forms of holiness in Quakerism and its central role differ from the position taken in this study. Rather than identifying holiness as a central tenet of Quakerism and revivalism as a form of renewal, he considers holiness as revivalism to be revolutionary. Revivalism is thus a transformation imposed upon Friends from outside rather than arising from within historic Quaker spirituality (1988, 74). Since Hamm's work is confined to a particular time period, he does not make any substantial comparisons of the Holiness revival among nineteenth century Friends with the enthusiasms of early Friends, and thus does not notice the strong continuity of experience. Instead, he contrasts the revival with the late eighteenth century Quietists who are upheld as the norm of Quakerism (1988, 74-76). Hamm thus regards the renewed energy of holiness in the revival period as more destructive to Quakerism than creative (1988, xiv). Hamm contends that Quakerism is not essentially evangelical, but was absorbed into that stream by cultural forces (1988, xv). This study challenges some of Hamm's divisions between holiness leaders and renewal leaders, as well as his tendency to portray the two as essentially different, rather than viewing all renewal leaders along a spectrum of Quaker holiness of that era (1988, 43-45, 79-81).[94] Hamm's final mapping of Quakerism results in "modernism" as the mainstream of the evolution of Quakerism and the positive fruit of the renewal movement, and Holiness as a definite (and eccentric) side (1988, 176).

1.7.9   Summary of Previous Theories

No historian to date has isolated "holiness" as the key to understanding early Quaker history, nor viewed it as a framework in which to trace the evolution of later forms. Roberts (1953, 1959, 1967, 1993), Punshon, (2001, 1984), Barbour (1964), Moore (2000), Nuttall (1992), and Bailey (1993, 1992) identify the concept of perfection with the goal of holiness variously understood, as a distinctive Quaker element in its beginnings. But only Roberts and Punshon, and Barbour to a lesser degree, emphasize holiness throughout Quaker history and claim it as a defining characteristic. All three of these scholars would concur that Quakerism is revivalistic, in the sense of a renewal and reawakening of a more intensive experiential Christianity, and thus recognize nineteenth century adaptations as valid theological continuities. Both Roberts and Punshon would concur that Quakerism is firmly embedded in orthodox Christianity, and thus modern evangelical Quakerism is seen by them as a natural outcome of historical Quakerism. But neither of these scholars recognize fully the degree to which mysticism shaped Quaker holiness, and thus both give minimal weight to Rufus Jones' pioneering work. Punshon rightly recognizes the debt to Quietism in the evolution of holiness, but Roberts

---

[94] This study also strongly questions his view of the role of women in the renewal movement as subordinate, and in particular his glaring omission of one of the leading Holiness Quakers, Hannah Whitall Smith (see 5.4).

does not value early Quietism and its later manifestations as a necessary stage of holiness or as an essential bridge to the later Holiness Movement. Roberts, however, has come to affirm and value a mysticism which he describes as Christ-centered and evangelical and desires to recover this spiritual dimension for contemporary Quakerism.

While Jones and the newer work of Bailey place much greater emphasis on the mystical, both fail to see Quaker mysticism as having deep connections and foundations in Christian orthodoxy, and specifically in Protestant Puritan mystical experience. Jones presents Quaker mysticism in modern Liberal guise, and Bailey in an esoteric, new age guise. Jones traces Quakerism to the radical reformers of the sixteenth century, but less so to the medieval Catholic mystics, or the Greek Fathers who were also Quaker forerunners in their emphasis on deification (an area he hardly explores).

Endy (1981) provides an excellent critique of Jones and Puritan theories, and offers a mediating "spiritualist" theory of Quaker origins, which has important affinities with holiness theory, but like Jones and others, he overlooks the inherent orthodoxy of Quakerism. Benson's work recaptures the undeniable Christocentric approach of Fox, but overlooks completely the mystical component.

Hamm's (1988) exploration of the transformation of Quakerism in the nineteenth century fails to significantly link holiness to the mainstream of Quaker theology and thus contrasts sharply with the findings of this research. Gwyn's (1986) apocalyptic theory relates to one essential ingredient of Quaker holiness, and provides an important foundation for this work, but his concentrated focus on one element does not provide an adequate synthesis for understanding modern forms of Quakerism. Only holiness, when understood as the constellation of eight essential elements of early Quaker theology, provides a continuous identifiable theological framework to explain the evolution of Quakerism across time.

1.8 Chapter Summary

In Chapter One we have introduced holiness as the paradigmatic theme of Quaker history and theology. We have explored the range of meanings for the terms holiness, perfection and mysticism, and set the parameters for the way the terms will be used in this study. By identifying eight different types of holiness, a model has been developed to help describe the patterns of holiness in history (See Figure 3). This chapter has also shown how Quakerism uniquely combined these features of separate holiness traditions, reinterpreting them into a radical and new type of holiness movement. By establishing a criterion for Quaker holiness consisting of eight essential elements found in the earliest movement, it becomes possible to locate the differing emphases of these elements in the writings of early Friends and in Quakerism thereafter.

This chapter has argued that Quaker holiness recovered for Reformation Protestantism the experiential and transformational aspect of the Christian mystical tradition as expressed by the earliest church. We have concluded that Quaker holiness, though in conflict with established seventeenth century institutional and dogmatic forms of Christianity, nevertheless remained firmly grounded in the historical, theological and biblical framework of orthodox Christianity. We have surveyed previous scholarship which has explored the sources and complex relationships between Quakerism and other spiritual traditions and evaluated their findings in relation to the holiness theory. Thus we have laid the foundation of the thesis that holiness is a critical key to unlocking the complex interpretative problems that revolve around the origin of Quakerism, its relationship to other spiritual movements, and its place within the broader Christian tradition.

The next chapter focuses on two of the most significant figures of the "Enthusiastic period," George Fox and James Naylor, who represent two expressions of holiness in the "first wave" of Quaker spirituality. Both have presented difficulties for modern interpreters in understanding their claims about holiness and their unusual behavior. The chapter examines Fox's ecstatic mystical experiences and the claims he made about holiness, and James Naylor's misapplied literal expression of holiness and his final more existential understanding. Chapter Two also introduces the first explicit Statement of Faith concerning holiness in the writings of Edward Burrough.

Two early leaders of the "second wave," Robert Barclay, the major theologian of Quakerism, and Thomas Story, a leading minister who bridges the early period and classical period of Quietism, are examined as well in order to determine the degree of continuity of thought between the first and second wave of Quakerism.

Chapter 2

Quaker Development – Holiness Interpreted

2.1 Mysticism, Perfection and Puritanism in the Seventeenth Century

In Puritan England in the beginning of the seventeenth century, just prior to the birth of the Quaker movement, a common theme in much popular devotional literature concerned a perfection as deification or personal union with God[1] The writings of the Rhineland mystics – Ruysbroeck, Suso, and Tauler – and the *Theologia Germanica* were enjoying a resurgence of interest among radical Puritans, with the availability of new English translations. All of these writings describe the process of union with God as deification, reviving the favorite concept of the Eastern Church Fathers. Tauler's concept of union with God, for example, while using fourteenth century language and imagery, contains elements that are reflected in later understandings of Quaker holiness:

> The Godhead bends and nakedly descends into the depths of the pure waiting soul, drawing it up into the uncreated Essence, so that the spirit becomes one with Him…No one can unite himself to God in emptiness without true love; no one can be holy without becoming holy, without good works. (Inge, 1899, 189-190, 194)

---

[1] See Smith, 1989, 107-143 and Jones, 1914, 208-339. These writings were German mystical treatises translated into English by radical Puritans, primarily the anonymous *Theologia Germanica*, a standard devotional text for the Lutheran Reformation, and the writings of Johan Tauler. These works show the influence of Meister Eckhart, as do most German mystical writings, but simplified his thought, eliminated the speculative aspects, and as most historians concede, were within the boundaries of Christian orthodoxy. They also combined the apophatic thought of Eckhart with the affective, kataphatic devotional literature of the Latin mystics, Bonaventure and Bernard of Clairvaux. These texts adjusted mysticism for the common person (Packull, 1977, 17-34). Through these kinds of devotional writings, with their various modes of *unio mystica*, the medieval mystical tradition was passed on to English Puritans. These works were read by all varieties of sectarians, from respectable Quietists to Ranters. The pioneering historical research of Robert Barclay of Reigate (1879) and later Rufus Jones (1914) in establishing Quaker indebtedness to medieval, lay, ascetical spirituality, cannot be discounted. Pre-reformation Catholic continental mysticism shaped the way God-seeking Puritans read their Bible.

This description of union as both mystical and ethical holiness includes the Quaker emphasis on "pure waiting" and a union of "one spirit," the necessity of the apophatic emptiness, and the affective element of "true love," and concludes with the essential fruits of holiness, the necessary outcome of which is "good works."

Indigenous devotional writings of the fourteenth century English mystics, such as Richard Rolle, Julian of Norwich, and Walter Hilton, and the *Cloud of Unknowing* also describe intense experiences of union with God, both apophatic and affective, as divine indwelling which results in perfection. The influence of these native writings on seventeenth century radical Puritanism is still virtually unexplored.[2] The teachings of the Spanish mystics of the sixteenth century, Teresa of Avila and John of the Cross, were found in the popular devotional manuals of the French and Italian Quietists, the best known of which were Molinos, Guyon, and Fenelon. Quietism as a form of lay devotion in France and Italy arose at the same time as Quakerism in England and elicited the same kind of suspicion and persecution as that of the Quakers. The Quietists taught a perfection possible through union with God via the "prayer of quiet" by a somber emptiness and self-negation, yet resulting in an ineffable joy beyond words. The spirituality of the French and Italian Quietists had such strong correspondences to Quakerism that by the early eighteenth century the writings of the most prominent Quietists had become virtually a part of the "Quaker canon."[3] The synchronicity of thought between early Quakerism (even in Fox) and continental Quietism is so evident some transference of thought into Quakerism must be assumed. (See further discussion of Quietism in 3.1.)

But despite the prevalence of mysticism and perfectionism in widely read devotional materials and their appropriations by radical and separatist movements in England in the Reformed theology which permeated Anglicanism, the doctrine of perfection became either negligible or suspect. The call to perfection as union with God was seldom heard in establishment Protestant preaching in seventeenth century England and the promulgation of such ideas were denounced and censured (Smith, 1989, 142). George Fox and other Quaker leaders who wrote and preached consistently on perfection were not developing a new doctrine but appropriating an ancient one. Robert Barclay, who was well acquainted with patristic and medieval theology, drew on a rich

---

[2] Stephen Hobhouse, who has extensively researched the mystical sources of the English devotional writer, William Law, in the eighteenth century concludes that the four great English mystics "were, with the exception of Juliana, not readily procurable and probably unknown to Law" (1938, 366).

[3] The first person to translate Guyon's writings into English was a Quaker, Josiah Martin, in 1727. But an even earlier work linking Quakerism and Quietism can be found in a tract published in 1698 called *Quakerism a la Mode or a History of Quietism, particularly that of the Lord Archbishop of Cambray and Madame Guyone* (Hobhouse, 1972, 157).

heritage in formulating a Quaker doctrine of perfection. Nevertheless, the doctrine, being out of favor with the main currents of Protestant theology, drew considerable opposition and became a lightning rod for pamphlet wars and public debate (Smith, 1989, 142; Moore, 2000, 87-89).[4]

Although the concept of perfection is much broader and more inclusive than simply the question of freedom from sin, the popular debate revolved around the possibility of reaching a state of sinlessness. The Quaker claim to perfection meant an overcoming of the power of sin through union with God (see 2.3 on Nayler and 2.5 on Barclay). Although numerous biblical texts as well as a long tradition within orthodox Christianity supported such a concept of perfection as both an ideal and an attainment, when George Fox made such claims he was attacked from all sides and denounced as a blasphemer (Moore, 2000, 87).

Thus Quakers found themselves immersed in vitriolic debate with the established church over this teaching. George Fox confidently claimed to have reached a state "in which Adam was before he fell" (Nickalls, 1952, 27), and preached this message to disillusioned seekers. In his journal he described an even higher state, "another or more steadfast state than Adam's in innocency, even into a state in Christ Jesus, that should never fall" (Nickalls, 1952, 27). Few first wave Quakers made as bold a claim as Fox, or experienced such an elevated kind of spiritual rapture. But for Fox, locked as he was culturally in the Puritan prison of total depravity and election, the power of his vision became the divine gestalt to make the radical break with accepted Calvinist doctrine. He also challenged his contemporaries with a message that set Quakers apart from all other radical sectarians of the time.[5] Other groups proclaimed perfection, but only the Quakers combined mystical, eschatological perfection with the moral rigor of self-denial and perfect obedience. The Quaker call to perfection was born of mystical experience and a mystical consciousness. But it was not a private experience of initiation (in a Gnostic sense), or an absorption into God in a pantheistic sense, but a theistic sense of being filled with God, reborn and transformed.

---

[4] In Gershom Scholem's insightful study of mysticism, he notes how doctrines which are routinely accepted in certain times and places without causing conflict can become at other historical times the focus of great conflict (1965, 24-5). The doctrine of perfection as deification, a key doctrine of the patristic period, is one famous example. The teachings of Quietism are another. When formulated by Teresa of Avila in the sixteenth century, they were generally acceptable, but when taught by Madam Guyon in the late seventeenth century, they were condemned (Scholem, 1965, 25).

[5] Scholem uses Fox as one famous example of how mystics transform religious authority (1965, 23-24). On a personal note, when I first picked up Scholem's work on Jewish mysticism (*On the Kabbalah and its Symbolism*), I did so only hoping to find background materials and sources for a comparative study, and was completely surprised to find Fox and Quakers specifically mentioned in this work.

The German theologian Dorothee Soelle, in describing the mystic's relation to established religion, provides an insightful snapshot which captures beautifully the first wave Quaker experience:

> First, mystics have very rarely separated themselves from existing historical religions; without externally changing a single letter, they understood the meaning of these religions more deeply. They did not deny revelation but appropriated it differently. Second, conflict was part and parcel of the case: confrontation has to come between too much love for God and the institution that is concerned with regularity and order. (2001, 45)

First wave Quakers challenged the institutional church and created new kinds of spiritual communities, yet remained thoroughly and essentially orthodox, but radically so. They understood how to be Christian in a deeper, more authentic way – the way of perfection. Soelle also observes that mystics "erase the distinction between a mystical *internal* and a political *external*" (2001, 13), another prominent feature of early Friends. Perfection was not primarily private piety; it was communal and social. To live in the Light meant moral, ethical, social and political holiness. Fox's interior ecstasies (openings, as he called them) paradoxically both separated him from the world (he wrote often of being "above the world" and bringing people "off from the world") and united him with the world (he experienced a unity with all creation (Nickalls, 1952, 2, 110). They also thrust him out of his own spiritual despair and self-absorption (Smith, 1998, 28).[6] But the greatest impact of his openings is the emphasis on "overcoming the world" (Nuttall, 1973).

Fox's perfectionist message came as the result of a rapturous, ecstatic experience that left him with a deep, inward certainty of union with God. He also expected that others could come to that same kind of unity.[7] Other first wave leaders may have had less dramatic experiences, but the doctrine of perfection was never theoretical. It emerged from an existential encounter that resulted in the same deep inward certainty of union with God.

Isaac Penington, for example, a more reflective writer than Fox, describes perfection contemplatively rather than ecstatically: "I have met with the true peace, the true righteousness, the true holiness, the true rest of the soul, the

---

[6] See discussion of this concept in Geoffry Nuttall, "'Unity with Creation': George Fox and the Hermetic Philosophy." *FQ*, July 1947, 139-143.

[7] "Great things did the Lord lead me into, and wonderful depths were opened unto me, beyond what can by words be declared: but *as people come into subjection to the spirit of God, and grow up into the image and power of the Almighty,* [my emphasis; this is perfection for Fox] they may receive the Word of wisdom, that opens all things, and *come to know the hidden unity in the Eternal Being* [my emphasis; this is a classic expression of union with God]" (Smith, 1998, 28).

everlasting habitation which the redeemed dwell in" (1:1681, 4). While the first wave leaders used different images and metaphors to explain similar experiences, they had complete agreement on perfection as the goal of the Christian pilgrimage. Robert Barclay, a second wave Quaker, was the first to attempt to explain and interpret the Quaker spiritual experience in an organized, systematic fashion. He devoted his ninth proposition to a doctrine of perfection, and related perfection to other themes in his *Apology*. (Barclay's conception of perfection will be explored in section 2.5.)

2.2 George Fox

George Fox, the principal founder of Quakerism, organized the early movement around the concept of perfection, initiated with a direct, immediate experience of God and resulting in holiness becoming embodied within the individual. Fox was a Puritan lay mystic whose own personal experience transformed him and convinced him that holiness (perfection) could be embodied in all lay persons through a direct experience of God. He appropriated the medieval and monastic conceptions of holiness but taught they were available to all (e.g., a lay mysticism). However, unlike Reformation soteriology, holiness was not simply imputed and legal, but rather a dynamic, supernatural power which would be embodied and encountered relationally.[8] Fox felt divinely and morally driven to bring others to this experience.[9] As such, he became the spiritual guide and charismatic teacher in whom holiness was "embodied."

Holiness in Quakerism comprises a soteriology much closer to the pre-Reformation *via Triplex* (the stages of perfection of classical mysticism – purgation, illumination, and union) than Luther's *sola fides*. This understanding of the *via Triplex* of the mystical tradition seemed to be reflected in Fox's teaching to a potential young disciple, John Taylor, who described his guidance by Fox in this way:

> When I first went to him, he treated me in meekness as a lamb; he took me by the hand and said "Young man this is the word of the Lord to thee. There are three scriptures thou must witness to be fulfilled; first thou must be turned from darkness to light; next, thou must come to

---

[8] For a relevant and insightful discussion of charisma, conversion, embodiment and holiness see Douglas J. Davies, "The Sociology of Holiness: The Power of Being Good," in Barton, 2003, 48-67.

[9] Fox's most explicit statement of his vocation to bring people to the light that would give them "power to become sons of God" and that the "manifestation of the Spirit of God was given to every man" can be found in the beginning of his *Journal* (Smith, 1998, 34).

the knowledge of the glory of God; and then, thou must be changed from glory to glory.[10]

"Turned from darkness to light" represents the stage of purgation, "knowledge of the glory of God," illumination, and "changed from glory to glory," the transformation of union. ("Changed from glory to glory" is a common reference to deification in the patristic tradition.) In the Protestant version known as the *ordo salutis*, this last stage is referred to as "glorification" (justification, sanctification, glorification). Glorification is reserved for eternity. But for Fox and early Quakers, perfection was an earthly form of glorification and could be experienced in the real world.

Quoting Jesus' admonition in the Sermon on the Mount, "Be ye perfect even as my heavenly father is perfect," Fox gave his interpretation of what Christ meant:

> ...he who was perfect comes to make man and woman perfect again and bring them again to the state God made them in; so he is the maker up of the breach and the peace betwixt God and man.... But I told them Christ was come freely, who hath perfected for ever by one offering all them that are sanctified, and renews them up in the image of God, as man and woman were in before they fell; and makes man and woman's house as perfect again as God had made them at first. (Nickalls, 1952, 367-8)

Fox understood perfection as the return to the original God-likeness in which humanity was created, which Christ had restored through his incarnation and atonement.

George Fox's most dramatic expression of perfection as recorded in his Journal occurs sometime around 1648 when he experienced an ecstatic rapture, metaphorically expressed as being in the "Paradise of God." The experience itself was so overwhelming that Fox found words inadequate, yet he, like all mystics, was nevertheless compelled to try and express the inexpressible:

> Now was I come up in the spirit through the Flaming Sword, into the Paradise of God. All things were new, and all the creation gave another smell unto me than before, beyond what words can utter. I knew nothing but pureness, and innocency, and righteousness, being renewed up into the image of God by Christ Jesus, so that I say I was come up to the state of Adam which he was in before he fell...But I

---

[10] Testimonial of John Taylor, 1691 (Fox, 1831, 4:6). "Changed from glory to glory," a phrase often used in the Eastern Church to describe deification, is found in Scripture in II Cor. 3:18.

was immediately taken up in spirit to see into another or more steadfast state than Adam's in innocency, even into a state in Christ Jesus that should never fall. And the Lord showed me that such as were faithful to Him, in the power and light of Christ, should come up into that state in which Adam was before he fell, in which the admirable works of creation and the virtues thereof may be known, through the openings of that Divine Word of wisdom and power by which they were made. (Nickalls, 1952, 27-28)

Later, George Fox in his testimony at trial for blasphemy in Derby, refered to this state of being "in the Paradise of God" as sanctification. Here Fox is giving witness to Christ abiding in him in a state of continual presence through the Holy Spirit:

At last they asked me whether I was sanctified.
I said, "Sanctified? Yes," for I was in the Paradise of God.[11]
They said, had I no sin?
"Sin?" Said I, "Christ my savior hath taken away my sin, and in him there is no sin."
They asked me how we knew that Christ did abide in us.
I said "By his Spirit that he has given us.[12] (Nickalls, 1952, 51)

George Fox never developed a concise theology of perfection, or a clear doctrine of it. He never claimed to be a theologian. He had dramatic, rhapsodic experiences, which he expressed metaphorically and existentially: "I knew nothing but pureness, and innocency, and righteousness, being renewed up into the image of God by Christ Jesus" (Nickalls, 1952, 27). Fox had a subjective experience of being transported into union with God through Christ, convincing him that he had freedom from and power over sin, "a state in Christ Jesus that should never fall" (Nickalls, 1952, 27). What might appear to be arrogance or

---

[11] In Jewish mysticism, to enter "Paradise" means entering the realm of mysticism (Scholem, 1965, 26). In Christian mysticism the journey back to Paradise is through contemplation. See, for example, William H. Shannon in *Thomas Merton's Paradise Journey: Writings on Contemplation*, 2000, 3-4. Although Fox is not normally identified as a contemplative, Merton's description of a pure contemplative fits Fox: "...contemplation is a supernatural love and knowledge of God, simple and obscure, infused by him into the summit of the soul, giving it a direct and experimental contact with Him." Several places in his journal, Fox alludes to being infused with this love, for example: "...I was taken up in the love of God..." (Nickalls 1952, 14) and "...I saw the infinite love of God..." (Nickalls, 1952, 19). and "...I saw into that, which was without end, and things which cannot be uttered, and of the greatness and infiniteness of the love of God, which cannot be expressed by words..." (Nickalls, 1952, 21).

[12] Fox antagonized his Puritan opponents by accusing them of "pleading for sin and imperfection" and preaching salvation *in* sin rather than *from* sin (Nickalls, 1952, 18).

audacity is related to the ecstatic state, which gave him an unshakable certainty of the *unio mystica*, as well as profound insights, and assurance of the verity of his call.

Fox began his career as an itinerant lay mystic, whose experiences and teachings were similar to many great preachers of the late medieval period, including his assurance that he was led by the Spirit and lived in the divine presence. [13] Fox employed a variety of metaphors to try to describe mystical union, the source of holiness: "the paradise of God," "Adam's perfection" (the image of God that humanity had before the fall, clear and pure and without [original] sin), "growing up to the measure of the stature of the fullness of Christ," "the same power and spirit of the prophets and apostles," "Christ in you, the hope of glory"[14] (Nickalls, 1952, 32-33, 56). Other images used by Fox to describe the "life in Christ" which comes through union included the mystical "grafting" and marriage metaphors:[15]

> Wait in his Power and Light...that you may be grafted into him, the true Root, and built upon him, the true Foundation....and by this Truth you may be made free, by which ye may be espoused and married to Christ Jesus, for the Marriage of the Lamb is come and coming.[16]

Fox never exalted his mystical raptures, nor made them paradigmatic for his disciples, nor encouraged them to seek mystical states of sinless perfection. Moore's extensive and careful research of Quaker documents from the earliest period shows no evidence of "a personality cult centered on Fox" or that he was ever considered divine, despite his reputation for healing and performing miracles (2000, 78). Fox never claimed to be equal to Christ, though he and other Quakers were accused of blasphemy by the civil authorities.[17] He wrote,

---

[13] George Tavard compares him to the Spanish Dominican Vincent Ferrer (1350-1419) in "George Fox Among Christian Mystics" *QT*, 2000, vol. 2, no. 1, 38. He finds the doctrine of the Light of Christ within, the inward Light, a central theme in the Franciscan theologian, St. Bonaventure (2000, 41) and claims that the metaphor of the light is commonly used in the Christian mystical tradition, and was hardly a new concept discovered by Fox. The language of the Light, as employed by Fox, is both biblical and orthodox (John 1:9 is a key verse), and its usage by early Quakers is not far from the *lumen fidei* of standard Catholic teaching today, according to Tavard (2000, 42).

[14] Col. 1:27. (See 4.3 for later Quietist emphasis on this phrase for expressing the concept of holiness through union.)

[15] The metaphor of spiritual marriage is one of the most common images for mystical union in the medieval tradition.

[16] Epistle 288 (1672), qtd. in *A Day-Book of Counsel and Comfort from the Epistles of George Fox*, compiled by L. Violet Hodgkin (1937, 234-5).

[17] In a few rare instances Fox wrote that he was "the son of God" (see, for example, his letter to Oliver Cromwell, 1654, in Appendix III of Nigel Smith's edition of *The Journal* (1998, 493). While this could be construed as blasphemy, or at the very least the height

for instance, of being questioned at Derby for claiming to be Christ: "They temptingly asked if any of us were Christ. I answered, 'Nay; we are nothing; Christ is all'" (Nickalls, 1952, 51). Despite his answer, Fox spent the next six months in prison as a blasphemer (Nickalls, 1952, 51). Fox and other Quakers were often charged with blasphemy because they were perceived to be deifying themselves by claiming perfection, or being "godded" as Richard Bailey concludes (see 1.7.5).[18]

The apostle Paul, himself, writes of being rapt into the third heaven, and refers to an "out of body experience," yet is so cautious in expressing this mystical ecstasy that he creates distance by writing in the third person as an observer of his own experience.[19] "I know a man who.... was caught up to the third heaven" (II Cor. 12:1-4). Paul never refers directly to this experience again in his letters. Ecstatic states were graces, "openings" as Fox called them, and infusions of love, revelations of divine love, or what Catholic theologians call locutions, consolations or gifts of the Spirit. Fox described many such "openings" in which he was given remarkable visions and revelations, but he did not teach his followers to seek visions, nor canonize his own experiences. Nothing in his writings gives evidence that he would ever be satisfied with mystical exaltation, nor the seeking of otherworldly delights.[20]

George Fox's teachings on perfection have been interpreted widely, from Richard Bailey's identifying him as an "avatar" with divine union taken literally to mean the "celestial flesh" of Christ assumed by the saint (1992) (see 1.7.5) to a simple, biblical growth in grace: "Fox's belief in perfection is not to be distinguished sharply from a simple faith in or obedience to Christ....To him the state of grace brings a securer and stable relationship in which Christ gives the power of continued obedience and faith" (Jones, 1955, 149). The latter has been the dominant modern understanding of the meaning of Quaker perfection.

---

of arrogance, it seems more likely, in light of the totality of his writings, that it is meant as a metaphor of the new birth, divine sonship, by which Christians are changed into "sons of God." (See, for example, II Cor. 6:18.)

[18] Ranters, a more extreme sect which arose in England during the civil wars, were pantheistic and some of their leaders did claim to be Christ incarnated and divine. Thomas Edwards sums up their beliefs in *Grangraena or a Catalogue and Discovery of many of the Errours, Heresies, Blasphemies and pernicious Practices of the Sectarians of the time* (1740). Quakers were often confused or lumped together with this sect, which is not surprising, since many early converts to Quakerism came from this and other radical sects of the times.

[19] George Fox alludes to this experience of Paul and identifies with it (Nickalls, 1952, 21).

[20] In Fox's famous *Journal* passage outlining so concisely his ministry and mission, "I was to bring People off from all their own ways to Christ..." (Geoffrey Nuttall calls this passage his "marching orders" [1973, 145]), there is no mention of bringing people to visions or raptures, but only to "Christ the new and living Way" to "know the Spirit of Truth in the inward Parts...." (Nickalls, 1952, 35).

Arthur Roberts, a Quaker scholar who recognizes the centrality of holiness in early Quakerism, calls Fox's perfection a "prophetic perfectionism" which is Christ-centered (1953, 61). Roberts claims that one legacy of Fox was "the Christian doctrine of holiness, which he lifted out of the Scriptures..." (1953, 59):

> The perfection which he experienced and taught was made possible only through Christ. Here is not pantheistic perfection, nor absorption into the infinite...The mysticism of Fox certainly adheres to Christ's redemption and to the mystery of that fellowship. (1953, 61)

Robert's summary of Fox's theology of perfection is consistent with evangelical beliefs:

> Fox held that perfection, or life above sin, is possible in this life; that the "body of death" which is destroyed is original sin, or the Adamic nature which every man has. He asserts that this sinful nature is destroyed, purged, or cleansed from the heart by God's baptism with the Holy Spirit. Such is the purpose of the atonement, making the outward sacrifice of Christ meaningful inwardly as a result of God's grace and man's faith. (1953, 62)

Roberts considers perfection the completion of sanctification, begun at justification, but distinguishes Quaker soteriology from popular Wesleyan versions which speak of two works of grace (1953, 62):

> And justification and sanctification are one...not two things really distinct in their nature, but really one. This grace is received by steps or crisis, until there comes the completion of the work of cleansing, and the assurance of victory. (1953, 63)

Roberts is correct in differentiating Quaker holiness from the later two-stage process so emphasized in the Holiness Revivalism that developed from Wesley's teachings. But Wesley's most typical teaching on holiness is not far at all from Fox's notion:

> By salvation I mean, not barely, according to the vulgar notion, deliverance from hell, or going to heaven; but a present deliverance from sin, a restoration of the soul to its primitive health, its original purity; a recovery of the divine nature; the renewal of our souls after the image of God, in righteousness and true holiness, in justice, mercy, and truth. This implies all holy and heavenly tempers, and, by consequence, all holiness of conversation. ([1831] 5:35)

Fox spoke of perfection as coming "into subjection to the spirit of God" and growing up "into the image and power of the Almighty" (Smith, 1998, 28), as well as a present deliverance from sin.

The subtle distinction between embodied holiness, materialized and realized in an individual, such as the orthodoxy of *imitatio Christi* as found in the lives of the saints, and the crossing over into a dangerous and unacceptable form of divinization became explicit in the early movement, in the curious dynamics between Fox and another equally charismatic and revered leader of the early period, James Nayler.

2.3 James Nayler

The fine line between holiness as Christ *in* them, witnessing Christ, and Christ *as* them, incarnating Christ, became clarified for early Quakers through their near-undoing by the seemingly irrational behavior of one of their greatest early leaders, James Nayler.[21] Nayler articulated a theology of perfection which echoed Fox, but was less mystical and metaphorical (he did not record any raptures or ecstasies) and more literal than Fox (Damrosch, 1996, 89-90). Nayler followed Fox, as well as later Quietists (both Quaker and Catholic), in describing perfection as the annihilation of the self in which "Christ is all and the creature nothing" (Nayler, 1650, 23; Damrosch, 1996, 109-114). He also clearly anticipated Barclay (see 2.5) in his understanding of perfection as a gradual process and not a static state, and that each individual is perfect "in measure" (Damrosch, 1996, 100). Nayler corrected and defended the Quaker position on the relative nature of perfection, as well as its gradual process to his Puritan opponents: "It is a lying slander that we say every saint is perfect: for we witness the saints' growth, and the time of pressing after perfection" (1655, 6).

Nayler also formulated an early Quaker credo: "If I cannot witness Christ nearer than Jerusalem, I shall have no benefit by him" (1653b, 32). For Nayler, to "witness Christ" was manifestly the literal "imitation of Christ," as his actions ultimately implied. In 1656 Nayler felt compelled to imitate Christ by riding into Bristol with his followers shouting "hosanna" as a reenactment of Jesus' entry into Jerusalem, an incident that caused him to be convicted of blasphemy by the Puritan Parliament and tortured as punishment. The emerging Quaker movement in which he was a rising leader (second only to Fox) was

---

[21] James Nayler, a Yorkshire farmer and soldier, had a dramatic conversion experience around 1651, which prompted him to leave his farm and family to become an itinerant preacher. Shortly after meeting George Fox, he became one of the most prominent evangelists and the chief spokesman and pamphlet writer for Quakers in the early period (Moore, 2000, 35).

scandalized by this incident (Damrosch, 1996, 230-1). George Fox personally condemned Nayler's actions and referred to his behavior as having "run out...into imaginations" (Smith, 1998, 201).

Three years prior to this incident, which is commonly referred to as his "fall," Nayler wrote and witnessed to this understanding of perfection:

> ...Jesus Christ...is the eternal word of God, "by whom all things were made," and was before all time, but manifested to the world in time...which "Word became flesh, and dwelt amongst" the saints (John 1:2, 3, 4, 5, 14), who is "the same, yesterday, today, and forever," who did and doth dwell in the saints; who suffered, and rose again, and ascended into Heaven...who fills all places: is the light of the world, but known to none but those that receive and follow him, and those he leads up to God...by his pure light in them, whereby he reveals the man of sin; and by his power casts him out. And so prepares the bodies of the saints a fit temple for the pure God to dwell in: with whom dwells no unclean thing: and thus he reconciles God and man: and the image of God which is in purity and holiness, is renewed: and the image of Satan, which is all sin and uncleanness, is defaced: and none can witness redemption, further than Christ is thus revealed in them, to set them free from sin: which Christ I witness to be revealed in me in measure. (Gal. 1:16, II Cor. 13:5; Col. 1:27) (Nayler, 1653b, 15-16)[22]

James Nayler's prefall theology of holiness is an explicit doctrine of perfection as divine indwelling. The Christian becomes the temple and the dwelling place of God. Because the Word was incarnate in Christ, man could also be deified, as in the classic formula of the early Greek Fathers.[23] (See 1.7.5 and 2.1.)

---

[22] What separates Nayler (and Fox and early Quakers) from Ranters and other Pantheistic sectarians was their maintenance of the transcendence of Christ (Christ seated in heaven) along with his immanence in humanity and all things. Nayler and other early leaders used traditional orthodox language when speaking of the nature of the role of Christ as a sacrifice and propitiation for sins (Damrosch, 1996, 93), but Nayler also held initially to a panentheism that Christ "is the body of all creatures, and filleth all things in heaven and earth." (The phrase "body of all creatures" was edited to a less literal "the life and upholder of all creatures" in the 1716 edition of Naylor's writings; see Damrosch, 1996, 110.)

[23] The classic formulation of Irenaeus of Lyons is "The Son of God became man that man might become son of God," found in *Against Heresies*, III, 19, I. Gregory of Nyssa expressed the concept of deification as "The Word, in taking flesh, was mingled with humanity, and took our nature within himself, so that the human should be deified by this mingling with God: the stuff of our nature was entirely sanctified by Christ, the first fruits of creation" (*Against Apollinarius*, 2).

The motivations and meaning of Nayler's actions in Bristol continue to be debated by Quaker historians (Fogelklou, 1931; Nuttall, 1948; Carroll, 1972; Hill, 1972; Trevett, 1990; Mack, 1992; Ingle, 1994), but the general consensus is that however the event may be interpreted, it marked a shift in Quakerism from prophetic mysticism to apologetics and "domesticated Nonconformity" (Damrosch, 1996, 247; Moore, 2000, 47). Perfection as deification and divine indwelling – as Nayler claimed, Christ "did and doth dwell in the saints" (1653b) – became more muted after Nayler's trial and punishment, but never rejected.[24]

One can only speculate what prompted Nayler to ride into Bristol in 1656. This study hypothesizes that he did so because he truly felt he was revealing Christ in him by reenacting Christ's passion and literally following "the way of the Cross." Nayler may have desired martyrdom in literal imitation of the suffering Christ, as many early Christians did (Spencer, 2001). One of the earliest Christian martyrs, Polycarp of Smyrna, was placed upon an ass as he was led to his martyrdom, a celebrated story in Christian tradition that may have been familiar to Nayler.[25]

Damrosch, in exploring this incident in depth, argues that "...what was diagnosed as 'madness' even by fellow Quakers, was at a deep level an imaginative understanding of principles that all antinomians, [26] and many orthodox, claimed to accept" (1996, 5). Damrosch also contends that Nayler's action represented a "coherent context of antinomian symbolism" (1996, 7). However, Damrosch's explanation of the Quaker position is a more accurate description of holiness than antinomianism: "The Quaker position was that the law was still binding, but that participation in Christ made it possible to live up to its demands instead of endlessly failing to do so" (1996, 5).

This study argues that Nayler's "madness," rather than being labeled antinomian, would be more accurately described as an imaginative understanding of the doctrine of perfection, and the symbolism he embodied was that of the *imitatio Christi*. Damrosch concludes that Nayler did not

---

[24] Damrosch explains the difference between the Quaker and Puritan understanding of divine indwelling as a difference of "degree only, not of kind": "The favorite Quaker phrase 'that of God in thee' indicated not just the indwelling presence of God, which any Puritan would accept with the caveat that the person inhabited by God remained vile and alien to the divine inhabitant. To the Quakers it implied a resemblance between the human being and God that reflected a difference of degree only, not of kind" (1996, 93-94). This study argues that Quakers followed the classic patristic formation that "what he is by nature he makes us by grace" (Cyril of Alexandria), though without knowing the ancient sources.

[25] See *Anti-Nicene Fathers*, Concerning the Martyrdom of the Holy Polycarp, http://www.ccel.org/fathers2/ANF-01/anf01-13.htm#P912, 10/27/03.

[26] Damrosch defines antinomian as "the replacement of an external moral law by an internal, spiritual one," which is essentially the New Testament understanding of grace and conversion (1996, 5).

"literally or personally think he was the Messiah," nor did his followers, but rather as he had written earlier, Christ was "revealed in me in measure" (Nayler, 1653b). Nayler was acting out the *imitatio Christi*, in a way not so very different from the imitation of Christ in his poverty and suffering of the Franciscan mendicants who lived the apostolic life of wandering beggars.[27] The fatal flaw of Nayler, as Damrosch concludes, was to make literal what was normally figurative in Quaker spirituality (1996, 5).

Rosemary Moore interprets this incident in a more conventional way, as evidence that perfection, even with Christ within, did not guarantee success or sinlessness, though perhaps some of the early Quakers initially believed so (2000, 43). But as she points out, "back sliding happened," even among its greatest leaders, and penitence was needed (2000, 43). However, repentance led to restoration, and for Nayler, in the final analysis, a humbled spirit and the realization of his limitations and his "measure." Christ dwelled in him, but he was not Christ, and there would always be a distinction between himself and Christ. Moore found that Nayler's later works were concerned with his own sin and repentance, and his desire to be reunited with the Quaker community: "....in this journey I have seen the slothful servant overtaken with a fault which he had once cast behind him" (Moore, 2000, 43).[28]

Just before his death a few years later in 1660, a chastened, humbled and much wiser Nayler described the existential nature of perfection in what is, in the annals of Quaker history, perhaps the most powerful and moving testimony to the spirit of holiness. Nayler eloquently described perfection as a growing process of compassionate awareness which comes through suffering, a testimony that echoes the spirit of the desert Fathers as well as the later spirituality of St. Francis of Assisi:

> There is a spirit which I feel, that delights to do no evil, nor to revenge any wrong, but delights to endure all things....Its hope is to outlive all wrath and contention, and to weary out all exaltation and cruelty, or whatever is of a nature contrary to itself. It sees to the end of all temptations. As it bears no evil in itself, so it conceives none in thoughts to any other: if it be betrayed, it bears it; for its ground and spring is the mercies and forgiveness of God. Its crown is meekness, its life is everlasting love unfeigned, it takes its Kingdom with entreaty and not with contention and keeps it with lowliness of mind. In God alone it can rejoice, though none else regard it, or can own its life. It is conceived in sorrow and brought forth without any to pity it; nor doth it murmur at grief and oppression. It never rejoiceth but through

---

[27] An even more dramatic embodied manifestation of the complete identification with Christ would be St. Francis' stigmata, considered a visible sign of sainthood.

[28] Damrosch, on the other hand, maintains that Nayler only reluctantly recanted in the face of banishment from the Quaker community (1996, 5).

suffering;...I found it alone, forsaken. I have fellowship therein with them who lived in dens and desolate places of the earth, who through death obtained their resurrection and eternal holy life. (Nayler, 1716, 696)[29]

What Nayler described at this stage of his life, just before his death, was not a moralistic or ethical perfection, or even the process of perfection, nor a concise doctrine, but rather the inherent qualities of holiness. He captures the "spirit" of perfection: "There is a spirit which I feel..." (Nayler, 1716, 696). (It was generally thought that perfection, if ever attained, came just before death.) As J. Rendel Harris, another holiness Quaker said almost 300 years later, reflecting on Nayler's words: "In our earlier stages of experiences we are made humble by our sins; as we advance, by our failures, and when we are made perfect, by our limitations" (1914, 9-10) (see 6.2). Harris is echoing the concept of perfection "in measure" so often invoked by early Quakers, and Nayler in particular, who could thus claim perfection in Christ, yet admit to the imperfection of human failure and limitation:

It is true, the Light is but manifest in the creatures by degrees, but the least degree is perfect in its measure, and being obeyed, will lead to the perfect Day, and is perfect in its self, and leads up to perfection all that perfectly follow it. (Nayler, 1716, 117-118)

2.3.1   Summary and Conclusions

Nayler is perhaps most unique in his manifestation of Quadrant 4 holiness: the Ascetical Imitation of Christ (see Figure 3). He is the strongest representative of the Anabaptist model of following the suffering Christ, even to the willingness to embrace humiliation and martyrdom. He discovered that he had erred in believing holiness could be embodied literally by a public demonstration of his total identification with Christ through a reenactment of an event in Christ's life. He gradually seemed to recognize that his actions were unacceptable, and harmful to the Quaker witness of Christ and damaging to the community. But in a sense, he was also exhibiting Type 7 holiness, monastic obedience and renunciation. Just as blood martyrdom evolved into "white martyrdom" in monasticism, and later "green martyrdom" in wandering itinerancy, he followed the symbolic martyrs' path as he left family and wealth behind to obey the voice

---

[29] First published in 1660 immediately after his death (Damrosch, 1996, 266). For a review of the evidence of the authenticity of Nayler's words see Ormerod Greenwood, "James Nayler's 'Last Words'" *JFHS*, 8 (1958): 199-203. Damrosch concludes that Nayler's statement is consistent with his later writings, though probably edited, since they are "too artfully rhetorical for a dying man" (1996, 267).

of God to become an itinerant preacher. But then he went one step further and attempted to witness to a new kind of martyrdom, giving a literal form and body to the *imitatio Christi*. However, the censure of his actions by all but a few of the Quaker community show that while Quaker holiness was radical for its time, it was not revolutionary, and lines established clearly in the deep roots of Christian orthodoxy were not to be removed from Quaker holiness. Nayler appears to have submitted to the discipline of the community and ultimately to the authority which resided in Fox as the charismatic leader with the most authoritative powers. But Nayler's "error" does not disqualify him as a charismatic embodiment of Quaker holiness. He represents in a striking manner the fact that Quaker holiness was not held to be sinless perfection, that some singularly individualized manifestations of holiness were unacceptable to the community, and that if a person lapsed in judgment, even as a leader, restoration was always possible.

Nayler also shows strong elements of Quadrant 3 holiness, especially type 6: *unio mystica,* which like Fox is the mystical basis of his transformative experience. Quadrant 1 is represented by his emphasis on faith.[30] Quadrant 2, Experiential, is also strongly represented by his stress on rebirth and divine guidance (type 3), and the charismatic (type 4), "by the immediacy and completeness" in which he, as did other Quakers, claimed to receive the Spirit (Damrosch, 1996, 89).

The eight elements of Quaker holiness are all fully embraced by Nayler. In relation to eschatology, Nayler is especially representative of the internal apocalypse, an atemporal interiority of a realized eschatology, but also an expectation of a future second coming (Damrosch, 1996, 91). The element of suffering is also highly characteristic of Nayler, who writes that the spirit of holiness "...never rejoiceth but through suffering" (Nayler, 1716, 696) and is a decisive form of authentication of holiness. The spirit of non-resistance and bearing the consequences of grief and oppression is also evident: "...if it be betrayed, it bears it" (Nayler, 1716, 696).

Nayler's "post-fall" deathbed description of holiness as a way of being and feeling is free from legalism and contrived symbolic displays, representing a mature understanding of holiness learned through suffering and the hard lessons of life experience. It is also remarkably free from bitterness, anger, and judgmentalism.

---

[30] Quakers like all Puritans affirmed the "absolute priority of faith" (Damrosch, 1996, 104). Nayler wrote: "A right faith is the only ground of man's eternal happiness...and without it is impossible to please God" (Nayler, 1716, 427).

2.4   Edward Burrough

In 1657 Edward Burrough (1634-1662)[31] wrote the most explicit statement of belief concerning holiness of the Early Period even expressing it in a "creedal" form in a manner that sounds like a confession of faith. He clearly stated what Quakers believed about perfection in *A Declaration to All the World of our Faith*:

> We believe that the saints upon earth may receive forgiveness of sins, and may be perfectly freed from the body of sin and death, and in Christ may be perfect, and without sin, and may have victory over all temptations by faith in Christ Jesus. And we believe every saint called of God, ought to press after perfection, and to overcome the Devil and all his temptations…and we believe they that faithfully wait for it shall obtain it, and be presented without sin in the image of the father, and such walks not after the flesh, but after the Spirit, and are in covenant with God, and their sins are blotted out and remembered no more. (Barbour and Roberts, 1973, 301)

Perfection here is both a gift and grace that is infused, and also ironically something which must be pursued: "press after perfection and overcome the devil." He describes paradoxically both a waiting and an active pressing after, faith and works together, a seeking and a doing. This same dynamic is found in Robert Barclay's *Apology* written some twenty years later, showing continuity of belief from the Early Enthusiasts to the second wave of the Restoration period. The next section examines Barclay's theological formulations.

2.5   Robert Barclay: Theology of Perfection

Robert Barclay formulated the most comprehensive theological description of perfection in his *Apology for the True Christian Divinity*, first written in Latin in 1676.[32] Barclay wrote the *Apology* in order to defend, explain, and justify the

---

[31] Burrough was one of the earliest Quaker evangelists and leader of the Quaker mission in London. He was imprisoned in 1661 and died in Newgate prison about a year later. He was a major political and theological pamphleteer in the Enthusiastic period (Moore, 2000).

[32] The Scotsman Robert Barclay (1648-1690) was one of a small and rather elite group of educated, intellectual leaders among early Quakers. Few early Quakers had theological training or respect as scholars in the wider community as Barclay did. Barclay was educated in both Protestant Calvinist and Catholic traditions (Scots College in Paris), providing him with a somewhat broader cultural and religious perspective than others of his time (Trueblood, 1968).

spiritual lives of ordinary, unlearned men and women who made up the vast majority of the early Quaker movement.[33] He attempted to formulate a systematic epistemological basis for the spiritual beliefs and practices of a misunderstood and persecuted group of dissenting Christians (Braithwaite, 1979, 387). He also sought to explain the meaning of his own religious journey, which had found its final expression among the Quakers.[34]

The perfection of the period of "Early Enthusiasms" became formulated doctrinally with some modification and much greater nuance in Barclay's *Apology*. The doctrine was grounded in what Barclay refers to as the "divine mystery," which meant the mystery of "the Father, Son and Spirit," "the divine supernatural light or seed," and the incarnation – "the flesh and blood of Christ which came down from heaven." In one of the few instances in which he grasps for a theological term not found in Scripture, Barclay refers to this "mystery" as the *vehiculum Dei*[35] (Sippel, 2002, 120):

> . . .but we understand a spiritual, heavenly, and invisible principle, in which God, as Father, Son, and Spirit, dwells; a measure of which divine and glorious life is in all men as a seed, which of its own nature, draws, invites, and inclines to God; and this we call *vehiculum Dei*, or the spiritual body of Christ, the flesh and blood of Christ, which came down from heaven, of which all the saints do feed, and are thereby nourished unto eternal life. . . as this seed is received in the heart, and suffered to bring forth its natural and proper effect, Christ comes to be formed and raised, of which the scriptures makes so much mention, calling it "the new man"; "Christ within, the hope of glory." [Col. 1:27] This is that Christ within, which we are heard so much to speak and declare of; every where preaching him up, and exhorting people to believe in the light, and obey it, that they may come to know Christ in them, to deliver them from all sin. (Sippel, 2002, 120)

---

[33] Barclay concludes his Apology with this benediction: "Unto him who has begun this work, not among the rich or the great ones, but among the poor and the insignificant, and has revealed it not to the wise and learned, but to the lowly, to babes and sucklings" (1991, 440).

[34] Barclay's *Apology* is closer to the traditional category of "Mystical Theology" than Systematics. See, for example, Eeg-Olofsson on Barclay: "The most powerful impulse in Barclay's theology is the attempt to express the mystical content of the knowledge of God, a knowledge of God that has been gained neither by intellectualism nor by moralism but is entirely a gift of God" (1954, 128).

[35] "Vehicle of God," usually interpreted by Quakers as the Light, seems to reflect a strong Trinitarian understanding of the Godhead – the *vehiculum Dei* is an "invisible principle in which Father, Son, and Spirit, dwells" (Sippel 2002, 120). This invisible principle is experienced in history as the "spiritual body of Christ" which came down from heaven as "flesh and blood" – Christ's role in the Mystery of the Trinity in the incarnation, an extension of the Trinity into the world which is in all humanity as a seed.

This statement by Barclay summarizes the Quaker understanding of the Gospel, the universal light as a seed in all persons (grace), which when received in the heart (justification) and allowed to bring forth its natural effect (sanctification),[36] causes Christ to be formed within, to deliver from all sin (perfection). Barclay affirms in his next section that this "seed, or light, or grace" is a "real spiritual substance, which the soul of man is capable to feel and apprehend; from which that real, spiritual, inward birth in believers arises called the new creature, the new man in the heart" (Sippel, 2002, 121). Because he recognizes how strange this may seem to those who have not experienced it (the "carnal-minded"), he adds a bit of personal testimony, "we know it, and are sensible of it, by a true and certain experience...we are made capable of tasting, smelling, seeing, and handling the things of God" (Sippel, 2002, 121).

Barclay also insists that the doctrine of the seed in no way devalues the life and death of Christ, "the flesh [incarnation] and blood [atonement] of Christ" which he calls "the history": "The history then is profitable and comfortable with the mystery, and never without it" (Sippel, 2002, 123). The history is not sufficient without the mystery, but the mystery can be known without knowledge of the history.

Lastly, to correct any misconception that Christ is in all persons "formed and brought forth," Barclay makes an important distinction between the seed and the indwelling Christ:

> Neither is Christ in all men by way of union, or indeed, to speak strictly, by way of inhabitation; because this inhabitation, as it is generally taken, imports union, or the manner of Christ's being in the saints. As it is written, "I will dwell in them, and walk in them" (2 Cor. 6:16). (Sippel, 2002, 124)

The Light is universal in its seed form, but not in its Christ-form of inhabitation or union. Union with the risen Christ as indwelling is reserved only for the saints, those who "put on Christ" by cooperating with grace (*synergism* is the patristic term for "working with" grace). "To be a coworker with the grace" is Barclay's phrase (Sippel, 2002, 129).[37] In his description of the doctrine of perfection we find the same dialectical nature of both God's work (the holy birth) and humanity's work (pressing after). Barclay's concept can be

---

[36] Note Barclay's explicit use of the term "suffered" – sanctification always includes struggle.

[37] Barclay cites Augustine as his source on this: "He that made us without us, will not save us without us" (Sippel, 2002, 129). A standard criticism of Barclay's *Apology* made by both Braithwaite and Jones, and echoed by many later Quaker interpreters, is its emphasis on passivity. "It leaves little place in the Divine purpose for the active faith which springs from the human will reaching out to the Divine will" (Braithwaite, 1979, 390). Such statements fail to recognize Barclay's clear teaching on synergism.

summed up as never ending growth in grace, in proportion to one's measure (in relation to the potential of each individual). Barclay named perfection as the "growth of the holy birth into its fullness."[38] But even that fullness will "still admit of a growth" and is a "perfection proportionable and answerable to a man's measure" (Sippel, 2002, 205-207). It is a reaching for something that is always beyond. But its fruit is manifest in this life in the growth of pure love. Barclay concludes in one of his later works, *Universal Love*, "perfection consists in loving God above all" (1692, 190).

Barclay's theological formulation of perfection became the basis for John Wesley's development of the stages in sanctification in the eighteenth century, which culminated in Christian perfection, or "perfect love." For Wesley, as with Barclay, perfection was full or entire sanctification, "the holy birth in all its fullness," but never a static state of perfect sinlessness; "...this perfection still admits of a growth; and there remaineth always in some part a possibility of sinning, where the mind doth not most diligently and watchfully attend unto the Lord" (Sippel, 2002, 205). He further refutes sinless perfection by employing the term "measure": "Only a perfection proportionable and answerable to a man's measure." He illustrates his point in two ways: "even as a little gold is perfect gold in its kind, as well as great mass" and like "a child hath a perfect body as well as a man, though it daily grow more and more" (Sippel, 2002, 207).

Barclay also uses the Pauline expression "pressing after" (Phil. 3:14) in relation to perfection, in the sense that one is always reaching forward to something that is beyond (Sippel, 2002, 207, 223). He is careful to note that even when one has attained a "measure" it is possible to fall back, and that many holy persons who "have arrived to everlasting life, have had diverse ebbings and flowings of this kind" (Sippel, 2002, 207). Sin may temporally weaken a person, but through the Spirit within they can rise again.

There is a dynamic, existential quality to the writings of Barclay, which has often been missed because of his scholastic, systematic style. (Even John Wesley, a century later, borrowing heavily from Barclay, patronizingly called the *Apology* that "solemn trifle" [1748, 10:187]). Using the rational style of his day to defend Quaker beliefs, Barclay attempted to demonstrate a dialectical process as a kind of spiraling ascent, in which the goal is (and can be reached potentially, but never statically) Christian perfection, the holy birth of Christ fully formed within, or union with God. Barclay himself (like John Wesley after him) never taught or claimed sinlessness (Sippel, 2002, 207).

---

[38] Barclay's phrase is echoed among contemporary scholars such as Hans von Balthasar, who describes perfection, i.e., the mystical life, as "a full expansion of the Christian life of grace" (qtd. in Yarnold, 1986, 16).

2.5.1 *Perfection,* Epektatis, *and Detachment*

Barclay's use of measure and proportion and the dynamic movement toward perfection have similarities to the Greek patristic concept of *epektatis,* formulated originally by Gregory of Nyssa in his *Life of Moses* (Malherbe and Ferguson, 1978, 113-16). *Epektatis* is Gregory's way of describing the spiritual journey to God as one of a perpetual forward motion, a continual movement beyond. One never arrives, because wherever one is, there is always a step beyond. And at the same time whatever the proportion of one's measure, it is enough, yet not enough. In other words, perfection is eternally endless, just as Barclay recognizes; it always admits of growth. It is not a static perfection, in the Greek sense, but dynamic movement.[39]

The source of Gregory's concept of *epektasis* is found in Phil. 3:13-14.[40] Barclay also finds inspiration for his treatise on perfection in this text. Barclay concludes his argument by quoting Phil. 3:14. He describes those who go on to perfection as those who "daily go on forsaking unrighteousness, and forgetting those things that are behind, 'press forward toward the mark, for the prize of the high calling of God in Christ Jesus'" (Sippel, 2002, 223).

Perfection as *epektatis,* therefore, is related to the process of detachment and separation from the inferior pleasures of the world, and thus is directly connected to his final ascetical fifteenth proposition, "Concerning Salutations and Recreations." Perfection is the way of living amidst all the cares, pressures, evils, addictions, compulsions, and seductions of the world without being distracted and defeated by them. Tempted, yes, but with power to overcome the world because "It is no more I, but Christ alive in me..." (Gal. 2:20) (Sippel, 2002, 216). Barclay also quotes this verse in relation to his proposition on justification (2002, 200).[41] Barclay describes the outcome of perfection as a way of life equivalent to monastic perfection, but uncloistered:

> God...hath produced effectually in many that mortification and abstraction from the love and cares of this world, who daily are conversing in the world (but inwardly redeemed out of it) both in

---

[39] Gregory, using more philosophical language writes: "...its augmentation in the good cannot be circumscribed by any limit, and yet the actual good, even if it appears the greatest and most perfect possible, is never anything but the beginning of a superior good. Consequently, here also is verified the word of the apostle that by expectancy towards what is ahead, the things which had formerly appeared fall into oblivion" *Sixth Homily on the Canticle*; P.G. XLIV, 885A-888A (qtd. in Bouyer, 1968, 364-5).

[40] For the complete text see Malherbe and Ferguson, 1978.

[41] He adds further emphasis on the indwelling Christ with "*Christ alive in* us" and "the Spirit of Christ and the grace of God *in* us" [Barclay's emphasis] (Sippel, 2002, 200). He seems intent on affirming the early Quaker belief in divine indwelling. Sippel notes that "alive" is replaced with "liveth" in later editions (2002, 216).

wedlock, and in their lawful employments, which was judged could only be obtained by such as were shut up in cloisters and monasteries. (Sippel, 2002, 435)

In a later work, *Universal Love,* he reflects further on this topic of renunciation with his most contemplative statement on perfection:

> If we are really in the love of God we will keep the commandments, so it is apparent that love without purity is but a false pretence, and that whatsoever hinders from the practice of this love of God...is to be denied...And as from the true love of God (having taken place both upon the understanding and will) there ariseth a great fervency and desire of mind, that it may be wholly united with the Lord, and made conformable unto his will in all things. (Barclay, 1692, 3:190-191)[42]

Again, we see Barclay's insistence that the goal of the Christian life is perfection, which is to be "wholly united" with God, *spiritus unitas*, one will, perfect love. Such an exalted "being-in-love" results naturally in a stripping and detachment from all other competing desires, hence his almost monk-like asceticism in the fifteenth proposition. When Barclay is read with recognition of how his own deeply felt inward experience has informed his theology, his writings take on a different quality than that of a scholastic tome. The dogmatic and moralist tone of the Scottish Puritan Scholastic becomes the authentic reflections of a mystical theologian who has had a transforming inner vision, yet is still bound by the intellectual disciplines of his Calvinist-Catholic training in which to attempt to communicate them.

As a theologian known as a formidable opponent in public debates on fine points of doctrine, as well the object of criticism by later generations for his dogmatic abstruseness, it is ironically fitting that his most eloquent description of growth into perfection is his description of his own spiritual experience:

> ...I myself, in a part, am a true witness, who not by strength of arguments or by a particular disquisition of each doctrine, and convincement of my understanding thereby, came to receive and bear witness of the Truth, but by being secretly reached by this Life: for, when I came into the silent assemblies of God's people, I felt a secret power among them, which touched my heart; and as I gave way unto it, I found the evil weakening in me and the good raised up; and so I became thus knit and united with them, hungering more and more after the increase of this power and life whereby I might feel myself perfectly redeemed: and indeed this is the surest way to become a

---

[42] Written from Aberdeen Prison, Jan. 1677.

> Christian; to whom afterwards the knowledge and understandings of principles will not be wanting, but will grow up so much as is needful as the natural fruit of this good root, and such a knowledge will not be barren nor unfruitful.... (Sippel, 2002, 300)

Barclay was aware that all of his tightly reasoned arguments, however brilliantly he might explain them, would not bring a certainty of faith to anyone, unless it was divinely disclosed through an inward experience of the "secret power," the divine mystery. It is worth noting that he refers to this as the manner in which "We desire therefore all that come among us to be proselytized..." (Sippel, 2002, 301), thus a "worship-evangelism." He adds that though thousands may be "convinced in their understandings of all the truths we maintain, yet if they were not sensible of this inward life, and their souls not changed from unrighteous to righteousness, they could add nothing to us." He refers to this kind of transformative heart experience as "the cement" that joins us to the Lord and to each other (Sippel, 2002, 301).

This leads into a final key element of Barclay's concept of perfection which the above quote points to. Perfection is not merely individual – it is a corporate holiness – a purely individualistic sanctification would be inconceivable for Barclay. For "Came not Christ to gather a people out of sin into righteousness..." (Sippel, 2002, 211). The church itself (the pure and holy church which he calls "catholic") has been sanctified and consecrated by Christ (Eph. 5:25-27) (Sippel, 2002, 212).

The manifestation of perfection is love – love of God, of neighbor, and most revealing of all because it is the most difficult love, love of our enemy. Thus, the doctrine of perfection is also the foundation for the Quaker peace testimony. Perfection is growth in love, a continuing expansion of the heart to include even one's enemies and the ultimate test of the ethical side of holiness because it is so humanly unnatural. This leads to one distinctive aspect of Quaker holiness that diverges from later Wesleyan forms – the integration of pacifism and holiness.

2.5.2 Summary and Conclusions

Within 100 years, Barclay's proposition on perfection was almost entirely appropriated by John Wesley and formed the basis for the doctrine of Christian Perfection of the Wesleyan revival in England and the subsequent formation of the Methodist movement.[43] Wesley carefully investigated and compared the

---

[43] Dean Freiday, in his introduction to Barclay's *Apology in Modern English*, discusses the relatively unexplored influence of Barclay's theology upon Methodism (1967, xxxiv-xxxviii). Freiday points out that John Wesley, though publicly distancing himself from Quakerism, nevertheless borrowed portions of Barclay's *Apology* to use in his own

entire *Apology* with his understanding of Christianity, and although he found differences with Barclay on several propositions, in his assessment of the eighth proposition on perfection, he concluded, "There is no difference between Quakerism and Christianity" (Wesley, 1748, 10:179). Wesley's articulation of the doctrine of Christian Perfection was in full accord with Barclay's formulation. However, he did note that the language used by Barclay, "This holy birth brought forth" was an "uncommon expression" taken from Jacob Boehme.[44] And he contends that many other Quaker expressions and sentiments were also taken from Boehme, reflecting Wesley's bias against mystical elements in Quakerism and his own love-hate relationship with mystics (Wesley, 1748, 10:179).[45]

For the majority of Quakers, Barclay's *Apology* remained the "official" and most complete explanation and analysis of Quaker faith and experience well into the nineteenth century. Even during the first divisions in American Quakerism between Orthodox and Hicksite, both sides could still appeal to it to support their positions. It continues to be held in high regard by most evangelical Quakers and some Conservative Friends, but is considered antiquated and outmoded by most liberal Quakers today.[46]

Barclay's *Apology* remains the definitive theological expression of Quaker holiness. Being neither Catholic nor Protestant, it integrates all of the historical Quadrants of holiness: Quadrant 1, symbolic (Christ "for us" in the atonement), and the Reformation, *Sola fides*; Quadrant 2, the experiential and charismatic elements of being Spirit-led and filled; Quadrant 3, the Quietist passivity and interiority, and divine indwelling; and Quadrant 4, a new worldly monasticism, an ascetical life-style of renunciation and obedience (proposition fifteen, Salutations and Recreations) (see Figure 3, p. 20). All of these elements of holiness are blended into a Neo-holiness mystical ethic for the late seventeenth century, in which an interior sanctification leads to an exterior ethic of love, for neighbor and even one's enemy.

---

publications. In 1741 Wesley published an abridged version of Propositions V and VI on the "Universal Redemption of Christ," resulting in a 26 page pamphlet entitled *Serious Considerations on Absolute Predestination, extracted from a late author* (Freiday, 1967, xxxv). He claims that Wesley's pamphlet "in most places was so close to the original wording that the differences can be determined only by close comparison" (Freiday, 1967, xxxvi).

[44] Wesley refers to Boehme as Behmen.

[45] Of all the mystics, Wesley had the strongest aversion to Boehme. See Tuttle, 1989, for an indepth study of Wesley and mysticism. (See also Appendix C on relationship between Quakerism and Methodism in the eighteenth century.)

[46] Howard Brinton writes, "About the beginning of the twentieth century nearly all Quaker writers were critical of Barclay's *Apology* which had up to that time largely expressed the character of Quaker thought" (Brinton, 2002, 63).

2.6 Thomas Story: Holiness in the Transitional Period

Thomas Story (1663-1742) became a Friend towards the end of the 17th century after the waning of the Enthusiasms of the First Wave. He left a two-volume account of his life, which describes in detail and depth the progress of his spiritual journey and his Quaker ministry (Kendall, 1832). His writings capture the flavor and essence of Holiness Quakerism after the passing of the toleration act, which ushered in the period known as Quietism. His ministry links the Second Wave of early Friends (he was a friend of William Penn) to the beginnings of Quietism. Story continues the fervent and mystical holiness of the earlier period into the more settled Quietist one, and clearly challenges the stereotype of the Quietist.

Story had a conversion in 1689 as dramatic and remarkable as many earlier Friends had experienced. Filled with despair and self-hatred, his inner devastation turned to elation, as the God of judgment was experienced as the God of love. Like Fox, he experienced (in solitude) the euphoria of an exalted state which resulted in "sweet repose," peace and calmness, and the serenity of inner healing. Note in the excerpt below that he used the therapeutic and holistic terms "all-healing" and "divine healing":

> ...alone in my chamber, the Lord brake in upon me....quick as lightning from the heavens, and as a righteous, all-powerful, all-knowing, and sin condemning Judge; before whom my soul...trembled...and filled with such awful dread as no words can...declare. But, in the midst of this confusion and amazement ...a voice was formed and uttered in me,... "Thy will, O God! Be done; if this be thy act alone and not my own, I yield my soul to Thee."...I quickly found relief: there was all-healing virtue in them; ...all my fears vanished, ...and my mind became calm and still, and simple as a little child; the day of the Lord dawned, and the Sun of Righteousness arose in me, with Divine healing ...and He became the center of my mind. In this wonderful operation of the Lord's power, denouncing judgment in tender mercy... I lost my old self... I now saw the whole body of sin condemned in my own flesh; not by particular acts, as whilst traveling in the way to a perfect moral state...but by one stroke...of the all-awing Judge of all the world...the whole carnal mind...was wounded, and death begun; as self-love, pride, evil thoughts, and every evil desire, with the whole corruption of the first state and natural life. Here I had a taste...of the agony of the Son of God, and of his death...upon the cross...Now all my past sins were pardoned and done away....the mysteries of religion were over...my sorrows ended... and this true fear being to me the initiation into wisdom, I now found the true Sabbath a holy... and free rest, and most sweet repose. (Kendall, 1832, 34-35)

Such born-again conversion experiences are typical of revivals. But also, as is typical of revivals, once the fire dies down, the emotional experience often produces no lasting effects. The doctrine of perfection taught by Quakers, and later the Wesleyan and Holiness Movements, was the antidote to the elation of ecstasy reverting to despair.[47]

After a dramatic conversion experience, Story had a further ecstasy which he described as "my whole nature and being, both mind and body, were filled with the Divine presence, in a manner I had never known before, nor had ever thought that such a thing could be; and of which none can form any idea, but what the holy thing itself doth give" (Kendall, 1832, 35). Story was attempting to communicate the experience of mystical union.[48] God was experienced as both light (illumination, beyond powers of reasoning) and finally love (affective feeling):

> The Divine essential Truth was now self-evident; there wanted nothing else to prove it. I needed not to reason about Him; all reasoning was superseded and immerged, by an intuition of that Divine and truly wonderful evidence and light which proceeded from Himself alone,

---

[47] Augustine of Hippo set the pattern for Western Christian conversion in his description of his own journey to God in *Confessions*. He described just such an experience of rapture reverting to despair. Augustine had a rapturous experience of transcendence, an ascent to God not unlike Fox's "coming up into the spirit through the flaming sword," but rather than empowered by the experience, Augustine was afterward left with a consciousness of his own frailty and loneliness. He wrote, "by weight of my imperfections I fall back again, and I am swallowed up by things customary: I am bound, and I weep bitterly, but I am bitterly bound." His conclusion was that life on earth is marked by isolation and prevents us from actual union with God, and thus real communion even with each other. He wrote with a sense of deep sadness how "every heart is closed to every other heart." For Augustine an impenetrable wall isolates people from one another, just as it does between God and humanity and thus casts a shadow of melancholy on all of his writings. Only in heaven will the gap be closed, and humanity glorified.

The Quaker experience is very different. Although a period of intense struggle often ensues (when freedom is glimpsed, one feels the pain of being chained), the final catharsis brings a genuine sense of victory over sin, a release from bondage. In the end the release of love into the heart brings union with God, and power and victory over sin. A mystical theology of holiness, as union with God, became for Quaker spirituality the antidote for the kind of religious regression and despair that Augustine describes.

[48] The culmination of all of his ecstasies is a unitive experience. He describes a transporting rapture in which he sees (like George Fox) the unity of all creation, (Nickalls, 1952, 27-28) and their dependency on each other – of "animals, reptiles, and vegetables, sun, moon, stars, the innumerable host of heaven …that boundless space which they move and roll in …as all depending one upon another, as meet helps and coadjutors; all connected without a chasm…" (Kendall, 1832, 38).

leaving no place for doubt... I saw Him in his own light...by that eye which He Himself had formed and opened, and also enlightened by the emanations of his own eternal glory. Thus I was filled with perfect consolation, which none but the Word of Life can declare or give. It was then, and not till then, I knew that God is love, and that perfect love which casteth out all fear. It was then I knew that God is eternal light, and that in Him is no darkness at all. (Kendall, 1832, 35-36)

Not long afterwards Story attended a Friends meeting and found the worship experience for which he had been seeking. He described his experience of worship in familiar Quietist language:

Heavenly and watery clouds overshadowing my mind, brake into a sweet abounding shower of celestial rain; and the greatest part of the meeting was broken together, dissolved and comforted in the same Divine and holy presence and influence of the true, holy, and heavenly Lord; which was divers times repeated before the meeting ended; and, in the same way, by the same Divine and holy power, I had been often favoured with before when alone. (Kendall, 1832, 70)

Story had already described in some detail, in the emotive style of the period, his private ecstasies. He now claimed to have those same favored consolations he experienced alone with God, in a group setting. He had discovered a like-minded group of people who shared the same mystical sensibility as he did and had similar break-through experiences, and thus as a group, had the ability to "break through" together, to go beyond the usual limitations of the self. The use of the term "celestial showers" seems to connate a "breaking in" of heaven, a transcendence of self.

Once he had found a community, a spiritual home, he made a complete break from his old way of life, quitting the profession of law, joining with Friends and traveling in the ministry. He described a "Dark Night of the Soul" experience that parallels accounts of many Christian mystics. He was overcome with a sense of utter desolation, as though God had withdrawn from him.

Having been deprived of all sense of the Divine presence for many days, and destitute of all comfort... deeply mourning for some weeks, till all hope was vanishing, the heavens became as brass, and shut up as with bars of iron; and nothing remained but a bare remembrance of former enjoyments. (Kendall, 1832, 128)

He identified with Paul, the Apostle, who said: "Woe is unto me, if I preach not the Gospel" (Kendall, 1832, 128). The struggle with answering a call through a long "dark night" and hearing the words of Paul are common in the accounts of holiness ministers.

In 1693, Story met William Penn and they formed a deep spiritual bond: "I contracted so near a friendship in the life of Truth, and tendering love thereof in many tears, as never wore out till his dying day; and in which his memory still lives, as a sweet odour in my mind..." (Kendall, 1832, 122). This ability to form deep friendships and to speak and write of the other using such intimate language was characteristic of these mystically inclined Quakers (see Appendix A on love mysticism).

An example of the Quaker Gospel he preached during his many travels can be found in a passage in his journal that was prompted by a Roman Catholic who questioned him concerning the principles of Friends, and asked of what use were silent meetings. His response testified to his own spiritual pilgrimage, presented as a commonly shared Quaker experience:

> That we had been as other men, subject to common infirmities and ignorant of God, as to any experience of his Presence and Divine working in us, till it please Him in his goodness and mercy to visit us by the Spirit of his Son Christ, through which we had known a time of condemnation and humiliation for sins past, and true repentance and forgiveness; and believing in Him through the work of his Spirit and power in our minds, He, with the Light and Life of his Son, became the object of our faith; by which also He sanctified our hearts, and reconciled us unto Himself: so that the enmity being slain, and we made temples of the Holy Ghost, we now worshiped the Father through the Spirit of his Son, in a state of faith and obedience; whereby we draw near unto Him, even through that blessed medium which Himself hath appointed, partaking of the nature of man; not of flesh and blood only, as the son of man, but also being clothed with a holy human mind; by Him we are made partakers of the Divine nature as the sons of God; as it is written; "He shall take of mine, and give it to you." (Kendall, 1832, 176-77)

Story's words evidence a clear affirmation of Trinitarian belief: "we now worshipped the Father through the Spirit of his Son," as well as the incarnation, the human and divine nature of Christ "partaking of the nature of man, not of flesh and blood only...but also being clothed with a holy human mind," and perfection (deification) with the classic standard reference to II Peter 1:4.

Story preached a clear holiness message of freedom from sin – the same message, he claimed, found in the teachings of the Church of England, but ignored: "... things opened well on several points, especially concerning freedom from sin in this life, and the necessity of it" (Kendall, 1832, 2:93). This truth, he reminded them, was found even in the "great vows and promises" of the catechism of the Church of England (Kendall, 1832, 2:93):

I directed them therefore to God's covenant of Light, and to that grace which came by Jesus Christ, which they mention in their catechism, though they regard it not in practice, but commonly dispute that no man can be free from sin in this life, yet that is the only means to attain such freedom and perform those vows. (Kendall, 1832, 2:94)

Story had the heart of an evangelist and found spiritual complacency not just a concern, but a form of unbelief. He observed that declension and a tendency toward "forms" had already taken effect among Friends in 1716 (Braithwaite, 1919, 539).

Braithwaite quotes an intriguing comment Story made about a large meeting in Kendal consisting mostly of young people, which he visited in 1733. Story compared the meeting to Paul's experience with the Samaritans in Acts 8:16, who had not yet received the Holy Ghost, though they believed in Christ and the Light, "yet the Spirit Himself is not fallen upon many of them, as a sensible and experimental dispensation of life and power; which is properly the Gospel and the former is rather previous and introductory" (Braithwaite, 1919, 539).

2.6.1   Conclusion: The Poetry of Perfection

Based on this brief survey of Story's spiritual experiences and ministry, if he is normative of this period (which Braithwaite indicates he is) the evidence seems conclusive that holiness as a second and deeper experience was the Quaker Gospel being preached in England at this time. This "second blessing" holiness was prior to the Wesleyan Revival and Wesley's formulation of the Doctrine of Christian Perfection. John Wesley's *Plain Account of Christian Perfection,* his *summa theologica* of the doctrine, did not appear until 1766, although as early as 1733 he had begun to reflect seriously on the implications of it. Like Story, Wesley found perfection in the essentially ignored creeds, confessions, and prayers of the Anglican Faith (Peters, 1985, 32).

Story's mystical experiences inspired one of the most poetical expressions of holiness that can be found in Quaker literature. Story pens a consecration hymn, modeled after the poetry of the Psalms, to witness to his extraordinary experience of divine love:

> I called unto my God out of the great Deep:
> > and He had compassion upon me,
> > because His Love was infinite and
> His Power without measure.
> > He called for my Life and I offered it at His Footstool;
> > but he gave it to me for a prey,
> > with unspeakable addition.

He called for my Will:
    and I resigned it at His Call:
    but He returned me His own in token of His love.
He called for the World,
    and I laid it at His feet with the Crowns thereof:
    I withheld them not at the beckoning of His hand.
    But mark the benefit of Exchange!
For He gave me, instead of Earth,
    a Kingdom of Eternal Peace and in lieu of the
    Crowns of Vanity, a Crown of Glory.
(Kendall, 1832, 49-50)

The parallels between Thomas Story's Quietist Quaker holiness and the later nineteenth century Holiness Movement are numerous and striking. Rendel Harris (see 6.2), a Quaker modernist who espoused holiness in the early twentieth century, found Story to be a powerfully inspirational figure. Harris believed firmly in the Quaker doctrine of continuing revelation and thus could claim that inspired writings did not end with the closing of the biblical canon (Wood and Harris, 1929, 2-7). Harris decided to search for examples of literature "not too dissimilar from the Scriptures in their style and in every way comparable with them for insight and for spiritual intensity" (Wood and Harris, 1929, 5). Among several selections of Quaker writing which he fully believed were inspired is an excerpt from the journal of Thomas Story. Harris informs us that it was composed at the beginning of his life of faith "as a Consecration hymn or psalm... a direct reminiscence of the days when he surrendered himself to the life of God."[49]

Story's prayer is also significant in this study of Quaker holiness in the compelling way it captures all of the essential facets of holiness experience as surrender of self. The phrase, "He called for My Will...and He returned me His own in token of His love," is a moving expression of the "union of wills" in which the transcendent God becomes the intimate beloved so frequently claimed by the mystics. Harris, 200 years later, found this prayer genuinely inspired because he recognized in Thomas Story a kindred soul who had put into words the ineffability of his own experience. (See 6.2 on Harris.)

---

[49] The psalm is found in his journal (Kendall, 1832, 49-50), written as he emerged from a period of silence. He prefaced his prayer with these words: "I was silent before the Lord, as a child not yet weaned. He put words in my mouth, and I sang forth his praise with an audible voice." Harris firmly believed that "If these sentences had been found in Hebrew we should have recognized them at once by their kinship with the Psalter for genuine inspirations" (Wood and Harris, 1929, 7).

2.7 Chapter Summary: Holiness in Post-Restoration Quakerism

Post-restoration Quakerism, though sometimes considered the beginnings of Quietism, could as easily be called the beginnings of Quaker orthodoxy. This period was decisive for the formation of Quakerism as an organized entity. The leadership of this period was responsible for forming loose communities of enthusiasts into an organized structure, with a body of common beliefs, practices and forms of worship. Moore writes that respectability and preservation of their community became a primary concern (2000, 215). Quakerism, because of its own internal conflicts (perhaps more so than external conflicts, after the restoration), had to go through a difficult process of self-identification, marking lines in the sand beyond which Quakerism would not go. In the process, claims Moore, their theology became increasingly orthodox (2000, 214). Moore argues, "Pressure from opponents affected the expression of the Quaker faith, forcing a prophetic inspiration into theological subtleties" (1993, Abstract). While Moore, Ingle and others are certain that the response of their opponents and desire for respectability motivated Quakers to become more interested in doctrinal and theological subtleties, the work of Davie and Dobbs argues that Quakers were essentially orthodox from their inception, and core convictions of Christian belief were inherent rather than a later imposition (Davie, 1992, 40; Dobbs, 1995). Davie concludes that Quakers accepted the core of conviction of Christian belief (1992, 40).

Quakers were dissenters from the mainstream of the Reformation, but they were not heretics, and nothing in their normative teaching and preaching was a novelty or heterodox. This study argues that Quakerism contained some modern theological trajectories, but the heart of Quakerism is to be found in their blending of the biblical mysticism of the Apostle Paul with the spiritualizing of the Johannine tradition. The "Christ in me" language of Paul is blended in Quakerism with the "union" language (which modern interpreters find so unsettling) in the Gospel of John.[50] Quaker antecedents (proto-Quakers, and "Quakers before Quakerism") seem to appear everywhere in Christian history, and the reason is simple – Quakerism was more a look backward than forward, for Quakerism reflected the idea of perfection found in the patristic mysticism of the early church of the first four centuries and the medieval mystics who continued to develop that tradition through the Middle Ages.[51] Quakers were

---

[50] See McGinn, ch. 3, especially p. 7, on the mysticism of the early church.

[51] A standard criticism of early Quakerism is its lack of emphasis on the atonement. The focus on atonement only came to the fore in the Protestant Reformation. Quakers, like the church fathers, emphasized the risen and glorified Christ rather than the historical Jesus. "The later Protestant concentration of Christian Faith on the death of Jesus as an atonement for our sins cannot be found in that form in the church fathers. Generally speaking they attached just as much importance to the incarnation and resurrection and

innovative only in that they appropriated the long history of the search for Christian perfection (which *is* the basis of Christian mysticism) into a holiness movement in a Puritan, Post-Reformation, and politically revolutionary context. They combined elements of all of the various styles and forms which holiness had taken within the boundaries circumscribed by Christian orthodoxy, though generally a minority tradition, and in some eras of the church a suppressed tradition. One reason why this has been so hard to see in the past is that boundaries of Christian orthodoxy and orthopraxis are much wider and more flexible than those of the institutional church of any historical period. Experiential Christianity is always in tension with institutional Christianity and even the great mystics who are now recognized as saints were often viewed with suspicion, suffering oppression and betrayal from the institutional church at some point in their lifetime.[52]

Perfection, the spiritual transformation of being changed "from glory to glory," (see 2.2) and the reality of such union, would be evidenced through outward expression or response of action, as well as moral purity, obedience, compassion, and humility. The puritanical morality and asceticism of early Quakers served to differentiate them from Ranters, and other antinomian sectarian groups, who claimed to be beyond the law. Barclay's *Apology* includes a lengthy section outlining a distinctly Puritan ethic of separation from all worldly activities including sports, games, and recreations (Sipple 2002, 429-478). William Penn's widely read devotional work, *No Cross, No Crown*, is similar in spirit (1682). These and other Quaker writings advocating a this-worldly asceticism were necessary to correct common misperceptions and to differentiate themselves from the libertarianism of some of the more extreme sectarians. Quakers were determined to convince their opponents they were orthodox Christians who observed a biblical morality. They were like monks without vows who lived in families and pursued vocations in the midst of the world, but separated themselves from the culture of the world. Strict renunciation and puritanical asceticism were the antidotes to tendencies of pride, a constant temptation among perfectionists. This ethical and behavioral asceticism of early Quakers was so strong that it became the dominant ethos of the next century of Quaker faith and practice. Such a disciplined and ascetical way of life was as necessary for Quaker mystics as it had been for Catholic mystics. Structures and disciplines were needed to contain the excesses and prevent the dangers of delusions, which can result from mystical experiences.

---

glorification of the Son of God" (Roukema, Riemer, *Gnosis and Faith in Early Christianity*, 1999, 164).
[52] Some notable examples: St. Francis of Assisi, Teresa of Avila and John of the Cross. Most women mystics came under suspicion at some point in their lives.

CHAPTER 3

Holiness in the Golden Age of Quietism

3.1 Quietism and the Apophatic

The seventeenth century had been a heroic and enthusiastic period for the Quaker movement with a focus on conversion, mission, and the creation of a deeply experiential, Spirit-filled and Spirit-guided religious community. By the close of the century, the enthusiasm of the first and second wave began to give way to the maintenance and nurture of a distinct Quaker culture (Vann, 1969, 167). As consolidation and definition increased, beliefs and practices were formalized.[1] A radical holiness movement transformed itself into a settled and industrious, but still austere way of life that came to be called Quietism in the eighteenth century.

Although the period of Quietism is often equated with the Golden Age or Classical period of Quakerism when Friends created a unique religious culture, some historians, such as Rufus Jones, view the period as one of decline. Jones casts a fundamentally negative impression of Quietism. He views Quietist spirituality as repressive of human nature with its concern for the annihilation of self and the expectation that all action must have divine impulse (1921, 60-64). A lack of understanding of the apophatic approach to union with God has contributed to such pejorative views of Quietism. Union with God was still central to Quakerism in this period, though often now spoken of in terms of continental Quietism's "union of wills" (Dubois, 1986, 412-413). Rufus Jones defined Quietism as "an act of faith in supernatural divine action, operated in those who succeed in suppressing all human activity" (1921, 60). Howard Brinton, who is more sympathetic towards Quietism than Jones was, defines it as "the doctrine that every self-centered trait or activity must be suppressed or quieted in order that the divine may find unopposed entrance to the soul" (2002, 81). Kathryn Damiano, who also has a more positive appreciation of the spirituality of Quietism than Jones, defines it as a form of religious expression that "called for an emptying of all actions motivated by human will to be open to the guidance of God" (1988, 38). Damiano understands the difference

---

[1] Rosemary Moore marks the end of the early period with the document called "The Testimony of the Brethren," written in 1666, which she claims as the first standardization of belief and organization, giving final authority to the "Church", i.e., the Quaker business meeting (2000, 224). This study uses 1666 as the transition from the enthusiastic radical period to the second wave, the formative period, and 1689, the date of the toleration act, as the movement into the third wave of Quietism.

between "emptying" and suppression. These definitions are attempts to grasp the apophatic way of Christian mysticism that can be traced back through the Spanish Carmelites and the Rhineland School to the Desert Fathers (Dupré, 1996, 132). George Maloney, a modern interpreter of this type of mysticism, in describing the apophaticism of the Greek Fathers, might well be defining Quaker Quietism when he writes, "It was a call to worship and receive God's revelation in a prayerful mystery that was a positive knowledge of God given by God's Holy Spirit to the pure of heart" (1987, 2). This chapter shows how two Quietist leaders, Anthony Benezet and Stephen Grellet, both embodied the apophatic as well as the kataphatic in their zeal to "spread holiness over the land."

3.2 Anthony Benezet and the First Quaker Reformation: Holiness Renewed

Jack D. Marietta, a historian of eighteenth century Friends, documents the first renewal movement within the Society of Friends in 1748. He describes this radical alteration as a reformation which took place in the American colonies among Pennsylvania Friends and spread throughout the Society (1984, xi). By the 1750s, a century after its founding as a counter-cultural and radical holiness movement, the second and third generations were now mostly birthright members who had not experienced the kind of dramatic conversions, faith-testing persecutions and spiritual trials of their parents and grandparents. Those who were raised in the Quaker colony of Pennsylvania had even become part of the cultural and political establishment. Philadelphia Friends had accumulated wealth, prestige and power, and inversely, according to a group of concerned Quaker ministers, spiritual and moral decline. Marietta describes this renewal movement as one of purification and withdrawal from the mainstream of society. He casts it as a movement of reversal from established church back into sectarianism. He views this reversal as a positive and necessary direction for a religious society which had compromised its own principles and was desperately in need of spiritual reform and renewal (1984, xii).

Because holiness, in any organized form, as in monasticism, represents a more intense form of spirituality and a detachment from all that distracts from the pursuit of union with God, it tends towards cultural separatism. Thus, holiness movements are inevitably counter-cultural. But essential Quaker holiness, as has been shown, always includes strong outreaching elements, a zealous desire to awaken others to the Light of Christ through evangelization and mission. While holiness creates a condition of being inwardly detached from the world and emptied of the ego-self, it also impels the "pure in heart" back into the world to spread the Quaker message and to promote justice.

This renewal movement, described by Marietta, came about through the leadership of a small group of radicals, who had strong "pietist"[2] leanings (1984, 37). The broader context of this revival in Quakerism was the "Great Awakening" in the American colonies, spearheaded by George Whitefield, Jonathan Edwards, and Gilbert Tennant. The Quaker revival, unlike the "Great Awakening," was not geared primarily to the evangelization of the masses (though evangelization was not absent), but rather focused on a renewal of the spiritual vigor and prophetic power of its own society – in other words, a renewal of holiness. The reformation of its own Society became the Quaker response to the broad movement of spiritual awakening, which was itself a response to the rationalism of the Enlightenment and the low state of spiritual life in the American colonies in general (Finke and Stark, 1992, 24).

The Quaker reformation (like the Wesleyan revival in England in the eighteenth century) reemphasized Christian perfection, a desire for purity and holiness. The political, cultural and social context of this awakening was obviously quite different from the original radical Quaker Holiness Movement of the 1650s, as well as from the revivalistic Holiness Movement of the nineteenth century, yet many of the aims, in spiritual, moral, and social reform, were the same. All of these reform movements had an express concern for moral reform with a call to personal purity, simplicity, honesty, and integrity, and an equally strong agenda of social reform – in particular, abolition, temperance, anti-wealth and materialism, concern for the poor, educational reform, pacifism, and equality. The nineteenth century Holiness Movement placed a major emphasis on evangelism and a deeper spiritual life (conversion and sanctification) but had a strong social outreach as well. The eighteenth century Quaker movement placed its primary emphasis on the deepening of the spiritual and moral life of its meetings. Social outreach had an important place, but its immediate challenge, eliminating slavery from within its own ranks, became paramount in its desire to be a holy community.

One of the most prominent and intriguing figures of this renewal movement was Anthony Benezet (1713-1784), who was a convinced Quaker, not a birthright one.[3] This section examines the life and thought of Anthony Benezet

---

[2] Pietism was a seventeenth century renewal of holiness and experiential Christianity among Lutherans.

[3] Benezet was born into a wealthy family with ties to Huguenots in St. Quinten, France, in 1713. Persecution led the family to seek refuge in Holland and thence to London where his father became associated with Quakers (Vaux, 1817, 11). In 1731, at the age of 18, Anthony moved with his family to Philadelphia and probably joined with Quakers at that time (Brookes, 1937, 16). There is no record of Benezet's convincement or date of membership with Quakers. He married Joyce Marriott, a Quaker minister, in 1736, before Philadelphia Yearly Meeting. The Benezet family had great admiration for the Moravians and two of their most well-known leaders, Nicholas von Zinzendorf, founder of the Moravians in Germany, and a notable Protestant mystic, and August Spangenberg,

as a figure representing the continuing thread of holiness perfectionism that emanated from the Quietist period. If Quietism, as John Punshon claims, "preserved the soul of Quakerism" (1984, 102), Anthony Benezet and the radical reformers preserved the soul of Quaker holiness. Benezet exemplified the deep inwardness of the Quaker way, the mystical sensitivity to the Divine, and the power of love that characterizes the holy life. In addition, he expressed what this study will show is that unique dialectic of Quaker holiness, the "separated" life, detached from the secular world, yet moving within it, with the expansiveness of vision that reaches compassionately into it, desiring to mend it.

Benezet was a close friend and exact contemporary of John Woolman, another of the Quietist radicals, and they shared the same ideals and ethical principles.[4] Based on the evidence in Irv Brendlinger's study of Benezet, he "was the greatest eighteenth century influence on the ending of British slavery and the slave trade" (1996, 81). Benezet, like Woolman, was a thoroughgoing Quietist, with the same kind of deeply interior spirituality and sensitivity to human suffering. Benezet has not been immortalized in a journal like Woolman, but collections of his letters and pamphlets and several devotional writings reveal both his theology and spirituality and the depth and breadth of his reforming zeal. Benezet was a far more public figure than Woolman, and he left deep impressions upon his contemporaries, both within and without the Society of Friends.[5] We know less about him through his own eyes (as in Woolman, in

---

founder of the Moravian Church in America, were visitors at the Benezet home. In 1743 Benezet's father, and subsequently his three sisters, left Friends to join with the Moravians. Anthony had ample opportunity to learn and absorb the Moravian faith. The Moravians were a holiness movement that emerged out of the Lutheran Church as a community of renewal in Germany. Moravians had much in common with early Quakers, e.g. perfectionism, mysticism, strong community orientation, emphasis on new birth, evangelism and mission. Anthony, his mother, and three brothers remained with Friends (Brookes, 1937, 19-20). Not much is known about the relationship between Quakers and Moravians in the American Colonies, a topic worth further exploration.

[4] John Woolman (1720-1772) has become the best known figure of this period, "canonized" by the Quaker poet-reformer, John Whittier, in the nineteenth century for his life of simplicity, integrity and testimony against slavery expressed so authentically in his *Journal,* reprinted by Whittier in 1871. Benezet, like Woolman, was both a reformer and a mystic, but without slighting the contribution and significance of Woolman, Benezet's mission, and the arena of his influence in his lifetime, was much broader. Woolman's impact ultimately became greater over time, beginning with the 1774 publishing of his *Journal,* considered a literary masterpiece, which continues to inspire contemporary readers.

[5] In 1780 his book written in French and English, entitled *A Short Account of the Religious Society of Friends Commonly called Quakers,* was "esteemed the best succinct view of the principles, as well as discipline and economy of the Society, that had then appeared" (Brookes, 1937, 110). He also published a small work in 1782 entitled *On the Plainness, and Innocent Simplicity of the Christian Religion.*

his *Journal*) but more through the eyes of his contemporaries, including his biographer Roberts Vaux (Vaux, 1817).

But more significantly for this study, he left, in addition to his many writings on slavery, two devotional works published under his name, though not actually penned by him, which reflect his deep holiness orientation: *The Spirit of Prayer*, a description of the apophatic approach to mystical union, and a tract on perfection called *The Plain Path to Christian Perfection*. *The Spirit of Prayer*, included in a volume of tracts bound together under his name, was actually a reprint of the work of William Law (see Appendix C). *The Plain Path to Christian Perfection* was Benezet's translation of an anonymous mystical work originally published in Germany in the early sixteenth century, and translated into French.[6] Since Benezet's name is ascribed to them both, we can assume the message of these writings was adopted as his own. The fact that they were published by Quakers and reprinted many times demonstrates that they were not just Benezet's idiosyncratic preferences, but were read and accepted by the Quaker community. Much like Guyon's *A Guide to True Peace*, these writings became part of the canon of Quaker orthodoxy.[7]

Benezet was a true apophatic mystic. One of his favorite phrases, "It is in nothingness that God is found," was taken from *The Spirit of Prayer* and quoted in his letters (Marietta, 1984, 251). He was also a man well ahead of his time in many areas of social justice. In addition to his championing of the slave and the rights of Native Americans, he was an advocate for temperance a hundred years before it became a social issue.[8] Benezet is known primarily for his anti-slavery

---

[6] The full title is *The plain path to Christian perfection, showing that we are to seek for reconciliation and union with God, solely by renouncing ourselves, denying the world, and following our Blessed Savior, in the regeneration*. It was first published in Philadelphia by Joseph Crukshank in 1772.

[7] Stephen Hobhouse identified *The Spirit of Prayer* as a "little self-contained treatise" which "gained great favour with members of the Society of Friends" (1972, 295). Whole portions were reprinted by Quakers in 1815, 1822 (in French), 1836, 1875, 1876, and 1886 (1972, 295, n2). Hobhouse, however, was unaware that Anthony Benezet much earlier, in 1780, had reprinted *The Spirit of Prayer* with his own introduction and that the work even came to be ascribed to him.

[8] A generation before Benezet, George Keith, an influential Quaker leader who for many years worked and traveled with Fox, Penn, and Barclay, spoke out against the practice of slavery in a pamphlet entitled "An Exhortation and Caution to Friends Concerning Buying or Keeping of Negroes." It was printed in New York in 1693. Keith later challenged the Quaker leadership on some doctrinal and authority issues which needed clarifying. Unfortunately, his personally provocative, argumentative, and apparently graceless manner eventually cost him his influential voice, and he was disowned. The critique on slavery was largely muted with his departure, though the occasional voice was heard via William Edmundson and George Fox in England. In the colonies in 1688 a "Minute Against Slavery" was addressed to Germantown Monthly Meeting (http://www.qhpress.org/texts/oldqwhp/as-1688.htm, Dec. 11, 2003). (For more

work and the many tracts he wrote about the slave trade. One in particular, his 1771 tract, *Some Historical Account of Guinea, Its Situation, Produce and the General Disposition of its Inhabitants with an Inquiry into the Rise and Progress of the Slave Trade,* became the most influential due to its being "borrowed" and edited (now we would call it plagiarized, though an accepted practice then) by John Wesley in 1774 (Barclay, 1991, xxxiv; Ayling, 1979, 283). Wesley called his tract *Thoughts on Slavery* (admittedly a catchier title than Benezet's). Benezet's connection with Wesley and many other luminaries of the time is significant because it contradicts the general impression of Quietists as being withdrawn from the world, and only ministering and associating within their own society.[9] Benezet's connection with Wesley is also significant at this time because it reveals a degree of mutual appreciation between Methodism and Quakerism already existing in the eighteenth century, which became more pronounced in the nineteenth century. Two of Benezet's main social concerns, the incompatibility of wealth with the Gospel and the sin of slavery were also major concerns of John Wesley. Both also believed fervently in Christian perfection, though they expressed it somewhat differently. Benezet remained solidly anchored in a mystical, apophatic Quietism, which Wesley came to resist (see Appendix C).

Benezet's reputation as a social reformer has been noted by many historians (Brookes, 1937; Jones, 1921; Marietta, 1984; Brendlinger, 1996). His social reform was an integral part of his spirituality and his understanding of holiness and perfection. But most modern historians who have taken notice of him focus only on his role as a radical social reformer and do not relate his passionate social witness to his mystical pursuit of holiness. (Brendlinger is the exception.) Marietta, who has written the only in depth scholarly study of the reformation movement, finds Benezet's writings valuable as evidence of his interests in antislavery and asceticism, yet oddly concludes that his letters show less breadth of reformist interest than other material (1984). Yet his life of social activism included reform in education, distribution of wealth, treatment of Native Americans, abuse of alcohol, slavery, racial and ethnic prejudice, opposition to war, and all forms of oppression (he also took up the cause of the Acadian refugees who were forced off their lands). His life demonstrated there need be no dichotomy between prophetic religion and mystical religion. In Quaker holiness the mystical and the prophetic are always a dialectic, not a

---

information on Keith, see J. William Frost, *The Keithian controversy in early Pennsylvania,* 1980.) Benezet revisited the slavery issue after it had been eclipsed by the Keithian controversy. Benezet also reaffirmed the pacifist position of holiness Quakerism in his opposition to all war during the fervent patriotism of the American War for Independence.

[9] This was truer of Woolman, and may be one reason for the misleading impression that eighteenth century Quakers were isolated and insulated from the outside world.

dichotomy. Benezet's life, work, and ministry became a true integration of the mystical and the prophetic.[10]

Benezet was a prophet of the *via negativa*, a category Rufus Jones found difficult to assimilate with his theory of Quaker affirmative mysticism (Jones, 1931, 12-13) (see also 1.7.1). And most importantly for this study, Benezet taught a spirituality of perfection through union with God (mystical perfection) and imitation of Christ (ethical obedience) via the path of renunciation (apophatism). We find these themes contained in the two devotional works to which his name is attributed, *The Plain Path of Christian Perfection* and *The Spirit of Prayer*. The perfection of which he writes is not the Methodist doctrine of holiness developed by John Wesley, but the more ancient perfectionist tradition as it is found in medieval monastic literature. Benezet's perfection is the holiness of the monastic, who lives in the world, yet is detached from the world. It is consistent with that of Barclay and early Quakerism. It is the perfection found in the fifteenth Proposition of Barclay's *Apology* on the renunciation of the world, and devotional works such as William Penn's *No Cross, No Crown*. Quaker perfection in the Quietist era remained attached to the ascetical mystical tradition. Wesley, too, discovered it there, and explored the mystical tradition through his own reading of the mystics. In the end, he separated perfection from the *via negativa*, but he appropriated aspects of the mystical tradition which he felt were valuable, including the Quaker favorites, Guyon, Fenelon, and Molinos (see Appendix C).

Although he wrote, conversed, and interacted with leaders from many different religious perspectives, from the deists (Ben Franklin) to the Methodist founder, John Wesley, and could easily be viewed as an ecumenist, he retained a staunchly Quaker anti-worldly asceticism. Benezet was a classic example of one who lived in the world and had the respect of those who shared his reformist views, yet maintained an identity and practiced principles in opposition to the world. He maintained a "pure," plain Quaker identity even while hobnobbing with worldly, aristocratic non-Quakers. (He may have been viewed as a charming eccentric by some.) In this respect he anticipates to some degree Joseph John Gurney (a nineteenth century Quaker reformer, see 4.2), yet he was never perceived as Gurney was – despite Gurney's plain dress and speech – as "worldly" and liberal. One reason for this may be his continual emphasis on a mystical interiority, his monk-like asceticism, and his strident invectives against wealth, all of which became platforms of the Quaker renewal movement.

---

[10] The title alone of Benezet's tract is indicative of a contemplative in action, showing his integration of practical mysticism and social activism, and how the former flows out of the latter: *An Extract from a Treatise on the Spirit of Prayer or The Soul rising out of the Vanity of Time into the Riches of Eternity with some Thoughts on War: Remarks on the Nature and bad effects of the use of Spirituous Liquors and Considerations on Slavery* (1780).

3.2.1 The Spirit of Prayer: Quietist Spirituality

Benezet wrote the preface to the Quaker version of William Law's *The Spirit of Prayer* framing it in the context of Quaker holiness[11] (see Appendix C). Benezet wanted to be certain it was read in the light of the Gospel of Christ. Thus he offered this treatise on prayer as a distillation of the Gospel which he called "the watch words of Christianity to all true followers of Christ" (1780, 2). He distilled this Gospel into the incarnation and atonement: Christ "came down from his father's glory, took upon him our nature and suffered death for us" (1780, 2). The purpose of this work of Christ is to restore us to that "spirit of life of meekness, purity, and love, that being dead to sin we should live unto righteousness" (sanctification, perfection), as well as "leaving us an example that we should follow in his footsteps" (imitation) (1780, 2). He specified what imitation means: to love our enemies and follow the new commandment – "love one another as I have loved you." And he further reminded his readers that the meek, the merciful, and the pure in heart are to be the particular object of divine regard. Our pattern of life is to be based on Christ's ethic of love, not the world's. (This is also the theological basis of the holiness ethic of John Wesley.) He then contrasted this vision of the Gospel message of love with war, which requires killing and destroying our neighbors and our enemies, thus including a distinctive Quaker testimony to holiness (not found in Wesleyan holiness). He concluded his introductory remarks with: "God is Love – and he that dwelleth in God dwelleth in love and God in him" (mutual indwelling or union) (1780, 2).

The treatise itself contains many passages that resound with Quaker concepts and expressions, and indeed, most Quaker readers probably assumed Benezet penned them (Law's name does not appear as author):

> It is manifest, that no one can fail of the Benefit of Christ's Salvation, but through an *Unwillingness* to have it ...But if thou wouldst still farther know how this great Work, the *Birth* of Christ, is to be effected in thee, then let this joyful Truth be told thee, that this great Work is *already* begun in every one of us. For this holy Jesus, that is to be formed in thee, that is to be the Saviour and new Life of thy Soul, that is to raise thee out of the Darkness of Death into the Light of Life, and give thee Power to become a Son of God, is already *within* thee, living, stirring, calling, knocking at the Door of thy Heart, and wanting nothing but thy own *Faith* and *Good Will*, to have as real a Birth and Form in thee, as he had in the Virgin *Mary*. For the eternal *Word*, or

---

[11] William Law (1686-1761) was an Anglican priest, non-juror, and early mentor to John Wesley. His works range from the stern, moralist tome, *A Serious Call to a Devout and Holy Life,* to the mystical heights of *The Spirit of Love*, inspired by the writing of Jacob Boehme and French Quietism.

Son of God, did not then first begin to be the Saviour of the World, when he was born in *Bethlehem* of *Judea*; but that Word, which became Man in the Virgin *Mary*, did, from the Beginning of the World, enter as a *Word* of Life, a *Seed* of Salvation, into the first Father of Mankind, and inspoken into him, as an ingrafted Word, under the Name and Character of a *Bruiser of the Serpent's Head.* Hence it is, that Christ said to his Disciples, *the Kingdom of God is within you*; that is, the Divine Nature is within you, given unto your first Father, into the Light of his Life, and from him rising up in the life of every Son of *Adam.* Hence also the holy Jesus is said to be the *Light, which lightest every Man that cometh into the World.* (1780, 11) [all emphases are his]

Following the pattern of the Quaker focus on John 1, *The Spirit of Prayer* then offers a classically Quaker meditation on that text. The description of the new birth includes many of the common phrases used by early Quakers.[12] The new birth is presented as a conscious decision one must make to the seed of salvation already sown within, and thus has the tone of an evangelistic sermon, a preacher fervently desiring that his or her hearers will make a response to the offer of salvation. The emphasis is on the inward opening of the heart in order for Christ to be born within, but the same Christ born in the person of faith is also the Christ born of Mary. Both the universality of the *offer* of salvation and the necessity of choice cannot be missed.

"The Pearl of Great Price" is a common metaphor of the New Birth and is described in traditional Quaker fashion:

When this Seed, of the Spirit, common to all Men, is not resisted, grieved and quenched, but its Inspirations and Motions suffered to grow and increase in us, to unite with God, and get Power over all the Lusts of the Flesh, then we are born again, the Nature, Spirit and Tempers of Jesus Christ are opened in our Souls, the Kingdom of God is come, and is found within us. (Benezet, 1780, 19)

Perfection, or union with God, is described as:

...this longing Desire of thy Heart to be *one* with Christ. [his emphasis] From this desire of Union on *both sides* [from God and

---

[12] Images and descriptions of this New Birth in Christ include the "Pearl of Great Price," "New Heart," "willingness" that comes through faith (always a free choice), "self-love dethroned," "new nature," "new birth from above, and Kingdom of Heaven to be opened within," "a Spark of light and Spirit of God, as a Supernatural Gift of God, given into the Birth of his Soul, to bring forth by Degrees a New Birth of that Life which was lost in Paradise" (Benezet, 1780, 20).

human, thus synergy] the vegetable Life arises, and all the Virtues and Powers contained in it. (1780, 21)

In describing this union the writer uses an analogy, which he calls a "Similitude," of a grain of wheat in the light and air and describes how they are interconnected, though not the same (1780, 21).

A distinct emphasis in this writing, common to Christian mysticism, is that the "Desire for Union" is on both sides (1780, 21). God's desire for us is met by our longing for Him, though first the corrupt self must die:

> But this Desire on both sides cannot have its effect, till the Husk and gross Part of the Grain falls into a State of Corruption and Death, till this begins, the Mystery of Life hidden in it, cannot come forth. ...we may here see the true Ground and absolute Necessity of that dying to ourselves and to the World to which our Blessed Lord so constantly calls all his Followers. ...Self-denial... is not a Thing imposed upon us by the mere Will of God, is not required as a Punishment, is not an Invention of dull and monkish Spirits, but has its Ground and Reason in the Nature of the Thing, and is absolutely necessary to make Way for the New Birth, as the Death of the Husk, and gross Part of the Grain, is necessary to make Way for its vegetable Life. (1780, 21)

Here is sounded the oft-repeated Quaker call to renunciation, yet it is not forced or invented by "monkish spirits" but is the response of love. "The Pearl of Eternity" is the "Wisdom and love of God within Thee" (1780, 22). The writer proceeds to use the metaphor of "The Pearl of Eternity" to develop an orthodox theology of creation, fall, and redemption. The Pearl of Eternity is:

> ...the Light and Spirit of God within Thee, which has hitherto done Thee but little Good, because all the Desire of thy Heart has been after the Light and Spirit of this World...When Man first came into Being, and stood before God in his own Image and Likeness, this Light and Spirit of God was as natural to him, as truly the Light of his Nature, as the Light and Air of this World is natural to the Creatures that have their Birth in it. But when Man, not content with the Food of Eternity, did eat of the earthly Tree, the Light and Spirit of Heaven was no more Natural to him, no more rose up as a Birth of his Nature, but, instead thereof, he was left solely to the Light and Spirit of the World. And this is that Death which God told Adam he should surely die, in the Day that he should eat of the Forbidden Tree...But the Goodness of God would not leave Man in this Condition; a Redemption from it was immediately granted, and the Bruiser of the Serpent brought the Light and Spirit of Heaven once more into the human Nature. Not as it was in its first State, when Man was in Paradise, but as a Treasure hidden

in the Center of our Souls, which should discover, and open itself by Degrees, in such Proportion, as the Faith and Desires of our Hearts were turned to it. This Light and Spirit of God thus freely restored again to the Soul, and lying in it as a secret Source of Heaven, is called, Grace, Free Grace, or the Supernatural Gift, or Power of God in the Soul, because it was something, that the Natural Powers of the Soul could no more obtain. (1780, 16-17)

The writer strongly affirms the doctrine of the incarnation and the necessity of the new birth to occur, and promotes the distinct Quaker theme of the inward and the outward Christ:

This Love, or Desire of God towards the Soul of Man is so great, that He gave His only begotten Son, the Brightness of his Glory, to take human Nature upon Him, in its fallen State, that by this mysterious Union of God and Man, all the Enemies of the Soul of Man might be overcome, and every human Creature might have a Power of being born again according to the Image of God, in which he was first created. The Gospel is the History of the Love of God to Man. Inwardly he has a Seed of the Divine Life given into the Birth of his Soul, a Seed that has all the Riches of Eternity in it, and is always wanting to come to Birth in him, and be alive in God. Outwardly he has Jesus Christ, who, as a Sun of Righteousness, is always casting forth his enlivening Beams on this inward Seed, to kindle and call it forth to the Birth.... (1780, 21)

The Spirit of Prayer includes a classic description of the inwardness of Quaker worship:

...this Pearl of Eternity is the Church, or Temple of God within thee, the consecrated Place of Divine Worship, where alone thou canst worship God in Spirit, and in Truth....all outward Forms and Rites, though instituted by God, are only the Figure for a Time, but his Worship is Eternal. Accustom thyself to the Holy Service of this inward Temple. In the Midst of it, is the Fountain of Living Water.... (1780, 27)

It includes the necessity of the Lord's Supper, but inwardly celebrated:

There the Mysteries of thy Redemption are celebrated, or rather opened in Life and Power....There the Supper of the Lamb is kept...When once thou art well grounded in this inward worship, thou wilt have learnt to live unto God above Time and Place... For every day will be Sunday to thee, and wherever thou goest, thou wilt have a priest, a church and an altar along with thee. (1780, 27)

The Spirit of Prayer is, in effect, a Quaker Quietist manifesto:

Now all dependeth upon thy right Submission and Obedience to this speaking of God in thy Soul. Stop therefore all Self-activity, listen not to the Suggestions of thy own Reason, run not on in thy own Will, but be retired, silent, passive, and humbly attentive to this new risen Light within Thee. Open thy Heart, thy Eyes, and Ears to all its Impressions. Let it enlighten, teach, frighten, torment, judge, and condemn. (1780, 30-1)

A critical corollary, and often overlooked aspect of holiness as union with God, is that the new self which has been purified, detached from the world, and baptized by the Holy Spirit, is now able to use all of the "things of this world" and the human faculties for good and Godly purposes:

And that Man, baptized with the Holy Spirit, and born again from Above, should absolutely renounce Self, and wholly give up his Soul to the Operation of God's Spirit, to know, to love, to will, to pray, to worship, to preach, to exhort, to use all the Faculties of his Mind, and all the outward Things of this World, as enlightened, inspired, moved and guided by the Holy Ghost; who, by this last Dispensation of God, was given to be a Comforter, a Teacher, and guide to the Church, who should abide with it forever. (1780, 34)

This self-denial, "absolute self-renunciation" which the modern mind finds so repugnant, even dehumanizing, ultimately results in the greatest freedom of all, and thus the individual, baptized with the Spirit, can return to the world with a whole new perspective and a new way of being in the world. Early Quakerism was also characterized by this withdrawal from, but also a return to, the world. This pattern was thought to have been given by Christ. Later interpreters have claimed that Quietists withdrew from the world without any desire to return to it, and erected an impenetrable sectarian hedge (Marietta, 1984, 84-85). Certainly many did, but in a different manner from what is described in this passage, or for example in William Penn's admonition: "True godliness don't turn men out of the world, but enables them to live better in it and excites their endeavors to mend it: 'not hide their candle under a bushel, but set it upon a table, in a candlestick'" (Penn, 1726, 1:370). This familiar quote by Penn is found in his most world-renouncing work, *No Cross, No Crown*.[13] The statement appears in the midst of a comparison of true (Quaker) asceticism or

---

[13] See 3.3 on the impact of this book on Stephen Grellet.

holiness vs. monastic asceticism, which for Penn (as a Protestant) is pseudo-holiness.[14]

Despite the Quietist passivity throughout this document, Benezet is not advocating a flight from the world. He is a contemplative in action, which his life powerfully demonstrates. His pattern of holiness corresponds to the mission-oriented lifestyle of George Fox and the First Publishers of Truth.

Like most early Quaker writings, *The Spirit of Prayer* is full of repetitions of phrases and variations on the same themes, with ample use of biblical metaphors and symbols to illustrate thoughts and instructions. It is didactic and sermonic in tone. Like Fox's writings, it contains no biblical references, but is filled with texts and phrases from the Bible. *The Spirit of Prayer* captures poetically and mystically the essential nature of the holiness of the early Quietist period, its grounding in death of self, the centrality of the new birth or conversion, detachment from the world and union with God. This is the essential nature of the kind of perfection that flows from a life lived moment by moment in the presence of God—"born of the Spirit," "animated by the Spirit" and "governed by the Spirit" (Benezet, 1780, 34). The key phrase for Quaker holiness is "born of the Spirit," which, theologically speaking, is the experience and process of justification/ sanctification/perfection.[15]

3.2.2 Summary and Conclusions

In relation to the typology of holiness, the following types and subtypes are most prominent in Benezet and the period of the Quaker Reformation:

---

[14] It is worth noting that Penn develops this "withdrawal-return theme" by adding in later editions (1694) of his work this concluding paragraph: "Not that I would be thought to slight a true retirement, for I do not only acknowledge but admire solitudes. Christ Himself was an example of it. He loved and chose to frequent mountains, gardens, seasides. They are requisite to growth of piety, and I reverence the virtue that seeks and uses it, wishing there were more of it in the world. But then it should be free, not constrained. What benefit to the mind to have it for a punishment and not a pleasure? Nay, I have long thought it an error among all sorts that use not monastic lives that they have no retreats for the afflicted, the tempted, the solitary, and the devout, where they might undisturbedly wait upon God, pass through their religious exercises, and, being thereby strengthened, may with more power over their own spirits enter the business of the world again, though the less the better, to be sure. For divine pleasures are found in a free solitude" (qtd. in Tolles & Alderfer, 1957, 49). Later in his life Penn understood the need, even necessity, for withdrawal, periods of solitude, and spiritual retreats in order to spend time alone in deep prayer with God.

[15] *Justification* is release from the guilt of sin; *perfection* is release from the power of sin. This basic formula is consistent in holiness theology from the early period through the modern period.

1. The experience of union as a movement toward God which brings intimacy is strongly reflected in the devotional writings published by Benezet. A mystical spirituality dominates this period. Holiness in its fullness is union with God, mystical holiness, *unio mystica*. For Quietists the real presence of Christ in group contemplative prayer (the spiritual sacraments) is the essence of true worship, and silence becomes elevated in this period. The apophaticism of the "prayer of Quiet" is taught as a path to God. (See Figure 3, Quadrant 3: Union with God.)
2. Radical self-surrender to the activity of God, dying and rising with Christ, and perfect obedience in imitation of Christ continues to be a strong theme. This is essentially biblical, Pauline mysticism. Detachment and renunciation is present in a strong degree, and most elevated during the Quietist period, which is still based on a semi-monastic, ascetical approach to holiness as *The Plain Path to Christian Perfection* makes clear. This is Anabaptist, ascetical or semi-monastic holiness. (See Figure 3, Quadrant 4: Imitation of Christ.)
3. Christ born in the soul, in the heart, or the internalization of the atonement is still the way of salvation-sanctification-perfection. Conversion continues to be essential, as seen in the centrality of the new birth in *The Spirit of Prayer*, but now as a second generation religion, the tendency is for faith to be "inherited" rather than experienced. The need now is for individuals who have grown up in the faith to rediscover it or *own* it for themselves. Faith must be experienced and illuminated. All of the reformation ministers were strongly influenced by the Pietist movement – Benezet, in particular, with his family ties to the Moravians. A constant sense of presence, divine guidance, and filling of the Spirit and an assurance of empowerment for service and mission with evangelistic, social, and prophetic vision is also characteristic of this period. In the eighteenth century Quaker reformation the emphasis, as reflected in Benezet and Woolman's crusade against slavery and human oppression, is on the social and prophetic. This prophetic empowerment is a result of "baptism of the Spirit" (the term later used by evangelical holiness Quakers in the nineteenth and twentieth centuries for sanctification). This is charismatic holiness (but not to be confused with tongues-speaking). (See Figure 3, Quadrant 2: Experiential Holiness.)

Quietists maintained a strong Christological framework, with a traditionally orthodox view of the work of Christ rooted in the incarnation and the atonement. Early Quakers called this the "history" or the outward Christ, which referred to the humanity of Christ and his saving work. But belief in the "history" or the humanity of Christ was not in itself sufficient for holiness; the risen Christ had to be born within (Barclay's "holy birth"). Quietists looked to Barclay's *Apology* as the standard exposition of Quaker doctrine (Punshon, 1984, 122). "Simple" faith, *sola fides*, is a necessary ingredient for salvation, but experiential or illumined faith is necessary for holiness.

Stephen Grellet: Evangelical Social Holiness

Several historians of Quakerism (Jones, 1921; Punshon, 1984) have noted that by the end of the eighteenth century the majority of the most active and effective ministers were converts from other faiths: William Savery, a Huguenot; Mary Dudley, a Methodist; David Sands, a Presbyterian; Thomas Shillitoe, an Anglican; Rebecca Jones, an Episcopalian; and Stephen Grellet, a Catholic who became a Voltairian atheist. All of these ministers rose to prominence at a time when Quakerism still clung to its Quietist, mystical ways, yet all, even Shillitoe, "one of the most pronounced quietists in the Society," (Jones, 1921, 281) are called evangelicals. The fact that such powerful and evangelically oriented leaders would find their spiritual home with Quakers speaks to the depths of Christ-centered mysticism that set apart Quietists from other Christian denominations in this period.

All of these ministers retained the Quietist ethos, embodied a holiness ethic, and were true Quaker mystics. Because they were not "birthright" Quakers, nurtured from childhood in Quaker culture, suspicion has sometimes been cast on their "purity" or commitment to genuine Quakerism (Jones, 1921, 277). Since they were all convinced Friends who had experienced dramatic conversions, they brought to their new-found religion vibrancy and vitality that those who inherit their faith often lack. Rufus Jones writes:

> ...they were for the most part born in other folds and nurtured outside the Quaker atmosphere. They "came in" from the outside and brought with them a psychological attitude somewhat different from that of the inbred Quaker, and quite unconsciously they added a tinge and colour of their own. (Jones, 1921, 277)

While Jones' observation may be partly true, it must also be admitted that these leaders found something in Quakerism itself that resonated deeply with their own experience and yearnings that the "inbred Quaker" may have ritualized or lost touch with.

All of these figures are worth examining historically for their impact on Quaker holiness. But the most compelling of all is Stephen Grellet because of the uniqueness of his background, his unlikely entry into Friends, and the unusual breadth and depth of his ministry.[16] While his life is a fascinating narrative in its own right, he is a key figure for purposes of this study for the insight he sheds on Quaker holiness at another turning point in Quaker history (the transitional period at the turn of the century that became the precursor to conflict in the shift from Quietism to modern Evangelicalism and rationalism). Grellet, who was known for his compassion and spiritual sensitivity, and not his polemic, nevertheless found himself painfully swept into the storm of the Hicksite-Orthodox separation in the latter part of his ministry (see 4.1). His memoirs fill two detailed volumes of over 800 pages, so extensive records of his reflections, experiences, observations, and beliefs are accessible for analysis.

Rufus Jones cannot conceal his mixed feelings about Grellet in his history of Quakerism (1921). He names Grellet's call to the ministry "one of the most important events in the Quaker history of the eighteenth century" (1921, 206) and his third journey to Europe "perhaps the most important single piece of Quaker itinerant labour in the nineteenth century" (1921, 212). Jones describes the atmosphere of "Stephen Grellet and his immediate circle of intimate friends" as "charged with evangelical fervour" (1921, 284). But rather than see his zeal and passion as being in the mold of George Fox and the earliest Quakers, Jones claims Grellet "belongs with Bunyan rather than Fox, and he shows the evangelical temper of Wesley and Newton rather than the mystical outlook which characterized the religious body into which he came" (1921, 284). Yet as this study shows, Grellet was intensely mystical, recorded a number of visionary experiences (unlike Wesley and the others named) and theologically was typical of this period of Quietism. Yet, Jones concedes Grellet was "the most gifted Minister in the Society in America" (Jones, 1921, 285) and describes him in the most laudatory terms:

> ...he had an unmistakable unction from above, and he often seemed carried beyond himself with an inspiration which none who heard him at such times could doubt...he felt intensely the burden of the world's suffering, and he yearned with apostolic zeal over those who were astray in the deeps of sin....he was a tender prophet, appealing in love rather than moving by emotions of fear and terror. (1921, 285)

Yet, according to Jones, he did not have the "mystical" outlook which characterized the Society, and in spite of such high praise, Jones contends that Grellet preached the gospel of Wesley and Whitefield, not Quakerism (1921, 285). Ironically, in Jones' opinion the most gifted minister of the Society, with "unmistakable unction from above," did not fit the mold and criteria for a *Quaker* minister.

---

[16] Grellet's extraordinary life might even cause a skeptic to admit the possibility of a divine hand in it.

3.3.1 Conversion

Grellet was raised as a Catholic in France and attended a Jansenist college.[17] His early mystical leanings are evidenced in some religious "openings" he had while a student at Lyons. He wrote of celebrating the sacrament of the Lord's Supper at the close of his college years, in which he felt a vivid sense of God's presence that lingered for some time after. But then, he confessed, after the feeling passed, he sought the "happiness of the world's delights" (Seebohm, 1862, 10).

In 1792 his aristocratic parents, wealthy porcelain manufacturers, were imprisoned during the French Revolution, and he and his brother were forced to leave France. He joined a royalist counter-revolutionary army. While in Germany, he secretly visited deserted monasteries and found himself attracted to solitude (Seebohm, 1862, 10).

He was taken a prisoner of war, but escaped to Holland, and then to New Guinea, where he first became aware of the horrors of slavery. By this time he had become an atheist and a disciple of Voltaire (Seebohm, 1862, 13). After two years in New Guinea he sailed to New York. He spoke virtually no English, but met a young woman who spoke French and she loaned him the works of William Penn. Having heard of Penn as a political leader, he was curious to read his works, and began painstakingly translating each word into French using his dictionary. Soon thereafter he had a mystical encounter with God, which he described in vivid language, echoing the experiences of many earlier Friends:

> Through adorable mercy, the visitation of the Lord was now again extended towards me, by the immediate opening of the Divine light on my soul. One evening as I was walking in the fields alone, my mind being under no kind of religious concern, nor in the least excited by any thing I had heard or thought of, I was suddenly arrested by what seemed to be an awful voice proclaiming the words, "Eternity! Eternity! Eternity!" It reached my very soul--my whole man shook,--it brought me like Saul, to the ground. The great depravity and sinfulness of my heart were set open before me, and the gulf of everlasting destruction to which I was verging. I was made bitterly to cry out, "If there is no God, doubtless there is a hell." I found myself in the midst of it.... After that I remained almost whole days and nights, exercised in prayer that the Lord would have mercy upon me, expecting that he would give me some evidence that he had heard my application. But for this I was looking to some outward manifestation, my expectation being entirely of that nature. I now took up again the works of William Penn, and opened upon "No Cross, No Crown." The title alone reached

---

[17] See Appendix B on Jansenism as a holiness movement in the seventeenth century.

> to my heart. I proceeded to read with the help of my dictionary, having to look for the meaning of nearly every word. I read it twice through in this manner. I had never met with anything of the kind; neither had I felt the Divine witness in me operating so powerfully before. I now withdrew from company, and spent most of my time in retirement, and in silent waiting upon God. I began to read the Bible, with the aid of my dictionary, for I had none then in French. I was much of a stranger to the inspired records. I had not even seen them before, that I remember; what I had heard of any part of their contents, was only detached portions of Prayer Books. (Seebohm, 1862, 16-17)

Grellet's experience contains many of the same elements as found in the conversion narratives of early Quakers (see 1.5.3 on conversion, and compare, for example, Thomas Story, 2.6).

Shortly after, he learned of a Friends Meeting to be led by two English women ministers, Deborah Darby and Rebecca Young, and felt led to attend. And without understanding their words, their presence alone became the catalyst for his conversion:

> The sight of them brought solemn feelings over me; but I soon forgot the servants, and all things around me; for in an inward silent frame of mind, seeking for the Divine presence, I was favoured to find in me, what I had so long, and with so many tears, sought for without me....I felt the Lord's power in such a manner, that my inner man was prostrated before my Blessed Redeemer. A secret joy filled me, in that I had found Him after whom my soul longed. I was as one nailed to my seat. (Seebohm, 1862, 17)

Again, this kind of inward apophatic experience, forgetting "all things around me" and "in an inward silent frame of mind," is distinctive of Quaker spiritual experience, and atypical of Wesleyan revivalism.

Later Grellet was invited to dine with a group of Friends, including the two women from England. After dinner at a "religious opportunity," Deborah Darby spoke and although he could barely understand a word she said, Grellet writes:

> It seemed as if the Lord opened my outward ear, and my heart.... She seemed like one reading the pages of my heart, with learning describing how it had been, and how it was with me. I was like Lydia, my heart was opened; I felt the power of Him who hath the key of David. No strength to withstand the Divine visitation was left in me. O what sweetness did I then feel! It was indeed a memorable day. I was like one introduced into a new world; the creation and all things

around me bore a different aspect, --my heart glowed with love to all.[18] The awfulness of that day of God's visitation can never cease to be remembered...I have been as one plucked from the burning--rescued from the brink of a horrible pit. (Seebohm, 1862, 18)

He continued to attend Friends meetings regularly, at first secretly feeling embarrassed to be seen with them, and then openly.[19] Worship was held in silence, no one spoke, and few people attended. (The meeting in which the two women ministers spoke had been a special "appointed meeting," not a regular meeting for worship.) He said he had no communication with anyone there for some time (Seebohm, 1862, 19). But in the silence he felt "Divine mercy... as a tender father," and the Lord instructed him (Seebohm, 1862, 19). He accepted this solitary journey to faith "with no outward dependence to lean upon" as "a favour." His individual, solitary approach in some ways parallels that of Fox. His rather unique experience also indicates that his movement towards God did not come about through the teaching or preaching of any particular religious tradition, though his Catholic upbringing and Jansenist training obviously provided the initial context. He seemed to be simply drawn towards God, and the Quaker silent worship provided a contemplative setting ideal for his experience. (Recall that even as a young atheist soldier he was drawn to abandoned monasteries.)

He described a period of purgation and detachment, alternating in tears of grief and joy, and culminating in a feeling of being surrounded by the love of God:

O how many things had to be removed out of the way, to give room for the heavenly seed to grow. The axe of God's power was lifted up against the root of the corrupt tree. As wave follows wave, so did my exercises. Yet I must testify of the Lord's unspeakable love extended towards me; it was great indeed. The sense of it was so much with me, that I do not know whether tears of joy and gratitude have not flowed

---

[18] Echos of Fox can be heard here: "All things were new, and all the creation gave another smell unto me..." (Nickalls, 1952, 27).

[19] He struggled for a while with both a compulsion to attend Friends worship and resistance against it. At the time he was living with a Presbyterian family who advised him against becoming a Quaker. Grellet wrote that "Quakerism was, at that time, [1795] very imperfectly understood, and little appreciated....by other denominations; much ignorance and prejudice still prevailed against it. It was by no means generally thought to be a creditable thing to assume the character and appearance of a Friend" (apparently 150 years had not improved their public image very much).

as plentifully as those of grief, which latter have not been few. (Seebohm, 1862, 20)[20]

He described one further mystical experience (which would be termed entire sanctification in the Holiness Revival period), also occurring in an entirely silent meeting, with further purgation and then a sense of complete forgiveness of past sins. This experience is described in classic evangelical holiness language. It concluded with a call to ministry:

> My misery was great; my cry was not unlike that of Isaiah, "Woe is me, for I am undone!" The nearer I was then favoured to approach to Him "who dwelleth in the light," the more I saw my uncleanness and my wretchedness. But how can I set forth the fullness of heavenly joy that filled me when the hope was again raised that there was One, even He whom I had pierced, Jesus Christ the Redeemer, that was able to save me?[21] (Seebohm, 1862, 20-21)

As he adopted the traditional Quaker ethos, the former French aristocrat began to think about simplifying his lifestyle and relinquishing his upper-class habits. The first luxury to go was powdering his hair. The reason he gave was two-fold: the expense of it when he realized the scarcity of necessities in France and, "the ground of which I knew to be pride" (Seebohm, 1862, 24). He finally adopted plain language, a decision that he referred to in the typical Quietist expression: "I took up my cross in that also, though it exposed me to much ridicule"[22]

---

[20] This is a classic description of what the early desert monastics called *penthos* – the gift of tears – an essential part of the journey to union with God. Individuals who experience *penthos* will subsequently exhibit in their lives a heightened degree of compassion, far beyond the ordinary. Grellet, as we shall see, embodied this kind of magnanimity characterized by boundless, undiscriminating love.

[21] Although Grellet embellished his account with language, unmistakably evangelical, the echoes of Fox in describing his own conversion after a long period of struggle and purgation, can hardly be missed: "Oh then, I heard a voice which said 'there is one even Christ Jesus who can speak to thy condition,' and when I heard it my heart did leap for joy" (Nickalls, 1952, 11). Some interpreters of Fox minimize any sense of guilt and release from sin in Fox's conversion (e.g. Jones, 1976, 30), but when read carefully, without this assumption, Fox's sense of being a sinner saved by grace is obvious. The "condition" Christ speaks to in Fox is the same "condition" Christ speaks to in Grellet— "woe is me, I am undone." (This phrase from Isaiah 6:5 was well-used by holiness Quakers.) Fox then added emphatically "For all are concluded under sin...as I had been" (Nickalls, 1952, 11). Other accounts of early Quaker conversions affirm this acute sense of sin; see, for example, Howgill and Dewsbury in 1.5.3.

[22] Adopting plain dress and speech became the eighteenth century equivalent for the early Quaker essential element of suffering. Respectable as they now were, no longer persecuted, the necessity of bearing the cross became symbolized by being visibly

(Seebohm, 1862, 24). He began to feel the effects of adopting the Quaker "testimonies" by its power to separate him from the worldly culture, its main purpose at this time serving as a hedge (as it continued to be in conservative branches): "Some who before had courted my company now turned away; and this became a blessing to me, for it tended quickly to make the separation great between me and the world" (Seebohm, 1862, 24).

He moved to Philadelphia where he was welcomed by Friends. He began to feel a part of the community: "I found fathers and mothers in a spiritual sense" (Seebohm, 1862, 25). He described feeling a constant sense of the Lord's presence and often swallowed up in God's love (Seebohm, 1862, 26). He began to read the Bible regularly, so absorbed he often spent a week pondering one chapter. His writing began to reflect typical Quietist language of deep exercises, sufferings, and baptisms.

A year after his conversion, the two women from England so instrumental in that experience once again visited. This time they personally ministered to him, "confirming him in the knowledge of Christ" (Seebohm, 1862, 27). This is the first mention of any specific instruction from the Quaker community. Whether through their influence, or purely his own needs, he began to feel he should witness to his new-found faith[23] (Seebohm, 1862, 27). Thus far, all of his experiences were described in both the language of evangelical holiness and the *via negativa* of Quaker quietism.

Clearly the formative first year of his life as a Christian was shaped with minimal outside influence by others. This resulted in part from the nature of Quaker worship, where spiritual formation occurs mainly through nurture in the family (Damiano, 1988), and in part because of the initial language barrier.

January 20, 1796, was the date of a significant breakthrough. It was the first experience given an exact date, recording the moment of his first spoken words in meeting after the typical long period of Quietist angst (Seebohm, 1862, 29). The experience of speaking in worship seems the equivalent of going to the altar for consecration in the later holiness movement. His description of the

---

different from mainstream society, and bearing ridicule. This decision became a double "cross" for Grellet to bear because the French revolutionaries, responsible for his parents' imprisonment, had adopted the Quaker "plain speech," and he felt compelled to write to his mother and try to explain this new way of speaking. Apparently French revolutionaries idealized certain counter-cultural aspects of Quakerism, including plain dress – totally separated, of course, from their religious beliefs – and adopting this peculiarity of speech and dress became a trendy revolutionary badge. This idealization is related to why Ben Franklin, who dressed in the Quaker style, was often mistakenly called a Quaker by the French.

[23] Testifying to one's sanctification became a symbolic ritual in the Holiness Movement. It developed out of the Methodist class-meetings. The Quietist's decision to speak in the Spirit for the first time publicly in worship was a similar kind of compulsion, and served a similar purpose.

push-pull to speak and the "deep baptisms" are commonly found in Quaker journals of the period. As an outsider and a foreigner not born into the Quaker culture, and not yet recorded in the ministry, the dilemma to rightly discern the time to speak would be even more intense. He described the struggle:

> Meeting after meeting I was under the pressure of exercise to stand up and speak a few words; but the sense of the awfulness of the engagement prevented me, time after time, till the Lord's displeasure was felt to be kindled against me. O the depth of my baptisms, in those days! ...I could not believe that such a poor creature as I was, such a great sinner as I had been, could be fit to engage in such a solemn work. (Seebohm, 1862, 28-29)

Finally he had a breakthrough to speech, though he does not record his words, only his feelings afterwards, and the affirmation of others (recognized ministers), which was most significant:

> It was on the 20th of 1st month, 1796, the third day of the week that I first opened my mouth in the ministry. For some days after this act of dedication, my peace flowed as a river, whilst mine eyes were like fountains of tears of gratitude, in that the Lord had so mercifully continued to bear with me. Besides the internal evidence he gave me of his Divine approbation, several of his dignified servants, as William Savery, Samuel Emlen, Rebecca Jones, &c., stood up after me, bearing testimony to the Lord's power, and the sufficiency of his Divine Truth, as displayed on my behalf. (Seebohm, 1862, 29)

After this event, the meeting took great care to nurture and support him. He received spiritual guidance from Friends who now recognized his "tender and exercised state of mind." He wrote that they supported him with "feeling and affection," acting as "nursing fathers and mothers." But they did not push him to become a member. He was absorbed in his own personal relationship with the Lord, and did not yet think about joining with a community (Seebohm, 1862, 29). But as he began to consider the "ground of my faith, the nature of the testimonies I had already borne publicly" (his speaking in meeting, but also adopting simple dress and speech and his separation from the world by no longer socializing with friends or following cultural customs such as powdered hair), he began to seriously reflect on membership and whether his faith and experience truly corresponded to those of Friends:

> For I saw that it would not do for me to become a member of that religious society unless I was established in their Christian principles, and was convinced also that these principles were *consistent with the Truth as it was in Jesus* [my emphasis]. I thought that because Friends

professed principles similar to those which I had been led to adopt, through the teaching of the Holy Spirit, and because I had so often found among them the flowings of the Divine Light and life, to my great refreshing, this was not a sufficient ground for me to conclude to become one of their body. (Seebohm, 1862, 29-30)

He sought for guidance with much prayer, watching, and fasting (Seebohm, 1862, 30). He carefully re-examined all the principles professed by Friends in order to see again "the foundation upon which they stand, even the eternal rock – Christ Jesus, that I could feel satisfied to join them in outward fellowship" (Seebohm, 1862, 30). The principles he listed he called "the first rudiments of the Christian religion" or the basic core convictions:

the fall of man
my own fallen and sinful condition
redemption and salvation by Christ alone
the true Christian baptism
the supper
Divine inspiration, worship, ministry & c
(Seebohm, 1862, 30)

By the fall of 1796 (approximately a nine-month process) he felt clear to become a member and united with Philadelphia Yearly Meeting (Seebohm, 1862, 30). He took this step with much prayer, discernment, and deliberateness, feeling an extra measure of responsibility and caution coming from outside into the Society. He felt he must join at the "right door" of both "conviction and conversion," otherwise, he wrote, "we cannot be of profit to them or be profited by them," and added, "No man, nor any religious body, can save any, salvation cometh from God alone" (Seebohm, 1862, 30). His recognition that he must be united with Quakers both doctrinally and experientially and that he had no misgivings after making that commitment through careful discernment (Seebohm, 1862, 32) is evidence that his evangelical convictions and his mystical experience both corresponded to what was then mainstream Quietism. His biographer affirms Grellet's "missionary life" to be perfectly suited to the Friends where no other Society in quite the same way allows "full scope to the operations and leadings of the Holy Spirit, and admits of the free exercise of every spiritual gift, in whatever direction the rightly authorized ambassador for Christ may be called to labour" (Seebohm, 1862, 33).

Grellet attended his first yearly meeting in Philadelphia soon after, joyfully observing that the Yearly Meeting was in a healthy spiritual state with many distinguished faithful servants of the Gospel (Seebohm, 1862, 33). Apparently the reformation of Benezet and others was still in effect among Philadelphia Quakers at the end of the eighteenth century.

When he thought of his parents in prison in France and learned of the betrayal of those who had been his father's intimate friends but were now his enemies and persecutors, he found his faith put to the test. But with the ground of his religion being divine love, he found that he could pray for the enemies of his father and desire their salvation (Seebohm, 1862, 34). This reflects an important aspect of Quaker holiness, the ability to love even one's enemies. (See 1.5.6 on suffering and 1.7.6 on peace testimony.)

3.3.2 Asceticism

As with many saints and mystics who have come into the Light, Grellet found himself in a period of testing, a dark night experience, that included further detachment and renunciation through asceticism. For five years he practiced a highly disciplined and ascetical life, in eating and drinking, including becoming a vegetarian and a personal boycott of the products of slave labor, "for the sense of the sufferings of that people was heavy upon me" (similar to the lifestyle of Benezet) (Seebohm, 1862, 37). But he wanted to be very careful that he was not simply being legalistic, or imposing his personal disciplines on others who were not under the "same scruples" (Seebohm, 1862, 37).

After this long period of austere self-discipline and renunciation, he described a revealing and highly significant insight which led him to a new place of spiritual freedom:

> I continued about five years under that exercise, and when my release came, the free use of everything in the creation was set before me, so that I received it with thankfulness and moderation. Great was the fullness of the Lord's love at that time, and the sweetness of his presence. It seemed as if heaven was opened and the angelic host was about me, proclaiming the Lord's praise and glory, to which I was permitted to join my feeble accents. This took place at the house of my dear friends John and Esther Griffin, at Purchase, whilst traveling on a religious visit in company with my beloved friend John Hall. A holy solemnity came upon us all. (Seebohm, 1862, 37)

This could be interpreted in a variety of ways. It could be a departure from the ascetical holiness of the Quietist tradition reflected in "bearing the cross" by adherence to a strict discipline, or simply Grellet's feeling released from his severe practice of them. He clearly had an experience of spiritual freedom and release, though what precipitated this experience is not known. He did not specify that he had ceased to practice Quaker peculiarities, but only that he had modified them.[24] There are hints in prior Quaker writings of this kind of release from ascetical practices as a higher stage in an individual's spiritual development (see 3.2.1). When baptism with the Spirit is experienced, a new sense of freedom in regards to all of creation unfolds. In classical terms of the *via Triplex* this could be the movement from purgation to illumination and thence to union (see 2.2).

One additional event described in his journal, which strongly reflects his holiness spirituality, occurred in 1797 with his first call to a traveling ministry. He was called to minister at a place called Egg Harbour, a fishing village on the Atlantic coast amidst the desolate "pine barren" region of New Jersey, in order to "visit in the love of the Gospel, and to distribute Testaments and religious books" (Seebohm, 1862, 37-38). His Franciscan-like sensitivity and compassion and the inclusiveness of his ministry is reflected movingly in this account of his first missionary endeavor:

> I proceeded in it in much lowness of spirit, [humility] keeping close to my heavenly guide. He so condescended to me, that on coming into a family, a feeling of Divine love clothing me, I was enabled to communicate my concern for them, so as, in many instances, to reach the witness for Truth in their hearts. Many of those opportunities were favoured seasons, and proved visitations of love and mercy to the people. Most of them received us, and our books, with tears of gratitude. (Seebohm, 1862, 38)

Grellet eventually made four missionary trips to Europe, including Scandinavia and Russia. He ministered to emperors and barons, Catholic nuns and Mennonites, out-of-work weavers, thieves, slaves, and child prostitutes. He visited prisons, poorhouses, and asylums all over Europe.[25] After a visit to Newgate, he became the inspiration for Elizabeth Fry's life-long prison ministry. He even made a pastoral visit to Thomas Paine on his deathbed.

---

[24] This event occurred around 1802. Without reading too much into this account it does appear to be a significant shift from the *via negativa* to a balance of *via negativa* and *via positiva*. It may represent a shift from sectarian quietism to evangelicalism, represented by moving away from dependence on a legalistic, moralistic behavioral code to greater freedom in the Spirit.

[25] A British ex-Quaker, writing a critique that only a former Friend might freely publish, found Grellet to be one of the most inspirational and authentic Quakers, and expressed his admiration in these terms: "Grellet was an aristocrat who had that aristocratic 'roominess,' enhanced by what I believe was an uncovenanted grace of great measure, which made him superbly careless of his philanthropy. He always seemed quite at home in prisons, among Karaite Jews, with Pius VII, Spanish grandees, Lutheran barons, timbermen and other American backwoodsmen. He is rather singular in this respect among Quakers, who have developed a less catholic taste in their missionary and philanthropic enterprise" (Edwards, 1948, 416).

Judging from a brief survey of his memoirs, he appears to have visited almost every monthly meeting in the United States and Canada, including the most isolated and impoverished. He also held meetings in many small towns in which no Friends lived. He was sometimes invited to speak in Methodist, Presbyterian, and even Episcopal Churches. Most of his ministry occurred pre-separation; his darkest "dark night of the soul" was the Orthodox-Hicksite Split, which plunged him into the "deepest baptisms" of his spiritual life.

3.3.3 Summary and Conclusions

Aspects of the four quadrants of holiness continued in the Evangelical Quietism of Grellet, with emphasis on the mystical and experiential (see Figure 3). Applying the types of holiness to Grellet and evangelical Quietism we find:

1. This type of spirituality reflects Quadrant 3, the mystical (see Figure 3). Grellet does not often use "union with God" language (it was much less common in the eighteenth and nineteenth centuries, probably used only in Catholic spirituality at that time), but his spiritual journey is definitely reflective of a mystical movement toward God and a language of deep, personal intimacy with God. There are remnants of Catholic mystical language in his writings, either incorporated from his upbringing, or possibly adopted from Catholic Quietist literature widely read among Quakers (e.g. "adorable mercy" – a phrase which other Quietists also used). He appears to have a genuine mystical consciousness. (There are numerous dramatic examples of his mysticism not included for lack of space, which are applicable to this argument.)

2. This type also reflects Quadrant 4, Imitation of Christ, with an emphasis on detachment and renunciation, and asceticism (see Figure 3). Grellet went through a long period when this aspect of holiness was essential to him. He felt a release from his strict asceticism later and shifted towards the "new holiness" of perfect love more typical of the Wesleyan Movement, and later to characterize the Quaker revival of the 1860s. But the *via negativa*, or apophatic was a path he never really left. He was drawn to inward, silent worship. He came to Christ through silent worship, and he retreated to silence often.[26] (He was an unusually

---

[26] While Grellet greatly valued silent worship he recognized it sometimes lacked effectiveness or meaning for many people. For example, in 1804 on a trip to Western N.Y. he made this observation: "We had several silent meetings, to the disappointment of the people; for very few understand the nature of silent worship" (Seebohm, 1862, 73).

extroverted contemplative.) Radical self-surrender to the activity of God, dying and rising with Christ, and the perfect obedience of the Anabaptist also characterized Grellet. Some of the typical Anabaptist language became modified in him, but basic Anabaptist themes were all still central. Dying to self continued to be a common phrase, e.g. "Be also willing to die to thyself, that thou mayest live through faith in Him" (Seebohm, 1862, 51).

3. Christ born in the soul, the internalization of the atonement as the way of salvation/sanctification/perfection of Quadrant 2 (the Experiential) also characterized Grellet (see Figure 3). Pietist holiness, with its strong affective dimension of devotion to Jesus, was typical of Grellet. The atonement was both outward and inward. A constant sense of presence and guidance by the Spirit, who gives special gifts of discernment and empowerment for mission, was also typical of Grellet's holiness.[27] Holy Spirit language was prominent in his writing. Charismatic elements of holiness abounded. He spoke more of the "Holy Spirit in you" than "Christ in you." His rhetorical style was characteristic of evangelical holiness preaching, yet also reminiscent of George Fox: "I directed them to Christ and to his Spirit in them. The same who convinces men of sin, is able to deliver from sin."[28] His preaching was affective and heart-felt; he was not afraid of emotional response in his meetings. People were often visibly moved and shed tears; he sometimes cried with them. Grellet continued the Quietist adherence to a strong Christological framework, rooted in the incarnation and the atonement. He was

---

[27] Grellet had a special gift of discernment common to Quietist ministers. He wrote, for example, of this experience: "We had the next day a meeting at Bennett's Creek, where I was greatly oppressed under a sense of the wickedness, and even blood-guiltiness of some present, and I spoke to the people of the awful condition of those who thus follow the way of Cain. After meeting, I heard that three men were present who had been engaged in the murder of a black man; but, as the evidence of slaves is not received, the law takes no cognizance of their crime" (Seebohm, 1862, 131).

[28] This line comes from a message he preached to young French Canadian Catholics who came in off the street out of curiosity to hear him in 1804 (Seebohm, 1862, 76). After speaking to these young people, Grellet records that "several of them gave vent to their inward conviction by expression, and now and then cried out in French "c'est la verite" – this is the truth" (Seebohm, 1862, 76). Grellet often preached to non-Quakers and people of other faiths. Catholics were especially receptive to him; perhaps because of his own religious background he had a natural sensitivity to their spiritual needs. But although he "evangelized," he never seemed concerned about making Quakers out of them, or recruiting into Quaker meetings. His primary concern was to "save souls" to bring them into the love of Christ, to make Christians out of them, but not necessarily Quakers. This attitude was more typical of evangelical holiness Quakers in the next century.

convinced that the traditional core principles of the Christian faith were essential to Quakerism. In the theological and rationalist climate in which he lived, some core Christological beliefs were beginning to be challenged. He believed that relinquishing this framework would erode Christian spirituality and Quakerism. He had great concern that the Society of Friends maintain the "great and important testimonies, which, in the opening and power of Truth were committed to our forefathers..." (Seebohm, 1862, 141-2)

Grellet's preaching conveyed a clear Gospel message of holiness, with a three-stage process of salvation/sanctification/perfection. Although revival holiness did not emerge among Quakers until after 1850, Grellet's preaching was a foreshadowing of that type. His preaching on holiness at the turn of the century already contained elements of both the tradition of George Fox and the "New Holiness" of the Wesleyan movement. Holiness was indigenous to Quakerism, and Grellet, who came directly to Quakerism from atheism, found it there. As an example, here is a sample of Grellet's preaching at Newbegun Creek, North Carolina, in 1809:

I opened to the people the state in which Adam was before the fall, then described the mournful condition of man in the fall, and the impossibility for him by any efforts or wisdom of his own, to extricate himself from it, and to regain the state of purity and acceptance with God, and paradisical felicity which he has lost by sin; that we have all sinned, and have come short of the glory of God. Then I unfolded the great Gospel treasure – Salvation through faith in Christ Jesus the Lord; what He has done for us, without us, through the blood of his Cross, his meritorious death and most holy and acceptable offering of Himself for our sins, whereby we are reconciled to God; and what, through his eternal Spirit and Divine Grace, He does for us, within us; that, through the obedience of faith, we may be renewed again through Him, by obtaining remission of sin, and witness a newness of life, and finally an entrance into his glorious kingdom of everlasting blessedness, where Satan, the grand deceiver, the old adversary, has no more place, and the purified spirits can never fall. (Seebohm, 1862, 129-30)

Contrary to Jones' contention that Grellet sounds more like Wesley than Fox, this study argues that an examination of Grellet's journal shows more evidence of Foxian thought than Wesleyan. For example, in the concluding statement in the passage above concerning entry into the "everlasting blessedness"... where "purified spirits can never fall," we find a clear allusion to Fox's description of mystical perfection: "being taken up in spirit, even into a state in Christ Jesus, that should never fall...and... such as were faithful to him... should come up into that state" (Nickalls 1952, 27). Grellet does not make a clear distinction between potential "glorification" and perfection in this life, or only in the future state of heaven. His meaning appears to be left, perhaps deliberately, to the reader or hearer. (Appendix C explains this critical area of the meeting and intersection of holiness in the Quaker tradition with that of the "New Holiness" of the Wesleyan Revival.)

3.4   Chapter Summary

Anthony Benezet, John Woolman, John Churchman, and other reform leaders in the mid-eighteenth century represent a second Holiness Movement in Quakerism – a perfectionist movement of re-awakening to a deeper spiritual life, a reformation of morals, a strictly disciplined life accountable to the community, and a passion for social justice. The Quietist creation of a Quaker "hedge" came as one by-product of the renewal movement, and as described by Marietta, led to the final transformation into a sectarian Quietism (1984, 83-85). American Quakers after the American Revolution became a community in exile. But this study argues that an "evangelical revival" was also a by-product of the renewal movement, and emerged within and broke through the sectarian Quietist culture, with the leadership of evangelists such as Stephen Grellet and William Savery.[29] This later period, 1775-1830, can be identified as "Evangelical Quietism." Thus while Quietism became a traditional way of life solidified with a high degree of cultural conformity, it was not as isolationist or non-evangelistic as is often assumed.[30] Quaker ministers continued to pursue an energetic peripatetic itinerant ministry of religious service within Quaker communities as well as public meetings for convincement. "Public Friends," those who addressed the general public, were the Quaker evangelists of the Quietist period (Brinton, 2002, 226). And perhaps the greatest "Public Friend" in the Quietist period was Stephen Grellet, one of a group of evangelical Quietist ministers – though not revivalists – with their deep concern for spiritual nurture of the Quaker community, and a passion for outreach, both evangelistic and social. This chapter detailed through Benezet's publishing and Grellet's life and ministry their embodiment of both a mystical and ethical holiness.

---

[29] Howard Brinton designates the Quietism of the eighteenth century as the "period of cultural creativeness" (2002, 213). He also identifies this century as the "period of mysticism," a cultivation of inward holiness which he calls "the right inward state" (2002, 226).

[30] See Clarkson, *Portraiture of Quakerism*, 1806, for the classic description of the culture of the "golden age" of Quietism by an admiring outside observer. See Jones, 1911, xxiv-xxvi, and 1921, 178, 192 for a more penetrating, though not always justified, critique of what he perceives as the spiritual decline of this period.

Mystical perfection continued to be central to Quakerism through the eighteenth century. Although expressed with some variation in a different cultural setting and ethos (the Enlightenment period), the message of direct experience culminating in union did not change. Perfection remained connected to both mystical experience and core traditional Christian doctrines. The emphasis on perfection also played a major role in both spiritual renewal and reform, and provided impetus for compassionate social concerns in Quaker Quietism.

The Quietist period continued to manifest all of the essential elements listed as criteria for Quaker holiness (see 1.5). 1) The Quietist view of Scripture was essentially unchanged from the early period. Scripture was God's revelation, read with spiritual eyes (*lectio divina*). But the Spirit remained the final authority, and revelation was not confined to Scripture. 2) Eschatology was internalized, "realized" in this life, and understood mystically. Eternal life began with union with God in the present and continued into heaven. 3) Conversion was still a necessary turning point of the spiritual life and a highlight and focus in journal narratives (sometimes dramatically, as in Grellet's experience). Sanctification was always the outcome of conversion and a continual process of deepening faith. 4) Evangelism as itinerant ministry of both spiritual nurture and social witness was evident in the many Quietist leaders known as "Public Friends." Benezet and Woolman were renowned for their work on behalf of the slave and the poor and their work to change structures of oppression. Grellet represented the height of the missionary spirit. 5) Charisma, meaning Spirit-filled and Spirit-led, continued to be a prominent feature of Quietist spiritual life. Holy Spirit language became more pronounced in evangelical Quietism. 6) Suffering meant bearing the cross of Quaker plainness and adopting the "peculiarities" of the Quaker witness, including commitment to the peace testimony. 7) Mysticism as a direct experience of God continued to characterize Quietism. The elevation of silence in prayer and worship kept the apophatic dimension prominent. 8) Perfection as union with God, or divine indwelling, was the goal of the spiritual life and provided empowerment over sin. (See Figure 4 for a comparative analysis with other periods of Quakerism.)

CHAPTER 4

The Breakdown of Holiness and Divergent Paths

4.1 Schism

From its inception, Quakerism has contained two seemingly opposite impulses arising from a theology of holiness: on the one hand is the impulse to sectarian perfectionism wherein holiness is measured by purity, asceticism, and moral rigor, and results in uniformity of behavior. On the other hand, holiness generates the impulse towards universal love, inclusiveness, freedom of conscience, and religious tolerance, which results in challenging sectarianism. Since both of these seemingly opposing impulses are found within Quakerism, it was perhaps inevitable that Quaker Quietism would be critiqued and challenged from within. And so it was, painfully, in the Great Separation of 1827-28 in America, which created two branches of Quakers, the Hicksites and the Orthodox.[1]

The most serious repercussion of the crisis of separation for holiness theology was its rending of the fabric of the seamless garment of Quaker spirituality, a holiness delicately balanced between a kataphatic and apophatic spirituality. This section will examine ideas and teachings related to the holiness of Elias Hicks (1748-1830),[2] and compare them to three of his contemporaries: Stephen Grellet, William Savery, and Job Scott.

Elias Hicks, a farmer-minister from Long Island New York, became an outspoken opponent to all forms of modernity (Doherty, 1967, 27.)[3] Yet despite his ultra- anti-modern strain he had little confidence in the traditions and wisdom of the Quaker elders. He antagonized the Orthodox by telling youth they need not obey the traditions of their elders, but rather the dictates of their conscience (Doherty, 1967, 29). His elevation of the individual conscience and human reason took precedence over religious tradition and its authority. He had a reputation as an eloquent and powerful preacher with a well-established

---

[1] For studies of the Great Separation, see Grubb, 1914b; Ingle, 1986; and Holden, 1988.

[2] Hicks was an enigmatic figure, a mixture of opposites that are hard to reconcile. Two major studies give very different impressions of Hicks. Bliss Forbush, in his biography, *Elias Hicks: Quaker Liberal*, argues, as his title indicates, that "he was a true liberal" (1956, 176) and the "turbulent prophet of Liberal Quakerism" (1956, 3), as well as "the chief exponent of Liberal Quakerism" (1956, 142). On the other hand, Doherty insists Hicks was neither modern nor liberal, but essentially "a prophet of the past" (1967, 27).

[3] Hicks was opposed to all "outward helps" – even books, and all signs of progress, including public schools, science, railroads, cities, commerce, urban life in general, and the Erie Canal (Forbush, 1956, 300).

ministry among Friends and a devoted following. Yet his published sermons are unremarkable and uninspiring.[4] Since they were originally oral messages, an impassioned delivery might make them more compelling, but they are hardly liberal manifestos. Barbour and Frost, in attempting to explain such polar opposites in Hicks, conclude that "the character of Hicks's thought is best described as that of an extreme Quietist or spiritualist tinged with rationalism" (Barbour, 1988, 174).

Although the Hicksite side of the Great Separation found its popular leader in this rationalist, but anti-modernist minister, the real innovators among the Hicksite reformers were radical deist-leaning modernists whose goal was to accommodate Quaker thought to Enlightenment rationalism. Doherty argues that because of Hicks' devoted following of rural folk, the more radical "free thinkers" used Hicks' popularity to promote their own liberal vision of Quakerism. These radical and influential freethinkers developed a highly organized movement that directly attacked Christian orthodoxy (Doherty, 1967, 84-87).

Even though Hicks himself preached against deism and distanced himself from Unitarianism, his protest against centralized authority, his principle of the light in the conscience, and his strong appeal to individual reason allowed his ideas to attract liberal thinkers. Hicksite ideas were diffuse enough that a traditional or sectarian Quietist, a spiritualist, a Unitarian, a Transcendentalist, or a liberal freethinker could all interpret Hicks within their own framework (Doherty, 1967, 89).[5] Some historians see Hicks as "almost incidental" to the actual schism, but his assertive and combative style and his large circle of influence undoubtedly became the catalyst for the controversies which swirled around him and led to the way the divisions developed (Barbour, 1988, 174). The major doctrinal differences between the two sides revolved around core Christian doctrines, the reality and meaning of the incarnation, the atonement, the divinity and humanity of Christ, and the authority of Scripture, deeply held beliefs for many Quietist Quakers.[6] Besides theological issues, conflict was greatly fueled by mutual fear on both sides (Punshon, 1984, 174).

One of the earliest references to concerns about Hicks' challenging of orthodox Christian doctrines came from Stephen Grellet. After a public meeting

---

[4] Reading his *Journal* confirms the estimation of Edward Grubb that it "is a singularly colourless document, and contains little that could not have been written by any Friend who traveled in ministry" (1914a, 59).

[5] An interesting side light to the conflict is that it even included a ranter-like group known as the "New Lights," who espoused radical individualism and came to be associated with the Hicksites. Most "New Lights" who remained Christian became Unitarian (Ingle, 1986, 93-94).

[6] In 1806 grounds for disownment in Philadelphia Meeting included "unsound" views such as denial of the divinity of Christ, direct revelation of the Holy Spirit, and the authority of Scripture (Punshon, 1984, 172).

in 1808, Grellet believed that Hicks had advanced some views which Grellet felt were "unchristian" (Seebohm, 1862, 125). He felt pushed to publicly disavow Hicks' views. Grellet firmly maintained that "as a religious Society, we had uniformly received and maintained the fundamental Christian truths, in harmony with clear Scripture doctrine" (Seebohm, 1862, 125). Both Grellet and Hicks used familiar Quietist expressions, though both had their own personal style, favorite phrases, texts, and themes. Their style of voluntary, itinerant ministry, their manner of worship and respect for silence, their maintenance of the traditional testimonies, their strict adherence to the Discipline, their preaching against slavery – in all these aspects they shared complete identity (Ingle, 1986, 75). Doherty claimed that Hicks "pushed quietism so far that he destroyed the balance among different strains of Quaker thought" (1967, 27). Rufus Jones offered a similar conclusion: "He made a fragment of truth do service for the immense reality which would make genuine religion an integral and rounded whole" (1921, 1:457). This study explores the implications of these critiques by examining some of the ideas related to holiness in Hicks' *Journal* and sermons, and compares his views to some other leading contemporary ministers.

4.1.1 The Gnostic Theology of Elias Hicks

Hicks, whose formal schooling did not go beyond a limited elementary one, became a self-taught theologian.[7] He read the standard Quaker literature, but also some contemporary works (despite his opposition to book-learning), such as David Hume, Joseph Priestly (*History of the Corruption of Christianity*) and John L. Mosheim, one of the first "German Rationalists" (Forbush, 1956, 175). This study argues that Hicks, despite his usual identification as a hyper-Quietist and a mystic, in his embracing of rationalism in his mature life, departed radically from the Christ-centered mysticism found in traditional Quietism and early Quakerism. He came to a position which disavowed a doctrine central to Quaker holiness – the incarnation (see 1.6). The incarnation is the chief doctrine that separates Christian orthodoxy from Christian Gnosticism; it is the defining

---

[7] Few, if any, Quietist ministers (unless they happened to come from another Christian tradition) had any formal theological training. J. J. Gurney, who will be examined in the next section, became the first Quaker minister with biblical and theological training since Barclay, Penn, Fisher, and other early leaders. Although the majority of early itinerants were untrained lay preachers, it should be noted that a substantial number had been educated at Oxford and Cambridge, and some had been Anglican clergyman before their convincement (Wright, 1932, 8-9). Thus the level of theological knowledge, critical thinking and creative engagement with doctrinal formulations would have been greater in the first 50 years than in the subsequent 150.

belief that transformed neo-Platonism and Greek thought into the Christian catholic faith in the early centuries of the church.[8]

Edward Grubb (a prominent liberal Quaker in the early twentieth century, though far more Christo-centric than Hicks) concluded that Hicks fell into docetism in a pronounced form[9] (1914a, 95). Hicks' opponents accused him of denying the divinity of Christ, which they rightly maintained had always been a central truth for Quakers (Grubb, 1914a, 61-62).[10]

Unlike most Quaker preaching, Hicks' sermons were taken down in shorthand and thus we have access to the ideas he passed on to the many Quaker meetings he visited. An example of his preaching on Christ begins with a text from John 16:7 where Jesus tells his disciples:

> "It is expedient for you that I go away, for if I go not away, the Comforter will not come." He speaks nothing but the truth: for so long as the Jews had him to look at, they never could rise any higher, – while he was bodily with them. That part must be entirely taken away. It must be dissolved, and be so no more. We must have no remembrance of it; because, if we did worship it, it would be the worship of an image. Let us only remember the glorious works which he did; but no more remember the flesh and blood. Let us have no hand in it. It was only an organ through which the power of God passed, and brought about all these effects; effects supernatural to the power of man; to any ability or power of his own. (Hicks, 1825, 261)[11]

This sermon illustrates the extreme apophatic position taken by Hicks. There was no room for images or materiality in Hicks' spirituality. He seemed to imply that the humanity of Jesus was an encumbrance to be forgotten.[12] Only

---

[8] Christian Gnosticism is notoriously difficult to define, but most scholars agree that the core ideas include a dualistic understanding of reality that sees materiality as inferior to spirituality, claims some form of the innate divinity of the soul, and teaches salvation through special knowledge (McGinn, 1991, 90-91).

[9] Docetism is a form of Gnosticism that considered the humanity and suffering of Jesus as only apparent and not real.

[10] Grubb contends Hicks found the source of his docetism in early Friends, which this study disputes (1914a, 62).

[11] Grubb claims this example is typical of his whole position and quotes similar kinds of statements. While Grubb insists his message was meant to be Christian and spiritual, he concludes, "It does not ring true to Christian experience" (1914a, 63).

[12] Several other unusual aspects of his Christology digress significantly from historical Quakerism, such as his belief that Jesus was the Savior of the Jewish people only, rather than the Savior of the world, and that Jesus was the not pre-existent Word (as Fox consistently insisted), but "adopted" after his baptism (Forbush, 1956, 197). His teaching that Jesus was only the Savior of the Jews was one of the most puzzling to the Orthodox, and when he claimed that the atonement for Christians was not only unnecessary but also

the ethics of Jesus – "the glorious works that he did" – have meaning; the mystery of the incarnation itself, God taking human flesh, was incidental, simply a form the power of God passed through. Although Grubb was not unsympathetic towards Hicks, in the end he concluded that for Hicks, "Spirit was all that counted in the religious sphere; the outward or visible could not possibly be divine or have any religious significance" (1914a, 95). In this sense Hicks moved beyond tendencies toward Gnosticism to become a full-fledged Christian Gnostic. His final position resulted in the extreme body-mind dualism of the Gnostic. One of his central thoughts, according to Grubb, was that "spirit can only beget spirit" (1914a, 96). There was no place for Christ as the bodily image of the invisible God in his theology.

4.1.2 The Theology of Job Scott

Hicks has been compared by Quaker historians to Job Scott, a contemporary who died young and avoided the painful experience of the Great Separation[13] (Jones, 1921, 288). Scott has been referred to as "the most creative Quaker theologian in the eighteenth century" (Barbour, 1988, 366). Rufus Jones claimed Hicks' teachings were a more extreme, though slightly mistaken, version of Job Scott's. But Scott's theology and spirituality, unlike Hicks', included a balance of the apophatic and kataphatic, the inner experience of the Light and the external historical Christ. Scott centered the substance of faith on the necessity of "Christ being born in you," but without denying the significance of the humanity of Christ (Grubb 1914a, 56-57). Jones (like Barbour and Frost) found Scott the most compelling and original of all the Quietist ministers (1921, 288). The "new birth" spirituality of Scott is strikingly reminiscent of the spirituality of Benezet and Law and the Anabaptist-Pietist emphasis of the Quaker reformation of 1748 with its mysticism and the necessity of the born again experience. But this tradition of holiness, I argue, is an incarnational spirituality which never separates the birth of Christ in the soul from the human Jesus who came in the flesh.

"vulgar" he was the most offensive: "The mode of redemption generally held by professing Christians as being effected by the death, or outward dying of Christ Jesus upon the outward wooden cross...I consider a vulgar error, that came in with the apostasy from primitive Christianity...I consider that the offering of the body of Jesus Christ, on the outward cross, applied only as a matter of redemption, to the Israelites." (1824, 11-12)

[13] Scott was born in Rhode Island in 1751, became a Quaker by convincement in 1770, and died in 1793 in Ireland of smallpox.

Job Scott's conception of holiness, which Grubb recognizes as Pauline mysticism, was based on Gal. 4:19.[14]

> In all ages, the true mystery of godliness was and is God manifest in the flesh etc, not in the flesh of that one body that was born of Mary, only; but in the flesh of all the godly. For there never was any true godliness without the manifestation of the very life and power of God in the creature, bringing forth a *new birth* of "the incorruptible seed and word of God." [his emphasis] (Scott, 1831, 1:443)

For Scott, "this birth of the Divine in the human soul seems to him to be a part of the Incarnation" (Grubb, 1914a, 57).

The main theme of Scott's preaching was the new birth, the focal point of all his theology. Here is Scott's vivid description of the new birth as union with God that results in perfection:

> The Father, by the overshadowing of the Holy Ghost upon the willing mind, which embraces and yields to the visitations and operations, and wooings of his life, begetteth and produceth a true and real birth of that which is truly and properly his only begotten forever, being one in all his spiritual offspring. This is he that is born again of God, or the incorruptible seed and word of God....In the production of this conception, generation, and birth, there is both Father and Mother. He that begets, is the only possible Father of this the only begotten. The soul in whom this conception and birth is effected, 'tis the mother; and here the man is not without the woman, nor the woman without the man in the Lord![15] This conception and birth cannot possibly be effected by the Mother without the Father, and is never produced by the Father without the consent of the Mother. [the implication is cooperation with grace, or synergy, see 1.7.2 above] There must be a celestial union a real cooperation, wherein two become one. Of twain the one new man is made, which is God and man in the heavenly and mystical fellowship and Union. This is the mystery of Christ...this is the new creature, that being born of God sinneth not; indeed, cannot sin, and that for this very reason, because his seed remaineth in him, and he cannot sin, because he is born of God as real so, as one was ever born of another in natural procreation. (Scott, 1831, 1:490)[16]

---

[14] Paul writes to the Galatians, "I am again in the pain of childbirth until Christ is formed in you."
[15] A reference to I Cor. 11:11, but using Paul's word allegorically in a different context.
[16] See also Appendix A where this passage is used as an example of bridal mysticism.

Scott did not evidence the reaction against the flesh that Hicks did. He did not divorce the new birth from God's manifestation in the world of the humanity of Jesus. But he was aware that he might be called a heretic, as early Quakers often were, because he did not believe that salvation was simply imputed, but instead a real transformation of the whole person that required intimate fellowship with Christ:

> Some may call me a heretic when I confess unto them that I expect no final benefit from the death of Jesus, in any other way than through fellowship with him in his sufferings. But after the way in which they call heresy, I worship the God of my fathers, truly believing in the history of Christ's life, death, resurrection, ascension and glory. (1831, 1:221)

This study argues that following the teachings of early Quakers, "final benefit" does not mean *no* benefit. The death of Jesus provides for universal atonement. Christ died so that all might be saved, but the *final* or full benefit is "fellowship with him in his sufferings," the indwelling Christ, or in classical terms, mystical union. Thus, the final benefit for Scott was holiness.

As for Scott's teaching on holiness, Jones contended he "went far beyond the orthodox position and insisted on a process of life which reproduced the Christ-Spirit and which conquered sin and exhibited real holiness of life in man's nature" (1921, 290). This study fully agrees with Jones' description of holiness as continuing the essential Quaker tradition, but argues that Scott, unlike Hicks, did not go beyond the orthodox Christian position. Scott taught a mystical path of holiness in the tradition of early Quakers (Jones, 1921, 290). He was, as Jones claimed, "a thorough-going mystic" (1921, 239), challenging conventional faith, as many mystics do; but as this study contends, he remained a fully Christ-centered Quaker within the Christian mystical tradition.

> In all ages it has been a real birth of God in the soul, a substantial union of the human and divine nature; the son of God and the son of man, which is the true Immanuel state. (Jones, 1921, 290)

For Scott, perfection *is* mystical union.

Scott's mysticism followed the teaching of the early Greek Fathers on *theosis* (see 1.4). *Theosis,* or divinization, as the Fathers termed it, was for Scott the "Immanuel state." Scott's mysticism was akin to Fox's, and a few of Scott's statements are startling to Protestant ears. But unlike Hicks, he was never a center of controversy during his lifetime, nor accused of being "unsound." Only some years later after his death in 1793 when his Monthly Meeting wanted to publish his *Journal* and their request was blocked, did his writings seem controversial. By then his teachings sounded too similar to Hicks (though upon examination as shown, were quite different), and the Yearly Meeting was in a reactionary mode. However, it was not Scott's mysticism, which followed closely the stream of the Christ-centered mystics, but rather Hicks' Christology that took Quakerism "far beyond the orthodox position" (Jones, 1921, 290). Hicks cut the umbilical cord of connection, in effect wrenched the new birth from its roots in the incarnation, and with it any need for the reality of Christ's death other than as a model for self-sacrifice:

> Who was his [Jesus'] father? He was begotten of God. We cannot suppose that it was the outward body of flesh and blood that was begotten of God, but a birth of the spiritual life in the soul. We must apply it internally and spiritually. For nothing can be a son of God, but that which is spirit; and nothing but the soul of man is a recipient for the light and spirit of God. (1825, 10-11)

In this passage Hicks still appeared to claim divinity for Jesus, but for him the Word was *not* made flesh. The Incarnation was dismissed. This led him to further assert: "And this immortal spirit in man, is what constitutes the Son of God. Nothing but the immortal soul can become a Son of God"[17] (1825, 33). Hicks' spirituality was disembodied. He failed to see human beings as holistic – body, soul, and spirit. Unlike Scott, with whom he is often compared, Hicks became an extreme dualist and essentially a Gnostic, a position incompatible with Quaker holiness.

4.1.3 Quietist Conversion Narratives

Most Quaker historians claim that the source of Quaker theology was "personal experience of the divine" (Forbush, 1956; Jones, 1921; Grubb, 1914b). If then, Quaker theology, including holiness, is based on "religious experience," (Barbour, 1964, 149) then a question worth exploring is whether different kinds of mystical experiences, or interpretations of them, even within a closely conforming religious community, might lead individuals to adopt different kinds of theological beliefs. In comparing the journals of three traditional Quietist ministers, Elias Hicks, Stephen Grellet, and William Savery, I show how this may be the case.

All traveling ministers were expected to keep journals of their spiritual experiences. This discipline provided an outlet for their emotions and served

---

[17] Rufus Jones holds that Hicks eventually adopted a Unitarian position: "To Christ in Spirit, but not in Christ as man," Hicks wrote to Phoebe Willis in 1820, "I ascribe all true divinity. Divinity cannot be ascribed to any corporal matter (i.e. any person in the flesh) only in similitude or shadow" (qtd in Jones, 1921, 452). This position is beyond Unitarianism and is inherently Gnostic with its devaluing of the humanity of Jesus.

didactic purposes and as models for later generations. Since most ministers kept detailed journals of their inner lives, as well as observations about the state of the meetings they visited, the first place to locate divergent thinking might be found in comparing their journals. All Quaker journals followed a standardized formula and style, which included the writer's early visitations of God, a period of youthful frivolity, religious questioning and a struggle to submit, convincement, a struggle with the call to ministry, breakthrough of first speaking in worship and adoption of plain dress, and a record of travels and impressions of spiritual states of meetings (Brinton, 1972, 4-5).

Hicks' experiences of the Divine were similar in many aspects to his "evangelical" opponents, though, based on his own descriptions in his journal, less intense, dramatic, and emotional. That they were less affective may simply reflect Hicks' personality, but in addition they were less personal. Hicks' experience of the Light was that of a "principle" and not a person. Hicks' *Journal* followed the conventional patterns expected of Quietist ministers – impressions and visitations of grace, as well as times of "great dryness" and "poverty of spirit" (Forbush, 1956, 56-57). Hicks, like all Quaker ministers, described a period of struggle with temptation, sin, vanity and frivolity as a youth that led to a final spiritual turning point of confession and pardon (a few years after his marriage). He described this event as a "visitation of grace," but not as a conversion or convincement:

> But, about the twenty-sixth year of my age, I was again brought, by the operative influence of divine grace, under deep concern of mind; and was led, through adorable mercy to see, that although I had ceased from many sins and vanities of my youth yet there were many remaining that I was still guilty of, which were not yet atoned for, and for which I now felt the judgments of God to rest upon me. This caused me to cry earnestly to the Most High for Pardon and redemption, and he graciously condescended to hear my cry, and to open a way before me, wherein I must walk, in order to experience reconciliation with him; and as I abode in watchfulness and deep humiliation before him, light broke forth out of obscurity, and my darkness became as the noon-day. I had many deep openings in the visions of light, greatly strengthening and establishing to my exercised mind. My spirit was brought under a close and weighty labour in meetings for discipline, and my understanding much enlarged therein; and I felt a concern to speak to some of the subjects engaging the meetings...which often brought unspeakable comfort to my mind. (1832, 15)

But it was not until after considerable struggle to be faithful in obeying the intimation to speak that he felt a sense of release and peace:

...but O the joy and sweet consolation that my soul experienced, as a reward for this act of faithfulness; and as I continued persevering in duty and watchfulness, I witnessed an increase in divine knowledge, and an enlargement in my gift. I was also deeply engaged for the right administration of discipline and order in the Church... (1832, 16)

It is striking that Hicks' experience of God is described in the same breath (there is not even a paragraph break) as his performance of duty to speak in meeting and his concern for administration of discipline and church order. It was the act of obedience and fulfillment of duty that brought peace to his soul, different from the Protestant salvation by faith through grace, and as this study argues, a different kind of experience than that of the earliest Quakers. It is closer to salvation by sanctification (works), rather than justification by grace. It is similar to the kind of understanding which Wesley a century earlier had accused Quakers and William Law of holding (falsely) – "flat justification by works" (see Appendix C). Although Hicks recorded the joy his soul experienced, affective love and deep intimacy with God seem strangely absent.

For comparison, here is an excerpt from the conversion narrative of Stephen Grellet (greatly condensed since the fuller text is found in 3.3.1):

...I was favoured to find in me, what I had so long, and with so many tears, sought for without me....I felt the Lord's power in such a manner, that my inner man was prostrated before my Blessed Redeemer. A secret joy filled me, in that I had found Him after whom my soul longed....It seemed as if the Lord opened my outward ear, and my heart... was opened; I felt the power of Him who hath the key of David.... O what sweetness did I then feel! It was indeed a memorable day. I was like one introduced into a new world; the creation and all things around me bore a different aspect, – my heart glowed with love to all. (Seebohm, 1862, 17-18)

Grellet, as stated previously, found Christ after a journey from Catholicism through Voltarian atheism, thus it might be expected that his conversion experience would be more dramatic. The freedom, peace and feeling of love which he experienced came from the visitation of God by grace, and were not dependent upon any performance of duty. (Grellet, not long after, also experienced the struggle to be obedient to his call to speak, but that event for him was affirmation of his acceptance into the community, not his acceptance by God (see 3.3.1).

Unlike Grellet, William Savery's (1750-1804) background was almost identical to Hicks'. He was born into a Quaker family, flirted with worldliness, and became a strict Friend after his marriage. He was recognized as a minister in 1781 about the same time as Hicks. Both he and Hicks had commercial interests in the tanning business (Barbour, 1988, 365).

Jonathan Evans, a Philadelphia Quaker to whom Savery was "a beloved brother," compiled and edited Savery's *Journal*. In the preface written in 1837, Evans tells his readers that "His [Savery's] affable disposition, his catholic spirit, and his truly Christian principles, endeared him to those who knew him" (1844, iv). Evans described Savery's ministry as "generally more of a doctrinal nature, than that of many other Friends, accompanied with a fervent engagement that his audience might be brought to a heartfelt experience of the unspeakable love of God" (1844, iv). Evans himself seemed intimately acquainted with this love of God, which he described in classic holiness language, "the unspeakable love of God, in sending his dear Son, our Lord Jesus Christ into the world to save sinners; of the propitiatory sacrifice and the sanctifying power of his Holy Spirit, who hath by his own blood obtained eternal redemption for all that come unto Him in true faith" (1844, iv). This is what Hicks called "dogma" and preached against. In Hicks' preaching, salvation was not described in a personal, affective way; it was not a "heartfelt" experience. Salvation came through obedience. Savery, on the other hand, found his attempts at obedience to fall short and led him to despair. He described, as do so many others, a period of divine visitations, spiritual struggles, and final submission:

> ...notwithstanding my regularity of behavior and all my boasted attainments, I fell far short of that purity, which all the vessels in the Lord's house must come to; and that I was yet under the law, which cannot make the comers thereunto perfect, not having passed under the flaming sword, nor felt the day of the Lord to be come, which burns as an oven.[18] This brought great distress and anxiety of mind over me, and sometimes I was ready to doubt the truth of these divine revelations; and was exceedingly desirous to find, if possible, an easier way to peace and happiness, than by submitting myself to the cross, of which I had as yet experienced but little.... One evening, sitting in my house alone, great horror and trouble seized me – I wept aloud...my distress was so great, that it almost overcame me...My spirits at length being nearly exhausted...I grew cold like one near death, a clammy sweat covered me, and I was to appearance stupid. In this state I was, through adorable mercy, released from the horror that before surrounded me, and was comforted with a sight and feeling of a state of inexpressible happiness and joy; and when so far come to myself to have utterance given me, I cried aloud on this wise, "Oh! now I know that my Redeemer liveth!" Oh! the sweetness I then felt, in being

---

[18] This statement is significant because it illustrates how Fox's flaming sword vision was understood as an experience of sanctification and perfection. Grellet, too, in his account alluded to Fox's experience when he wrote, "I was like one introduced into a new world; the creation and all things around me bore a different aspect" (Seebohm, 1862, 18).

favored with such an evidence of the goodness and mercy of God! It far surpassed everything I had before experienced.... Tears of joy ran freely down my cheeks,...I could not restrain them nor scarcely utter a word for a considerable time; and my dear partner, who shared with me in my affliction, was also made a partaker with me in my exceeding great joy. (Evans, 1844, 26-27)

The difference in affect and degree of rapture in these accounts may simply relate to differences in temperament. But more significant than the difference in emotional heat that may vary with personalities is the actual interpretation of the experiences themselves.[19] In most studies of the Hicksite-Orthodox split, differences between preaching "doctrines" and preaching "experience" is generally highlighted (Evans, 1844; Grubb, 1914a; Forbush, 1956; Ingle, 1986). This study contends that both sides were preaching experience *and* doctrine. Hicks preached from his experience of being opened to the light, which he formulated as obedience to the light and to that alone; Christ was not experienced as a mediator. Grellet, Savery and other evangelical Quietists preached from their experience of the love of Christ felt in their hearts and the indwelling Holy Spirit that sanctified and guided.

Both sides were expressing important aspects of early Quaker theology and spirituality, but the conversion narratives of Grellet and Savery more closely capture the Christ-centered mystical experience and the holiness language of George Fox and early Quakers than that of Hicks. The schism between Hicksite and Orthodox was fueled by doctrinal disputing, as well as the interplay of sociological factors and of opposing cultural trends towards rationalism on the one hand and revivalism on the other, but the source of the conflict initially may have been different interpretations and formulations of their own personal religious experiences. Grellet's and Savery's experiences were mediated by Christ, their divine redeemer. Hicks' way of perfection was described just as doctrinally as Grellet and Savery's, but more rationally, and less intimately and mystically. Many expositions of it can be found in the pages of his journal, for example:

...I was led, in a clear manner, to show the ground from whence all this darkness and unbelief proceeded; that it was from a want of due attention to, and right belief in, the *inward manifestation of divine light,* which reveals itself in the heart of man against sin and uncleanness; and at the same time shows what is right and justifies for right doing. Therefore while men disregard this inward divine

---

[19] Emotions, however, do play a part in mystical experience. Paul Mommears, in a recent study of mystical experience, explains that a mystic's consciousness is touched in an "unforeseen and incomparable way" as "the divine Object makes itself known through the human subject's own emotion" (2003, 53).

principle, of grace and truth, and <u>do not believe in it, as *essential and sufficient to salvation;*</u> they are in danger of becoming either Atheists, or Deists – these are also in danger of becoming so blinded as <u>not to believe in that necessary and very essential doctrine of perfection</u>, as contained in that <u>clear, rational, and positive injunction</u> of our dear Lord: "be ye therefore perfect, even as your Father which is in heaven is perfect." And we <u>cannot rationally suppose</u> they can ever be otherwise, while they continue in this situation; as nothing but <u>this light is sufficient to produce the knowledge, on which this belief is founded.</u> (1832, 122) [underline my emphasis, italics his emphasis]

The divine principle was "grace and truth," but justification came from "right doing." Hicks named this divine principle the *light within,* and emphasized that "it is by *obedience to this inward light only*, that we are prepared for an admittance into the heavenly kingdom" (1832, 122) [his emphasis]. Hicks was not always clear as to what he meant by the light within, but it was not the saving light of Christ. He referred to Jesus as "our blessed pattern" rather than "our blessed savior" as the evangelical Quietists did (1832, 123). The "inner light" theology of modernist Quakerism finds its source in Hicks.[20]

Grellet and Savery's concept of holiness was explained doctrinally as well, but intimately and mystically as an affective experience, rather than rationally as belief and knowledge. Though often accused by later interpreters of not using "Quaker language" or teaching Quaker doctrines, this study argues they were closer to early Friends in their theology and in their concept of perfection as an experience of union with Christ than was Hicks. As an example, here is Grellet's preaching of the Gospel, articulated in distinctive Quaker fashion, which, I argue, would meet the approval of Fox and Barclay:

> I was largely engaged in setting forth what is the Christian baptism, by which a man, being regenerated or born again, becomes qualified to partake of that living bread, which nourished the soul unto eternal life; then I showed how all the former dispensations were pointing to Christ, the end of all shadows. (Seebohm, 1862, 132)

4.1.4 Summary and Conclusions

Although on the surface doctrinal controversies became the center of the storm that caused the Great Separation, an underlying issue was a distrust of the elders. The Hicksite "reform" was actually a revolt against the tradition of the elders, in effect the established hierarchy (which Hicks called the papacy), as

---

[20] In Joseph Pickvance, *A Reader's Companion to George Fox's Journal*, it is shown that Fox himself never used the term "inner light," and used "inward light" rarely (1989, 89).

well as the faith, practice and discipline which had been passed down as a Quaker apostolic succession from the early leaders. Both Hicksite and Orthodox had departed in some significant ways from their founders. All traditions change over time, but these groups were moving in radically different directions. They were both dismantling, in different ways, the Quaker hedge which had maintained unity for over a century – the Orthodox by joining in interdenominational activities, such as Bible and Tract Societies, the Hicksites by adopting the rationalistic, progressive, and individualistic political thought of Enlightenment America.

But in Hicks' challenge to the controlling elders, he became the symbol of the common folk who felt oppressed by the rule of a powerful Quaker oligarchy. His theology, strange in some respects and a clear departure from historical Quakerism, still sounded like the Quaker faith to those whose main concern was individual freedom and who were not much interested in the doctrinal issues anyway. According to Doherty, few of those called Hicksites actually adopted Hicks' theology (1967, 32). But the influential liberal minority soon came to dominate Hicksite leadership (Doherty, 1967, 85-86). They agreed with Hicks' basic principle of the inward light and individual freedom, and felt Hicks had the right to preach whatever he wanted (Doherty, 1967, 85). Liberals determined the content of responses to the Orthodox through radical liberal publications such as *The Berean* (Doherty, 1967, 86).

Hicks, perhaps without consciously intending it, led a large portion of Quakerdom to a position which relinquished belief in the incarnation and atonement – key components of Quaker Christology and essential to maintaining the delicate balance between the inward Christ and the outward Christ, so distinctive of Quaker holiness. Although Hicks is generally called a mystic (Brinton, 2002, 231), this study argues that his spirituality was more rationalistic-moralistic than mystical. His religious experience, as he described it, did not appear to flow from personal intimacy with God through Christ as found in earlier Quaker mysticism, though he was strongly apophatic in the sense of dispensing with all images in worship. Hicks was primarily concerned with behavioral codes (those which he deemed most important), maintaining a strict Quaker hedge and a rural, agrarian way of life, and not with mystical experience. Hicks' theology in his later years evolved into a rationalistic Christian Gnosticism. In reaction to Hicks, whose position seemed like a major departure from both historical Quakerism and core Christian beliefs, the Orthodox gradually relinquished "mysticism" (which had now become erroneously equated with Hicksism), and strengthened doctrines for safety, as an anchor in a storm. Among the Orthodox, Quaker holiness with its balance of kataphatic and apophatic holiness, the humanity and divinity of Christ, and Christo-centric mysticism remained strongest with the evangelical Quietists.

Applying the four quadrants of holiness (see Figure 3) to Hicks and Hicksites, the following conclusions can be drawn:

1. The Hicksites were the first branching movement to eliminate Quadrant 1, Sacramental holiness. Hicksites did not follow early Friends' belief that Jesus Christ was the incarnation of God. Salvation by faith through the atonement of Christ was gradually repudiated (Jones, 1921, 454; Grubb, 1914a, 95-96).
2. As to Quadrant 2, Experiential holiness, only divine guidance was emphasized. Affective feelings were generally muted. Hicks essentially dispensed with all forms of kataphatic holiness.
3. Regarding Quadrant 3, Mystical holiness, it is debatable whether Hicks was a genuine mystic, though stronger leanings toward mysticism can be found in Hicks' early career. But his spirituality became increasingly rationalistic, though silence and emptiness were still characteristic modes of worship for him. Mystical holiness was pursued by some later nineteenth and twentieth century followers, but separated from any grounding in the other Quadrants. Hicksism thus gradually spun out of the circle of holiness.
4. Quadrant 4, Imitation of Christ as moralistic or behavioral holiness, was actually Hicks' strongest quadrant. His spirituality was an extreme *via negativa*, but unconnected to the kataphatic half of the circle.

To summarize, Hicks' holiness was no longer Christocentric, but became an "inner light mysticism." The ethics of Jesus were patterns to be followed, but the incarnational grounding was severed. Holiness became purely ethical actions. The spiritual narratives of other Quietist leaders such as Job Scott and William Savery conformed to traditional expressions of Quaker holiness, blending all four Quadrants, and maintained a strong mystical consciousness with a Christocentric focus, both doctrinally and experientially.

The next section examines the Orthodox branch and the theologian Joseph John Gurney as the leading representative of evangelical Quakerism in the nineteenth century. Gurney moved away from Quaker holiness to an Anglican non-mystical type of religion. He prepared Orthodox Quakers for a renewal of holiness through revivalism (though he himself did not embrace revival), but his legacy altered the shape of holiness for American evangelicals.

4.2 Joseph John Gurney and Orthodoxy: Non-Mystical Holiness

As was shown previously (3.3, 4.1.3), an evangelical renewal, shaped by ministers such as Stephen Grellet and William Savery, began to impact Quaker Quietism in America. Rufus Jones called the period from 1775-1830, "The great age of evangelical ministry," spearheaded by the missionary travels of Public Friends. An "atmosphere charged with evangelical fervour" appeared on both sides of the Atlantic (Jones, 1921, 284). This religious awakening emerged out of the Quaker holiness model of Quietism through the vibrant personal religious experiences of its leaders. Quaker evangelicalism in this period was a heart-felt, Christ-centered mysticism, with conversion as its centerpiece, holiness as its goal, and evangelism and outreach as its mission. Evangelicalism became more pronounced among the Orthodox after the Separation of 1827-28 when non-evangelicals, anti-evangelicals, and radical liberals united to form the Hicksite branch. In London Yearly Meeting, which never experienced a distinct Separation as in America, evangelical Orthodoxy held sway until the 1870s (Punshon, 1984, 165).[21]

In America, Quaker "Orthodoxy"[22] took a different turn. "Orthodoxy," after the 1820s, became the designation for the larger faction of Friends united against the heretical views of Hicks (Hamm, 1988, 19). The Orthodox maintained a traditional Christology, holding doctrinal views similar to evangelicals of other denominations (Abbott, et al., 2003). By the mid-nineteenth century much of Orthodox Quakerism began to converge with the American Holiness Movement and its Methodist roots, and through the Holiness Revival, "The Friends Church" was born in America around the turn of the century.

Most historians agree that all evangelical Friends trace their heritage through a British Friend, Joseph John Gurney, an Oxford trained biblical scholar[23] (Punshon, 2001, 15, 21). Edward Mott, an early leader in the Friends Church, described Gurney as "a clear exponent of Evangelical faith" (1948, 154). This study argues that Gurney helped prepare the way theologically for the Holiness Revival, but Gurney himself was not a revivalist and was only marginally within the stream of Quaker holiness. In many respects, Gurney's

---

[21] Evangelicalism today makes up two-thirds of the Quaker world and is growing most rapidly in third world countries. Approximately 100,000 Friends belong to Evangelical Friends International, an organization which holds to "the centrality of Christ both historically and experientially" (Abbott, et al., 2003, 94-95).

[22] Hamm maintains that Quaker Orthodoxy represents a decisive break with traditional Quakerism (Abbott, et al., 2003, 201). I argue that both Hicksism and Orthodoxy broke with the traditional Quaker understanding of holiness, the essence of Quakerism.

[23] Joseph John Gurney was born in Norwich, England, in 1788, the tenth child in a family of eleven, of parents who were prominent heirs of an influential banking family. He grew up on a huge estate called Earlham Hall. He studied for two years at Oxford under private tutors, and became a scholar in biblical studies and Patristics. No other Quaker had this level of education or competence in biblical languages since the apologist, Robert Barclay (a distant relative). By 1830 Gurney had become a leader among British Friends, though his views were sometimes challenged. In 1837 he came to America for a three-year visit as a traveling minister. The most visible result of his visit was a split in Orthodox Quakerism, which became known as the Gurneyite-Wilburite split beginning in 1845. He died, age 59, in 1847, two years after this major schism. For biographical information on Gurney see Swift, 1962 and Braithwaite, 1855.

evangelicalism was a departure from the evangelical holiness that had characterized earlier Quakers, and though Christ-centered, he was decidedly not a mystic. Thus modern Quaker evangelicalism is constantly in tension with its own mystical holiness heritage (see 4.2.4).

Joseph John Gurney built on the evangelical awakening within Quietism and emphasized one additional element – biblical authority. Gurney's view of Scripture, however, was more intellectualist and scholarly and diverged from the contemplative spiritualized reading of Scripture which characterized earlier Friends. He developed a defense of scriptural authority based on enlightenment thought and a nascent historical-critical hermeneutic of progressive revelation[24] (Swift, 1962, 159). But he continued to maintain the Quaker understanding of Scripture (see 1.5.1) which emphasized Spirit over letter (Christ is the "Word of God," the Bible, the "words" of God):

> But I object to the common technical use of the term "the word of God," as the name or title of the Bible, because such a use of that name has the effect of excluding, or, at least, *appearing to exclude*, all other communications to mankind." (Braithwaite, 1855, 447-8)

But for Gurney as a scholar, defense of the letter in light of current biblical scholarship became more critical. Gurney's view of Scripture was a modernist form of scholasticism, but never fundamentalistic. It was however, a new turn within Quakerism towards rationalism and biblicism, and became the foundation for a new kind of Quaker biblical scholarship, both evangelical *and* liberal in the twentieth century. All subsequent Quaker religious scholars owed an immense debt to Gurney, whether they acknowledged it or not.

Thus this study contends that the Gurneyite movement which he spawned split into two streams. One stream, emphasizing biblical authority, merged with the Holiness Movement and became the Friends Church;[25] the other merged with mainstream ecumenical liberalism and the Social Gospel movement and became a modernist Friends Meeting – the lines at first were blurred, but became clearly etched by 1905.[26]

---

[24] Swift notes that Gurney's statements on the relationship between Scripture and science were "notably relaxed for an Evangelical committed to the Bible as inspired revelation" (1962, 159).

[25] In 1887 most Gurneyite meetings adopted a uniform "confessional" statement known as the Richmond Declaration of Faith, a synthesis of modern evangelical and traditional Quaker views on doctrine and practice. Today most evangelical yearly meetings include the Richmond Declaration in their books of discipline. Modernists Friends, however, have been divided over endorsement of the Richmond Declaration since 1902 (Abbott, et al., 2003, 247).

[26] I suggest 1905 as the turning point because it is the year Walter Malone (Holiness evangelical) broke with Rufus Jones (liberal modernist) as co-editor of the *American Friend* (the Orthodox journal) and began publishing the *Evangelical Friend* (Hamm,

Arthur Roberts maintains that Gurney was strongly ecumenical and pointed Quakerism towards the world, but "ecumenical" then was characteristic of evangelicalism rather than being identified with liberalism, as it was in the twentieth century (personal correspondence, Jan. 6, 2000). While Gurney may have paved the way for revival by opening Quakerism to the wider world, his theology in several major areas was quite divergent from the course of the Holiness Revival which followed him. Thus, while he became a revered figure within the Quaker evangelical movement, he was nevertheless an unlikely forerunner. I suggest this for three reasons: firstly, because Gurney was not a conversionist (he did not stress a consciousness of a conversion experience) and thus differs from both evangelicals and seventeenth century Puritan Quakers to whom a distinct conversion experience was central (see 1.5.3). Secondly, he did not hold a formal doctrine of perfection, a key element of Quaker holiness. And thirdly, he was not in touch with the biblical, "being-in-Christ" mysticism so characteristic of Holiness Quakerism, thus did not grasp the mystical aspect of perfection, which continued to be an essential element of Quaker holiness.[27]

To understand the basis of the transformation within the Orthodox wing of the Society of Friends in America, Joseph John Gurney's life-long struggle to forge new paths for a more ecumenical Quakerism is pivotal. This section considers three aspects of Gurney's thought: conversion, perfection and mysticism, and compares his theology to Quaker models of holiness and Wesleyan understandings.

4.2.1 Conversion

As we have seen, early Quakers emphasized the conversion experience, perhaps more emphatically than any group of their time. They created their own term for the experience, calling it "convincement" (see 1.5.3). An ongoing contemporary debate revolves around whether or not convincement meant conversion or sanctification in the early movement (Punshon, 2001). While the issues in that

---

1988, 167). The designation "Church" usually indicated that the meeting had adopted pastoral leadership and "programmed" (planned worship) rather than silent worship, though many meetings which eventually called permanent pastors still retained the traditional term of "meeting."

[27] Both movements (modernist and holiness) at first repudiated "mysticism" as an antiquated form of Quietism. Rufus Jones eventually reclaimed it in a modernist form, (see 6.1.1), realizing it was the only way to retain the heart of the Quaker message amidst the deconstruction of an intellectualist liberalism. Not surprisingly within the revivalistic fervor of the Holiness Movement, mysticism took the form of Pentecostalism, seriously fracturing the integrity of the revival. On Pentecostalism see Hamm, 1988, 170-1. This Pentecostal phenomenon also occurred in the broader American Holiness Movement, which, at the turn of the century, divided with great animosity over tongues and the meaning of divine healing (Dieter, 1996, 250-53).

debate are obviously relevant here, its resolution is not necessary for this argument, for sanctification does not equate with perfection. It would be the rare Quaker convert who was not already Christian in some form, so convincement was not a turning from pagan to Christian or from no faith to the Christian faith. It was, however, a mystical experience that included repentance and commitment of the will (on the human side) and a transformation of one's whole being (on the divine side).

Whether convincement is defined as conversion or sanctification, or both, justification-sanctification, in every account, is described as a *crisis* event (usually occurring as the culmination of a process of spiritual seeking bringing about radical change). It is an event that occurs at a certain place and time, analogous to a birth. Born again or rebirth is a common metaphor with its gradual gestation period, climaxing in the birth of the "new" man or woman. Unlike Baptists, who required adult baptism to testify publicly to the conversion experience, early Quakers had no outward ritual to point to it. Therefore, every individual had to experience in a deep, intensive, and usually dramatic way, the mystery of dying and rising with Christ by an *internal* rather than *external* baptism. By the eighteenth century, Quietists would write and speak of many deep baptisms, internally intense experiences described as sufferings and desolations necessary to bring one into perfection – that total dying to self, the symbol of the complete transformation of mind and heart.[28] The experience of being reborn, the mystery of entering into the baptism of repentance, and resurrection of the new person in Christ was central to traditional Quaker understanding of conversion.

In the Wesleyan Holiness tradition, conversion is the beginning of sanctification, and perfection, the culmination of the process (Peters, 1985). One difference generally noted between early Quaker and Wesleyan understandings of perfection is that Wesleyans emphasize a two-stage "crisis" experience rather than an ongoing process: the crisis of conversion, and sanctification following in an instantaneous event, though Wesley himself admitted to both crisis and process, and was never entirely consistent on this issue (Punshon, 2001, 265-8). The American Holiness Movement spawned by Wesley's teachings naturally embraced the two-crisis theory, shaped as it was by charismatic revival preachers calling people to the altar for decisions. Punshon describes the early Quaker experience of sanctification as a natural process of growth in grace, but differentiates that process from *entire* sanctification (also known as the second blessing) that can come in an instantaneous rapture (2001, 265-8). For early Quakers, as has been shown, perfection was a never-ending process of continual spiritual growth (*epektasis*) (see 2.5), but with crisis experiences often occurring as markers along the way.

---

[28] Damiano's study of spiritual formation in eighteenth century Quakerism provides many examples of this process which she terms "eschatological mysticism" (1988, 143-148).

In the final analysis, the question as to the pattern of sanctification as progressive growth or crisis experience has never been settled by either Quakers or Wesleyans.

But unarguably, conversion or convincement is central to Quaker religious experience (see. 1.5.3). Conversion narratives are turning points in lives that alter a person's sense of self. Although the cultural context always shapes the experience, a direct encounter with God through the immediate presence of Christ and the power of the Spirit is an essential aspect of Quaker holiness. Quaker conversion is an experience of immanent transcendence when for the first time a person feels the difference between belief and experience. It can be an ultimate crisis to a long process, or a sudden breaking in by which another reality is glimpsed, but in one way or another conversion is central. Yet, surprisingly, in Gurney's journal, he recorded no distinct conversion experience. He described, using the familiar language of Quaker Quietists, sensing the presence of God as a child, through "precious visitations of Divine love, which often draw the young mind to its Creator, and melt it into tenderness" (Braithwaite, 1855, 22). But he admitted that "... I cannot now recall any decided turning point in this matter, except that which afterwards brought me to plain 'Quakerism'" (Braithwaite, 1855, 22).

For Gurney, the outward adopting of plain dress became symbolic of spiritual transformation, rather than a mystical, or conversion-type experience (Braithwaite, 1855, 36-40). However, the decision to embrace plainness was not simply a doctrinal or rational one, but came about as a sense of "visitation" by God in which a pitting of wills took place – God's will for him vs. his own ego. For Gurney, the submitting by faith to obedience to God became centered on the struggle to sacrifice the dress that symbolized his privileged place in society as an upper class Englishman and the humiliation of adopting the Quaker icon of plain dress, which symbolized identification with his humble spiritual roots and ultimately to Christ. This occurred over a period of four years through a gradual process of renunciation. The first activity he gave up was "field sports," even though he had "often taken great delight in the pursuit of them, but am in my heart convinced that they are morally wrong. I have this day come to my determination, and have solemnly renounced them for ever" (Braithwaite, 1855, 40). He continued the renunciation process by adopting plain speech, then plain dress, and finally, after struggling with the spiritual sacraments, was able to say with conviction, "I have been enabled to unite with Friends in their spirituality, and have thought I had reason to be satisfied with their mode of spiritual worship" (Braithwaite, 1855, 92). He continued however, to harbor some doubts about "silent waiting" (Braithwaite, 1855, 100).

Realizing the central place of a conversion experience in evangelical Christianity, he defended his gradual turning to plain Quakerism as its equivalent by noting:

> Cases of this description are, in my opinion, in no degree at variance with the cardinal Christian doctrine of the necessity of conversion, and to the new birth unto righteousness. The work which effects the vital change from a state of nature to a state of grace, is doubtless often begun in very early childhood – nay it may open on the soul, with the earliest opening of its rational faculties; and that its progress may sometimes be so gradual, as to preclude our perceiving any very distinct steps in it, we may learn from our blessed Lord's parable. (Braithwaite, 1855, 22)

He continued by quoting Jesus' parable of the seed cast into the ground which brings forth fruit, "first the blade, than the ear, than the full corn in the ear" as a biblical teaching for a gradualist conversion (Braithwaite, 1855, 22).

In *Essays* (1884, 528) Gurney alluded to Paul's experience on the Damascus road, yet did not make this dramatic and mystical conversion example paradigmatic. He contrasted Paul's experience with that of most Christians, and described new birth in this way: "But, in general, this vital change is very gradual, and its precise commencement, as well as the daily progress of its growth, are often impalpable alike to the regenerate man himself, and to the persons by whom he is surrounded" (1884, 528). He was unequivocal, however, that "the celestial plant is known by its fruits" (1884, 528).

Despite Gurney's gradualist view of conversion, more of a "Christianization" process as in Anglicanism, his spirituality was nonetheless cast into a modern classical evangelical mold by contemporary Evangelical Quakers. This can be seen, for example, in Donald Green's introduction to the 1979 reprint of Gurney's *Observations on the Religious Peculiarities of the Society of Friends*. Green wrote that "Gurney came to a full surrender of his life to the leadership of Christ at the age of 24" (Gurney, 1979, iv).

Gurney never used the phrase "full surrender to the leadership of Christ." He used the biblical term "new birth" but described it as "the progress of the work of religion – a work, in general, slow and gradual, of which the commencement is regeneration, and the end salvation" (1884, 528). Note that for him the end was salvation – not "entire sanctification" as with Wesley, nor perfection as with historic Quakerism, nor union with God as in Christian mysticism. Salvation for Gurney meant imputed righteousness – one's sins have been atoned for and one is assured of heaven (Jones, 1921, 507).[29] Gurney's doctrine of salvation can be summed up by this statement from his journal:

> The natural and infallible consequence of continued sin is death. There is but one means of escape,– justification through the blessed Saviour.

---

[29] In *Essays* Gurney states that Paul teaches that " 'righteousnesss' is 'imputed' to the believer in Jesus" (1884, 493).

And in this justification we have no part if we are not sanctified by his Holy Spirit, and *always* walk in obedience to his will. (Braithwaite, 1855, 75)

For Gurney, unlike Fox, Barclay, Wesley, and the whole of the Christian mystical tradition, the goal of the Christian life is salvation, consisting of justification-sanctification-obedience, but not perfection. (Unlike Wesley and traditional Quakerism, and in line with Reformed and Lutheran exegesis, Gurney interpreted Romans 7, where Paul describes his inner conflict with sin, as post-conversion struggle rather than pre-conversion struggle)[30] (Gurney, 1884, 529).

4.2.2 Perfection

Gurney never made sanctification a main theme. Perfection was mentioned even more rarely. When he did mention perfection, it was in conjunction with Matthew 5:48, Christ's "a*wful* injunction" (as he calls it), to "be perfect as your Father in heaven is perfect." But he did not elaborate on what this might mean. For Gurney, perfection seemed to mean continual striving to be obedient. His most complete, though still ambivalent, statement on perfection appeared in the context of his comments on Romans 7 and 8:

> Although, therefore, the conflict between the flesh and the Spirit, which strive within us, and are contrary the one to the other, is often long-continued, and perhaps is seldom entirely finished, until the moment when the thread of the Christian's life is cut, and death is swallowed up in victory, we ought, nevertheless, to be consoled and encouraged under the assurance that divine grace is omnipotent, and to press forward with holy diligence and magnanimity towards the only practical standard proposed to us by the Gospel – the standard of uninterrupted piety, charity, and holiness. (1884, 529-530)

Arthur Roberts concurs that Gurney's view of holiness diverged from the traditional Foxian-Barclayan view because he "moderated an earlier more eradicationist understanding of sanctification by offering a more progressivist model" (personal correspondence, Jan. 8, 2000). Although Barclay also offered a progressivist model in that perfection was "never-ending," Barclay's concept included the mystical dimension of becoming "partakers of the divine nature" (see 2.5). Perfection included obedience, but went beyond it into union with

---

[30] "For I do not do the good I want, but the evil I do not want is what I do" (Rom. 7:19, NRSV).

God through Christ (see 1.5.8 and 2.5). For Gurney, this movement into the transcendent did not happen until heaven.[31]

Gurney's doctrine of salvation, therefore, was closer to the mainstream Protestant concept of justification by faith than to the traditional Quaker belief in justification/sanctification completed with perfection (Davie, 1992, 60). Perfection as the holy birth in its fullness was not at the center of his theological vision, as it was for the early Quakers and later Quietists.

Gurney's goal was to bring the Society of Friends into mainstream Protestantism with its emphasis on salvation by faith (1884, viii-ix, 547ff). He wanted to correct any misunderstandings that Quakerism was other than thoroughly Reformation Protestantism. Gurney was sensitive to the fact that even "holiness" could be misunderstood to mean salvation by merit or effort and was careful to point out how this had been misunderstood. For example, he wrote:

> Our frequent declaration of the Christian principle, that without holiness none can see the Lord, or enter into his kingdom, has led some persons to imagine that our Society underrates the importance and necessity of faith. Yet there is probably no truth on which Friends have been more accustomed to dwell, than the Scripture doctrine, that the "just shall live by faith." (1979, 5)

Gurney accentuated the doctrine of justification by faith more forcefully than most earlier Quaker writers, and in the elevation of Protestantism's "faith alone," he was intentionally "correcting" the more Catholic and mystical Quaker doctrine of perfection.

4.2.3 Mysticism

Gurney was a biblical scholar – one of few great ones Friends have produced – and a man of deep and sincere faith. But he did not seem to understand, nor be in touch with, the mystical dimension of Quaker experience. In fact, he seemed to have an antipathy to mysticism (Grubb, 1914a, 67; Wilbur, 1845, 316). Unlike Barclay and even Wesley, who borrowed liberally from Quakers on holiness (see Appendix C), Gurney's spirituality lacked a mystical theology of perfection.

---

[31] William Hodgson, Jr., a nineteenth century Quietist historian, critiqued Gurney's writings and concluded, "there is an entire omission of the doctrine of Christian Perfection; which our early Friends suffered so much for, which they uniformly held forth as an integral part of Divine truth, and which they maintained was to be aimed at by the disciple, and experienced also…" (1856, 18-19).

Edward Grubb notes this missing element in Gurney, and contends that he had "a constitutional incapacity to grasp the meaning of the mystical element in the teaching of the early Friends, and behind them, to early Christianity itself" (1914a, 70). Grubb notes further that Gurney overlooked:

> ...the mystical teaching of John and Paul in regard to the actual indwelling of Christ in the Christian soul. "Christ liveth in me" – "Christ in you, the hope of glory" – "I am the vine, ye are the branches" – "If we love one another, God abideth in us." – this is the language of the deepest Christian experience, but Gurney either barely notices it, or else explains it away. He was learned in patristic lore; but there is no sign that the deep mysticism of the early Greek Fathers touched him in the least. (1914a, 70)

Grubb's critique echoes that of Rufus Jones, who also claimed Gurney was "non-mystical, even anti-mystical" (1921, 529). Grubb, an early liberal Quaker, may be biased against Gurney, yet he has captured one of the difficulties with Gurney's theology in relation to holiness. Gurney's conception of the spiritual life was closer to an evangelical Anglicanism than to Quakerism or Wesleyanism[32] (Punshon, 2001, 21).

Thomas Shillitoe, a leading Quietist evangelical minister from London, made this startling observation about Gurney:

> [He]...is no Quaker in principle. Episcopalian views were imbibed from his education and remain with him. I love the man, for the work's sake, so far as it goes; but he has never been emptied from vessel to vessel, and from sieve to sieve, nor known the baptism of the Holy Ghost and fire, to cleanse the floor of his heart from his Episcopalian notions. (Wilbur, 1845, 344)

Shillitoe, who had been an Anglican himself before joining Quakers, was speaking the language of holiness when he declared that Gurney had never been "emptied from vessel to vessel" nor "known the baptism of the Holy Ghost and fire."[33]

---

[32] Punshon asserts that the first English evangelical Quakers resembled Anglicans in ideas, culture, and philanthropic causes. "It was an elite faith, unsympathetic to Methodist enthusiasm, and hostile to the doctrine of holiness" (2001, 21).

[33] This quote reflects a double irony in that Shillitoe and the Quietist opponents of Gurney claimed that Gurney never experienced the "baptism of the Holy Spirit and fire." This very phrase (with or without the addition of "fire") became the byword of the Quaker Holiness Movement (which looked to Gurney as its model and theologian). It became the designated term for the second work of grace, entire sanctification or perfection (Mott, 1935, 76-80).

Though Gurney was a modernist and an ecumenical, he did not want to relinquish his Quaker identity and thus preserved Quaker distinctives, while reshaping his theology to be in greater conformity to a rationalistic centrist Protestantism. While the trajectory of his thought points more towards liberalism than holiness or evangelicalism as found in pastoral Friends, it is nonetheless American Quaker Evangelicals, known today as the Friends Church, who look at Gurney through a twentieth century lens, and consider him one of their greatest proponents.

Grubb concluded with this evaluation of Gurney's impact on the state of Quakerism in the first quarter of the twentieth century and what he deemed lacking on both sides:

The result is that since his time the Society of Friends, the world over, has been speaking with two voices, and has had no clear and ringing message for the world as it had in its early days. Most of us, in our devotion to doctrine and the historic side of faith, have been in danger of losing the inward Christ, and with this the heart of Quakerism; a minority have maintained the latter, but (for the most part) without the large outlook and the missionary spirit that marked our founders, and which seems to require, as its inspiring force, a devotion – not to doctrine or tradition – but to the person of the historic Jesus as the Redeemer and Healer of man. (1914a, 71)

This is an interesting, almost prophetic comment from a self-identified Quaker liberal who seemed to be lamenting the loss of traditional beliefs, yet could not resonate with Gurney as a bridge between the two voices, even though this seemed to be Gurney's goal and theological vision[34] (Swift, 1962). Quaker mysticism in the early twentieth century began to detach itself from traditional, orthodox Christian doctrine. Rather than a mysticism built on the atonement and incarnation as in historic Quakerism, a "new mysticism" or "natural mysticism" based purely on experience without biblical or doctrinal moorings came into being and became the hallmark of liberal Quakerism. Since Hicksism was developing in a similar way (see. 4.1), by the later twentieth century the liberal Orthodox and the Hicksites were gradually reconciling (Punshon, 1984, 198). Thus, liberalism focused on mystery without moorings; evangelicalism focused on doctrinal moorings but neglected the mystery.

---

[34] He wrote in his journal toward the end of his life, "I adopt and have professed with the utmost openness the middle line, on which account my name is cast out as evil on both sides to a remarkable degree. I wonder I do not mind it more" (Swift, 1962, 182).

4.2.4 Summary and Conclusions

Gurney was indelibly shaped by his intellectualist Oxford education, his Anglican friends and his rational scholarship. He was evangelical in the same sense that mainstream Anglicanism was evangelical in his era. He was not a revivalist, and though his conception of holiness has some similarities to Wesley, in the final analysis he was not Wesleyan, and he would not have been comfortable in the enthusiasms of the American Quaker Holiness Movement, of which he is considered a forerunner. He was an ecumenical Quaker evangelical scholar who espoused what were "centrist" understandings of Christianity current in the mid-nineteenth century. He thought Quakers elevated Barclay's *Apology* too highly and disagreed with Barclay on both perfection and his view of Scripture (Swift, 1962, 177-78).

In comparing Gurney with the historic models of holiness (see Figure 3) this study suggests the following:

1. Gurney did not experience or describe holiness as union with God (Quadrant 3). He lacked the mystical consciousness characteristic of historical Quakerism. He was wary of mystical experience, and frequently condemned all mysticism as close to heresy (Grubb, 1914a, 67). His only work which reflects a touch of the mystical spirit is a devotional writing called *Essay On the Habitual Exercise of Love to God Considered as a Preparation for Heaven* (1840), perhaps his best work. This essay is his most contemplative writing, occasionally touching on deep connections with divine presence, but this work did not have the impact or the broad influence of his doctrinal writings. The title of this essay is a clue to his view of perfection. Our life on earth is only meant to prepare us for perfection in heaven, rather than a seamless garment in which we enter into perfection through an earthly union with Christ.

2. In relation to Quadrant 4, "Imitation of Christ" was not a term used by Gurney; he preferred to speak of the necessity of being committed to "the guidance of this inward Monitor" (1979, 91) He urged the taking up the cross in a "spiritual sense" (1979, 91) which for Gurney, became equated with adopting plain dress and other Quaker distinctives. He rarely spoke of the deeper, mystical aspects of "dying and rising with Christ" which results in total transformation of the whole person. Although he spoke often of obedience, the Anabaptist model of total surrender and death to self was not his usual language; rather he employed a more moderate phrase "daily self-denial" (1979, 91). But again, Gurney's adoption of plainness in speech, dress, and lifestyle (in contrast to his social status) is a relic of this kind of ascetical

holiness. In fact, Gurney felt that Quakers had been led "to adopt a higher and purer standard of action...more exactly conformed to...divine law" than that of other Christians (1979, 376).

3. In relation to Quadrant 2, experiential/charismatic holiness, Gurney is widely seen as representing a turning to an evangelical faith. But emphasis on the new birth, conversion experience, or direct, personal encounter with God was not central to his own experience or the theological vision he formulated. Gurney did emphasize the doctrine of the Holy Spirit, with guidance of the Spirit being a central theme. (Gurney referred to the Light of Christ, or the Inward Light, in the language of the Holy Spirit.) Gifts of the Spirit – even supernatural gifts – were *not* relegated by Gurney to the early church. To do so would have been to deny a foundational tenet of Quaker ministry. The gift of prophecy (as preaching) was paramount for Gurney. However, he did not describe baptism of the Spirit (in a more charismatic sense) as a rapturous experience, but rather a constant sense of presence, guidance, and assurance. Although he attached great prominence to the Holy Spirit, he elevated the Bible above the Spirit as a safeguard against any kind of charismatic heresy or ecstatic enthusiasm, unlike early Quakers.

4. Gurney's thought was anchored in Quadrant 1, the Sacramental/ Holiness model. The rational, cognitive aspect of religion was fundamental to Gurney. He focused much of his writing on a rational defense of Christian orthodoxy. Worship as a sacramental experience, the real presence, in the traditional Quaker sense was prominent in his thought. But unlike the Greek Fathers, he does not connect the incarnation (the Word made flesh) with the potential for perfection (becoming divinized) as early Quakers did. He did not connect the incarnation with its counterpart, *theosis*. Strong emphasis on "faith alone," the mainstream Protestant concept of justification by faith, was the center of his theological vision; sanctification was important, but not as central as in early Friends.

Gurney's three-year ministry in America prompted the second major schism in Quakerdom when the Orthodox split into two branches: the Gurneyites and the Wilburites. The next section examines holiness in Gurney's fiercest Quaker opponent, John Wilbur.

4.3   John Wilbur: Radical Holiness

History has not been kind to John Wilbur.[35] But this section counters the received tradition of Wilbur as a deficient representation of authentic Quakerism and argues instead that he embodies a significant stream of Quaker holiness. While some historians acknowledge the holiness of Wilbur (Hamm, 1988, 29), he is usually presented as a rigid obscurantist clinging to "dead" rather than living tradition, terrified of any kind of change (Jones, 1921, 512-3). Jones failed to fully understand or recognize the issue of deepest concern to Wilbur – the experience of "Christ within, the hope of glory" (Wilbur, 1859, 7-8). Jones found Wilbur's beliefs paradoxical and inconsistent; he had difficulty accepting that Wilbur could hold evangelical beliefs along with the doctrine of the inward Light: "In one compartment the doctrine of an inward Light held complete sway and was the central fact. In another compartment, separated by impervious partitions, he carried along almost all the beliefs of the evangelical churches" (1921, 514). Jones found this a contradiction because he disregarded the fact that early Quaker mystics experienced the divine through the inward Christ, yet also accepted core Christian doctrines, including belief in the historical Christ and the atonement.

Walter Williams' history of Friends, written from an evangelical perspective, echoes Jones on the centrality of the inward Light in Wilbur's thought. Wilbur was a man who "felt certain that in his own life the inward Light was infallible" (Williams, 1987, 175). Hamm concurs that Wilbur "was constantly attentive to what he perceived as the guidance of the Inner Light" (1988, 28). Despite this general agreement among historians (both evangelical and liberal) that Wilbur's spirituality centered on the guidance of the inward Light, these terms are rarely found in his writings. To cast his spirituality as essentially one of "Inner Light" guidance tends to be misleading. Wilbur's phrase of choice was rather "Christ within," or more specifically, "the work of Christ within us," and as I will show, he was careful to remain faithful to Robert Barclay's doctrinal formulations of salvation through Christ alone. Williams does, however, add that Wilbur "held the orthodox doctrines of the Christian faith, *as did early Friends*" [my emphasis] (1987, 175). Jones, on the other hand, contends that Wilbur's orthodoxy is evidence of "how fully the doctrines of orthodox faith had filtered into the minds of even the most conservative

---

[35] Wilbur was born in Hopkinton, Rhode Island, in 1774, the devout son of Quaker parents. He was a part-time teacher, farmer, and surveyor, and a Quaker minister. Identified as a spiritual leader in New England Yearly Meeting, he became an elder in 1802, and was recorded as a minister in 1812 (Barbour and Frost, 1988, 377). Two primary sources exist on Wilbur: *Journal of the Life of John Wilbur, A Minister of the Gospel in the Society of Friends; with Selections from His Correspondence, & c* (1859) and *A Narrative and Exposition of the Late Proceedings of New England Yearly Meeting* (1845).

Friends" (1921, 514). Wilbur was a true disciple of Barclay, and all of his doctrines without exception found their source in a Barclayan theology. What seems to be most paradoxical about Wilbur is why, if he held, as Jones claims, "almost all the beliefs of the evangelical churches," he would become Gurney's staunchest opponent.

Wilbur had been concerned about the spiritual state of Friends for years when a journey to England in 1831-2 provided opportunity to speak out with great relief. He recorded in his journal the grounds of his deep concern for the spiritual state of London Yearly Meeting:

> In this meeting, great professions of faith in the mediation and atonement of Jesus Christ our Lord, were made, and this profession was abundantly reiterated; but still I mournfully felt a great want of that precious sweetness and savor of life, which gives weight and solidity, as well as power, to a meeting; and without which, all the professions of faith, however high and glowing, as to words, are but as sounding brass, and a tinkling symbol. And I am more and more confirmed in the belief that the most full and literally sound acknowledgment may be made, of faith in the blood and sacrifice of Jesus Christ, our blessed Redeemer, and without any reserve too, but still it may be not more than in the oldness of the letter, and that, for want of believing fully in, and of being really and practically quickened by the living power of the gospel, that calls to, and enables to keep the commandments of Christ our Lord, by whose spirit and grace we are sanctified through obedience, and those who are thus sanctified, cannot be otherwise than believers. (1859, 123-4)

Wilbur vigorously affirmed the propitiatory atonement of Christ, but his fears revolved around the ease with which the doctrine was merely *professed* and not experienced internally, resulting in obedience. What was missing for Wilbur amidst eager "professions" of faith in the atonement was a sense of the "sweetness and savor of life" (true spiritual joy) as well as "power" – being "really and practically quickened by the living power of the gospel" (1859, 123). Wilbur's passionate concern for the authenticity and power of true sanctification was the essence of Quaker holiness.

His descriptions of other meetings during his travels in England reveal a soul keenly sensitive to the real presence of the Divine, and also reveal the heart of an evangelist. For example, he described a meeting:

> …which was pretty long silent and painful, but at length the clouds were dispelled, and the trumpet of alarm was blown among them, and my companion joined me in calling them to the life and power; and the meeting ended well…. Next day…had an open, soul-solacing meeting, in which the invitation of the gospel of Christ ran forth like the limpid

stream, to the watering and contriting of several tender minds among the young people; and, I believe, that all were sensible of the precious descending of the celestial shower that fell upon us.... (1859, 127)

He often compared "a painful, silent meeting" with "a heavenly, solacing meeting" (1859, 127). He recorded what could only be described as an evangelistic meeting with "the town's-people" in Warwick in which "it appeared to be my business to open the plan of Christian Redemption, through the blessed mediation of Christ Jesus, outwardly and inwardly, and, as I continued speaking, the power rose and increased and it became a solid, baptizing time" (1859, 128).

Wilbur concisely summed up his understanding of Christian redemption in this way: salvation is both "the work of Christ within us" and the "work without us" (1859, 587). Wilbur concluded, "if we reject either of these provisions for our salvation, we cannot be saved" (1859, 587).

4.3.1   Divine Indwelling

Under the heading in his *Narrative* called "The anointing – Christ in man," Wilbur contrasted Gurney's views of the indwelling Christ with his own (representing historical Quakerism) (1845, 315). The dispute revolved around their different interpretations of a key biblical passage for Wilbur (also a key text for Barclay, and the Christian mystical tradition in general) (Sippel, 2002, 120).

The biblical text in question is Colossians 1:26-7: "the mystery which hath been hid from ages and generations, but now is made manifest unto the saints." Vs. 27 explains what this mystery is: "that God would make known what is the riches of the glory of this mystery among the Gentiles which is 'Christ in you,' the hope of Glory'" (Col. 1:27). Wilbur quoted Gurney's indictment that the words "'Christ in you' are often recited by mistake as 'Christ within'[36] and that these expressions are sometimes used amongst us as a synonyme (*sic*) for the light of the Spirit of Christ in the heart – a view which some have imagined to be supported by the apostle's treating the whole subject as a "mystery"[37] (1845, 315). Gurney's interpretation of "mystery" was that it referred only to the incarnation of the Son of God – God's coming in the flesh as a human being (Wilbur, 1845, 316). Thus, Gurney limited the term mystery to the incarnation as a historic event. But for Wilbur, the "mystery" clearly encompassed much more, that of the mystical indwelling Christ, as Paul himself clearly points out in vs. 27: "the mystery which is 'Christ in you, the hope of glory.'" Thus,

---

[36] This is Barclay's rendering; see Sippel, 2002, 192, from the earliest English ed., 1678.
[37] Mystery is the translation of the Greek word *mystikos*, from whence comes the term mysticism.

mystery in Wilbur's understanding referred both to the incarnation – God in Christ, in fleshly human form – and also the other glorious side of the mystery, divinization – "Christ within, the hope of glory"[38] (1845, 315). This was the full and complete Christian mystery as realized by Wilbur and early Friends. It was a more "mystical" view, but also a biblical one, the heart of Pauline mysticism, and as valid an interpretation as Gurney's more limited one. Indeed, it is a long-held interpretation in the Christian tradition (see 1.2, 1.5.7 and 1.7.5). Gurney's limiting the mystery to the incarnation of Christ only is evidence of his more rational interpretation and lack of a mystical consciousness. Gurney defended his view by quoting the official position of London Yearly Meeting:

> As the Holy Spirit influences our hearts, and enlightens our understandings, we are brought to a lively apprehension of the character and offices of the Messiah, and Christ received by faith into the soul, and, ruling there by his Spirit, becomes our sure and only hope of glory. (Wilbur, 1845, 316)

The actual experience of Christ, which Gurney was describing, may not have been ultimately very different from that which Wilbur so ardently defended, but the language of Quaker mystical piety was much less pronounced. It was less intimate, less mutual, and less mysterious, and was deliberately meant to be so, as Gurney then explained, "Here then is a full testimony to vital, practical, inward religion, but no mysticism" (Wilbur, 1845, 316). Gurney was, in effect, giving a nod to "inward religion," but the experiential relationship to Christ that he preferred was a non-mystical and less overwhelming one – the Spirit influences the heart and enlightens the understanding, thus allowing the mind to apprehend the character and offices of Christ, and by faith the Spirit rules in our souls. For Wilbur (just as for Fox, Barclay and other early Quakers), "Christ in you" meant divine indwelling and union with God, an utterly overwhelming experience. "Christ in you" was a state of being which is often called *perfectio* (perfection or union) in classical Western theology and *theosis* in Greek theology (Soelle 2001; Louth, 2003, 221-3) (see also 1.7.5).

The aftermath of the Hicksite split gave mysticism a bad name among the Orthodox. Gurney, I suggest, was equating mysticism with Hicksism. The quote from the General Epistle was written as a reaction to the Hicksite controversy. Hicksites were considered "mystical," and thus mystical was equated with heretical. It was in this context that Gurney explained why a "mystical" interpretation of "Christ within" diminishes Christ. Gurney conceded that his alternative interpretation of "mystery" had long been held, though it remained relatively unnoticed and nonproblematic until highlighted by the "opposition" [Hicksites]. The Hicksites used it to support their excessive elevation of the inward Light, which Gurney called heresy (and Wilbur named apostasy)

---

[38] This significant difference was recognized by Edward Grubb; see. 4.2.3.

(Wilbur, 1859, 278). Both men believed Hicksites, in effect, denied the incarnation and divinity of Christ. Thus, Gurney could say,

> ...the errors themselves have naturally enough been suffered to pass with but little notice. But with some who have seceded from us in America, they have evidently *been the means of aiding* that tremendous process in heresy, by which the Eternal Word, or Son of God, is gradually converted into a mere influence, and finally becomes nothing at all but a seed sown in the hearts of all men. (Wilbur, 1845, 316-7)

Robert Barclay defended the "inward Christ" in his *Apology* in the fifth and sixth proposition, "Of Universal and Saving Light." In this context he highlighted the phrase so loved by Wilbur, "Christ within the hope of Glory," as the central theme of Quaker preaching: "This is that Christ within, which we are heard so much to speak and declare of, everywhere preaching him up, and exhorting people to believe in the light, and obey it, that they may come to know Christ in them, to deliver them from all sin" (Sippel, 2002, 120-1; Wilbur, 1845, 317). Thus, it was Barclay's doctrine that Gurney was in effect considering an "error" and equating with mysticism. Barclay never reduced Christ to a seed, but argued for the universal light – the seed in all humanity, which, when the spiritual birth occurs, allows the seed to grow into the full, entire, holy birth of perfection, or holiness. Barclay (and Wilbur who quoted him on this) was careful to make the critical differentiation between being "in Christ" and claiming equality with Christ: "...we do not at all intend to equal ourselves to that holy man the Lord Jesus Christ" and also to refute the charge that Quakers do not value the person of Christ, either as a real man or glorified in heaven: "so neither do we destroy the reality of his present existence.... as we believe he was a true and real man" (Wilbur, 1845, 317-8).

The crux of the dilemma for Gurney came in expanding "the mystery" to "Christ in you" (which Gurney implied was a Quaker error to start with – but little noticed), in that it opened the door to heresy. Suspicion and distrust has often been the accusation against the mystic.[39] Wilbur, however, posed an interesting dilemma because he was an excellent example of an "orthodox mystic," which Gurney, and later, Jones, both considered an oxymoron. For Gurney, orthodoxy was not compatible with mysticism. For Jones, a generation later, mysticism was not compatible with orthodoxy. However, the patristic and medieval understanding of "the mystery of Christ" referred to the mystery of the incarnation *and* the indwelling Spirit. This mutual indwelling, the doctrine of the incarnation completed by humanity's perfection or deification, was summed up by Athanasius in the familiar refrain, "God became man that man

---

[39] A common denigration of mysticism is found in this oft-quoted quip: "Mysticism begins in mist and ends in schism."

might become God." [40] Wilbur's understanding of the Christian mystery, the incarnation, salvation, perfection and divine union – the inward and the outward Christ – followed a long strand of mystical piety within the orthodox Christian tradition (divine union is called *perfectio* in medieval theology, e.g. Aquinas). This mystical piety was neglected by the Protestant Reformation and subsumed by the scholastic theology it left in its wake, but was revived by a broad movement of awakening of "heart religion" in the seventeenth century, of which Quakerism became one of its prime manifestations and enduring forms (Campbell, 1991) (see also Appendix B). They discovered anew the mystery of Christ – the indwelling Christ – by experiencing it firsthand.[41]

4.3.2 Quaker Communion

One other significant area in which Wilbur contrasted Gurney's views with those of an earlier Quakerism is somewhat of a surprise (given Gurney's appreciation for traditional Quaker silent worship) (Jones, 1921, 96). However, Gurney struggled with the spiritual nature of Quaker communion, and this is reflected in his differences with Wilbur concerning the spiritual nature of Quaker communion and its relation to the "body and blood of Christ."[42] Wilbur quoted Gurney's references to numerous passages in which Christ speaks of his body and blood – and the eating and drinking of it. For Gurney, all references to the body and blood refer only to Christ's "atoning sacrifice," his historical death on the cross. The body and blood of Christ did not take on mystical meaning as they did for Wilbur. Even when Gurney quoted Jesus saying, "Except ye eat the flesh of the Son of Man, and drink his blood, ye have no life in you," he was still able to maintain that "the flesh *always* means his human body – that body which was born, died, and rose again – and that his blood *always* means his very blood, which was his natural life, and which was naturally shed on the cross for the remission of sins" (Wilbur, 1845, 320).

---

[40] This ancient formulation was developed in Western spirituality as "mutual indwelling through love" by no less than the greatest Dominican scholar and champion of Christian orthodoxy, St. Thomas Aquinas, in his *Summa Theologica*.

[41] Barclay, in one of several instances where he is compelled to provide personal testimony in his *Apology*, on his doctrine of divine indwelling writes, "This seems strange to carnal-minded men, because they are not acquainted with it: but we know it, and are sensible of it, by a true and certain experience. Though it be hard for man in natural wisdom to comprehend it, until he come to feel it in himself" (qtd. in Wilbur, 1845, 318).

[42] Swift explains, "The Quaker practice which Gurney found hardest to accept was abandonment of sacraments. He had some reservations about it in 1812, when he decided to become a plain Friend, and he still struggled with it in 1826 after he had done his best reasoning defending Quaker practice" (1962, 134).

Wilbur compared Gurney's view of the body and blood of Christ with Barclay, who though discarding the use of the material elements, continued to understand communion as the body and blood of Christ in a true sacramental sense as Christ's real presence, and as "a mystery hid from all natural men" (Barclay, 2002, 374):

> The body then of Christ, which believers partake of, is spiritual, and not carnal; and his blood, which they drink of, is pure and heavenly, and not human or elementary, as Augustine also affirms, which is eaten in his *Tractat.* Psalm. 98. Except a man eat my flesh, he hath not in him life eternal: and he saith, The words which I speak unto you are Spirit and life; understand spiritually what I have spoken." (Sippel, 2002, 374)

Eating the body and blood of Christ thus represented more than a symbolic designation of the objective doctrine of the atonement; it referred to an inward experience of mystical communion, "fellowship and communion with God" (Wilbur, 1845, 321). Although Barclay was refuting transubstantiation, he was not denying the mystical aspect of communion (the mystery of participation in the body and blood of Christ, the divine-human encounter that really happened in Quaker communion). Barclay and Wilbur had a much higher, more sacramental view of communion than did Gurney. Again, Gurney's lack of a mystical proclivity or sensitivity seems evident in his objective view of the atonement and distancing from Barclay's explanation.[43]

One other significant point of difference between the two is that Gurney treated sanctification as *subsequent* to justification (following Wesley's formulation). Wilburites (as did early Quakers) believed you could not be justified unless you were also sanctified. In fact, sanctification was often mentioned first – Wilbur quoted Barclay, who was in fact quoting Scripture (I Cor. 6:11): "as we are sanctified, so are we justified in the sight of God" (Wilbur, 1845, 2; Sippel, 2002). This position of Gurney's, following Wesley's *ordo salutis,* helped pave the way for Wesleyan holiness to supplant Quietist holiness among Orthodox Friends.

---

[43] The Quakers' attack on their contemporaries' *use* of the sacraments must not be understood as spurning any need for participation in the "body and blood of Christ," but as a protest against the *abuse* of those rites which had become merely a ceremony covering over lives devoid of true holiness, yet allowing its participants to nonetheless claim it. Luther's denouncing of monasticism as masking true perfection in light of rampant abuses of those monastic vows can be seen as a parallel protest – the unmasking of a false holiness – rites or vows as "works," which by themselves justify no person.

4.3.3 Summary and Conclusions

In 1845, Wilbur and his supporters separated from New England Yearly Meeting and set up a new Yearly Meeting with the same name (Cooper, 1999, 4-5). Wilburite sympathizers in other Yearly Meetings soon joined the Wilburite movement, and thus a third branch of Quakerism formed, known as the Wilburite Friends. By the mid-nineteenth century three separate branches of Quakers existed in America: Orthodox (Gurneyite), Hicksite, and Wilburite. By the twentieth century, Wilburites came to be known as Conservative Friends, maintaining primitivist traditions and Quietist sectarian ways.

Wilbur's primary criticism of Gurney's practice and ministry he called "the spirit and friendship of the world." Wilbur deeply desired to maintain "plainness and self-denial" and "the Quaker hedge." Wilbur represents holiness lived out in a semi-monastical form, an ascetical withdrawal from the world, a radical detachment, which turns its back on the culture and allurements of the world. Wilbur's great fear was that Gurney would pave the way for "easy union with the world" (1859, 567).

Wilbur used the ascetical language of the monk or mystic, commonly spoken by the true Quietist: "to die with Christ," "true self-denial," "conformity to the cross of Jesus Christ," and "yielding up the will" (1859, 272-3). These were the phrases cherished by Wilbur to express his understanding of sanctification. Sanctification was "submitting to die with Christ, and to abide the painful struggle of yielding up the will and wisdom of the flesh" (1859, 273). Worldliness was simply incompatible with sanctification. Wilbur maintained one could not be a true follower of Christ without possessing so much of the spirit and power of the cross as to enable the "mortifying of the deeds of the body; to the sanctifying of the spirit, and to the subjugation of the will of the flesh" (1859, 593-4). This is indeed the language of strict asceticism. Wilbur did not think Quakers were the only spiritual community to "take up the cross," but often pointed out that the Society of Friends from its beginnings:

> ...found it needful to adhere to greater purity of manners than other professors had done, in order to be more perfect followers of his example, as well as of his doctrines of the strait and narrow way which leads to life; believing indeed the verity and truth of his sayings. (1859, 594)

Wilbur felt passionately that holiness, symbolized by bearing the cross, was a special calling of Friends given to them as a deeper spiritual insight. It was Quakerism's *raison d'etre:* "as a people we have seen more clearly than others the necessity of bearing about in the body the dying of the Lord Jesus Christ" (1859, 594). And this meant detachment from the culture and allure of the world, "denying all desires after the maxims, manners, fashions, and customs of this vain world" (1859, 594).

Wilbur contrasted Gurney's views on sanctification with his own by showing the implications of Gurney's position:

> Christ's incarnate suffering and propitiatory sacrifice upon the cross ...as the *whole* covenant of salvation, and by him thus accomplished without them; and, consequently, it is feared are carnally believing and trusting in this alone for justification, without its essential concomitant, the true obedience of faith, and the work of sanctification wrought in the heart. (1859, 273) [Wilbur's emphasis]

Wilbur essentially accused Gurney of "cheap grace," to use Bonhoeffer's familiar contemporary terminology.

Gurney believed in the incarnation as passionately as did Wilbur, but Wilbur suspected (apparently correctly) that Gurney did not believe in perfection as that "whole covenant of salvation," but instead taught only the necessity of belief in an external, historical event. Just as later holiness revivalists would urge the necessity of "pressing on to perfection," Wilbur preached that faith is made manifest in obedience. Instead of a gospel of justification by faith alone, Wilbur claimed the gospel is justification by faith and obedience. Free grace, yes – but justification included sanctification, or the cooperation with grace by obedience, which is the fruit of faith (1845, 14-15; 1859, 286).

Gurney and Wilbur both felt they were remaining true to spiritual Christianity and loyal to Quaker tradition, but Wilbur conformed more closely to Barclay and early Quaker understandings of holiness and perfection than Gurney. Theologically they may have been but a hair's-breadth apart, but they emphasized what they considered crucial distinctions. Their conflict reflects the danger of an emphasis becoming exclusive. As the tendency to emphasize the difference escalates, positions harden, and alienation occurs. The difference becomes critical, and then it must be vindicated at all costs or the spirit of the distinction will be lost. The volumes of letters and verbatim on Wilbur's opposition to Gurney is evidence of this spiraling effect. Wilbur firmly believed he was called as a prophetic voice to uphold traditional Quaker testimonies, doctrines, and practice, and if they could not be maintained without controversy, then they must be maintained with controversy. For Wilbur, "...the cause of the blessed Truth is worthy both of controversy, and of a warfare too, under the banners of the Prince of Peace" (1859, 595).

Wilburite spirituality falls within all four holiness quadrants (see Figure 3). His emphasis on the historical, sacramental view of Quaker communion as well as the necessity for faith in the historical atonement draws on Quadrant 1. But he was also insistent that faith must be manifested by the kinds of holiness in the other three Quadrants: it must be experiential, be discovered through silence and mystical union, and result in imitation of Christ through obedience.

His attention to the guidance of the Spirit and the expectation of Spirit-filled worship ("celestial showers") drew heavily on the experiential aspects of Quadrant 2. The mysticism of Quadrant 3 is unmistakable; especially prominent is the apophatic dimension of silence. And the insistence on obedience with an ascetical lifestyle of cross-bearing finds its source in Quadrant 4.

That Wilbur stands well within the radical holiness tradition of early Friends is attested to by his staunch commitment to a Barclayan theology, with a mystical and ascetical perfection remaining a central theme. Perfection is realized through the mystical experience of "Christ within, the hope of glory," and evidenced by a life of imitation of Christ in his suffering and humility. The cross becomes the symbol *par excellence* of Wilbur's spirituality, which he bore through the dark night of the *via negativa*.[44]

4.4 Chapter Summary

In the nineteenth century, holiness in Quakerism took many divergent paths. The first branching off of the historical holiness path came with the Hicksite-Orthodox separation. The rationalist enlightenment liberalism of the Hicksite branch emphasized the ethical aspects of holiness and gradually severed its ties to the historic Christ and core Christian doctrines. The Orthodox became more rationalistic as well, and with Gurney holiness became decidedly less mystical. Biblical authority and orthodox Christian doctrines were emphasized, but with a reduced focus on divine indwelling of the mystical Christ. A subsequent division between the Gurneyites and Wilburites caused a further polarization between advocates of a more apophatic spirituality centered in the mystical Christ of Quietism and the kataphatic spirituality of the historical Christ of Quaker orthodoxy.

Thomas Hamm concludes that Wilbur's resistance to Gurney was based on his fear of any compromising of Friends' stance toward holiness. Doctrinal differences between Gurney and Wilbur, however much Wilbur split hairs with Gurney (and they seemed important hairs at the time), were actually quite slight; this study argues that the way to holiness was the central issue between the two. Wilburites "feared that contact with the world, even with the most benevolent and humane interactions, would distract Friends from the great struggle of the soul towards holiness" (Hamm, 1988, 28). Wilbur's prime consuming ideal that led him to resist Gurney's evangelical activism was his

---

[44] From a contemporary perspective Wilbur's spirituality of cross-bearing could be taken as an example of the deeply ingrained tradition of Christian masochism. Some might even consider it a mask for piety, but the intensity of his devotion and passion has an unmistakable authenticity about it. For Wilbur, the cross is strength, power, life, and even joy (Wilbur, 1859, 124, 127).

passion for holiness. Wilbur preached against what he discerned to be Gurney's diminished concept of holiness. Perhaps Orthodoxy's repudiation of Wilbur depleted their spirituality of some of its mystical richness, and left many Orthodox meetings with their own form of Quaker scholasticism. Perhaps the departure of the Wilburites with their primitive mystical piety left a vacuum for the emergence of a new and more emotionally charged form of revivalistic holiness to explode upon the next generation of Orthodox Friends, whose quest for perfection burst out of the monastic-like cloister of Quietist holiness in the 1860s. The next section will examine Quaker reactions to the Holiness Revival of the later nineteenth century.

In comparing Hicksism, Wilburites, and Gurneyites (Orthodox) to the eight essential elements (see 1.5) we find that (1) for Hicksites, Scripture became completely subordinated to experience; for Gurneyites, Scripture became the primary authority and it was interpreted less mystically-symbolically and more rationally-literally (despite the fact the Gurney claimed to hold the traditional Quaker position). Wilburites maintained the historical balance between Scripture and the Holy Spirit. (2) Eschatology was not a major concern for any of the three branches. Both Hicksites and Wilburites would most likely assume the traditional view that Christ had come again within them. Gurney did not address eschatology. (3) For Hicksites, conversion meant obedience to the Light within, and in time became subordinated to bonding with the community. For most Gurneyites, conversion became a gradual process of conforming to Christian principles and Quaker practices. For Wilburites, theologically conversion meant justification-sanctification and it continued to be a deeply spiritual moment of self-transcendence. (4) For Hicksites, evangelism gradually diminished in importance, though ministry within the community continued to be essential. For the more progressive Hicksites, radical politics replaced evangelism. For Gurneyites, evangelism and social reform were integrated and became important forms of outreach. Wilburites became increasingly sectarian, and isolation from culture and society restricted ministry to community nurture. (5) All three branches maintained a strong focus on charisma as the leading of the Spirit. Among Hicksites, this leading became a guiding tenet, but the spirit (the Inner Light) became a principle in the conscience rather than a relationship to a divine person, and not necessarily identified with Jesus Christ. Gurneyites also emphasized guidance of the Spirit, but more intentionally used the language of the Holy Spirit. Wilburites maintained the most mystical understanding and expectation of charisma in the manner of early Friends. (6) All three groups replaced suffering with embracing the testimonies (plainness and the peace testimony), which continued to be an important source of differentiation from other religious groups. Wilburites were the most ascetical and maintained the strongest ethic of redemptive suffering. (7) Apophatic mysticism was retained in silent worship for all three branches. Only Wilburites maintained a strong emphasis on mysticism as essential to a holy life. Gurneyites became increasingly suspect of mysticism, and even viewed it as heretical. They were also increasingly open to the possibility of other forms of worship as they became more ecumenical and accommodated themselves to mainstream evangelicalism. (8) For Hicksites, perfection consisted in obedience and ethical action. For Gurneyites perfection as a doctrine became increasingly marginal. Only Wilburites maintained the historic Quaker doctrine of perfection as both mystical and ethical (see Figure 4, p. 323).

CHAPTER 5

Quakerism and the Holiness Revival

5.1 The American Holiness Movement

Beginning in the 1830s and reaching its peak in the 1870s, the holiness revival vitalized American denominations. Religious leaders preached personal and social "holiness unto the Lord." They taught a heightened spirituality, often termed "Christian perfection" (Dieter, 1996). The movement first arose from within mainstream American Methodism as a reaction to the perceived neglect of John Wesley's doctrine of perfection. Leaders within the Methodist Church became convinced that the neglect of the doctrine manifested itself in declension in the church. The doctrine of perfection had been the "crown jewel" of Methodism, its primary spiritual legacy to the Protestant church. These revival evangelists were found chiefly among the Methodists, but prominent leaders arose within every American Protestant denomination (Smith, 1980 [1957], 135-6). The Presbyterian minister, Charles G. Finney, the leading revivalist of the period, is well-known for preaching a message of Christian perfection. Even some of the more culturally separatist Mennonite and Brethren communities were impacted by the holiness revival during this era. But no other non-Methodist tradition came under the spell of holiness to the depth and degree as the Society of Friends. Under the influence of the Holiness Movement, entire communities of Quakers, particularly in the Midwest and far West, adopted new forms of worship, theology and ecclesiology that transformed traditional Quaker meetings into evangelical churches (Jones, 1974, 60-61).

Thomas Hamm has documented the radical changes within Quakerism during the nineteenth century. His work provides a sociological analysis and framework to understand the various forces that shaped and altered Quaker traditions in that period (1988). He presents Quakerism as a striking, yet complex, example of the inevitable processes of acculturation to the dominant values of mainstream society that shape every "sectarian" group. Hamm examines the Holiness Movement's impact on Quakers as one manifestation of this overall phenomenon. But the process of acculturation cannot fully explain the most intriguing aspect of this phenomenon. Why were Quakers so receptive to *this particular form* of the revival movement and why did it captivate and re-radicalize a vast segment of the tradition as a whole? Hamm provides some insights into the period that help us understand why the Society of Friends was ripe for change and renewal (1988, 88). Acknowledging that a combination of sociological, cultural, and even economic factors ultimately played a major part in the divisions and transformations of Quakerism, as Hamm (1988) and others have shown (Barbour and Frost, 1988), this study argues that the holiness revival met the spiritual longings of so many Friends because of its strong connections to the Quaker holiness heritage of early Friends, a heritage rooted in a Christ-centered mystical vision of perfection.[1] The optimistic perfectionism of the Holiness Movement re-ignited among nineteenth century Quakers the Christ-mysticism that had permeated and fueled the Quaker awakening of the seventeenth century.

The vision of perfection reclaimed by holiness theology produced a very intentional, transformative spirituality that promoted both personal piety and an activist social ministry -- in effect, an "ethical mysticism" that resonated with the Quaker call to holy living. Unlike earlier American revivalism, personal salvation/conversion was not the primary concern of the American Holiness Movement. The primary concern was sanctification, the fruits of conversion lived out in a holy life of devotion to God and neighbor. The holiness revival was clearly evangelistic in its outlook and deeply concerned with saving the sinner and redeeming the backslider. Nevertheless, it focused primarily and uniquely on persuading people to seek and experience the mystical moment of

---

[1] In addition to the ideal of perfection rooted in mystical theology, the Holiness Movement also embraced a spirituality that affirmed the value and authority of women's experience. With a significant core of female revivalists promoting and defending women's right to preach, the historical parallels with early Quakerism were obvious. The Holiness Movement tapped into a stream of spirituality that appropriated both imagery and authority from the female mystical tradition. (See Kate Galea, "Anchored Behind the Veil: Mystical Vision as a Possible Source of Authority in the Ministry of Phoebe Palmer," *MH* 31, 1993, 243-247.) One of the most obvious external parallels within the Holiness Movement and Quakerism is the role that women played in the leadership and development of both traditions. The founder and initial force behind the holiness revival was a Methodist woman, Phoebe Palmer, a grass roots organizer, preacher, teacher, devotional writer, popular theologian, and humanitarian (White, 1986). Phoebe Palmer's *The Way of Holiness,* one of the most widely read holiness publications, is full of feminine mystical imagery (Galea, 1993). Madame Guyon, the French mystic, was immensely popular among holiness adherents. A biography of Guyon written by a well-known holiness leader, Thomas Upham, became a best-seller. When the goal of perfection as well as the goal of spiritual equality merged within a popular renewal movement, the resulting spiritual vision proved irresistible to many Quaker women. For example, Hannah Whitall Smith, nurtured in the mystical Quietism of traditional Quakerism, found spiritual renewal and inspiration within the Holiness Movement and became one of its leading evangelists (see 5.4). In fact, a substantial number of Quaker holiness leaders were female. (Thomas Hamm mentions at least ten by name; see 1988, 78-84.) Among Orthodox Quakers in the 19th century, a number of women influenced by the holiness revival became social activists with culturally radical agendas. They became the "evangelical" counterparts to the radical Hicksite feminists, such as Susan B. Anthony and Lucretia Mott. (See Spencer, "Evangelism, Feminism, and Social Reform," *QH* 80, 1991, 24-48.)

entire sanctification that occurred subsequent to conversion. Holiness advocates saw entire sanctification as a breaking in of the Holy Spirit that empowered the individual to live a righteous and obedient life. This experience was often referred to as the "Baptism of the Spirit," a phrase and concept familiar to traditional Quakers (Dayton, 1996, 88-89).

The Holiness Movement also resonated with Quakers because both traditions shared the same rootedness in the contemplative, inner life of devotion and prayer. The energetic combination of piety and prophecy characteristic of the holiness revival found a ready audience among Quakers yearning for a deeper experience of religion. Among many younger Quakers especially, the long periods of silence that were so meaningful to previous generations seemed deadening and unproductive (Hamm, 1988, 88). The spirit of the Holiness Movement must have reminded Quakers familiar with their early history of the heady days of the charismatic exuberance of Fox and the first Quaker awakening.

The quest for perfection, both personal and social, of the American Holiness Movement resonated with nineteenth century Quakers to such an extent that it reshaped an entire generation of Quaker leaders. Within a span of less than forty years (from 1860-1895), about two-thirds of the Quaker constituency gradually moved from a Quietist, apophatic form of Christian spirituality to the pietistic, kataphatic spirituality favored by Wesley, which has permanently shaped American evangelicalism. The Quietist holiness impulses that predominated in religious circles of the late seventeenth and early eighteenth centuries moderated the behavior of the second generation of Quakers. The extremes of "enthusiasm" and ecstasy of the earliest Quaker spirituality have their parallels in groups within the Holiness Movement of the nineteenth century. In fact, by the turn of the century, American Pentecostalism emerged from the more radical fringes of the Holiness Movement to spin off a new spiritual movement, and drew into this new stream some Quaker leaders as well.[2]

It is the contention of this study that the nineteenth century holiness revival and the Quaker tradition of holiness had natural spiritual affinities that drew vast numbers of Quakers into its embrace, despite the difference in forms of worship. Ultimately many holiness Quakers adopted the forms and practices of the revival culture. Paid pastors, worship focused on preaching, hymn-singing, and altar calls became commonplace. Some congregations even practiced the rites of water baptism and communion with bread and wine. As Quaker meetings became Quaker churches, once again deep divisions polarized the Society of Friends. The next section will explore some reactions to holiness revivalism.

---

[2] One notable example is A. J. Tomlinson, an Indiana Quaker who founded one of the largest Pentecostal denominations, the Church of God, Cleveland.

5.2 Reactions to Revivalism: Joel Bean

Some historians portray Joel Bean[3] as the martyr of the "moderates" within the Orthodox body (Hamm, 1988, 139). Bean is usually cast as a moderate Quaker who only wanted to maintain tradition, but if that were the sum of the case, Bean would have aligned himself with the Conservatives (Hamm, 1988, 139). Bean, however, had a different agenda than simply preserving tradition. Like his predecessor, Joseph John Gurney, Bean's loyalty and appreciation for the traditional "form" of Quaker worship tended to mask what was in effect a significant new direction toward a broadly ecumenical vision for a new Quakerism. Bean, I maintain, was not a moderate in his time, but rather the voice of a Quaker modernist. His position represents the natural outcome of Gurneyite ecumenism.

In the early years of the revival, Joel Bean was among its cautious supporters. Hamm dates the beginnings of the first modern revival among Friends to a meeting at Bear Creek Meeting in Iowa early in 1867 (1988, 76). In 1867 Bean became clerk of Iowa Yearly Meeting, until his departure in 1872 when he felt called to visit Friends in Great Britain and also New England.

The Beans were then absent from Iowa for five years, which became a pivotal time for both the Beans and Iowa Yearly Meeting. While Bean absorbed British and New England forms of Quakerism and had exposure to the cultural and literary circles in the East, Iowa Yearly Meeting was being exposed to revivalist forms of Christian perfection preached by a new breed of dynamic Quaker evangelists. These evangelists were influenced by the interdenominational National Association for the Promotion of Holiness, a group organized in Philadelphia in 1867, with strong Methodist leadership, for the establishment of camp meetings as a method for promoting spiritual renewal. Bean and Iowa revivalists were traveling on two different highways, but since both desired leadership of the Yearly Meeting, they were on a collision course. Bean was moving towards the cultural-religious mainstream, and Iowa towards a more counter-cultural grassroots mystical pietism. Both adamantly claimed they were recovering true Quakerism – Bean the pure, spiritual, universalism of Quakerism, and the revivalists, the power of a transformational conversion and the experience of true holiness.

---

[3] Joel Bean (1825-1914), teacher and Quaker minister, was born in Alton, New Hampshire, and moved to Iowa in 1853. In 1858, Iowa, being then a part of Indiana Yearly Meeting, recorded Bean as a minister (Le Shana, 1969, 49). In 1859 Bean married Hannah Shipley, a daughter of wealthy Philadelphia Quakers who were prominent members of the Orthodox Arch Street Meeting (Le Shana, 1969, 49). The Beans were respected for their spiritual leadership in the West Branch Iowa community in the early years of the revival, and in part through their ministry, Iowa Yearly Meeting was established in 1863 (Le Shana, 1969, 52).

When the Beans returned to Iowa in 1877, the Yearly Meeting immediately appointed him again as their clerk. By this time, revivals of holiness had swept through the western meetings, and had the support of much of the leadership of western Quakers. But just as in the Methodist Church, where Christian perfection was the "grand depositum" of Methodism (Peters, 1985, 196) and enthusiastic revivals were part of the fabric of their tradition, the Holiness Movement nevertheless drew intense opposition from some quarters. Shortly after Bean's appointment as clerk, a conservative split occurred in Iowa Yearly Meeting. During the next 25 years, four more Yearly Meetings experienced conservative splits, but Iowa Yearly Meeting endured the most bitter divisions. The splits occurred over reaction to revivals, use of pastors, and understandings of the Inward Light (Barbour and Frost, 1988, 213-214). Joel Bean's attitude toward revivals changed during his time in England and New England, and soon after his return to Iowa he became a vocal opponent of revivalism. Yet, when Iowa Yearly Meeting split in 1877, the Beans chose to remain with the main body of holiness evangelicals, rather than the conservatives (Le Shana, 1969, 54).

Tensions continued and Bean began to write widely and influentially on his opposition to the revival movement (Le Shana, 1969, 59). In 1879 he wrote on "The Light Within" for the *Friends Review*, the Philadelphia Gurneyite Journal, and in 1881 spread his views to England with an article entitled "The Issue," his very personal critique of the Holiness Movement. When the *British Friend* published it in March 1881,[4] it created a storm of controversy, and marked the beginning of London Quakers' repudiation of evangelicalism and growing sympathy for Wilburites and Hicksites (Barbour and Frost, 1988, 213).[5]

At Iowa Yearly Meeting in September of that same year, David B. Updegraff, a visiting holiness preacher from Ohio, challenged the views expressed by Bean in "The Issue" (Hamm, 1988, 139). When Iowa Yearly Meeting gave Updegraff a "returning minute" (a formal affirmation of his ministry), Bean felt rejected. In 1882 the Beans moved to San Jose, California, to escape the tensions in Iowa (and perhaps as a reaction to the discounting of his once influential leadership in Iowa) (Barbour and Frost, 1988, 213; Le Shana 1969, 61).

---

[4] "The Issue," *BF*, 39, originally published March, 1881, 49-51. It was republished in *BF*, 41, November 1, 1883, 282-284.

[5] Only five years earlier, a respected British minister, Walter Robson, visited America and attended sessions at all of the Western Yearly Meetings during the height of revival enthusiasm. Other than his first exposure to a holiness devotional meeting in Ohio led by David Updegraff, which was an entirely new experience for him and left him initially with mixed feelings, his impressions of the spirituality of the Holiness revival were generally favorable and supportive. He himself entered fully into the spirit of the revival, preaching and praying alongside the most well-known revival ministers in America. (See Bronner 1970 , 41, 43, 49 and 5.3 for more detailed descriptions, and 5.3.1 following.)

Although the Beans had hoped to escape from revivals by moving westward, they found no relief; in fact, they were thrust deeper into the revival movement. Revival fires awaited them in California, where holiness evangelists also traveled with great effect and impact. Conservative opposition in the far West was minimal and Bean continued to be the vocal leader of a small, dissenting group. To compound his situation, the new western meetings were under the umbrella of Iowa Yearly Meeting, and despite the distance in miles, the revival pipeline to Iowa remained strong (Le Shana 1969, 83-85).

Not long after his arrival in San Jose, Isaac Sharp, a well-respected minister from England traveling from New Zealand, arrived in San Francisco where Joel Bean met him. Together they crossed the continent to attend Baltimore Yearly Meeting and visited meetings in many other states in succeeding months (Budge, 1898, 137). Bean's continual outspoken opposition to revivalism during his travels with Isaac Sharp antagonized the Iowa holiness leadership (Barbour and Frost, 1988, 213; Hamm, 1988, 140).

Controversy mounted and came to a head in 1885 when two holiness revivalists from Iowa visited San Jose Meeting (Hamm, 1988, 140). Bean claimed that the revivalists found little support (Hamm, 1988, 140); however, they had enough support for the meeting to split. Iowa determined that the leadership of San Jose Meeting was "unsound" (Hamm, 1988, 140). In the storm that raged as a result, Honey Creek Meeting determined that San Jose Friends were in a state of such confusion and disunity that they dissolved the meeting. English Friends and moderates in the East protested the action, calling it an "inquisition"[6] (Hamm, 1988, 141).

---

[6] The final demise of Bean's ministerial leadership within Iowa Yearly Meeting came about in 1893 when concern about his liberal doctrinal views (about which he was quite vocal) led Iowa Friends to request Bean and another minister at College Park, Benjamin Jones, to answer a list of queries in writing. Such queries were standard practice to determine whether recorded ministers of Iowa Yearly Meeting were in unity with Quaker Faith and Practice. Iowa was willing to put the matter to rest and reinstate College Park and its leadership if affirmative answers were given to all of the questions, including one asking for a "general expression of unity" with Iowa Yearly Meeting (Hamm, 1988, 141). Bean answered yes to all but one (on eternal punishment, which he rejected), which gave Iowa Yearly Meeting enough reason to depose the Beans from the ministry in 1893. London Yearly Meeting and many eastern Friends were again outraged (Hamm, 1988, 142). The Beans were not disowned, however, and remained members of New Providence Monthly Meeting, Iowa, until 1898, when a new Clerk, unaware of all the controversy surrounding the Beans, dropped their names from membership (along with 91 other inactive non-resident members, about 21 percent of its membership) for "disinterest" (Le Shana, 1969, 103-4). This action ignited a new round of protest from eastern and British Friends. (Determining unity with Faith and Practice of its ministers through the use of written queries on doctrine was common practice in Iowa Yearly Meeting, and is still used in recording ministers in evangelical meetings today. Bean was not being singled out by this procedure.) New Providence, in a gesture of reconciliation,

Bean and his supporters then formed a new meeting (Bean himself financed the new meetinghouse) which became College Park Friends, centered on silent worship and without the leadership of pastors or evangelists (later to be called "unprogrammed worship"). The meeting drew up a five-point statement of faith eschewing doctrinal or theological language that marked the first truly liberal (in the sense of modernist) meeting to come out of Gurneyite Quakerism. The statement of faith was so liberal for its time that it was far in advance even of Hicksism (Le Shana, 1969, 141; Kaiser, 1994).[7] There was no mention of perfection or holiness, salvation, Scripture, or conversion, theological themes dear to the hearts of revivalists – nor any mention of the atonement, the inward Light, plainness, or obedience, themes dear to the heart of conservatives.[8]

In 1889 the Beans and their supporters founded College Park Association of Friends as an independent, unaffiliated religious association unconnected with any Quaker monthly or Yearly Meeting. College Park became the prototype of the "college meetings" that formed around colleges or universities, drawing students, intellectuals and educated professionals. They were neither evangelical nor traditional, but were open to new thought and ideas, allowed a relaxed discipline, and had an ecumenical orientation.

---

then restored the Beans' membership and stated they could associate with any group that would receive them (Hamm, 1988, 146).

[7] The five points of Beanite Quakerism are: 1. Doctrine: Friends believe in the continuing reality of the living Christ, available to all seeking souls. 2. Worship: The worship of God is held in spirit and in truth, and shall be held on the basis of the leadership of the Holy Spirit. 3. Ministry: All Members and all Attenders are free to participate vocally in meetings, under a sense of God's presence. 4. Manner of Living: Friends are advised to conduct their private lives with simplicity and directness, ever sensitive to the world's needs and eager to engage in service. 5. Relation to the State: Friends are urged to feel their responsibility to the nation, and at the same time to recognize their oneness with humanity everywhere, regardless of race or nation, abstaining from all hatred (Le Shana, 1969, 141).

[8] Holiness Quakers re-established San Jose Meeting as a "Friends Church" and installed a pastor. They were recognized as a Meeting by Honey Creek in Iowa. The Beans, however, were still members of Honey Creek in Iowa. At one point they asked to be united with the new Monthly Meeting in either Oregon or Los Angeles, but this request was denied (Hamm, 1988, 141). Iowa, not really knowing what to do with the membership of the Beans (now an international *cause celebré*), finally transferred them to New Providence Monthly Meeting in Iowa (Hamm notes with tongue in cheek – two and a half miles closer to San Jose).

5.2.1 Anti-Revivalism

The article which set off the bombshell in Iowa Yearly Meeting and became a *cause celebré* in London Yearly Meeting was called "The Issue." "The Issue" was Joel Bean's devastating critique of the revival movement, as a new, but false manifestation of spirituality among Friends. Bean's intensely negative and highly personal reaction to revivalistic holiness, despite the fact that it renewed and energized the spiritual lives of countless western Friends, has become deeply ingrained in the minds of modernist and liberal Friends. Bean perceived revivalism as a kind of emotional blitz on unsuspecting worshippers. He saw no connection with revivalism to the conversion experiences of early Quakers, nor any parallels to the emotional fervor of the evangelistic mass meetings of the early Quaker itinerant ministers:

> The present condition of our Society shows how far we have drifted out of our first course, and how radical are the changes into which we have been swept. A great movement has set in, and borne the masses of our people along to consequences which they little anticipated, and which few of them see with entire satisfaction...It has been common to call it the "Revival Movement," and to denounce those who demur at any excesses connected with it as opposed to revivals and "opposed to the Lord's work." Many who were amongst the readiest to welcome signs of revival in our Society (using the word in its true sense), and who laboured earnestly and devotedly to promote it, have had to stand aloof from the movement, where it has adopted means which they felt to be hazardous and scattering to the Church and defeating to the very object desired....Those who recognized "foreign elements" introduced into the work, found their "influence narrowed" and made to feel their was no place for them in "the Church so dear to them....They did not doubt that the renewed interest and quickened life of many had been begun by the Holy Spirit. [But]....old, wild grapes were brought forth where a right vine had been planted and the blessings of heaven had been poured out." (1881, 49)

The dilemma for Bean and other protesters who found themselves at odds with the new holiness leadership was whether to withdraw (as the Conservatives had done) or whether to stay and resist "as good soldiers of Jesus Christ" within a meeting that had been "almost entirely changed" and where their message had been "rejected and their counsel set at naught." Bean's writing elevated as he described his pain: "For those who have not yet been led to separate, their portion is in suffering, as they see devastations which error and wrong are working in the Church, neutralizing more or less her power for good, and scattering from her folds" (Bean, 1881, 50). From Bean's perspective of the revival movement:

...is utterly diverse from essential Quakerism in almost every feature. Silent worship and silent prayer are treated as of questionable or doubtful reality, or sometimes with ridicule. The necessity of regular ministry is therefore, of course, taught. The singing of hymns by companies and Bible reading fill most of the spaces between other vocal exercises in many meetings. The duty to move in ministry or prayer, or singing, is urged upon all as enjoined by the Bible. (1881, 50)

The result of this approach, he noted, was not the building up of the community but instead, "Disorganization and disintegration are confessedly making rapid progress, and most rapid where protest is most silenced and conservatism most inert..." (1881, 50). Bean quoted directly from Luke Woodard and David Updegraff, two of the most prominent holiness evangelists:

"Salvation full and free" i.e., salvation not only from the guilt of sin, but to all the fullness of Christian perfection, seems perpetually to be taught as a thing fully wrought out and purchased for us by the blood of Christ, and offered for our simple acceptance by faith alone. Complete sanctification is claimed as a definite experience, instantaneously received, and defined to be "the eradication, not merely the subjugation, of the disposition to sin, in which our bodily propensities are restored to their normal healthful action."[9] All sinful perversion is to be eliminated; the diseased and distorted members are restored to perfect health and normal action; all the affections and appetites, and desires and propensities are purified, and brought back to a normal state. And this is an experience to be entered into at once. Thus comes the experience of the eradication of sin, and being filled with all the fullness of God, entered into by a single definite act of faith.[10] (1881, 50)

He further described the revivalists' teaching:

In this condition of perfect restoration of soul and body to "healthy normal action" and filled, moreover, "with all the fullness of God," that all impulses from the body must be right, and hence the full equipment and authority for public praise, and prayer, and exhortation, and teaching, and song, whenever one is inclined to do it. The one condition urged is faith; the one essential duty urged is confession with thanksgiving. (1881, 50)

---

[9] Bean is referencing Luke Woodard in *Christian Worker*, IV: 345.

[10] The reference in this instance is to D. B. Updegraff in *Christian Worker*, V: 65.

Bean's motive in stating these facts was not "detraction" but to "expose our condition" (1881, 51). In conclusion, he wished to "re-affirm my deepening faith in the principles of ancient Quakerism, in which all my Christian life has been nourished and sustained. And all who hold them in the heart-transforming and life-ennobling vitality...I would greet in heartfelt fellowship..." (1881, 51).

Part of the irony of Bean's critique can be seen in his closing impassioned words. Bean was certain that the revivalists had abandoned entirely the essentials of true Quakerism, while revivalists would counter that they were in fact recovering those very essentials in the call to holiness. Revivalists also would consider themselves to be "deepening faith in the principles of ancient Quakerism" and would greet in heartfelt fellowship all who shared in their "heart-transforming and life-ennobling vitality" (Bean, 1881, 51).

The problem with Bean's critique of revivalism is that in his reaction to change, the roots of genuine Quaker piety grounding the revival were overlooked and the experience of genuine transformation denied in his focus on the tendency toward hyperbole that inevitably occurs in revival periods. The declaration of holiness Friends that they were "filled with the fullness of God" (a biblical phrase from Eph. 3:19) is hauntingly similar to the kind of experiential claims made by George Fox and other early Quaker leaders. Bean's skepticism has the same ring of incredulousness as did the Puritan opponents to Quaker claims of perfection.

The majority of the doctrinal issues of the last quarter of the nineteenth century revolved around differing understandings of the inward Light, a term always difficult to precisely define and which gradually came to be used in many different ways by Quakers (Hamm, 1988, 122). The revivalists came to identify the inward Light with the Holy Spirit (following Gurney), and thus created the dilemma of whether or not the Holy Spirit could indwell unconverted persons. When they were forced to concede that the Holy Spirit only indwelled the converted, they sounded "un-Quakerly" to the traditionalists. Yet they also understood the Light as grace, available to all. The "moderates," as Hamm calls the Bean party, defined the inward Light as an internal guiding principle in every person. But as Hamm notes, "The tortured arguments both for and against the doctrine showed little understanding of what its meaning had been to the early Friends" (1988, 122).

Though doctrinal issues consumed much print, they did not seem to be the central issue in this polarization. Opposition to revivalism as a spiritual phenomenon was "the issue" for Bean. Though he claimed to be an ecumenical and inclusive Christian, he was not willing to include revivalism as a legitimate form of spiritual expression. He took a defensive stance toward the emotional expressions of revivalism. Worship must be subdued, refined, sedate, and rational in order to be pure, higher, spiritual worship. An example of his fear of engaging emotions, as well as an elitism inherent in separating "lower" and "higher forms" of Christian expression, can be found in his condescending attitude toward black worship, found in an excerpt from his journal (included in

Isaac Sharp's biography) describing a visit "among the coloured people at Southland College in Arkansas" (Budge, 1898, 138).

Bean wrote of "the emotions stirred among the coloured people by the old plantation songs," and how the effect of the tune and the emotions stirred "would have to be seen and heard to be understood" (Budge, 1898, 138). Bean commented:

> We could see how readily the coloured people could be wrought upon to a high pitch of excitement by these old songs…The evening closed with some remarks on the contrast which the purer worship "in spirit and in truth" presents, and with encouragement to those who see beyond these things, to labour for the elevation of the standard among the people. Morris Brown, a minister, and Charles Wade have been led out of these excitements." (Budge, 1898, 138)

The Quaker revivalists, on the other hand, valued and encouraged emotional expressions of spiritual experience, and had much greater understanding and appreciation of black worship. They allowed for a certain "contextualization" of worship experience.[11]

One factor which may have played a role in the Beans' repudiation of the Holiness Movement and their turn towards a more intellectualized and liberal form of religion may have been a sociological one. The Holiness Movement in America began in the 1830s among the "upper classes" in New York City with gatherings in the Victorian parlor of Phoebe Palmer, wife of a well-to-do physician. As the movement moved westward and southward, it became more emotional and enthusiastic, and attracted a less sophisticated and cultured crowd, as well as a more racially mixed one (Dayton, 1996, 77). Its identification with and appeal to those in more ordinary walks of life, rather than "high culture," may have prejudiced the Beans against the movement. Joel and his wife, Hannah (who came from a wealthy Philadelphia family), were more closely identified with the "cultural elites" of San Jose than were other western Quakers. During the summers they attended, rather than holiness camp meetings, the "Chautauqua Assembly," the upscale, educational version of revival camp meetings – more literary, intellectualist, and sedate (Dieter, 1996, 92, n58).[12]

---

[11] Walter Robson, in his journal describing the holiness revival among western Quakers, made note of meetings which had strong resemblances to the "call and response style" of black worship (Bronner, 1970, 41). He also mentioned that one of the recorded ministers present at Ohio Yearly Meeting who "offered a beautiful prayer" was a Negro, called a "son of thunder." He is identified by Bronner as William Allen, who was first a Methodist, then joined Friends (1970, 41).

[12] Although revival-style worship offended his Quaker sensibilities, he did not object to a tasteful and moderate use of elements of mainstream Protestant worship, such as reading

Ultimately, he seems to imply, if in a spirit of inclusiveness and progressive thinking it becomes necessary to abandon old forms, systems, and practices, then Quakerism should opt for a religion of higher culture rather than the inferior type manifested by the "new school" of the Holiness Movement (Bean, 1883, 287).

The great irony of the Beanite Friends is that Joel Bean, who denied having any separatist tendencies, nonetheless became the founder of a new independent Quaker group that arose without affiliation with any other Quaker Monthly or Yearly Meeting (Le Shana, 1969, 54, 137). The breadth of The College Park Association's ecumenism, pluralism, and toleration of a broad range of religious opinions (provided they were not of a holiness bent) was remarkable for its time. Beanite Friends also represented a groundbreaking shift from the historical roots of early Friends. The shadow of historical Quakerism remained in its form of worship, but connection to the eight essentials became minimal, tenuous or nonexistent.

5.2.2 Summary and Conclusions

In reaction to the revivalists' preoccupation with holiness as both experience and doctrine, Bean's stance on holiness tended to be reactive and skeptical. With Bean, perfection would become an imperative for social justice. Beanite Friends believed in "the continuing reality of the living Christ" (Le Shana, 1969, 141) as a spiritual principle, but no longer emphasized an intimate, personal relationship to Christ. Such vague language then paved the way for liberal Quakerism to become a modernist moral philosophy, as we shall examine in greater detail in the section on Rufus Jones (6.1). But before we follow the liberal trail, two other responses to revival holiness will be examined – that of William Robson, a sympathetic visiting British Friend, and Hannah Whitall Smith, who journeyed through revival holiness to rediscover her authentic Quaker roots. Both of these Friends were articulate and adept observers of their times. Unlike Bean, they were willing to see the positive value of revival means and methods (kataphatic worship, active striving) to lift

---

portions of Scripture, the singing of a hymn, or preaching and prayer. In an essay, "Why I am a Friend," written for the inaugural issue of *The American Friend* (1894), he wrote, "I would not deny the use of what our Father has made of beauty for the eye, or music for the ear, because of its misuse" (1894, 6). And further, "It is in the spirit of comprehension, rather than of exclusiveness, that I am a Friend" (1894, 7). He stated without reservation that Quakerism was not unique in its forms and practices: "But as for the principles of the Society I would claim no inflexible, invariable form of manifestation. They are principles of life, and in life there is growth, and variety, and adaptation to time and place" (1894, 6).

ordinary people towards a higher spiritual experience, a potential meeting with God, and growth in holiness.

Bean's relation to the four Quadrants of holiness (see Figure 3) shows a different pattern than the Quaker figures evaluated thus far. His ecumenical spirit and willingness to engage what he considered tasteful and moderate elements of mainstream worship forms (see 5.2.1, n12) places him more comfortably in Quadrant 1 than his predecessors. But he would be in tension with historical doctrinal underpinnings, since he claimed no fixed principles within the Society of Friends (see 5.2.1, n12). As for Quadrant 2, he affirmed the centrality of divine guidance and the leadership of the Holy Spirit, but resisted charismatic and revivalistic expressions of it. Like Gurney, he did not manifest a strong mystical consciousness, as found in Quadrant 3, other than his appreciation for traditional Quaker silence. His connections to the holiness of Quadrant 4 would be relegated to ethical and social witness, but not in cultural separateness. He represents a rationalist and intellectualist form of liberal Quakerism, more culturally affirming than radically countercultural, and strongly ecumenical in spirit.

The eight essentials were substantially reduced in Beanite Quakerism, and Bean represents a major shift towards modernism. Scripture was not mentioned in Bean's five points of Quakerism (see above) and was replaced by experience and reason as primary authorities. Eschatology, conversion, evangelism, suffering, and mysticism were virtually eliminated. Charisma was maintained in part with a strong emphasis on leading of the Spirit, especially in worship. Perfection remained as a fragment in the form of ethical idealism similar to Hicksism.

5.3 British Reactions to Revivalism

Although evangelical fervor marked British Quakerism for most of the nineteenth century, revivalism did not. Despite the fact that a constant stream of traveling ministers criss-crossed the Atlantic, thus cross-fertilizing British and American Quakerism, holiness in a revival setting never became a prominent feature in English Quakerism.[13] Reasons for the resistance to the holiness revival among British Quakers are not so much attributable to basic doctrinal differences nor a lack of concern for holiness as central to the spiritual life, but rather to a fear and even repulsion of public religious expression. There is profound irony in the fact that the British part of the Society of Friends, a religion of the heart based on direct experience of God, has succumbed to a

---

[13] The American Quaker evangelist Hannah Whitall Smith, with her husband Robert Pearsall, held prominent public holiness gatherings in England – they did so interdenominationally through the Keswick Convention, and not with Quaker backing. She was however, identified publicly as a "Quakeress" (see 5.4).

state of intense discomfort with the natural manifestations of the directness of such experiences. A good example of this repulsion of revival experience can be found in an article entitled "Religious Excitement," published in the *British Friend*, July 1, 1880. The article, excerpted from an Anglican work,[14] illustrates the need to find a broader base of support for an anti-revival stance beyond the rather weak claim that revivals are departures from Quaker tradition. The article was excerpted from a new edition of a work entitled "Holiness" by Canon Ryle. Ryle wrote that he was convinced real practical holiness did not get the attention it deserved, but at the same time he was convinced that "zealous efforts of some well-meaning persons to promote a higher standard of spiritual life are often not 'according to knowledge' and are really calculated to do more harm than good" (1880, 182). He may have been specifically criticizing what were called "Higher Life" and "Consecration" meetings which had become quite popular among British Evangelicals, or the Moody-Sankey revivals that also took Britain by storm in 1873:[15]

> Sensational and exciting addresses by strange preachers, or by women, loud singing, hot rooms, crowded tents, the constant sight of strong semi-religious feeling in the faces of all around you for several days, late hours, long protracted meetings, public profession of experience. (1880, 182)

The German theologian Dorothee Soelle has insightfully diagnosed how this kind of ecclesial repression is the greatest factor in church decline in Protestantism. Although she is speaking of the Lutheran Church, her diagnosis could be equally applied to Anglicanism and, I would argue, equally applied to what became normative, modernist forms of "traditional" Quakerism:

> In this self-imposed modesty, which has ecclesial sanction and imposes a prohibition of the mystical self, there lurks perhaps one of the difficulties central to modern Protestantism. Its defensive stance toward the emotions turns the enormously fetishized "faith" into a nonexistential category. The repulsion of experience, as well as the fear of engaging it, represents a kind of spiritual suicide that at the turn of this century continues to cause church membership to decline. (2001, 18)

---

[14] Quakerism in England in the nineteenth century had moved culturally closer to Anglicanism. See 4.2.3 on Gurney's connection to Anglicanism. See also Isichei, 1970, 4 and Punshon, 2001, 21.

[15] See Dieter, 1996, 135-141 for a description and analysis of the English holiness revival.

Soelle's analysis is a clear echo, though in different language, of the early Quaker charge against the Calvinists, the Anglicans, and other Christian "professors" of their day who turned religion into a "fetishized 'faith'" and belief that was never experienced.

In England, a few attempts at promoting spiritual renewal through revival and evangelism began in 1875. General Meetings, imported from the revivals among western Friends, were held with some success, but such evangelistic outreach in Great Britain was short-lived. Concerns about such "aggressive work" led to a reorganization of the Committee on General Meetings in 1883 into a Home Mission Committee, which continued to incorporate a moderate evangelism into its goals. But suspicion and tensions surrounded this venture as well (Kennedy, 2001, 123). General Meetings elicited fears that they would deteriorate into a full-blown revival along the lines of Moody and Sankey. Kennedy comments that suspicion of singing, prepared sermons, Bible reading, and emotional responses were not unmixed with "middle-class snobbery" (2001, 122).

Similar to the attitude of Joel Bean, Ryle also questioned the long-term effect of revivals in promoting the spiritual life, and implied there are no proofs that such "mass meetings" actually make people better Christians (1880, 182). Quaker echoes of this kind of critique of holiness gatherings appeared in article after article in *The British Friend*, *The Friend* (London), *The Friend* (Philadelphia), and *The American Friend*.

5.3.1 Walter Robson

In contrast to Bean's opposition to revivals, an unusually objective perspective on the western revivals was provided by English Quaker Walter Robson. His *Journal of Walter Robson* provides an ideal vehicle for a record of an inside observer. Robson traveled widely during the post-Gurney, pre-modernist transition in British Quakerism. He came to America in 1877 at the height of the Holiness Movement with no familiarity with the phenomenon of revivalism among Quakers. Everything he observed and experienced was new and different, and often startling. Sometimes he detected the "ludicrous," but most often he suspended judgment and allowed himself to enter the flow and partake of the spirit of the meetings.

Robson was an Orthodox Quaker and was accepted by American revivalists with "open arms." He displayed a nonjudgmental attitude and appeared to recognize the spirit of Quaker holiness when manifested in a different cultural context. He exhibited a radical openness to the movement of the Holy Spirit and a warmth that endeared him to all[16] (Bronner, 1970, 1).

---

[16] Robson was born in Saffron Walden, in Essex, near Cambridge in 1842. He earned his living in the family drapery business, Robson, Green, & Co., begun by his grand-parents.

Robson arrived in Philadelphia on August 19, 1877, and traveled to all of the various western Yearly Meetings where he experienced first-hand a Quaker world he had never known (Bronner, 1970, 4). At Indiana Yearly Meeting he witnessed a revival meeting conducted by two of the most prominent holiness ministers, David Updegraff and John Henry Douglas. Robson entered "wholeheartedly" into the meeting, which he called "an Altar of prayer" (Bronner, 1970, 6). He then traveled to Kansas Yearly Meeting where he preached, but tensions over the revival were high and he was interrupted and rebuked by a Conservative Friend.[17]

At the end of his visit, he found himself in Philadelphia sitting in the minister's gallery with the most conservative of Philadelphia Friends (Bronner, 1970, 7). Returning to England, after traveling 12,000 miles in four months, he concluded the writing of his journal with this testimony to his experience:

> He has blessed my own soul with a wondrous realization of the exceeding greatness of His power even to me, *baptizing me with the Holy Ghost & teaching me in a way I never experienced before – the completeness & fullness of the salvation wrought for us & in us, by His dear Son Jesus Christ.* May His felt presence ever keep me abiding in Him & he in my heart by faith, that so I may reflect His image.... (Bronner, 1970, 156) [my emphasis]

Robson clearly adopted the language of the Holiness Movement to describe his spiritual experience, yet I argue such language and experience does not in any way depart from historic Quakerism, and, in fact, is a valid interpretation and

---

He married an Australian, Christina Cox, during his travels there in 1869. She returned with him to England and they raised six children. Robson, in addition to being a Quaker minister and a businessman, was also borough treasurer and magistrate, clerk of his Monthly and Quarterly Meeting, and committee member of Saffron Walden Friends School for more than 50 years. (Bronner notes that Robson had "boundless energy" [1970, 1]). Robson died December 14, 1929, age 87, a few weeks after the celebration of his sixtieth wedding anniversary. Robson's obituary in *The Friend* claimed that his death signaled "the closing of an era in the Society of Friends, this passing of almost, if not quite, the last of the great ministers..." (*The Friend* [London] 70, 1930, 35-36, qtd. in Bronner, 1970, 4). Robson was 35 years old at the time of his visit to America. Prior to his American visit he had traveled to Australia, Tasmania, and New Zealand with a prominent English minister, Joseph James Neave, so had some cross-cultural ministry experience. Robson was recorded as a minister in 1871 by Thaxted Monthly Meeting in Essex (Bronner, 1970, 1-4).

[17] Kansas split a few years later when Conservatives separated from the Orthodox Gurneyite Meeting (Bronner, 1970, 6). By 1890 these Conservatives, who were anti-revival, merged with the Wilburites, and these Quakers became known as Conservative Friends (Hamm, 1988, 99-100).

description of the mystical experience of perfection in continuity with the heart of Quaker spirituality from its inception.

5.3.2　Robson's Experience of Revivalism

Robson's first experience of a western Quaker revival elicited this journal response:

> My dear friends at home have little idea of an American Friends devotional meeting. The groaning, responding, "Amen! Brother" "God hold thee sister", were just kept up all the while. Several hymns were just started by Friends all over the meeting & sung by any who inclined. David Updegraff who is looked on as one of the finest ministers in America presided & near the close, asked all Friends who decided then & there for Christ, to rise – several rose – then for all who wished conversion, & several more rose. Then all who were unconverted & several more stood up. Prayers were offered for each class. (Bronner, 1970, 41)

Initially he experienced a kind of religious cultural shock, e.g. "These meetings are very exercising to me. I almost dread them, & I think you had need pray that I may overcome my too keen sense of the ludicrous" (Bronner, 1970, 43). But he also described his own leading to preach and being "greatly blessed" by the response, as well as being moved by others' preaching: "A lady Friend, Esther Frame[18] (very young) spoke for an hour & a half, the most finished wonderful sermon I ever heard..." (Bronner, 1970, 43- 44). With candor he shared his conflicted feelings: "Dear Friends here, are very kind and loving. I am passing through great conflict of mind as to my position here. I feel truly like a dwarf among giants & often the query will come & it fills my eyes with tears" (Bronner, 1970, 43- 44).

His observations provide evidence that holiness revivalism affected persons from all branches of Friends and bridged separations:

> A rank Hicksite and a Wilburite were converted at about 11 o'clock last night. I see & feel it *is* the Lord's work & it is marvelous in my eyes. Old Friends of 80 in the straight-coats and bonnets rise, with the

---

[18] Esther Frame had been a Methodist, though she had Quaker roots. She joined with Friends in 1867 when her call to preach was met with opposition by the Methodists. She became one of the most prominent Quaker evangelists of that period and one of the first salaried pastors (possibly the first) in 1878 in Muncie, Indiana. See Nathan T. Frame, *Reminiscences of Nathan T. and Esther G. Frame*, 1907. See also Spencer, 1991.

tears pouring down their cheeks, to say, how happy they are in the love of Jesus & how he has delivered and saved them. (Bronner, 1970, 49)

Not all the preaching was done by revivalists, and not all the sessions were devotional. At Western Yearly Meeting, for example, Robson mentioned an educational conference, addressed by Professor Pliney Chase from Philadelphia, "considered one of the most learned men in America." Robson wrote, "His proof of scripture & science being one, were beautiful..." (Bronner, 1970, 69). Current biblical scholarship was apparently valued by the holiness Quakers, and they were not anti-intellectual.

Robson summed up his own message preached as "Christ and Him crucified with much liberty & power" and mentioned that afterward Professor Chase followed with "a striking scientific appeal to the truths I had declared." Robson preached to a packed meetinghouse, which seated 2,500 people. A separate preaching center was created outdoors for the throngs that could not fit into the meetinghouse, as well as many curious onlookers. Robson remarked that "Many only come for the spree of the thing, but I trust some 'who come to scoff, remain to pray'" (Bronner, 1970, 70). He estimated about 10,000 people were on the grounds (Bronner, 1970, 70).

At Indiana Yearly Meeting Robson met Hannah Whitall Smith, the most famous Quaker holiness evangelist, and her sister Mary Thomas, another respected minister (see 5.4).[19] The few comments in his journal about Smith seem to indicate a tremendous respect, even reverence, as well as a genuine and deep spiritual resonance and a growing friendship based on, I suggest, a mutual understanding and appreciation of authentic Quaker holiness. For example, he wrote:

> I escorted H. W. Smith home. I should be ungrateful if I did not acknowledge the great blessing to my own soul, association with this holy woman & her no less holy & gifted sister Mary Thomas, is more & more, every day. Truly they live in the power of God. (Bronner, 1970, 88)

At a meeting for worship at Indiana Yearly Meeting, Hannah Whitall Smith, Robson, and David Updegraff[20] comprised what would appear to be a rather

---

[19] Smith, a Philadelphia Quaker, became a leading holiness evangelist, in both England and America, and a best-selling devotional writer of the period (see 5.4). Her sister, Mary Thomas, was also a prominent Quaker minister, most active in social reform work. See Spencer, 1991.

[20] David Updegraff (1830-1894) from Ohio Yearly Meeting was one of the most prominent and controversial revivalist preachers. In 1884 he was baptized with water and began to preach "tolerance" of the material sacraments, which led to the creation of the

unique and unusual trio of speakers.[21] Smith began the ministry ("very excellent," he noted), Robson followed, and finally Updegraff concluded with "great power & when those who wished to consecrate themselves to the Lord were asked to rise, they rose in all parts of the house & the power of the Lord was with us of a truth" (Bronner, 1970, 88).

Robson provides one of the most moving descriptions of a holiness meeting:

> After the [Presbyterian] service closed, I gave H.W.S. my arm & we hurried off to the Friends meetinghouse where a scene of indescribable solemnity was being acted "an Altar of prayer." Friends old & young, smart & very plain, kneeling in rows, sometimes quite still, often ejaculating short earnest prayer for a baptism of the Holy Ghost, some praising God with a loud voice that their prayers were answered. Dear David Updegraff & J.H.D. quietly moving about among the kneeling throng, sometimes in prayer themselves & at others quietly whispering words of comfort or of counsel. I never realized such agonizing in prayer before. It was a scene never to be forgotten. (Bronner, 1970, 90)

This scene, however, was not unique, but replicated many times. The "Altar of prayer" became a familiar pattern of holiness devotion in Western Yearly Meetings (Bronner, 1970, 91).

At Kansas, the newest of the Western Yearly Meetings, Robson found the most tension he had thus far experienced (conservatives had not yet separated in Kansas.) He described painful moments of discord and opposition from those he termed "the Wilbur element." For example, a man interrupted David Updegraff "most tryingly" as he spoke and when he called for a silent prayer. A woman protested against another minister, Mary Rogers, when she "sang a hymn sweetly," condemning her for "singing a song out of a book" (Bronner, 1970, 100). He also experienced a devotional meeting, "*promising* much blessing, but marred at the close, by a long declamatory address from a minister name Cyrus Harvey of strong Wilbur tendencies who cannot bear the plain preaching of sanctification & Holy Ghost baptism."[22]

"water party." The controversy over the sacraments split the holiness revivalist Quakers. See Hamm, 1988, 132-33.

[21] Smith had major differences with Updegraff's approach to holiness. She thought him too extreme. Yet both, nonetheless, seemed to respect each other, and felt they were working towards the same spiritual goals (see 5.4).

[22] These Western conservative factions, though called "Wilburites" were of a somewhat different stripe than the original traditionalists who followed John Wilbur out of New England Meeting in 1845. Though both held tenaciously to the plainness and old traditions, there were subtle differences, and although they were a tiny minority, they split even further among themselves (Hamm, 1988, 99-102). In these Kansas conservatives, of whom Cyrus Harvey (mentioned above) was the leader, a reactionary

If Robson was indeed accurate in his recording of Cyrus Harvey's words, it is worth noting that he spoke of "the inner light" rather than "Christ within," the usual expression of the early Wilburites (and later modernists, such as Rufus Jones):

> His sermon alluded to having these doctrines [baptism of the Holy Ghost] dinned forever in their ears, making the young people profess what they knew nothing about, while the older ones who have lived the life of Christians by obeying the inner light, are thought little of. (Bronner, 1970, 102)

Harvey, apparently, could not conceive that young people might actually be having a genuine experience of God. Robson's attitude toward Harvey's diatribe is that "His discourse just seemed to pull back the blessing which was coming." And he added this insightful comment: "Thus do we Friends pay the penalty of our liberty 'to relieve our minds'" (Bronner, 1970, 102).[23]

Robson offered this insightful and accurate observation of the differences between western and eastern Quakerism in America:

> It is a curious fact that the Allegheny Mountains seem to cut Quakerism in two parts: *west,* they are all liberal in their actions as churches; *east* they are more like England—prudent, solemn & inclined to be conservative, no hymns sung, friends rise during prayer,

---

and ferociously combative fundamentalism seemed to have replaced the mystical sensibility of the earlier Wilburites. They were most energized, not by a positive affirmation of Quaker perfection, but by a spirit of negation and opposition. Harvey began publishing his own journal in 1879 called *The Western Friend*, which primarily focused on denouncing revivalists and revivalism. Ridicule and caricature were not beneath him, as he took special "delight in highlighting rumors" about revivalists and "never shrank from controversy or ferocious editorial wars with those who dared to oppose him." His favorite target was David Updegraff (Hamm, 1988, 101).

[23] At Kansas Yearly Meeting, Robson was exposed for the first time to a publicly expressed rejection of his ministry. He described poignantly this painful experience: "While I was speaking & many were in tears & a most solemn feeling was over us, a plain old man friend rose & said nearly these words 'Friends, I wish we might now have a really solemn sermon in the life, instead of this light lifeless talk which only causes levity.' I keep very calm & 'sweet inside,' for which I bless my blessed Master but physically these things always make me tremble, but a sort of whispered, 'go on dear brother' reassured me & I proceeded" (Bronner, 1970, 103). While the attack on Robson's preaching was disconcerting, it pales in comparison to the attack two days later on David Updegraff as he led a devotional meeting: "A minister (Cyrus Harvey) loudly declaiming against D.U. & his teaching & at last a recorded minister (a woman) went to him & said -- 'we read of a deceiver & an antichrist & thou art the man'" (Bronner, 1970, 104).

periods of silence are observed, and altogether after the five Western Yearly Meetings I have attended, the change to the proprieties of Baltimore is quite curious. But they are a sweet choice body of intellectual & spiritual Friends. (Bronner, 1970, 110)

The final meetings he visited before his homeward journey reflected the divisions within Philadelphia Orthodox Quakers, and were a microcosm of the Quaker world at that time. He preached in the morning at North Meeting in Philadelphia at the invitation of the Conservative minister Samuel Balderson. And that evening and the following day, he preached at 12th Street Meeting, a Gurneyite meeting.[24] And lastly, just before leaving, he spoke at the "Mission Room" of an independently minded Friend, Joshua Bailey, who ran his own self-governing urban Friends mission and was president of the American Bible Society.[25] Robson described his experience at North Meeting:

Samuel Balderson took me to sit next to him in the gallery & I never looked on such a sight of long bonnets of the oldest cut & broad hats all on the heads, & my heart felt ready to sink, but when I knelt in prayer, I was surprised at the whole great meeting rising without an exception. They often do not, but sit with their hats on, if it is a minister from the Western Yearly Meeting. I then spoke for about an hour, & I felt as if there was but little opposition, but I knew my beard & coat would stumble them. (Bronner, 1970, 143)

Robson called these Conservative Friends the "narrowest" because of their emphasis on ancient traditions such as rigid plainness of dress symbolized by the longest bonnets, oldest cut, and broadest hats. Apparently Robson's beard and cut of his coat made him acceptable to them and thus they received him respectfully, unlike the ministers from Western Yearly Meeting.

---

[24] At 12th Street Meeting Robson he gave his "missionary lecture" about his travels to the "South Seas" to an ecumenical audience of about 500 Friends and others (Bronner, 1970, 144).

[25] Robson described Bailey as: "One of the few Friends in this city who ventures to mark out a course for himself & having great wealth he consecrates to his Lord, feeds 4000 poor people every day; has a large temperance & mission room which he manages himself, entirely" (Bronner, 1970, 146). After having tea with Bailey, Robson preached in his mission room, along with Bible readings & hymns to a "solemn & attentive audience." The audience was quite diverse, ranging from some of the conservative enclave to an Episcopal priest (Bronner, 1970, 146). Bailey is representative of a revival holiness with his use of hymn-singing, diversity of his audience, as well as the breadth of his ministry and social outreach.

5.3.3 Summary and Conclusions

Walter Robson's journal provides intimate access to the heightened spiritual atmosphere with all the tensions, color, drama, and intensity of this crucial period in the evolution of American Quakerism. Despite the inevitable conflict which accompanies change, this period of the growth of western Quakerism was in its own peculiarly American way, a Quaker renaissance – and the last great flowering of holiness within American Quakerism. Robson captured some of this energy and mood in his illuminating journal. He provides a glimpse of Quaker holiness that is obscured, if not obliterated, by the wearisome doctrinal debates and anti-revival diatribes and invectives that consumed so much print during this time. Granted, this is but one individual's perspective, and that of a moderate evangelical. Yet it can be argued that it was as unbiased a view as could be uncovered since Robson was an English Friend who had never experienced revival or American Quakerism before. He did not appear to have come with a particular social or spiritual agenda. He believed Hicksites and Wilburites had strayed from the true path, but he was not hostile or unloving towards them, nor did he direct his preaching against them.

His culture shock at the emotional intensity of western "devotional meetings" disconcerted him, but the deeper recognition that this, too, was authentic Quaker holiness overcame his initial ambivalence. Edwin Bronner, the Quaker historian who edited and published Robson's journal almost 100 years after it was written and the first to give it public exposure (it was never published in his lifetime), does so with no particular Quaker theory to advance or ax to grind. Bronner makes a strong case for the significance of this work and its value for historians:

> Walter Robson maintained a degree of objectivity during these extensive visits, which enhances the value of his observations. Orthodox evangelical Christianity in London Yearly Meeting was quite different from what he saw in Ohio and elsewhere, and this provided the author of the journal with a perspective, which was highly significant. (Bronner, 1970, 1)

The value of his observations is also related to the question of how important his voice was and whether he was a significant figure in British Quakerism of that period. Robson is not mentioned in the two major histories of English Quakerism in the Victorian age (Isichei and Kennedy). Robson did not publish, nor was he one of the inner circle of London Yearly Meeting. But he was highly respected and had an important circle of influence. According to Bronner, at London Yearly Meeting of 1878 when two epistles were received from Western Yearly Meeting and London had to deliberate upon them, Robson recommended that a delegation be sent to Western Yearly Meeting to heal the schism and his plan was adopted.[26]

Robson's observations support the argument of this study that form of worship is not the key to enabling or mediating communion with God in Quaker worship. Robson valued worshipful silence, and probably preferred it himself, because ultimately he hoped London Yearly Meeting would not move to the American revival style (Bronner, 1970, 44). Yet he apparently saw no real inconsistency in the revival approach to worship and Quaker principles. For Robson, the essential reality of worship came in the existential moment of unity with the Spirit – when the power and the blessings would descend on the gathered worshippers. Holiness preachers referred to this as the Baptism of the Holy Spirit (a baptism Robson testified to having experienced during his visit-- see 5.3.1). Whether that happened at an "altar of prayer" or in the depths of silence was not important to Robson.

5.4 Hannah Whitall Smith: Holiness Evangelist

This section introduces one of the most striking and complex personalities in nineteenth century Quaker evangelicalism, and one of the most articulate exponents of holiness in the Victorian era, Hannah Whitall Smith.[27] In 1870, Smith, a Philadelphia Quaker, published *The Christian's Secret of a Happy Life*, the most popular devotional book to emerge from the nineteenth century Holiness Movement. Her book, still in print, became an instant best seller, going through numerous editions, and continues to be read by religious seekers. *Christian's Secret* is a popular expression of holiness theology and spirituality. The fact that a Quaker would write one of the greatest classics from the literature of the Holiness Movement strongly affirms the premise of this study that holiness is the key to understanding authentic Quaker spirituality. But it is curious that Quaker historians have hardly taken notice of her, despite her prominence in the religious world of the Victorian era.[28] Smith wrote over a

---

[26] Four weighty London Friends, including the weightiest of all at that time, J. Bevan Braithwaite, were sent to attempt mediation. Their efforts failed, but they nonetheless made helpful contributions to American Quakerism (Bronner, 1970, 16).

[27] The best academic study of Smith (1832-1911) is found in Dieter, 1996, 130-157.

[28] For example, in 1875 she and her husband, Robert Pearsall, held meetings for holiness in Brighton, England. One observer noted that more than 6,000 people gathered at her meetings, giving her a "congregation…larger than Mr. Spurgeon's" (Dieter, 1996, 148). In addition to her religious prominence, she also had connections within some of the same intellectual circles as Rufus Jones, knew and corresponded with William James, and was mother-in-law to Bertrand Russell. She wrote numerous books, several of which became bestsellers. Hamm relegates her to a footnote in his analysis of the Holiness Movement and its impact on Quakers, despite admitting, "She was unquestionably the most famous of all holiness Friends" (Hamm 1988, 201, n19). She is included in his long

dozen books in addition to *Christian's Secret,* including her spiritual autobiography, *The Unselfishness of God,* which provides valuable and fascinating documentation of the history of the Holiness Movement and its relationship to the Orthodox Quietism in which she was raised.

Smith became politically radical in later life (she joined the Labor Party, supported Christian Socialism and marched for women's suffrage) and revised some of her earlier more enthusiastic holiness views, but she never relinquished the essential holiness spirituality or her Quaker identity (Spencer, 1991). Throughout her writings, she conveyed a deep commitment to both holiness and the Quaker tradition, which in her mind were the same.

However, Smith claimed she had to be introduced to holiness by her Methodist seamstress, because the experience was essentially hidden to her within Philadelphia Quaker Orthodoxy. Thus, she admitted she had to learn from outside the Society what were in fact the foundational principles of Quakerism. She wrote of sharing with a Quaker friend her "new discoveries" of holiness teachings:

> [The Friend]...on hearing what I had to tell, had expressed surprise at its being new to me, as it was, she declared, what the Quakers had always taught. This seemed to throw light upon Quakerism that I had never dreamed of. My mother also said to me one day, but Hannah why does thee call this doctrine new? Thee is only preaching what all the old Friends have always preached. Yes, I answered, "I begin to see that this is the case, but they have never preached it in a way that

---

list of "Leading Renewal Friends, 1865," (1988, 45) but not in his list of "Holiness Quaker Revivalists," because, he notes, she left the Society of Friends in 1872, moved to England, and did not play "an important role in the revival." (1988, 201, n19). While it is true she resigned from Friends for a time, she rejoined in 1886, though she inquired about reuniting many years prior, and although not formally a member she was still active and involved in the revival as Robson's *Journal* clearly indicates (Bronner, 1970). Robson, who called her "a holy woman," had significant interactions with her at both Indiana Yearly Meeting and in Philadelphia (see 5.3.2 where Robson, Updegraff and Smith were all speakers at worship). Other than the footnote, she is given one line of text by Hamm: "Most [women in the renewal movement] were, at best, their husbands' partners, as were Hannah Bean and Hannah Whitall Smith" (1988, 47). Smith is a poor choice to support that dubious claim as she continued to be an active public figure and prominent holiness Friend, independent of her husband, long after his short-lived ministry ended in scandal. See Spencer, 1991. Hamm has difficulty knowing how to categorize Smith because she does not fit the stereotype of the Quaker revivalist, despite the fact that "she was the most famous of all holiness Friends" (201, n19). In Philip Benjamin's *The Philadelphia Quakers in the Industrial Age 1865-1920* (1976) Smith again is given just one line of text, despite her prominence in exactly that period of time and cultural context (1976, 164).

ordinary people could know what they were talking about. It seems to me that nobody, who did not know it already, could possibly get hold of it from their preaching." Certainly I never did, although I have been listening to their preaching all my life…But I came to the conclusion that my mother and my friend were right. It *was* true Quaker doctrine that we had discovered. (1903, 275-6)

She concluded that Quakers called holiness "the life hid with Christ in God" (Smith, 1903, 276). But she had not understood their preaching because they never explained "how" it could be realized. They urged "holiness of life but failed to tell the secret by which this holiness was to be attained" (Smith, 1903, 279). But as she discovered the interior life for herself she came full circle back to her Quaker roots and understood their meaning:

…the true inner meaning of Quakerism dawned upon me more and more fully day by day. It was the "way of holiness" in which they were seeking to walk. They preached a deliverance from sin, a victory over the cares and worries of life, a peace that passeth all understanding, a continual being made "more than conquerors" through Christ. They were in short "Higher Life" people, and at last I understood them; and the old preaching, which once had been so confusing, became marrow and fatness to my soul. The preaching had not changed, but I had changed. I had discovered the missing link, and had reached that stage in my soul's experience to which such preaching ministered. (1903, 280-1)

Smith explained that holiness was the "missing link," but not until she came to understand it and experience it herself did she realize it was the core of Quaker belief and action:

…nearly every view of divine things that I have since discovered and every reform I have since advocated, had, I now realize, their germs in the views of the Society; and over and over again, when some new discovery or conviction has dawned upon me, I have caught myself saying, "Why *that*, was what the early Friends meant, although I never understood it before." (1903, 55-56)

This study argues that Smith was correct about holiness being the foundation of Quakerism. Smith also identified and affirmed the mystical aspect of Friends and its essentialness to Quaker holiness with this observation:

A very wise thinker among [the Quakers] said to me lately that in his opinion Friends were meant to be a strong mystic society, but he feared they were degenerating into a weak evangelical one; and I could not but feel there was too much truth in his word. (1903, 281)

Smith realized that Quaker holiness, the "life hid with Christ in God," is both mystical and evangelical. Although she was a fervent evangelical herself, she understood that to be a strong mystical society also entails being a strong evangelical one. A weak evangelical one would promote faith as belief and doctrine without experience, profession without possession, as early Quakers called it (1903, 274).

She also mentioned in her spiritual autobiography a book given her by her father which always held a special place for her alongside her Bible because it "seemed to reveal the mystical pathway" (1903, 234). "It was called 'Spiritual Progress,'" she wrote, "and was a collection of extracts from the writings of Fenelon and Madame Guyon" (1903, 234). This book links Smith to the contemplative way of Quietist holiness.[29] She admitted that although she valued it highly because it was a gift from her father, she did not understand it, and viewed it ambivalently. But, she realized later:

> ...all unconsciously to myself its teachings had made a profound impression upon me; and, even while I criticized, I still was often conscious of an underlying hunger after the mystical side of religion set forth in this book. (1903, 234)

5.4.1 Smith's Religious Experience

Smith went through a period of religious doubt and skepticism in young adulthood until she realized that God was a God of love and not to be feared. She wrote: "God was a terror to me, until I began to see Him in the face of Jesus Christ" (1903, 13). The incarnation became key in her conversion experience. "To know God therefore, as He really is, we must go to His incarnation in the Lord Jesus Christ" (1903, 13).

Smith left Friends for a period of time, disillusioned with the rigid traditionalism of Philadelphia Orthodoxy that she experienced as a young woman and the Society's inability to meet or answer her spiritual needs at that time. Yet she returned to Friends later and, in fact, never relinquished her identity as a Friend (Spencer, 1991, 44; Smith, 1903).

---

[29] As has been noted previously, Guyon and Fenelon were two mystical writers greatly appreciated and admired by the nineteenth century Holiness Movement, thus a concrete link between revival holiness and Quaker Quietism (see 5.1, n1). On Guyon's influence on Quakerism see 3.2 and Appendix B on Quietism.

In 1858 at age 26, after losing a five-year old daughter, she happened to go to a popular "noonday" prayer meeting[30] out of curiosity and she had a mystical experience of God's presence to her. It was not a conversion experience, but simply a sense of God's reality and God's nearness, as she describes it:

> ....suddenly something happened to me. What it was or how it came I had no idea, but somehow an inner eye seemed to be opened in my soul...I do not remember anything that was said. I do not even know that I heard anything. A tremendous revolution was going on within me that was of far profounder interest than anything the most eloquent preacher could have uttered. God was making Himself manifest as an actual existence, and my soul leaped up in an irresistible cry to know Him...It wasn't that I felt myself to be a sinner needing salvation, or that I was troubled about my future destiny. It was not a personal question at all. It was simply and only that I had become aware of God, and that I felt I could not rest until I should know him. I might be good or might be bad; I might be going to Heaven or I might be going to hell – these things were outside the question. All I wanted was to become acquainted with the God of whom I had suddenly become aware. (Smith, 1903, 172)

Smith experienced what is the beginning of a mystical awareness, her "inner eye" was opened into a new reality; she had a direct encounter with God. Her description is similar to elements in many mystics' descriptions of divine encounters in which a presence is felt, though always difficult to describe in words. Thus her first mystical experience was also her entrance into the Holiness Movement, and it became the catalyst for her own spiritual transformation.

She decided shortly after to go on a spiritual retreat to spend time alone at the beach reading nothing but the Bible. While reading Romans chapter 5 she had a classic conversion experience, though at the time she did not know that

---

[30] She described these meetings as stirring the religious world from "twelve to one, in the business part of the city, and crowded with business men" (1903, 172). Her initial reaction to them was one of "a very languid interest, as I thought they were only another effort of a dying-out superstition to bolster up its cause" (1903, 172). Timothy Smith calls this ecumenical religious awakening "Annus Mirabilis – 1858," the beginning of the spiritual phenomena known as the Holiness Movement. His description of the mode of worship of these meetings shows interesting parallels to early Quaker worship (except for the time limitations): "There was no ritual or prepared plan. Any person present might pray, exhort, lead in song, or give testimony as he felt 'led,' only keeping within the five-minute time limit and avoiding controversial subjects like water baptism or slavery. Distinctions between the sects and between ministers and laymen were ignored" (Smith, 1976, 64). He likens these meetings to the rural Methodist camp meeting transferred to an urban setting (1976, 64).

what she had discovered was called "conversion." She began meeting with a group of Plymouth Brethren who told her she had become "born of God" and found herself drawn into their church. Almost immediately she became an "evangelist"[31] (Smith, 1903, 179). She described the initial reaction of Friends to her excessive zeal, and their eventual tolerance:

> And in spite of all the disapproval and opposition of the Elders and Overseers among the Quakers,[32] and of my own family as well, my enthusiasm gained me a hearing, and nearly every friend I had came, sooner or later, into a knowledge of the truths I advocated, and more or less shared my rejoicing; so that gradually the opposition died down, and in the end, while the "solid Friends" could not fully endorse me, they at least left me free to continue my course unmolested. (1903, 186-7)

But in spite of their tolerance she began meeting with the Plymouth Brethren "who were at that time making quite a stir in Philadelphia" because she desired to learn more of the Bible, doctrine and theology, and they were "great Bible students" (1903, 190). She considered them among her principal spiritual teachers during this time, but eventually left them because she could not accept their "extreme Calvinism" (1903, 195). Their doctrine of election, in particular, raised serious questions for her, and she eventually felt their doctrines were too "restrictive". They also strongly opposed her views on "restitution" as did other Orthodox Friends.[33] But what she appreciated about

---

[31] She felt compelled to share her experience because "It seemed to me the most magnificent piece of good news that any human being ever had to tell, and I gloried in telling it" (1903, 179).

[32] She was referring here to the strict Philadelphia Orthodox, of which she was a member, not Gurneyite Friends who had little or no influence in Philadelphia Yearly Meeting at this time. Even as late as 1893 when Rufus Jones identified the four types of Quakers, he observed that the broad, liberal Gurneyites, though numerous, were still at the Fringe of Philadelphia Yearly Meeting (1934, 26).

[33] Restitution refers to a belief in the "universal hope" that because God is unlimited love, he will eventually save everyone, somehow, someway. It is a kind of Christian universalism. She may have found the concept in William Law, though I have not found a reference to him in her writing. In *Spirit of Love,* Law came to a position of universal restitution. (Law, 1974, 3:37-40) Other Christian mystics, such as Julian of Norwich, though orthodox in every other aspect, also embraced a similar view of hope for everyone. About opposition to her views on "restitution" she wrote, "…on this ground I have always rather enjoyed being considered a heretic, and have never wanted to be endorsed by any one. I have felt that to be endorsed was to be bound…" (1903, 220). Smith was quite open publicly about her "heresy" and it did not damage her reputation as "the angel of the churches," nor prevent her from speaking engagements at the famous Keswick meetings in England or in other holiness circles (1903, 221-3). For a more

them was their great love for the Bible and their nurturance and development of her gifts as a Bible teacher.

When she and her husband moved from Philadelphia to the remote factory town of Millville, New Jersey, in 1867, she discovered a very different religious as well as social culture. She came into close contact with Methodists, and while attending a women's prayer meeting, a mill-worker introduced her to the experience of perfection which they called the entire sanctification or "Second blessing."[34] Regarding this concept in relation to her Quakerism she wrote:

> The Quaker examples and influences around me seemed to say there must be a deliverance somewhere, for they declared that they had experienced it; although they never seemed able to explain the "what" or the "how" in such a manner as I could understand it. (1903, 232)

She recorded her first response to the Methodist version of this concept in her journal in 1866:

> ...And this is the Methodist "blessing of holiness." Couched by them it is true in terms that I cannot altogether endorse, and held amid what seems to me a mixture of error, but still really and livingly experienced and enjoyed by them. I feel truly thankful to them for their testimony to its reality, and I realize that it is far better to *have* the experience, even if mixed with error, than to live without it, and be very doctrinally correct, as was my former case. (1903, 245)

This was a tremendous window of discovery for her, and although she never had an "instantaneous" crisis experience in the Methodist way though she walked down to the altar many times in revival meetings, she wrote that she believed in and experienced the truth of it in her life and explained it fully in her book *Christian's Secret of a Happy Life* (1903, 261, 287). She summed up by declaring:

> This new life I had entered upon has been called by several different names. The Methodists called it "The Second Blessing," or "The

---

detailed discussion of this controversial issue, see Dieter, 1996, 135-6. Ironically, her openly universalist position did prevent her from rejoining Friends in 1881 when she requested membership in Indiana Yearly Meeting and was turned down for her unorthodox belief in "restitution of all things." She finally was accepted back into Quaker membership by Baltimore Yearly Meeting where her sister was a leading minister (Spencer, 1991).

[34] She also wrote that "another influence that seemed to tell the same story" was the book given her by her father, "Spiritual Progress," extracts from the writings of Fenelon and Guyon (1903, 232).

Blessing of Sanctification;" the Presbyterians called it "The Higher Life," or "The Life of Faith;" the Friends called it "The Life hid with Christ in God." But by whatever name it may be called, the truth at the bottom of each name is the same, and can be expressed in four little words, "Not I, but Christ."[35] (Smith, 1903, 261)

She went on to become a recognized and highly respected Bible teacher, evangelist, and preacher. In 1874 she and Robert traveled to England as key speakers in evangelistic meetings held in Brighton and Oxford, England, that became known as "the Higher Life Movement" or Keswick holiness. She and her husband became international "Christian celebrities" (Dieter, 1996, 132-138).

Smith's understanding of holiness developed and expanded throughout her lifetime, from an initial desire to experience "instantaneous sanctification" by treading the path to the altar, to a mature understanding of holiness as the experience of the divine indwelling of pure love:

I feel myself to have gotten out into a limitless ocean of the love of God that overflows all things... "God is love," comprises my whole system of ethics. I find that every soul that has traveled on this highway of holiness for any length of time has invariably cut loose from its old moorings. (1905, 120)

5.4.2 Summary and Conclusions

Although she initially had to leave her strict Orthodox Quaker Meeting in Philadelphia because it seemed far too narrow for her youthful spiritual aspirations, she eventually returned "full-circle," but with renewed understanding of her Quaker roots, identifying holiness as the essence of Quakerism. Her full-orbed understanding and experience of holiness includes all of the four Quadrants. Quadrant 1 is represented by her strong emphasis on justification by faith and her belief in the core historic doctrines of Christian belief. She was appreciative of Quaker silent worship and communion as the real presence, but was open to experiencing God through different forms of worship in her ecumenical settings and numerous connections. She was obviously oriented to the experiential and charismatic in her embracing of the holiness revival in its camp meeting and mass meetings forms (Quadrant 2). The mystical element of Quadrant 3 is evidenced in descriptions of her own spiritual experiences. She described "union with God," the goal and essence of

---

[35] She was quoting Paul in Gal. 2:20: "I have been crucified with Christ; and it is no longer I who live, but it is Christ who lives in me," an oft-quoted text on the transformation that happens in union with God.

holiness as "the life hid with Christ in God." Lastly, she connected holiness to Quadrant 4, not so much in asceticism or sectarian isolation (although she never abandoned the Quaker style of dress), but in her embracing of a radical social agenda, such as women's rights, socialism, and the labor movement, yet always elevating Jesus Christ, both the historic and the mystical, as the ultimate model and source for a holy life. She remained all her life a Christ-centered political radical.

The prevailing opinion among historians has been that the holiness revival was a near-revolution, as Thomas Hamm terms it, and represented an assimilation of Quakerism into the dominant evangelical culture (Hamm, 1988, xiv). Undoubtedly, as Hamm describes it, Quakerism, as all denominations of the time, was absorbed in varying degrees into the mainstream evangelical culture. Hannah Whitall Smith's life not only spanned this period of immense change, but she was also directly involved with many of the events and personalities of the period. Her writings attest to the fact that she was a woman of deep spiritual insight and a keen observer of people and culture. As she looked back over the course of her own spiritual journey, her remarks about the relationship between Quakerism and holiness imply a different or at least more complex phenomenon than cultural adaptation. If her experience is at all typical or representative, her observations imply that a new generation was rediscovering Quaker holiness and expressing it in new ways.

Smith viewed the holiness revival as a broad, ecumenical religious awakening, a renewal of deeper spiritual life across denominations.[36] What is unfortunate in Smith's case is that Quakers during her lifetime were so conflicted, so divided over loyalty to tradition and the risk of new life, that Smith, who was one of the most lucid and profound minds in that era, was overshadowed and perhaps guilty by association with the more sensational, hyperbolic, and divisive of the holiness revivalists. She had difficulty finding a sense of place or appreciation within any of the Quaker bodies, though she also felt free not to be approved by any one group, because "to be endorsed was to be bound, and that it was better, for me at least, to be a free lance, with no hindrances to my absolute mental and spiritual freedom" (1903, 220-1).[37] This is not to imply that she had no influence among Quakers, for she had a significant circle of influence and was a consummate networker. But she

---

[36] She wrote "In all Denominations, even where in other respects they may seem to hold widely diverging views, there have been always those who have understood and lived the life of faith, not only among the Methodists, but among the Quakers and among the Catholics as well, and in fact it is I believe at the bottom of the creeds of every Church" (1903, 73-4).

[37] She also added sardonically, "...I have always rather enjoyed being considered a heretic..." (1903, 220). Rufus Jones, a younger contemporary, also admitted that as a young man he could not identify with any of the four Quaker types or groups of his time (see 6.1.2).

struggled to find a place of true leadership among Gurneyite Quakers, though she was highly respected by many as an evangelist, Bible teacher, temperance worker, and social activist. So when Punshon writes, "one should not underestimate the strength of resistance to these trends of holiness revival" (2001, 280), Smith's fate of being at that time in a state of perpetual Quaker limbo is an excellent example.

5.5 Chapter Summary

Holiness was never a monolithic movement among nineteenth century Friends. Advocates of holiness formed a spectrum from the holiness of the traditional Quietist (anti-revival holiness); to renewal within the bounds of the old forms; to those who whole-heartedly adopted Wesleyan forms such as Edward Mott (Mott, 1935, 1948); to radicals who wanted to eliminate anything related to "quietist mysticism," such as John Henry Douglas (Hamm, 1988, 82-83); to the "come-outers" who moved towards Pentecostalism and formed new denominations, such as Seth Rees (Dieter, 1996,264); to what I would term the synthesizers and loyalists, such as Smith, who retained strong identity to the core values and principles of Friends, but found those core essences appreciated and often explained more clearly in contemporary spiritual movements such as the Keswick movement and the Holiness Methodists. She also found no objections to adaptations of worship style or use of pastors, preaching, or singing in worship, based on her enthusiastic embracing of the holiness camp meetings.[38]

The revival of holiness in the second half of the nineteenth century took shape in America in the context of an ecumenical holiness movement among many denominations. But the holiness revival had, perhaps, its most profound effects upon Quakers, precisely because a new generation was rediscovering the essential aspects of Quakerism buried deep within its own tradition and

---

[38] She described camp meetings or "Meetings for the Promotion of Holiness" as "great open air Conferences of Christians of all denominations, from all parts of the country…living in tents under the trees, and spending a week or ten days in waiting upon God, and conferring together on the deep things of the Kingdom….They were a sort of culmination of the grand spiritual romance which my religion has always been to me, and I count them among the most entrancing times of my life" (1903, 284-5). Not surprisingly, I have thus far found no references in Smith's writings to Joseph John Gurney. If Gurney's evangelicalism prepared the way for the Holiness Movement among Friends, she seemed completely unaware of it. Perhaps because the extremely traditional Philadelphia Orthodox were more sympathetic to the Wilburites, she had no exposure to Gurney's writings or his evangelical views. Interestingly, Gurney's widow, Eliza, was still living in Philadelphia at the same time as Smith resided there, but it is not known if they had any contact (Bronner 1970, 145).

manifesting them in a different cultural context with different forms (though in many ways not unlike the enthusiastic and charismatic revival meetings of earliest Friends). This explains why a Quaker such as Hannah Whitall Smith could find holiness as preached by revivalists to be "true Quaker doctrine." It also explains, in part, strong reactions to revivalism among other Friends, such as Joel Bean, who viewed the holiness movement as a regression to a more primitive form of Christian expression rather than evolving, as he hoped, to a higher, more progressive, and cultured form (Bean, 1885, 287).

The next chapter examines two modernist, scholarly Friends, educators by profession, widely respected and influential in their time, both inside and outside of the Quaker fold, who became leaders of a new movement in Quakerism that Thomas Kennedy has called "the Quaker Renaissance" (2001). One, Rufus Jones, became the distinguished scholar of Quaker mysticism and a pioneer in the nascent field of mystical studies; the other, J. Rendel Harris, though less well-known today, was a pioneering biblical scholar and linguist, and a Quaker holiness mystic of the twentieth century.

Smith, born a generation too early and lacking academic credentials, was past her prime by the rise of the Quaker Renaissance, but she was intimately acquainted with some who were voices of a new progressive Quakerism. One of her close friends was Helen Balkwill, who married the scholarly J. Rendel Harris in 1880 (Spencer, 1991). She remained close to the Harris' circle because they shared a common identity as holiness Quakers. The next chapter establishes holiness in Quaker modernism; although experiential Quakerism was greatly enhanced by the Holiness Movement, it was not limited to the revival forms of the nineteenth century.

CHAPTER 6

Holiness and Quakerism in the Twentieth Century

6.1 Holiness and Modernity

If Quakers were to mark sacred sites beyond its "1652 tour" of Pendle Hill where Fox had his vision of "a great people to be gathered," a more recent holy site (far more picturesque and dramatic) for Quaker pilgrims would be Mürren, Switzerland, beneath the Jungfrau. Here in the summer of 1897 an intimate drama occurred in the encounter of two people who would change the face of Quakerism in the twentieth century– Rufus M. Jones[1] and John Wilhelm Rowntree. This event occurred as a private and intimate meeting between two persons who became the "prophets of the Quaker Renaissance" – one, of American Quakerism, the other, of British Quakerism (Kennedy, 2001, 156, 162). The creative energy of that encounter set off sparks that ignited a blaze which transformed Orthodox Quakerism on the same scale that the fires of revival transformed Quietist Quakerism a generation earlier (Jones, 1929, 191).[2]

Before they parted, they had covenanted together to work towards creating "a fresh and sound historical interpretation of the entire Quaker movement" (Jones, 1929, 195). Jones resonated with Rowntree's diagnosis and remedy for the renewal of Quakerism:

---

[1] Rufus M. Jones was born in 1863 and raised in the rural hamlet of South China, Maine, in the Orthodox New England Yearly Meeting where Wilburites had been cast out in 1845. Jones came to maturity in the moderate Gurneyism of Haverford College where he attended and later taught as professor of Philosophy (Hamm, 1988, 148).

[2] A third figure, often overlooked, who also played a major role in Quaker renewal, but whose vision for Friends moved in a somewhat different direction, was J. Rendel Harris, Jones' traveling companion in Switzerland, and an old friend who had taught at Haverford College (Jones, 1929, 189). It was Harris who presaged the tone of the historic occasion by quoting a Christina Rossetti poem at the meeting for worship that morning at the Hotel Mürren. Jones recounted the enchantment of that day: "That day, that Sunday at Mürren, in front of the splendor of the Jungfrau, saw… the birth of an unending friendship between John Wilhelm Rowntree and myself…It was a day of continual thrills – my first experience on a high snow mountain – but greater than the joy of climbing or of seeing sunrise on the Jungfrau or of plunging down a mountain top into space, was my highborn joy as I went on to discover in the remarkable character and quality of the new friend who was walking at my side. We both knew before the day was over that we were to be comrades for the rest of life" (1929, 191-192).

He saw that the true historical track had been lost in the mists of controversy and convention, and that *someone must rediscover the clue to early Quaker history*. This task seemed to be his own peculiar mission. (1929, 196)

Rowntree's mission became Jones' mission, and the two agreed to begin work on a scholarly and comprehensive history of the Quaker movement. Jones would focus on a study of the pre-Quaker influences of European mystical movements, and Rowntree would begin to examine Quaker beginnings in the seventeenth century.

Jones believed that Rowntree, who was already a leader among young Friends in Britain, was destined to be a true prophet. Jones wrote, "He was not a rebel or a revolutionist but a prophet…. A prophet who reveres the past, lives in the present and forecasts the future that ought to be" (1929, 197-198). From that day forward, they met almost every year until Rowntree's premature death eight years later in 1905, with Jones at his side (Jones, 1929, 196). After Rowntree's death, Jones would carry on the vision for both of them. In his autobiography, Jones described the impact of Rowntree's death and how he was able to overcome the unbearable loss:

His death, so unexpected and so moving, carried me farther perhaps than his continued life could have done. I felt at once that I had to live and work for both of us and no longer as one person. (1929, 198)

6.1.1 *Jones and Mysticism*

This was not the first time Jones had faced the crushing pain of the death of someone he loved deeply. In 1903, just two years before Rowntree's death, Jones lost his eleven-year-old son, Lowell, suddenly and unexpectedly, while he and his wife were on their way to England.[3] Jones wrote, it "altered everything on earth for me" (1934, 83). In several of his writings, Jones described the unusually deep mystical bond he had with his son. The night before he was to learn of his son's death he had the most profound sense of "being brought into direct contact with God" that he ever experienced (1927, 42-43; 1934, 84). He interpreted this experience as a divinely given gift, an endowment of strength that enabled him to bear and prevail over such an immense loss. He described it in these words in his autobiography:

This experience came suddenly, spontaneously. There were no steps of preparation for it. I heard no words. I saw no light. I was impressed

---

[3] Jones also suffered the death of his first wife, Sallie, in 1899.

only with a sense of invasion, a new tide of life coming in as from some mystic ocean, and with it I had the consciousness of being taken up into boundless love. (1934, 84)

In *New Studies in Mystical Religion*, he referred to this experience didactically as an example of mysticism, with a longer version of the account. Unlike Quaker figures reviewed thus far, the experience was not framed in specifically Christian language. One wonders if he modified the description to fit a broad audience, or if, indeed, he did not interpret it in a specifically theistic context:

It seems on these occasions as though a larger and fuller Life flooded in and connected the recipient with what is essential for his spiritual life, somewhat as the red corpuscles in the blood connect us with the oxygen which keeps our life going. Once at sea, in the middle of the night, when all unbeknown to me then my little boy, left behind in America, was dying, with no father by him to hold his hand, I suddenly felt myself surrounded by a mighty presence and held as though by invisible arms. At no other time in my life have I ever felt such positive contact, and on this occasion my entire being was calmed, and I was inwardly prepared to meet the message of sorrow which was waiting for me next day when I landed at Liverpool. (1934, 42-43)

He was traveling to England at the time to participate as a lecturer in the opening of a new Quaker experiment in religious education called Woodbrooke. Under the circumstances, most individuals would cancel their appointments. Jones did not. He delivered all of his lectures as promised. His mystical experience somehow fortified him for his weeks in England. He wrote of the paradoxical state of feeling "divided in being, with an essential part of myself irrevocably gone and yet with an extraordinary increment of life and power such as I had not felt before" (1934, 84).

It is unfortunate that the dominant rational side of Jones prevented him from developing a modern Quaker theology of suffering based on the "mysticism of the cross," so essential to historical holiness Quakerism as well as the Christian mystical tradition. His identity as both a scholar of Quaker history and thought and of mysticism, as well as his own experience of suffering and tragedy, had all the potential for him to create such a work.[4] But instead he chose to dismiss (or repress?) rather than to analyze and attempt to understand the *via negativa* of Quaker mysticism. One of the most obvious facts about the origins of the Quaker movement is that it arose and thrived amidst the reality of persecution and intense suffering and is, therefore, immersed in a

---

[4] Compare, for example, a contemporary, C.S. Lewis, also a mystic, who wrote a profound book on suffering after the death of his wife, Joy: *A Grief Observed*, Seabury, 1963.

spirituality of suffering. Yet Jones chose to ignore entirely that dimension of Quaker mysticism and concentrate only on "affirmative" mysticism. Thus he overlooked the potential to synthesize the dialectical and paradoxical nature of the early Quaker movement, which included both a joyous affirmation of life and the mystical embrace of the reality of suffering. Both of these dimensions, the joyous affirmation and the embrace of suffering, were personified in his own life, yet he did not explore the depths of their potential integration.[5]

6.1.2   Jones and the New Quakerism

The quest for Jones and Rowntree was to discover the "clue to early Quaker history." The key for Jones to unlocking the mystery of Quaker beginnings and understanding its modern relevance was mysticism:

> No other large, organized, historically continuous body of Christians has yet existed which has been so fundamentally mystical, both in theory and practice, as the Society of Friends. (1921, xiii)

It was a bold claim and an arguable one, but one which was accepted for the most part uncritically by modernist Friends on both sides of the Atlantic. These modernist Friends were determined to separate themselves from Quaker evangelicalism, and the mystical explanation as envisioned by Jones was anti-evangelical and compatible with liberalism. According to John Punshon, Jones' interpretation captured a whole generation of the "silent tradition" (1984, 227).

In 1893, several years before his momentous meeting with Rowntree, Jones was offered both the philosophy position at Haverford and the editorship of the Gurneyite journal, *The Friends Review*. Believing *The Friends Review* had no future – its sphere lay in a "small midway area between two extremes" (Jones, 1934, 50), he pulled off what seemed an improbable coup by merging *The Friends Review* with *The Christian Worker,* a western based holiness publication edited by J. Walter Malone, the leading holiness voice at the turn of the century (Hamm, 1988, 161; Jones, 1934, 51-53). [6] In 1894 the two old

---

[5] Jones wrote one brief essay on the subject of death in 1923 after meeting Rendel Harris and Herbert G. Wood in Cairo. Here he took time to write an essay called "Death as a Spiritual Fact" for the *Friend (London)*. In reference to his personal life he wrote, "I can only add my personal experience that much which I have done in the last twenty years has been done in conviction that I was left here to finish what those dearer to me than life would have been doing if they remained" (see Vining, 1959, 206 and *TF,* April 13, 1923, 262).

[6] Jones did not mention Malone in his *Trail of Life* series or any of his published works, despite the fact that he became the leading holiness Friend of this period. See Oliver,

journals were reborn as *The American Friend*, with Jones as editor and a variety of moderate and holiness Friends as associates (Hamm, 1988, 148). Jones utilized what he could from the thriving and vibrant holiness movement of western Friends as it coalesced under the leadership of J. Walter Malone, then discarded it. Later in his writings, Jones leaves no doubt about his attitude towards holiness: "The holiness teaching of the period, taken over from Wesley, was crude and artificial, and bore the marks of the eighteenth century" (1934, 58). Jones, whose rural Maine Gurneyite roots were planted in holiness soil, gradually distanced himself from all traces of his holiness past.[7] But as Hamm observes, "Jones walked a tightrope and, initially at least, did it successfully" (1988, 148). In John Oliver's account, Jones and Malone had friendly relations, and Malone felt certain of Jones' sympathy with a moderate evangelical position. If he had doubted Jones' orthodoxy, he would never have given up control of *The Christian Worker*, which had more than twice the circulation of the struggling *Friends Review* (1991, 64-68).

Jones identified the essential aspect and most obvious feature in vital Quakerism in all historical periods as: "the inward, immediate assurance of God which possessed its founder, George Fox, and his greatest followers in true 'apostolic succession'" (1934, 33). Early Quakers had "known God experimentally." Jones believed the most central fact of early Quaker belief was "that God and man were not separated by space – the far-off…the other down here in mutability." He emphasized the immanence of God in the human soul as the *sin qua non* of Quakerism: "Nothing except sin ever separates God and man, since they are spiritually inter-related" (1934, 34); God is "the eternal Seeker,

---

1991, for an in-depth analysis of the merger of the journals and an interesting comparison of these two contemporaries.

[7] His biographer, Elizabeth Vining, documents an interesting visit Jones made to Oregon and California in 1905. In Oregon he was the guest speaker for a Pacific College program. He spoke in the meetinghouse, which "filled up with Friends and after an impressive period of worship and devotion I gave the message which was on my heart." Friends bid him farewell by singing on the meetinghouse porch, "God be with you till we meet again." He wrote to his wife, "I never felt anything was more worth doing than this trip, and I never felt more drawn to a company of people than to these Friends in Newberg" (1959, 121). According to Vining, he met opposition in Pasadena, California, where John Henry Douglas, a leading holiness Friend and first Superintendent of Oregon Yearly Meeting, had persuaded the Committee of ministry to "condemn" his writings. When he met Douglas face to face at the meetinghouse, he wrote that Douglas was "a good deal flustered but he said the right things…" After Jones spoke, "hosts of friends came up to speak to me," he wrote, and "The ice was really broken." He then arranged to meet with Douglas. The results of this meeting are not known (1959, 122). It appears that Jones was quite the diplomat, but it's difficult to determine conclusively what actually transpired during this visit to the far western states where most Friends were strongly holiness. Obviously, Jones had become a controversial figure with holiness Friends in the years since he began editing *The American Friend*.

the infinite Lover of souls" (1934, 34); Man is "self-conscious spirit – made in the image of the divine Spirit – in reality unsundered from God" (1934, 34); "True 'life' begins when man finds that eternal Reality to which he 'belongs'...This inward junction of the soul with God, Fox and Quakers after him, called 'the Light within,' 'the seed of God,' 'something of God in man'" (1934, 34):

> The point I fixed upon as essential was this *mystical* aspect of the Quaker movement, God discovered within man and actually revealed as a present fact to prophetic and responsive souls, who have brought their lives into spiritual parallelism with Him. (1934, 34-5)

He defines mysticism innumerable times in his writings:

> Mysticism is a word very loosely used, and one from which many persons shy away, but it has always been used historically to signify a personal, first-hand discovery of God, a vital interaction between God and man. (1934, 35)

6.1.3   Jones and the Inner Light

Elizabeth Vining, one of Jones' biographers, noted that Jones seldom used the traditional Quaker and biblical term "Christ Within." Instead he used "Spirit," "Divine Spirit," "Spirit of Truth," "Holy Spirit," "Presence," "the Over-world," and "the Beyond that is Within" (1959, 216). Although he believed Christ was divine and human, and died and was resurrected, the most unique aspect of Jesus for Jones was Jesus' own "experience of God" (1959, 216). Jones' Christology could best be summarized by a statement made in a sermon quoted by Vining: "The greatest single thing about Christ is His *experience* of God and His transmission of the life of God into the lives of men" (1959, 261). The transmission of the life of God into humanity came via the "Inner Light," a divine principle within every person, sufficient to bring one to self-understanding and self-actualization. One of the key themes found throughout his writings, which he states many times with slight variations, is that "Man is self-conscious spirit – made in the image of the divine Spirit – in reality unsundered from God" (1934, 34). So in effect, Christ's death and resurrection, though important to the Christian "grand narrative" as the ultimate symbol of God's love for humanity, need not be interpreted as a necessary sacrifice or atonement for sin, since humanity, for Jones, was not separated from God as in the traditional doctrine of the fall.

The concept of the Light, originally interpreted by Barclay as "the Light of Christ," a supernatural and divine principle that is not "any part of man's nature" (Sippel, 2002, 125), was reinterpreted by Jones as a divine part of human nature. Jones could not tolerate a dualism such as divine vs. human or natural vs. supernatural, and believed that Barclay had altered Fox's original meaning.

Social Law in the Spiritual World, published early in his career (1904), is the closest Jones came to developing a modernist Quaker "theology." It was based on lectures he had given at three "Summer Schools" between 1901 and 1904.[8] It was the *Summa* of his theological reflections from his teachings and study as he entered mid-life (Vining, 1959, 103). It was here Jones formulated his first clear statement of inner light mysticism: "The Inner Light is the doctrine that there is something Divine, 'something of God' in the human soul" (Jones, 1904, 149). Jones wrote that five terms are used to name what the Divine something is: "The Light, the Seed, Christ within, the Spirit, that of God in you" (1904, 149). "This Divine Seed is in every person good or bad" (1904, 140). Jones summarized what he claimed were the three ways in which primitive Quakers used the term "Inner Light":[9] "...as a Divine Life resident in the soul, as a source of guidance and illumination, and as a ground of spiritual certitude" (1904, 152). The latter, he explained further, meant "the self demonstration of spiritual experience," a concept, he maintained, in harmony with the findings of modern philosophy (1904, 152). Hence he could claim that modern philosophy had "settled for all time that the criterion of truth is to be found in the nature of consciousness itself – not somewhere else" (1904, 152). Jones had thus eliminated the transcendent Christ and the revelation found in Scripture. The criterion of truth was not multifaceted for Jones. It did not derive from Scripture or tradition (faith handed down though time), but reason alone – the nature of consciousness itself. "Everything in religion is to be verified in personal experience" (1904, 153). Certitude comes through "enlightened" reason as it interprets personal experience. Jones shifted truth from a revealed message given in time and history and passed on through Scripture and tradition to the subjective and immediate experience of each individual. Experience itself became divine revelation.

Jones summarized his understanding of the Inner Light by asserting that "Man's spiritual nature is rooted and grounded in the Divine Life" (1904, 157) and thus "...the Inner Light...is both human and divine." It is the actual inner self formed by the union of a divine *and* a human element in a single undivided life.

---

[8] Scarborough in 1901, Woodbrooke in 1903 (both in England), and Haverford (in the U.S.) in 1904.

[9] Primitive Quakers rarely used this particular term. Based on the concordance to Fox's *Journal* as compiled by Joseph Pickvance, "No instance of this usage has been noted in Fox, and even, "the inward Light" is a rare usage (1989, 93).

6.1.4 Jones on Barclay and Calvin

In *Social Law in the Spiritual World*, Jones clearly states his differences with Barclay on the Inner Light. (Barclay did not actually use the term Inner Light, but "the universal Light of Christ.") Barclay's understanding of the Light, Jones asserted, was "unspiritual and contrary to the known facts of psychology," and he also claimed that Barclay denied the possibility of God as "the indwelling light and life of the soul, permeating all the activities" (1904, 174-176). He did not accept Barclay's *Apology* as an adequate formulation of Fox's thought. According to Jones, Fox was correct in completely breaking with Protestantism and Reformation theology, while Barclay had corrupted Fox's message by reattaching it to a Calvinistic theology. Jones often expressed his antipathy to Calvin. Ridding modern Quakerism of traces of Calvinism became a major aim of Jones. Jones' judgment was that:

> It was Calvin's aim and mission to develop a Church organization and to formulate a theological system which would compete on its own ground with the Roman Catholic Church...But it would be quite impossible to maintain that the vast system of theology or the solid structure of organization had much relation to immediate experience. (1904, 141-142)

Calvin reacted to the Roman church precisely on the basis of his own religious experience, that of his own unworthiness, God's love and grace, and God's sovereignty as revealed to him by Scripture and in nature. Calvin's experience of God emphasized transcendence, yet he could also describe God as personally and intimately as God being like a mother.[10] Jones emphasized God's immanence, which was akin to something innate in the soul, but without the personal intimacy that Calvin expressed. In *New Studies in Mystical Religion* Jones wrote:

> We ought to challenge the elaborate logical construction of bygone metaphysics, and base our interpretations on the sure ground of *vital religious experience* and on the unescapable (*sic*) implications of our minds as they cooperate with a universe which reveals rationality from outmost husk to innermost core." (1927, 24)

---

[10] For example, in a sermon on Job he described a relationship of personal intimacy: "Our Lord makes himself uniquely familiar; he is like a nurse, like a mother; he does not compare himself only to fathers, who are so benign and humane toward their children, but he says that he is more than mother, more than nurse" (qtd. in Bouwsma, 1997, 323-4).

Both Calvin and Jones looked at the universe and saw a rational creator, but Calvin was reduced to a sense of his own inadequacy and unworthiness, and Jones to his innate link to divinity. Certainty for Jones was religious experience and rationality. But whose religious experience is most rational? The hubris of Jones's optimism about human nature is as extreme in its own way as Calvin's pessimism about humanity:

> But one of the essential aspects of religion now and always is the experiment, made in the soul's inner laboratory, of the personal discovery of that more than ourselves whom we call God. (Jones, 1927, 24)

Early Quakers would never conceive of God as merely "more than ourselves" or the self fully actualized. For early Quakers, the self had to decrease; in fact, death to self had to occur before Christ could be born in the soul.

The missing element in Jones' mysticism of the Inner Light, when contrasted with Fox, Barclay, and other early Quakers, is that the realization of the image of God in the soul must come by the way of Christ and the experience of the cross. Jones put all the emphasis on our becoming "partakers of the divine nature" as already innate and immanent, but without the *imatio Christi*, the way of the cross so essential to Quaker spiritual formation and the Christian mystical tradition Jones so revered. Evidently, this deficiency in Jones' mystical Quakerism was recognized by one of his close friends, and fellow modernist scholar, J. Rendel Harris (see 6.2), writing to Jones in 1908:

> Thy book[11] will be of great service – but the quotations must be verified, and certain dangerous tendencies must be warned against. Thee will see it for thyself in going about. *A Christless Quakerism will neither save itself nor the people.* [my emphasis] (Pickard, 1978, 21)

Harris' insight has a strong prophetic ring, a foreshadowing of H. Richard Niebuhr's stinging judgment of liberal theology that "a God without wrath brings man without sin into a kingdom without judgment through the ministrations of a Christ without a cross, saving man without sin..." (1959, 193). Jones enthusiastically adopted the classical liberalism of his day that Niebuhr would soon ruthlessly critique.

Jones always upheld certain central tenets of Christian orthodoxy. He accepted the divinity and humanity of Christ, the incarnation, and the moral theory of the atonement (not a substitutionary theory). But he undermined his Christocentrism by continually emphasizing the soul as inherently divine, until the soul itself became the Light. For example, in *New Studies in Mystical*

---

[11] Based on the date of the letter, the book referred to would be *Studies in Mystical Religion*, published in 1909.

Religion, he concluded his study of the Christian mystical tradition with a quote from Upanishads. An ancient sage is asked, "What then is the light of man?" and the ancient sage replies, "When the sun is set, and the moon is set, and the fire is gone out, THE SOUL IS THE LIGHT OF MAN." [his caps] By ending with this statement so emphatically, Jones took Christ out of the Light, the soul itself was the Light, and the soul became divine (1927, 205). Thus Jones created an "inner light mysticism" in which the soul was its own authority, an elevated humanism which severed the inward light from Christ. Consequently, liberal Quakerism developed a humanistic confidence in the soul as supreme.

6.1.5 Jones and Cambridge Platonism

Jones' theory of the Inner Light was not uncritically accepted by all modernist Quakers of the period. For example, H. G. Wood, a British modernist, wrote a pamphlet entitled "What do We Mean by the Inner Light?" (1930). Wood, who continued to value the holiness dimension of Quakerism, did not specifically name Jones, but clearly challenged his theory of the Inner Light as the majority of liberal Quakerism understood it (1930, 3-9, 15).

Jones' mysticism had a firmer base in rationalism than either Barclay or William Penn, the most rational of the early Quakers. The mysticism that Jones "recovered" in early Quakerism was a mysticism of *theosis*, or union with God, but with more affinity to Thomas More and the Cambridge Platonists,[12] whose favorite text was "the spirit of man is the candle of the Lord" (Prov. 20:27), than to the Christ-centered holiness mysticism of George Fox and early Quakers. Of course "the candle" for the Platonists was lit by God and would bring us to God. But for the Cambridge intellectuals, the candle was both reason and a spiritual faculty, and *theosis* was the "Divine Life" as lived ethically and joyfully. They were great admirers of Plotinus, as was Jones. The Cambridge Platonists "deplored enthusiasm and false and furious zeal as much as superstition, and would have said that Christianity is not 'mystical'" (Wakefield, 1989, 269). Christianity, for the Cambridge Platonists as for Jones, was innately reasonable. The Platonists, like Jones, would "have no sharp dichotomies" (Wakefield, 1989, 279). As appealing as the Platonists' philosophy appears, and though it had some affinities with Quakerism (Barclay quotes them twice in his *Apology*), their thinking was far from the early Quaker position. The Quakers were supernaturalists, and divine illumination was not the same as natural reason. The early Quakers were quite clear that the inward light was not natural reason or a natural facility. The Cambridge Platonists did not believe that the highest authority was the Holy Spirit, but rather reason itself, which was divine. For the Platonists, *supernatural* revelation by the Holy

---

[12] See Wakefield, 1989, 257-293, for further discussion of Cambridge Platonists.

Spirit ended with the closing of the canon, a view completely opposed to early Quakerism (Wood, 1930, 6). Jones' intellectualism and Platonic idealism places him closer to the Cambridge Platonists than to the early Friends.

6.1.6 Conclusions

As much as he elevated mysticism, Jones' intellectual quest conditioned everything. He filtered mystical experience through a rationalistic and humanist idealism and the then-current optimistic liberal theology. Although he mined the Greek Fathers for his Quaker interpretations, he identified most fully with Clement of Alexandria, the most Platonic of all the Greek Fathers.[13] But Jones implicitly rejected the apophatic way of mystical theology, also predominant in the Greek Fathers, which he termed Quietism. The apophatic way of Quietism and the ecstatic side of holiness (which he equated with extreme evangelicalism) were both repudiated, despite the fact that both were strong elements of the original movement.

Jones was tied to the intellectual fashions of his age and the prevailing views of scientific method. He was a modernist attracted to the Christian mystical tradition because of its prophetic stance and parallels with many aspects of Quaker tradition. But other aspects of mysticism – the apophatic, *via negativa*, the spirituality of the cross and suffering, the visionary and ecstatic elements, and the personal intimacy of Christocentric mysticism, especially perfectionism, all elements found in the holiness tradition – he thoroughly rejected. The prophetic (as ethical social action), the joy-filled freedom and liberation aspects attracted him. But he was highly selective in how he appropriated mysticism and applied it to Quakers.

Thus far, I have argued that the spirituality of the nineteenth century Holiness Movement has a strong correspondence to the perfectionism of early Quakerism, and that holiness, in fact, answers the question, "What is the clue to understanding early Quaker history?" (as Jones put the question). Jones was certain mysticism was the clue, and spent a lifetime studying and writing on that theme. Jones was not misguided; he was on the right track, but he was only half-right. He had found an important clue, but only half of the equation. The clue to understanding early Quaker history and its subsequent development is to grasp the spirituality of Quaker holiness, which is strongly mystical, but always centered on Christ and the cross. The nineteenth century Holiness Movement,

---

[13] Jones' first editorial in *The Friends Review* was called "Christian Thought in the Early Greek Church": "I had already discovered the remarkable interpretation of early Christianity by the great Greek Fathers...and their message admirably fitted my outlook on religious thought" (1934, 40). Jones had previously published *Selections from the Writings of Clement of Alexandria* (1914).

which reshaped in a revivalist setting the Quaker doctrine of perfection, was also a mysticism centered on Christ and the cross. Jones, though he accepted the incarnation, the divinity and humanity of Christ and the moral influence theory of atonement, rarely spoke of the Inner Light in connection with Christ. The "inner light mysticism" of Jones minimized the experience of Christ and the cross and maximized the experience of God and human potential. H. G. Wood, critiquing "inner light mysticism" as it came to dominate modern liberal Quakerism, wrote:

> Our experience may in some way be wider, but is likely to be shallower if we prefer to speak of the Inner Light rather than the Inward Christ. The importance of this insistence on heart-knowledge of Jesus Christ can hardly be overestimated...The light is not simply within us...The inner light is not so much a normal element in human nature as an experience of a transforming friendship, which will make us to be what we know we are not yet. And everyone that has this hope set on Him, purified himself. "If we would indeed have our knowledge thrive and flourish, we must water the tender plant of it with holiness."[14] (1930, 15)

Jones' de-emphasis on Christ and overemphasis on the Light as a non-personal "principle" alienated holiness Friends from his position, and led later scholars to question even more rigorously his assumptions about the faith of early Quakers. Paul Anderson, for example, maintained that "...the weakness of Jones' thesis was that it failed to give proper credit to the biblical and Christ-centered thrust of Early Quakerism, which certainly provided the impetus for the ethical conviction and the religious experience of early Friends" (Williams, 1987, 255).

6.1.7 Summary

Jones put great emphasis on the mystical aspect of holiness, but shifted the trajectory from a distinctly Christocentric focus to a more humanistic one. Union with God is referred to as *theois* by Jones, and often defined as participation in God, so that his theory of mysticism appears to correspond to Quadrant 3. But with his separation of affirmative mysticism from the apophatic, he rejected and devalued a critical component of Quaker holiness, and presented a liberal, progressive, and idealist version that became much more acceptable to the modern, rational, and activist mind. His theory of

---

[14] This last sentence he put in quotes, but did not reference it. He may have been quoting his friend and mentor, J. Rendel Harris; see 6.2.

mysticism, while hugely influential within both Quaker and non-Quaker circles and while portraying Quakerism in an attractive and culturally acceptable light, was historically inaccurate. He substantially loosened Quaker ties to Quadrant 1. Faith in the historic Christ was minimized. Christ in his humanity was primarily an ethical model and exemplar, and not a mediator to union with God. Representations of the divine through doctrines were unnecessary encumbrances. Although the experiential (Quadrant 2) was a constant theme for Jones, a personal encounter with Christ, or a conversion experience was not essential in the Quaker liberalism that flowed from Jones. For George Fox and all early Quakers, the direct experience of God was not simply discovering one's divinity in the soul, but being remade as a new creation, an experience mediated through the person of Christ. Quadrant 4, imitation of Christ, finds ethical expression in Jones' admirable social witness and active work for justice. But the role of the indwelling Christ, the Christ within of the contemplative life, from which Quaker holiness takes form and shape, was not made clear in Jones' theory of Quakerism. Although Jones located himself within the broad Christian tradition, he reinterpreted his theory of mysticism through a decidedly modern and intellectually and culturally accommodating perspective. The incarnate Christ was not abandoned, but became more peripheral.

6.2 J. Rendel Harris: Modernist Holiness Mystic

Shortly before the close of the nineteenth century when much Quaker ministry in worship took more of a sermonic form, a respected Quaker leader delivered a homily on "union with Christ" at a meeting for worship in Cambridge.[15] The sermon was based on the text, "He that is joined unto the Lord is one spirit," from I Cor. 6:17. It was later published as one of a collection of addresses in a book entitled *Union with God* (1895), and thus provides a glimpse into the content of at least some Quaker preaching at the turn of the century:

> ...this great centripetal sentence...takes us up to the source from whence we come and from which we live, "He that is joined unto the Lord is one spirit." It is pantheistic, beloved, strongly pantheistic; but we do not propose to let the theosophists have all the pantheism to themselves. We have got some of it too. If you do not like the term pantheistic, say panchristic. I am not ashamed to say that I believe there is an experience of union with the Lord which is rightly characterized as pantheistic, in which God has met all the needs of the soul, and has become the indwelling power of the human spirit; that

---

[15] See Wood, 1951, for a discussion of ministry in worship in this period.

the man who is thus united to God moves as God moves, and acts as the Lord wills him to act in the body and in the circumstances in which he is placed. Of course it is somewhat pantheistic; but Christ can be all in all in the nineteenth century as well as in the first, and we do not need to think Him less than He wishes to be to those who trust in Him. (1895, 141-2)

What we find in this sermon are elements which have the kind of radical and provocative ring of early Quaker preaching on perfection as divine union, as Christ within. But it also has the tone and cadences of nineteenth century holiness preaching on Christ as the indwelling power, the "all in all." It is biblically based, being an exposition of a text from Scripture, and if we were to read the entire sermon in its full context, thoroughly evangelical as well.

The inspired preacher of this sermon was J. Rendel Harris, (1852-1941), one of the key leaders of the modernist movement in turn of the century Quakerism (Kennedy, 2001). He became the first director of Woodbrooke, a "permanent Settlement for religious and social study," which opened in Birmingham on Oct. 13, 1903 (Davis, 1953, 13).

Harris was speaking of divine union, sometimes called "divinization," or *unus spiritus* in the Christian mystical tradition, a Pauline concept which has always carried for Protestantism shades of pantheism, a fact Harris clearly recognized and was willing to meet in his own uniquely humorous way. Harris' wry sense of humor was one of his most distinguishing traits (Pickard, 1978), as was his ability to be startling and provocative. Harris was, in fact, quite orthodox and Trinitarian, but could often speak in unconventional ways.[16]

Harris was one of the key speakers at the Manchester Conference in 1895, a turning point for British Quakerism which heralded the decisive shift from evangelicalism to modernism (Punshon, 1984, 210-212; Kennedy, 2001, 148-156). Harris, along with most educated, scholarly voices, was convinced that Quakerism needed to join with the intellectual forces of the world and incorporate the best of modern ideals and scientific knowledge into its faith and life (Kennedy, 2001, 152). However, he also maintained a holiness spirituality.

This section shows how Harris integrated the evangelical, holiness, mystical, and modernist strands of his Quaker spirituality without becoming a tangle of contradictions. His interpretation of Quaker holiness illuminates the contrast between his modernism and that of his colleague and friend Rufus Jones.[17] Both men had great admiration and respect for each other's scholarship,

---

[16] One of his more assessable and fascinating scholarly works was on the Trinity, entitled *The Origin of the Doctrine of the Trinity* (1929). He also wrote *A Tract on the Triune Nature of God* (1900).

[17] The number of Harris' published works rivals Rufus Jones (50 plus). He wrote brilliant scholarly books in the area of textual criticism and the new "higher" criticism and translated and interpreted ancient Christian and pre-Christian texts from Greek,

but ultimately arrived at very different theological locations. Harris remained all of his long life a holiness Quaker and a modern Christian mystic. Jones abandoned his holiness and evangelical roots to become the voice of Quaker liberalism and a scholar of mysticism.

6.2.1 Harris and the Holiness Movement

Little is known about Harris' early family life or religious background, other than that he was born in 1852 and grew up in the Congregational Church (Free Church tradition) in Plymouth, England.[18] Sometime around 1880-1881, perhaps through the influence of his wife, he attended a Keswick Conference meeting and had a life-changing spiritual experience. Irene Pickard describes this turning point in his life:

> [He] shared with his wife a religious conversion, which involved a very deep sense of dedication to God. They took part in the Keswick Conventions, and the Holiness Movement of the nineteenth century. In addition, Rendel Harris experienced what was called "the Second Blessing." I once asked H. G. Wood what that meant, and he replied, "An experience of sanctification over and above the earlier conversion." Whatever that means, it set him free in pursuit of Truth in whatever direction his vocation and guidance led. Freedom meant a great deal to Rendel Harris. The story is told of his being led to a new room in Cambridge by the landlady's small son, of whom he asked, "How old are you, young man?" "I'm free," replied the small person with imperfect speech. "Praise the Lord, so am I!" said Rendel Harris. And indeed he was, and it was a source of joy in his life.[19] (1978, 3)

Hebrew, Syriac, and Aramaic. He discovered three early Christian documents, which had been lost for centuries (Wilson, 1941). He was a pioneer in the new field of comparative religion, studying what was then called "Primitive Folk-lure," examining the influence of pagan mythology on early Christianity. In addition, he wrote devotional works, mainly collections of his sermons and speeches, as well as a few less technical books to introduce his findings to a more general audience. He was an established and distinguished scholar of Christian antiquity and a pioneer in textual and historical criticism. Based on a large body of anecdotal evidence, he was also whimsical, disarming, and playful (Pickard, 1978; Wilson, 1941).

[18] He was known all of his life as a "militant non-conformist" (Scott, 1967, 45). Harris went to Cambridge in 1869, and entered Clare College in 1870 in Mathematics. In 1875 he was elected to Clare College and received a Lectureship in Mathematics. In 1880 he married Helen Balkwill, a Quaker itinerant minister who had recently returned from a religious visit to the United States, in Plymouth.

[19] This description was written by his personal secretary for 12 years (1911 to 1923), who collected memories of Harris. Harris explicitly stated he wished no formal

The quaint anecdote attached to this quote is included here because it points to one of the central themes in Harris' life and faith that resulted from his religious experience – his discovery of freedom in Christ. This exhilarating sense of freedom permeated his religious and intellectual life.[20] It allowed him to follow his intuitions, which he trusted to be Spirit-led, in research, and the impulses of his heart in religion.

H. G. Wood shed light on Harris' early religious experience and identified the experience of "Christian perfection" as the link to George Fox and early Quakers:

> His outlook was determined in his early days by the second evangelical revival, particularly by the mission of Moody and Sankey. Later he was drawn into the holiness movement, especially the mission associated with Robert Pearsall and Hannah Whitall Smith. The latter's book on *The Unselfishness of God* may well have impressed him [see 5.4]. At any rate he experienced something like a second conversion, an experience of sanctification over and above the realization of the forgiving love of God, which had come to him earlier. *This, I incline to think, was his strongest link with George Fox.* Like George Fox, Rendel Harris believed that sanctification and justification should go together. Like Fox, he wanted to learn the secret of an overcoming victorious Christian life. He would not sing the lines "And they who fain would love Thee best, Are conscious most of wrong within." They were not true of his experience of Christ's cleansing powers. If only we can reflect as in a mirror the glory of God as seen in the face of Jesus Christ, we shall be changed from glory unto glory. (1953, 21) [my emphasis]

Note how Wood changed his focus from interpreting Harris' experience in the third person "he" to including himself by using the first person plural "we" in the last sentence, as if he was deliberately inserting his own wrestling with the reality of the holiness experience (an allusion to II Cor. 3:18, an oft-quoted text on union with God). Wood then continued interpreting Harris' spirituality, shifting back to the third person:

> He was aware of the danger of talking about holiness and perfection and of claiming to have attained, but he was convinced of the reality of what used to be called the second blessing, and to an extraordinary

---

biography to be written about him and did not share details of his life (Pickard, 1978, 1-2).

[20] Compare his sense of freedom with that of Hannah Whitall Smith: "to be endorsed was to be bound ...it was better, for me at least, to be a free lance, with no hindrances to my absolute mental and spiritual freedom" (1903, 220-1).

degree he had been permitted to enter into the joy of the Lord here and now, to recover something of the lost radiance of the Christian religion, and to be at home in that happy realm where "love is an unerring light, and joy its own security. (Davis, 1953, 21)

This study argues that Wood (also a modernist scholar) could not have understood or appreciated Harris' experience of holiness, or articulated it in these precise terms, had he not shared a sense of the reality of it in his own life (Davis, 1953, 21). Wood concluded his description of Harris' spirituality by noting both its continuity with historic Quakerism and the contrast between Harris' faith and that of the modernist movement in general:

He had found Christ as his inward guide and teacher, but he did not divorce the Christ of experience from the Jesus of History or belittle all that Christ had done for him once for all on the Cross because he had discovered the joy and wonder of Christ's indwelling presence. (Davis, 1953, 21-22)

In addition to being a mystic and a scholar, Harris was also known as a great humanitarian. He was a prominent Pro-Boer (against British imperialism) when such a position was a minority one, even within Friends. He was also a dedicated pacifist. He signed a national peace manifesto with a few other Friends in 1900 at a time when Quakers were vacillating on the peace testimony (Hewison, 1989, 137). As was typical of holiness Quakers, his life was counter-cultural, and included an explicit social testimony.[21]

6.2.2 The Mysticism of J. Rendel Harris

Those who knew J. Rendel Harris often commented on his "mysticism." Kennedy writes that he always projected "a strong streak of Quaker mysticism" (2001, 187). Pickard asserts, "I saw Rendel Harris as a true mystic" (1978, 69). Even in his public and academic recognition, his mysticism was remarked upon. When he received his honorary degree from Birmingham he was referred to as "Mystic, Critical Student, and Literary Discoverer" (Pickard, 1978, 22). His mystical consciousness should have been a great asset in this period when Rufus Jones was proclaiming that Quakerism was "essentially mystical" to its

---

[21] In 1896 he and his wife traveled to Armenia to help relieve the sufferings caused during the Armenian massacre by the Turks in 1895. (200,000 Armenians were killed in the atrocities.) Harris was a man of immense compassion, and his interest in ancient literature aroused great sympathy for the plight of the Armenians who had been converted to Christianity in the third century. He published a book, *Letters from Armenia*, in 1897 about his experiences there (Pickard, 1978, 3).

core and was the greatest organized body of mystics (see 6.1.2). Yet, paradoxically, Harris' mysticism seemed to go against the grain of liberal Quakerism, despite his being a modernist. Quaker liberalism, Jones' vast works on mysticism notwithstanding, was evolving into a non-mystical, rationalist and altogether reasonable faith.[22]

The inevitable tensions arising from this divergence soon appeared at Woodbrooke College, the experiment in religious education that emerged from the Manchester Conference. J. Rendel Harris was invited to be its first director.[23] In 1904 William and Margaret Littleboy became wardens. Harris and William Littleboy differed considerably (see 6.3). Littleboy's most popular pamphlet, *The Appeal of Quakerism to the Non-mystic*, locates and highlights those differences. This pamphlet was first printed in 1905 by the "Committee of Yorkshire Q. M.," and became so popular it was reprinted in 1916, 1938, 1945, and finally as a "Quaker Classic" in 1964 (Kennedy, 2001, 188, n97). None of Harris' books were as popular.[24] Littleboy's pamphlet captured the mood of Quakerism as it moved rapidly away from its mystical essence. Even Jones' work on mysticism was eclipsed swiftly.[25]

Harris was a modernist who embodied Jones' affirmative and active mysticism – a distinguished scholar who combined the best traits of Jones' "positive mysticism." But he also embodied a warm-hearted love-mysticism which had its center in the indwelling Christ. The Light within was indeed Christ, but Christ was more than a principle or an ideal – Christ was the personal manifestation of God, a "beloved" to whom Harris was devoted. The rationalist and skeptical modernist had little appreciation for this kind of personal devotion, and considered it pure sentimentality. Holiness was repudiated, not because it was anti-modern and anti-intellectual, for Harris proved it need not be. It was repudiated because it was too mystical and affective. But in the first decades of Woodbrooke's existence, Harris' warm-hearted, holiness spirituality carried the day by the sheer force of his personality.

---

[22] See, for example, Turner, Frith, Pollard, *A Reasonable Faith*, 1884, a work of major impact on the development of British Quakerism (originally published anonymously).

[23] Harris was not the School's first choice. Rufus Jones had been asked, but he declined because he felt his destiny lay in America at Haverford College, and with *The American Friend* (Jones, 1934).

[24] Harris' New Testament studies continue to be of interest to biblical scholars. One of his most significant works, *Testimonies*, is the subject of a recent Ph.D. thesis (Falcetta, 2000).

[25] Historians point to the significance of the removal in 1955 of Jones' introduction to Braithwaite's *Beginnings of Quakerism* (1912). Both liberals and evangelicals approved the deletion, though for different reasons. For evangelicals Jones' introduction was not Christ-centered enough and too biased; for liberals it was still too Christ-centered and too mystical.

Evidence survives that something of a "revival spirit" (what Harris referred to as "filled with wonder, love and praise") actually emerged at Woodbrooke during his tenure (Pickard, 1978, 15-19, 21). Richenda Scott describes the atmosphere:

> In the spring of 1905 the last great religious Revival was sweeping through South Wales, and a party of Woodbrooke students went down to study the phenomena at first hand, and came back deeply impressed. A group of students left behind at Woodbrooke, H.G.[26] among them, had turned to a more careful study of I Corinthians XIII, Paul's great hymn to love, while their companions were away in South Wales. In the course of their work and discussion they came to realize how little they knew of the meaning of love in St. Paul's sense of the term. "Rendel Harris reminded us that Paul recognized no limitations to love and that he learnt I Corinthians XIII from the Cross." [This is apparently a direct quote from a letter of Wood to his brother.] To H.G. himself these hours of discussion brought a deep emotional experience. "As you know," he writes to his brother, "I have long pinned my faith intellectually to the Gospel of Incarnation. That is, to me the life and death of Jesus have seemed the one signal proof that God is, and is love. But that night the truth came into one's heart with a warmth and reality I had only guessed at before." (Scott, 1967, 30)

In 1908 Harris wrote to Rufus F. Jones, "Woodbrooke is flourishing and is the joy of my heart. We are often filled with 'wonder, love and praise'" (Pickard, 1978, 21).[27]

6.2.3   Harris' Writings on Holiness

Harris' devotional books were popular not only among Quakers, but also the Free Church. They consisted of collections of homilies he had given in Quaker meetings for worship. They were thus informal talks or reflections spoken in plain, common language, rather than perfectly polished sermons. Because he used innovative and often unconventional language to speak about God and religion, they were a breath of fresh air from the usual published sermons (Pickard, 1978, 21). *Memoranda Sacra* and *Union with God* were a result of his ministry among Cambridge Friends. *Aaron's Breastplate, The Guiding of God,*

---

[26] A reference to Herbert G. Wood.

[27] Harris' faith was a continual adventure leading him ever closer to God and to new intellectual and spiritual wonders. One of his most oft-quoted remarks, comes from his version of the Lord's prayer in which he changes the request to "Give us this day our daily discovery!" (Davis, 1953, 23).

and *As Pants the Hart* were based on homilies given in his Monday morning devotional meetings that opened each week of study at Woodbrooke (Pickard, 1978, 21). These meetings always ended with the singing of a hymn. In later years the closing hymn was the same: "How sweet the name of Jesus sounds, in a believer's ear" (Davis, 1953, 22). This hymn expresses the deep devotion to Jesus that was so prominent in Harris' spirituality. These collections of homilies reflect the nature and content of his spirituality. One of the most interesting and relevant titles for this study is *Union with God* (1895). This work documents both his mystical sensibility and his solid location within the holiness stream of Quakerism.

From his homily entitled "Union with a Praying Saviour" we find an example of the centrality of holiness in his spirituality:

> ...Christ is the teacher of holiness. All the situations of His life and all the teaching of His lips express one purpose – namely, the restoration of the image of God in man....Jesus Christ never preached any half-gospel; He neither gave us a deficient calling, nor offered to us a measure of grace that was insufficient for the calling. He never preached a series of impossibilities and offered them to you so that you might take hold of them as though they were possibilities, and then be deceived and disappointed by having taken hold of something which would not bear your weight. It is quite possible to have holiness teaching of a sentimental sort that will not stand a day of trial or a time of cross, but Jesus Christ's preaching of holiness is not sentimental holiness; it is not the holiness which is meant to make people happy in meetings and unhappy out of meetings. It is the holiness which is meant to swim the dark river with, and to carry us over every big stream of trial and difficulty that we may have to pass; it is the holiness which is meant to be an experience for the cloudy and dark day, which will keep our testimony bright, and which will keep us true, loyal, and happy, and full of the gracious Spirit. Such was the holiness of Christ, of this holiness those that believe are made partakers. (1895, 42-43)

Harris believed in the centrality of holiness as the full Gospel of Christ, but he was also aware of the shallowness in which it was too often understood, and offered a critique of sentimental, pseudo-holiness.

He described the work of the Spirit in healing, holiness, and bringing in the Kingdom, ending with a quote from early Quaker writer, Isaac Penington: "There is an intercessory Spirit abroad in the world, and there was an intercessory Spirit in the person of the Well-beloved" (1895, 46). He imagined the first intercessory prayer as the "Spirit of God brooding over the face of the waters" in the creation. He proceeded to expand that image to our personal lives:

We are all of us more or less in the chaos until the kingdom of God shall come. What puts us right is the spreading out of the holy wings of Divine intercession over us, the love of God for the creature, the Spirit of God descending, and moving, and working, and pitying those of us who are out of the heavenly way; and so when our Lord came on earth He came with the wings of the creating Spirit, He came with wings of healing. (1895, 46-7)

He described the effects of the divine indwelling: "Our conversion to God made us members of the body of an interceding Christ. We not only confess that "Christ liveth in me," but are also aware that "Christ prayeth in me" (1895, 48-9). Quoting from John 17 he further expanded on the concept of the mutual indwelling: "....ye know Him, for He dwelleth with you, and shall be in you." He then explained how he understood the two-fold nature of conversion:

Note the two stages of the indwelling of the Holy Ghost: "He dwelleth with you, and shall be in you." When you are hungering and thirsting, therefore, and are wanting a deeper life in God, and when your mind has been touched on the subject of holiness, either because you have seen it in the Scriptures, or because you have seen it shine out in the lives and from the lips of some dear brethren and sisters in God, or even if you have never seen it anywhere, only you have been inwardly convinced that it must be somewhere – when you get the conviction of the possibility of sanctification, then you have the prayer of Jesus like a sacred dove spread over you. This prayer is balancing itself, as it were, over your spirit. You are receiving the revelation of an unclaimed promise of God, which rests upon you just as certainly as it rested upon the saints in olden time who went apart to plead and claim the fulfillment of it for themselves and for the world in which they lived...Shall we let that promise be limited to a few? Or is it not a prayer, which claims...all people that are longing after holiness, and all those who are tired of themselves and anxious to find rest in God? (1895, 52-53)

This is a classic holiness sermon, with its informality, spontaneity, and personal application.

Harris expounded on Ephesians 3, calling this prayer of Paul's "a kind of Magna Charta of the holiness movement" (1895, 62). As a concluding dimension of the Quaker way of holiness, he emphasized the centrality of the Cross, a central motif in his sermon:

I do not believe there is any way of getting into the blessing of pure life and communion with God unless we find it by way of the Holy Cross, and keep it by the way that we find it... if God has really

offered to us purity and offered to us power, we may be quite sure that
He has offered it to us by the royal way of the Holy Cross. (1895, 64)

He addresses another key theme, union of wills, in his homily, "Union with the Will of God":

"Holy living" is another term for living in the will of God: those who are in the will of God are holy; those who are out of the will of God are unholy. The definition is sharp, as Christ's definitions usually are, and there does not seem to be a middle or third term. It is this will of God by which we are sanctified. Sanctity, or its equivalent Beatitude, is that condition in which the lives of believers have become, in their own proper measure and degree, the incarnation of the will of God on earth. (1895, 73)

And finally, he described the source of power which keeps us in the love of God, the Pentecost experience of baptism of the Holy Spirit:

There must be some way of being kept in the love of God, if there is any way of finding the love of God for ourselves. But the art of keeping what we find is an art which is only learned in an upper chamber on the day of Pentecost. [He was here speaking of what revivalists call the "baptism of the Spirit," which is what occurred on Pentecost.] Nor is there anything short of a direct occupation of our souls by the promised Spirit of God that will enable us to be "always what we sometimes are, and never what we sometimes have been." (1895, 80)

He could at times be provocative and unconventional as when he called union with God "pantheistic, beloved, strongly pantheistic" (1895, 141). But he was careful to maintain the distinction in divine union between the creature and the creator. He explained this distinction further in his *Woodbrooke Liturgies* where he defended a "pantheistic or panchristic" exultation used in his liturgy as an expression of the "sacramental perception of the Glory of God in nature." This is always to be "balanced by the two-fold statement, 'Thou in God and God in Thee' in order that humility may keep her place...and we may never lose sight of the Nothingness of the Creature when we are contemplating the All of God" (1914, 10). The same caution would apply to the concept of divinization in union with God.

A scriptural phrase often quoted by Harris is "he that is joined to the Lord is one spirit" (1895, 144). Commenting on this idea of *unus spiritus*, he wrote, "I have to a very great extent got rid of the idea of a frontier between two worlds...There is no separation for those who are joined to the Lord, and are one spirit with him" (1895, 144). The idea of there being no impenetrable frontier between two worlds – between heaven and earth – harkens back to the early Quaker belief that the Kingdom had, in fact, come and they were living in it. It is a way of speaking of "realized eschatology." Finally, he got to the real crux of human experience: "…there is nothing worse than loneliness. Nothing is so bad as being disjoined from those we love by those isolations which come necessarily in life" (1895, 145). He used John, the evangelist, exiled on the isle of Patmos as an example. John was severed from all his friends and loved ones, isolated on an island. John voiced his loneliness by saying "I was on the island," yet he could still say, "I was in the spirit." And thus Harris concluded:

> That will do; for he that is in the Spirit is joined to God. He is not lonely any more; and his pains are over and his isolation done, and… when he says…"I was in the Spirit" … [it] is the first sentence of…a great ladder which runs right up into heaven itself, and where you see not only God at the top, like Jacob did, but the Bridegroom and the Bride, and Bridegroom with his Bride, the everlasting Sabbath and the unchanging glory, where we are restored to all that we may have lost…from that great embrace of love that has gathered back the soul that was its object to itself, he looking down upon us who are hungering and thirsting after righteousness, and after love, which is the essence of righteousness…. (1895, 147)

The experience of union is symbolized by the traditional biblical imagery of a ladder to heaven, language common to the mystical tradition. It is this spiritual ladder that unites heaven and earth.

6.2.4 Quakerism, Modernism, and Holiness

In 1948, a former Woodbrooke student, William E. Wilson, delivered the Rendel Harris lecture entitled "Quaker and Evangelical." He introduced his topic with this description of Harris and the early Woodbrooke environment:

> In the early days of Woodbrooke…Rendel Harris was a puzzle to some of us ardent young Quakers. This was not only in the sense in which by his many-sidedness he was always a puzzle – a delightful and entertaining puzzle – to everyone who knew him. The puzzle which we encountered in him was to us neither delightful nor entertaining. It was disturbing. We, under the influence of the movement of thought which dates from the Manchester Conference in 1895, had begun to distinguish very sharply the pure, original Quakerism of Fox and the Early Friends from the Evangelicalism which had early in the nineteenth century begun to invade the Society. To us it was either Quakerism or Evangelicalism, but not both, and we definitely chose

> Quakerism. We were then naturally astonished, and even pained, to find the 'the Doctor,' where we should have expected him to speak in the good Quaker phraseology, which we thought spoke to our condition, more frequently, as it seemed to us, used expressions that were reminiscent of revival meetings or Keswick Convention....Then there were the Hymns. I don't think any of us really disapproved of hymns. But they must be the right kind, used with moderation and certainly not sung in a Meeting for Worship. The Doctor, in our view, had too many: every lecture he gave began with one, and sometimes more. Once or twice he had hymnbooks handed round at the morning devotional meeting. The hymns he chiefly loved were those of the Evangelical Revival by Newton, Cowper or Charles Wesley. He thus transgressed all three of our regulations for hymn singing. This led one of his contemporaries to say, "I think the Doctor is really a Primitive Methodist."[28] (1948, 3-4)

Was his Quakerism, therefore, only superficial? Wilson responded:

> Rendel was both undeniably an Evangelical and undeniably a Friend, and unlike some other Evangelical Friends, he compromised neither his Quakerism, nor his Evangelicalism. Was it then that they lay side by side in him, not clashing, only because never mixed? Something like that was, I think, the condition of some of us who inherited one tradition and accepted the other. It was not so in him. The two traditions did not merely lie in him side by side. They were fused into one whole. Or better still he had, consciously or unconsciously, *dug down to the roots of both and found them the same.* [my emphasis] (1948, 4-5)

This final observation provides a key insight in support of the argument of this study: Evangelicalism and Quakerism are rooted in the same essential religious experience. But the evangelicalism Harris embodied is of a particular kind, a Quaker holiness evangelicalism. This leads to a further, and perhaps more perplexing, dilemma – how then could Harris also be a modernist? Both Thomas C. Kennedy and Martin Davie, who have written the two most detailed studies of twentieth century Quakerism, put Harris squarely and without qualification in the category of the modernist Friends who reshaped Quaker

---

[28] In another account about Harris, these words were attributed to his cook, who said, "The doctor thinks he's a Quaker, but he's really a *Primitive Methodist*" (Pickard, 1978, 21). That Harris would feel an affinity for Primitive Methodism is not as surprising as it might seem at first. See Nuttall (1967) for an essay which traces the strong affinity between early Quakerism and Primitive Methodism.

faith and practice at the turn of the century (Davie, 1992, 93; Kennedy, 2001, 150-2).

At the Manchester Conference, Harris urged British Quakers to accept evolutionary theory, although with some caution and discretion. He applied evolutionary theory to the development of the creeds and to Christian theology. He did not suggest it is "all the keys of all the creeds" but "it certainly is one big key." (Manchester, 1896, 225). He admitted that biblical critics "...have not done criticizing their own criticism yet and in many points they will probably turn out to be wrong all round" (Manchester, 1896, 224). He accepted evolutionary theory because in his own study of the early church and the development of the creeds, he saw clear evidence of the progressive development of thought.[29] But he was certain evolutionary theory helped us towards a clearer understanding of our faith and not towards the destruction of faith.

Davie argues that Harris "rejected the Evangelical belief in the infallibility of Scripture" (1992, 93) by quoting from his Manchester address: " ...the internal discords of all scriptures and of all explanations of Scriptures ought to be enough to convince us that we have no infallibility in the house not a drop" (Manchester, 1986, 225). Harris was, in fact, arguing for the historic Quaker belief that Scriptures are not the "ultimate test of truth" (Manchester, 1896, 222), but that the immediate revelation of the Spirit is primary. And thus if the Scriptures are made to be infallible (by which he meant without error, or inerrant), then any criticism is "a gross impertinence" (Manchester, 1896, 222). And "while we have no infallibility we have some splendid probabilities, and one of them in particular is of such a high order that we call it 'the certainty of love, which sets our hearts at rest'" (Manchester, 1896, 223). His view of Scripture may not be a nineteenth century evangelical one, but it is Quaker and orthodox, and in agreement with the early Church Fathers. He capped his argument with a quote from John Chrysostom (which he said he almost hesitated to quote, fearing it may sound like Elias Hicks):

> 'It were indeed meet for us not at all to require the aid of the written word, but to exhibit a life so pure, that the Grace of the Spirit should be instead of books to our souls, and that as these are inscribed with ink, even so should our hearts be with the Spirit.' But since we have utterly put away from us this grace, let us at any rate embrace the second best course....This case [of not being reduced to dependence upon written words] was not only the case of the Saints in the Old Testament, but also of those in the New. For neither to the Apostles did God give anything in writing, but instead of written words He promised that He would give them the Grace of the Spirit. (Manchester, 1896, 223)

---

[29] See, for example, his *Origin of the Doctrine of the Trinity*, 1919.

As startling as this quote appears, Harris was making the case for a Quaker understanding of Scripture to be closer to the teachings of the early Church (he went back to Chyrsostom, third century) than the then current theories of biblical infallibility. He was, to be sure, challenging current evangelical positions, but from a strong Quaker and Christian basis and not one of rationalism.

The reason Harris had no fear of accepting biblical criticism and new scientific findings can be attributed to the certainty of his faith experience, that of a direct and mystical relationship to Christ. Harris was a Quaker mystic and a holiness evangelical. He began his lecture on evolutionary theory at Manchester with a reference to Madam Guyon:[30]

> Madam Guyon tells us, in summing up the results of certain remarkable religious experiences through which she had passed, that "the intellect as well as the heart had received an immense accession from God" ...and unless we are prepared to regard our spiritual and mental faculties as a part of the same Divine life within us and entitled to an equally free expansion, we shall presently find one of them becoming the victim of the other. (1896, Manchester, 222)

The last is a prediction which indeed became reality in much of twentieth century liberal Quakerism.

To make sure that his audience understood the historic Quaker position of Scripture and how that should enable Friends who love Christ to welcome rather than fear higher criticism, he testified, "They cannot steal from us the truth of immediate Revelation and direct communication with God, which was before the Scriptures and was the cause of them" (1896, Manchester, 222).

Harris, armed with a view of Scripture that freed him to be open to biblical criticism and evolutionary theory, was centered squarely in the camp of modernist Quakers. But in a real sense he had already moved beyond modernism, and theologically he does not fit in the mold of classic twentieth century liberalism in the way of most of the other modernists, such as Rufus Jones and Edward Grubb. For example, he did not reject original sin and embrace the liberal view of the inherent goodness of humanity, and he did not exalt the Inner Light to the extent that it overshadowed and subsumed all other Christian doctrines.[31]

---

[30] As noted previously, Guyon was a favorite mystic of holiness Quakers (see 3.2).

[31] In his essay on "Grace and Heredity," he was clear that he accepted the doctrine of original sin (1895, 159-160). He did not believe children are born good (but neither are they "totally depraved"). He claimed there is no such thing as "starting fair in the race of life.... We do come into the world with a deficit which grace removes" (1895, 160). He was Augustinian to the same degree Barclay was, believing that the heredity of sin is what necessitates a strong doctrine of grace. "It is the sense of the prevalence of

As a mystic and contemplative, Harris valued silence in corporate worship, but he did not elevate it as the only pure form of worship. Unlike Jones, he considered Quakerism to be in continuity with orthodox Christian doctrines and Reformation faith, and not a rejection of it. Nor did he accept the common Quaker cliché that emerged from modernist writings, "We believe in Life, not doctrines" (Wilson, 1948, 12). For Harris, it was both helpful and necessary to maintain some formulation of core convictions, though adherence to doctrines should never be a test of true faith. William Wilson wrote that he recalled Harris once saying in conversation, "As I grow older, I believe fewer doctrines, but those few more intensely"[32] (1948, 12). Finally he differed from other leading modernists in that he remained convinced that mission work and evangelism were still a necessary means of passing on the faith and conveying the Gospel message to a seeking generation. Thus, he embraced another key aspect of thought that keeps him firmly planted in the evangelical camp (Wilson, 1948, 11).

6.2.5 Summary and Conclusions

From the perspective of most evangelicals at the turn of the century, Harris' attitude toward the Bible was a "modern" and dangerous one. He embraced wholeheartedly the new biblical and historical criticism. Much of his most creative research engaged that end. He recognized, without apology, that Christianity had absorbed in both its stories and its liturgy much of pagan myth and literature.

Unlike many intellectuals and scholars who eventually find their beliefs shaken and their faith diminished by their increased learning, Harris' robust faith remained unassailable. Nothing he discovered ever seemed to shake his faith; rather he was energized and amazed. He recognized the hand of God everywhere and rather than diluting his faith, his biblical scholarship expanded it. The reason, I will contend, is that he held to the Bible in the manner of the earliest Friends, not as an infallible, inerrant authority, but as a revelation of love, speaking to his heart through the Holy Spirit as a vehicle of God's truth. For Harris, the authority of the Bible did not lie in its infallibility, but in its power to reveal the love of God. However, the Bible did not reveal its power

---

hereditary evil that makes us apprehend the greatness of the Catholic doctrine of Grace and the glory of the Gospel of Jesus Christ. For Grace is the antidote of heredity" (1895, 162). His view of original sin would separate him from many other modernists, including Rufus Jones, and from most liberals of the time, but it corresponds to the early Quaker view of sin and the need for grace.

[32] H. G. Wood remembered another way Harris had of expressing this idea in relation to the modern intellectual challenges to faith: "apropos of the surrenders which criticism requires of us, we get a smaller creed but a larger God" (Scott, 1967, 25).

unless one experienced the Light of Christ directly. Without an experiential faith, and the certainty that one had communed with God, it became necessary to hold on to the Bible as "proof" of Christ's divinity and miracles. Therefore any critical reassessment of the Bible had to be resisted, for faith hinged on the Bible as infallible evidence that Christianity was true.

Many Quaker evangelicals had come to this place (an essentially Fundamentalist one), and the liberals were correct in their assessment that a doctrinal view of the Bible was contrary to early Quakerism. The early Quaker view of Scripture was almost identical to that of the early patristic understanding, which Harris alluded to in his Manchester address. The early Fathers were trained in Greek philosophy. As cultured Greeks, much of the Bible, if taken literally, appeared crude and incredible to them. Yet when they read it, it spoke to their hearts. They concluded that beneath the literal meaning were deeper spiritual meanings, which meditation and contemplation or a reading in a spirit of prayer would open up to them. Thus the largest portion of the writings of the early Church Fathers consisted in commentaries on Scripture in order to unlock the mysteries it held. Such a view of Scripture is very similar to that held by Harris, who was a student of early patristic literature.

The distinction between reading the Bible as a contemplative (mystically) or as a non-contemplative (non-mystically) is an oversimplification, albeit a helpful one. Was Harris therefore an evangelical or not? It would depend on how the term is defined. If it means a belief in the inspiration of the Bible, yes he was. If it means a belief in the infallibility of the text itself, he definitely was not. The Holiness Movement did make Scripture a prominent focus in its teachings, and often it became reduced in the minds of its followers to a dogma. But genuine holiness was always an experiential encounter of the Holy Spirit, and that teaching was the most central to its genuine vision.

Harris maintained that "The vitality of early Quakerism depended upon its belief in the continuity of inspiration" (Wood, 1929, 10), and offered three significant implications of this conclusion for Friends: Firstly, he claimed, "It set them free from the kind of bondage which is so often associated with insistence on the literal acceptance of Scripture." Secondly, "It enabled Friends to escape from the Orthodox belief in the lot of the heathen. If the work of the Holy Spirit is only associated with Scripture then the heathen are lost, but if the appeal is not limited to Scripture alone, then we may have hopes regarding the non-Christian world." And thirdly, he insisted that "The claim put forward by the Quakers alone does justice to Christianity as it is set forth in the New Testament" (Wood, 1929, 10).

Harris' view of Scripture may have seemed "modernist" to many conservative religious thinkers of his time, but he was articulating the traditional Barclayan Quaker position, an approach to Scripture much older than Barclay, in accord with the early ancient patristic (pre-modern) method of biblical interpretation.[33] George Cadbury knew J. Rendel Harris well, and was essentially correct in his assessment that Harris was "thoroughly evangelical" and would not be led astray by higher criticism (Kennedy, 2001, 181). But Harris' brand of evangelicalism was specifically a Quaker holiness evangelicalism. It contained elements of Wesleyanism, but it was not Wesleyan Holiness. It contained elements of Keswick Holiness, but it was not Keswick. He was too much a modernist and held to a different (Quaker) understanding of Scripture. Harris' evangelicalism was of a different type than that of Gurney, who has been shown to have been only marginally holiness. Unlike Gurney, Harris had a distinct, transforming conversion experience, and he was significantly more mystical than Gurney.[34] What gives Harris' holiness its uniquely Quaker flavor is his view of Scripture as continuing revelation and the Word being identified with Christ and the Spirit's presence in the world.

In conclusion, if we compare Harris with the eight essential elements of historic Quakerism we find his spirituality contained all eight: conversion, Scripture, evangelism, mysticism, charisma, suffering,[35] perfection, and even a "kingdom now" realized eschatology. All eight elements are embedded in a framework of what was then considered modernism. In the arena of worship, he insisted on the greatest possible freedom. He was unique as a Quaker in his creation of original liturgies,[36] but resisted any tendency towards a "one-man ministry" (Wilson, 1948, 4), allowing Spirit-led and Spirit-filled worship to take a great variety of forms.

In relation to the four quadrants of holiness, Harris is represented in all four (see Figure 3). He maintained core orthodox doctrines and stressed the importance of faith. He had a deeply sacramental view of life, finding traces of God in all of creation. As noted above, he was not opposed to using symbolism in worship and experimenting with styles and rituals. Yet, his strong opposition to a pastoral ministry in which leadership would reside in one person was well-known (Wilson, 1948, 4) (Quadrant 1). As with early Quakers, the experiential

---

[33] Sandra M. Schneiders calls this the "biblical spirituality approach." See her *Written that You May Believe*, 1999, 16-17, for further explanation and validation of this approach to Scripture.

[34] I have found no reference to Gurney in Harris' writings.

[35] Although Harris was known for his positive, joyful spirituality, he also understood and addressed the element of suffering, which he termed "dark love," as a necessary part of holiness: "And so hath the Eternal two loves: the love in the light, which now encircles us; and the dark love on which our souls lean back to sleep. Those who have felt God's daylight kiss can trust Him for it in the dark. For thee to die will only be to lie back in the Everlasting's Arms" (1892, 90). He also wrote, "The highest experiences of the Christian life are close bound up, in the Divine will, with suffering" (1892, 89).

[36] Harris wrote and published three of his own liturgies, which he used for worship to begin each semester at Woodbrooke: for spring, "The Liturgy of the Skylark;" for summer, "The Liturgy of the Rose;" and for fall, "The Liturgy of the Falling Leaf." See Harris, 1914.

was crucial. His emphasis on the continuing revelation of the Spirit was based on early Quaker understandings. He clearly grasped how early Quakerism differed from Puritanism. His language and style of expressing his spirituality had a prominent charismatic bent, also strongly reminiscent of early Quakers (Quadrant 2). As a true mystic, he believed the goal of holiness was union with God, *unus spiritus*, as did early Quakers (Quadrant 3). Quadrant 4 may be less obvious, but his passionate social witness and willingness to go against the grain of secular culture by taking unpopular positions (such as his stance on the Boer War) locates him in the radical holiness of "Imitation of Christ" as well. Harris, this study concludes, taught and lived a spirituality marked by all the types of holiness found in the early Quaker movement, while still holding to a modern and even scientific approach to the interpretation of Scripture and the development of doctrine.

6.3 The Case of William Littleboy: Non-Mystical, Non-Holiness

Quakerism as holiness is inherently mystical; it implies a personal encounter, a touching and a meeting with the Divine Other. Rendel Harris represents Quakerism as holiness with a modernist outlook, but other than his influence on his successor, H. G. Wood, the type of holiness that Harris embodied finds scant continuity in British liberal Quakerism. A contemporary of Harris and a colleague at Woodbrooke, William Littleboy represents the more dominant trend in British liberalism toward a non-mystical and non-holiness rationalist Quakerism. Littleboy's religious outlook shows the shift from holiness as mystical participation "in Christ" that results in certainty of faith, expanded compassion, and spiritual empowerment, to a life marked by an "unknowing" and uncertain faith[37] that results in dutifulness, obedience and good works – a shift from *being* "in Christ" to *doing* "for Christ," and eventually simply *doing* good.

Littleboy, who became warden and teacher in the second year of Woodbrooke's existence, was of an entirely different spiritual bent than Rendel Harris. H. G. Wood described Littleboy's spiritual perspective as "often blurred and overcast" (1953, 33). He had no taste for mysticism or mystical experience (Wood, 1953, 33). Wood had much to say in praise of Littleboy and his contributions to Woodbrooke (1953, 34-5). He called Littleboy's most popular work, *The Appeal of Quakerism to the Non-mystic,* "an admirable pamphlet" (1953, 33). He emphasized the balance Littleboy brought to Harris' high-spirited, exuberant style of leadership. Littleboy could "supplement the Doctor's influence by getting alongside some who felt as he did that the Doctor

---

[37] Pink Dandelion terms this outcome in contemporary British Quakerism as the "absolute perhaps." See 'Implicit Conservatism in Liberal Religion: British Quakers as an "uncertain sect."' *Journal of Contemporary Religion,* 19, 2004, 219-29.

was too far ahead of them for them to keep pace with them" (Wood, 1953, 33).[38] The new warden "knew the value of order and routine, and ...did much to settle the pattern of daily life at Woodbrooke" (Wood, 1953, 32). But differences with Harris were not just due to temperament; some were also theological, and the differences were not with Harris alone. A serious disagreement in the very first year of Woodbrooke's existence took place when John Wilhelm Rowntree suggested William James be invited to speak on the psychology of religion. But when Littleboy read James' *Varieties of Religious Experience*, he became "seriously alarmed" (Kennedy, 2001, 187). He was uncomfortable with any suggestion that spiritual experiences of any mystical sort might authenticate the presence of the Light within, and opposed James' interpreting Quakerism as having any particular appeal to mystics (Kennedy, 2001, 187).

In *The Appeal of Quakerism to the Non-mystic*, Littleboy firstly reaffirmed the essential Quaker belief that "the Inward Light, a Seed of God ...is nothing less than the personal presence of... Jesus Christ....This personal presence transcends our personalities as to assure us that we are truly akin to God...and undertakes to lead us through the shadows until we attain to the glory of the liberty of the sons of God" (1916, 3-4). Secondly, he reaffirmed the fact that Quakerism is "above most other religious types, the exponent of the mystical idea in religion" (1916, 4). Thirdly, he defined mysticism as "a type of religion in which ...the soul finds itself in a love-relation with the Living God."[39] All of the above are true and distinctive of the "Quaker Gospel" (Littleboy, 1916, 4). Fourthly, he observed that most of the teachers and ministers among Friends are mystics in this sense, those who can "speak out of the fullness of a conscious experience" of God (1916, 5). Therefore he concluded, "those to whom we look to for instruction are drawn from a minority." And thus,

> In many of our most honoured leaders there is at least an implicit suggestion that...our nearness to God is to be measured by the standard of conscious fellowship with Him and the emotional enjoyment of his presence. (Littleboy, 1916, 5)

These observations are descriptive of Quaker holiness, but Littleboy lamented the difficulty of this to the non-mystic who has no sense of God's immediate presence (1916, 7).

He claimed that most mystics, as well as a long-standing Christian tradition, "habitually overemphasize the place of emotions in the spiritual life" (1916, 7). Littleboy believed that "To serve Christ, not to feel Christ, is the mark of His true servants" (1916, 7). He claimed that "the lack of sensitiveness

---

[38] I would suggest that what Wood was referring to in the phrase "too far ahead of them" meant too far ahead, both intellectually and in spiritual experience.

[39] He borrowed this definition from Jones' introduction to Braithwaite (1912, xxxiv).

to the divine Presence....is often chiefly a matter of temperament" (1916, 7). Lastly, he asked the inevitable question, if by temperament or by "some limitation in our spiritual outlook, we do not apprehend [the Light] as the Real Presence of God, how then can we recognize the fact if we have no 'conscious inspiration?'" His answer was that if we simply follow our call to duty and do what we *ought*, duty and service will become habitual "until it has become in measure *natural* ...to obey" (1916, 10-11).[40]

The flaw in Littleboy's argument, which Harris would likely have challenged, is his assertion that mysticism is reserved only for the few, the spiritual elite, those with a kind of "mystical" temperament. Harris would say that we are all mystics and the consciousness of God's presence can be felt and experienced by everyone, though its expression will vary by temperament. Undoubtedly Harris had experienced the elevated but fleeting "ecstasy," but it was the enchantment of ordinary life that permeated his spirituality.

What Littleboy was arguing for, rather than a healthy democratizing of mysticism, was the acceptance of a non-mystical approach to life, a disenchantment of the ordinary life, or a spiritual pelagianism. You do what you ought, *as if* you felt God's presence, out of duty, idealism and obedience, rather than the impulse of delight, love and joy: in sum, obedience to a code of ethics without a sense of a felt presence. Littleboy was deducing, based on his own lack of a felt presence, that mystical experience or a personal consciousness of God's love and grace is not accessible to everyone. On the other hand, in relation to his students, Harris "thought all his geese were swans" (1953, 32). In context, he was referring to their capacity for learning, but Harris, I would argue, would have applied that metaphor to their spiritual life as well. Harris believed the universality of the inward light meant there was a mystical germ in everyone; it simply needed to sprout. Harris desired to democratize mysticism by unlocking the door of the mystic in everyone; Littleboy was willing to abandon mysticism to science and modernity, because a felt sense of the presence of God was rare.

A letter from Littleboy to Rufus Jones upon accepting his new post as warden illuminates his pessimistic view of the spiritual life:

> I do believe that this absence of spiritual sunshine – this failure to grasp experimentally and consciously the love of God in our lives – is a very much more common difficulty than is often supposed. If one can be used to help such as those who have this disappointing experience to recognize some bright points amid the general greyness (*sic*) of the inner life, one feels that it is some compensation for being

---

[40] This concept of the spiritual life as a sense of duty has similarity to Gurney's essay *On the Habitual Exercise of Love to God Considered as a Preparation for Heaven*, 1840, though even less mystical and more oriented to duty and performance.

without conscious enjoyment of the deep Christian privileges oneself.[41] (Kennedy, 2001, 188)

Littleboy was here confessing, perhaps even lamenting, his own lack of experiencing what Jones had claimed in a variety of statements throughout his writings as the essence of Quakerism: to grasp experientially and consciously the love of God. See for example (1939, 251). Littleboy was openly admitting that he himself found the inner life to be one of "greyness" rather than "spiritual sunshine" (Kennedy, 2001, 188). The darkness of his inner world makes one wonder whether there might be an underlying suppression of consciously felt experiences of the love of God due to his own skepticism.

The best he could do would be to help those like himself to find some "bright points amid the general greyness of the inner life," which would be some compensation for his own lack of "conscious enjoyment of the deep Christian privileges" (Kennedy, 2001, 188). One must admire Littleboy's honesty, yet also admit that he was describing a growing shift in the Society of Friends to a non-mystical, non-experiential future, and a growing doubt and distrust of an existential faith. Kennedy comments on the contrast with Harris evidenced in this letter by imagining that "the impetuous fun-loving Harris…would probably have thought such somber words an odd approach to discovering 'bright spots'" (Kennedy, 2001, 188).

I would argue that the real turning point for Quakerism, the shift that tears it from its roots and its historic reason for being, can be found in this major turn towards a non-mystical or non-experiential Quaker spirituality that was already dividing the ranks of the modernists at the founding of Woodbrooke in 1903. Woodbrooke, at least through Harris' leadership, maintained the holiness tradition of Quakerism in its affective, experiential mode. (This mode continued, though more muted, in Harris' handpicked successor, H. G. Wood.) Harris' holiness spirituality carried Woodbrooke through its "Golden Age" as a school for prophets, as he envisioned it, with the unswerving support of George Cadbury (Kennedy, 2001, 181-183). Harris affirmed that holiness as a consciously felt and expressed experience of the love and grace of God was available to all.

But Littleboy, rather than conceiving of Quakerism as a movement that appealed to those seeking a more spiritual experience of religion as it had been in its past, determined that holiness was an extraordinary, and in a sense abnormal, experience reserved for the few. Littleboy's version of a non-mystical Society of Friends with a holiness that is ethical and dutiful, rather than a natural outflowing from a conscious, intimate relationship to God, gradually took hold.

---

[41] Original quote from Rufus M. Jones Papers, William Littleboy to R. M. J., 23 December 1903, *Haverford College Quaker Collection*.

This perspective became institutionalized in the Society of Friends in Great Britain with the abolishing of the recorded ministry in 1924. Logically, this was the natural outcome. If ministers, as Littleboy suggested, were mainly mystics and taught an elevated "higher life" to be realized in a consciously felt experience of God, and if the majority of Friends were unable to realize such an experience, then Quakerism was a spiritual aristocracy and had to be democratized by eliminating a special class of spiritual leadership. Thus, it was not higher criticism, or evolutionary thought, or even reformulating and reinterpreting traditional beliefs into contemporary forms that led to a functional agnosticism (Harris embraced all of these, without diminishing his faith one iota), but the marginalization of the mystic from the inner circle of leadership to the fringes.

The genuine loss to Quakerism can be found in its growing ambivalence to the quest for holiness as a conscious experience of the love of God through Christ. To relinquish the search for perfection as personal transformation, to no longer strive for the "something more" of the growth of the seed into the "holy birth...in all its fullness" (Barclay, 2002, 205), opened the door to a sense of resignation to "the greyness of the inner life." The heart and soul, and color of the Quaker spiritual life dimmed and gradually stunted the growth of Quakerism as a holiness movement in its liberal forms. But the ethical idealism of perfection remained in a new form in the strengthening of pacifism and its humanitarian activities, for which the Society of Friends has often been commended and respected. But ethical perfection was severed from mystical perfection, and the separation weakened both sides. Mysticism and resistance need each other, and when integrated, as in the early Quaker movement, the potential for real social and political change is greatly strengthened.[42]

6.4 Thomas Kelly: Holiness via Liberalism

By the early twentieth century, the Holiness Movement had lost awareness of its mystical heritage, and some parts of it became more focused on biblical literalism, doctrinal correctness, and a shift towards fundamentalism. Similar to the later period of Quietism a century before, much of the movement became disconnected from its original charisma and vision and became rule, ritual, and duty oriented. A new infusion of mystical holiness came to the Quaker world, both the intellectualized liberalism of the "Silent Quakers" and the doctrinal fundamentalism of the evangelicals, through the reawakening of a liberal

---

[42] See Dorothee Soelle, *Mysticism and Resistance,* 2001, for an analysis of how mystical and ethical holiness belong together, especially p. 2-6 for a synopsis of her argument. See also Smith, *Revivalism and Social Reform*, 1980, for a detailed study of a historical period (1840-1865 in America) when holiness and social change were deeply and fruitfully interconnected.

Quaker college professor, Thomas Kelly (1893-1941). The spirituality expressed in his writings continued the thread of holiness into the later twentieth century and conveyed the dynamic combination of evangelicalism and mysticism to the contemporary seeker thirsting for a sense of the divine presence. Kelly, like Harris earlier, emerged from a liberal, modernist Quaker environment, yet expressed an evangelical Christ-centered mysticism that found its source in early Quakerism, and continued the authentic stream of Quaker holiness into the contemporary world.[43]

Thomas Kelly's spiritual journey is a modern echo of the same kind of mystical encounter that transformed the lives of the earliest Quakers – the intensely intimate, life-altering encounter with the divine presence that is felt in the heart as overpowering love. Kelly wrote in *Testament of Devotion*:

> It is an overwhelming experience to fall into the hands of the living God, to be invaded to the depths of one's being by His presence, to be, without warning, wholly uprooted from all earth-born securities and assurances, and to be blown by a tempest of unbelievable power which leaves one's old proud self utterly, utterly defenseless....Then is the soul swept into a Loving Center of ineffable sweetness, where calm and unspeakable peace and ravishing joy steal over one...In awful solemnity the Holy One is over all and in all, exquisitely loving, infinitely patient, tenderly smiling. Marks of glory are upon all things, and the marks are cruciform and blood-stained...Death comes, blessed death, death of one's alienating will... (1941, 56-57)

The sense of direct Presence, ravishing love, joy, and peace, the image of the cross, and death of self that one finds in descriptions of early Friends and nineteenth century holiness Friends are found in Kelly's moving testimony to a divine-human encounter. He was also clear that all comes by grace: "I was much shaken by the experience of Presence –something that I did not seek, but that *sought* me" (Kelly, 1966, 102).

Kelly was raised in Ohio as an evangelical Quaker. His son, Richard Kelly, is certain that his father's spiritual roots were "squarely in the holiness camp" (1995, 53).[44] T. Canby Jones writes that Kelly was shaped by this holiness

---

[43] T. Canby Jones writes that at a colloquium on Thomas Kelly in 1993, he was surprised to find Kelly characterized as an "evangelical mystic." Jones admits he never heard anyone called that before (1995, 10). This remark highlights the chasm which had come to separate evangelical and mystical by the late twentieth century.

[44] Richard Kelly's research into the religious background of his father exposes some fascinating connections with the holiness stream of Quakerism. The Kelly family belonged to Londonderry Meeting, Ohio, a Quaker meeting founded by the famed holiness revivalists John Henry Douglas and Esther and Nathan Frame (Hamm, 1988, 82-83). It is not known whether John Henry Douglas and Kelly's grandfather and

evangelical background, and then introduced to mystics by Rufus Jones at Haverford who encouraged Kelly to pursue an interest in philosophy (1995).

In Kelly's intellectual pursuits and driving need for scholarly achievement and recognition (he longed to be a world-recognized philosopher), he looked with condescension on his humble holiness Quaker roots. Yet, Kelly's original desire was to attend seminary and become a missionary. During World War I he worked as an evangelist with the YMCA "seeking 'decisions' for Christ among the troops encamped on England's Salisbury Plain, and later among German prisoners" (Kelly, 1995, 53). But after the war Kelly's theology was shaped by modernist Quakers, Rufus Jones at Haverford, and liberal Protestants at Hartford Seminary, where he earned a Ph.D. Kelly was a striver and a perfectionist who relentlessly pursued academic excellence. He had an insatiable thirst for knowledge and seemed driven to achieve and succeed as a scholar and an academician. Not satisfied with a Ph.D. from Hartford, he decided to pursue a Ph.D. at Harvard. His striving for greater and greater knowledge, perhaps a disguised search for God, resulted in a period of disorientation, and he ultimately failed his orals. The devastation of this event caused a pronounced personal crisis and deep depression. Then something occurred that reoriented his entire life, a spiritual encounter which he never reveals explicitly.

His son writes that it was not until a "soul-overturning experience" in Nazi Germany in 1938, where he met "simple souls" who had experienced the reality of the spiritual world, did Kelly once again appreciate and appropriate his own holiness roots (1966, 102-105).[45] And out of his failure at Harvard came a new vocation – to write and speak about the spiritual life – and from then on his personal ambition receded.

He began speaking at his Quaker meeting, and then at larger Quaker gatherings regularly for the few remaining years of his life, articulating the essence and heart of a spirituality rooted in his holiness Quaker heritage and the tradition of the great mystics of the Christian church that he had come to know through Rufus Jones at Haverford. He told a Friend that the "lectures just wrote themselves." All of his spiritual writing came out of these last four years of his life. He died of a heart attack at age 47. After his death, his writings were collected and turned into a book called *A Testament of Devotion* by his friend and colleague, Douglas Steere, another Quaker contemplative writer. Much later, in 1966, his son Richard collected other essays and published *The Eternal Promise*.

---

namesake, Thomas William Kelly (who were exact contemporaries), had any direct, personal contact, but Miriam Douglas, John Henry's widow, kept up a correspondence with the Kelly family and took a particular interest in following the career of Thomas William Kelly, who became a Quaker minister (1995, 52-53).

[45] See also Paul M. Kelly, 1986, 183-208 for further information on Kelly's experiences in Nazi Germany.

Richard Kelly more recently has shed much new light on his father's Quaker holiness background (1995, 43-56). He traces his father's spiritual roots and life-long spiritual journey, a pilgrimage which came full circle back to an evangelical faith. He shows that even though his father was drawn into modernism, distanced himself from his early religious tradition, and remained the "intellectual scholarly man," he never could sever himself from his holiness roots. "The fervor of the evangelists of his youth comes hammering through, insisting that religious experience be dramatic, be specific, be tangible, be real, be felt" (1995, 54). Richard Kelly describes the affective devotion of a religion of heart-felt experience that is the key to both understanding early Friends and holiness Friends.

One of a group of old college friends who visited Kelly in 1940 writes of the transformation which had come over the intellectual, rationalist Kelly he had once known:

> He almost startled me, and he shocked some of us who were still walking in the ways of logic and science and the flesh, by the high areas of being he had penetrated. He had returned to the old symbols like the blood of Christ, that were shocking to a few of his old colleagues who had not grown and lived as he had. But he brought new meaning to old symbols, and he was to me and to some others a prophet whose tongue had been touched by coals of fire. (Kelly, 1995, 54)

Richard Kelly quotes from the closing pages of his father's *Testament of Devotion,* observing that "you can hear the cadence of the camp meeting" (1995, 55):

> Do you really want to live your lives, every moment of your lives, in His Presence? Do you long for Him, crave Him? Do you love His Presence? Does every drop of blood in your body love him? Does every breath you draw breathe a prayer, a praise to Him? Do you sing and dance within yourselves, as you glory in His love? Have you set yourselves to be His and *only* His, walking every moment in holy obedience? I know I'm talking like an old-time evangelist. But I can't help that, nor dare I restrain myself and get prim and conventional. We have too long been prim and restrained. The fires of the love of God, of our love toward God, and of His love toward us, are very hot. (1941, 119)

Anyone who has ever experienced the zeal of revival-style preaching will recognize the heart-felt pleading tone of an altar call of sanctification and consecration by an authentic evangelist who wants his hearers to know and feel the same kind of divine love-experience that he has known.

T. Canby Jones supports the argument of this study when he concludes his essay on Kelly, affirming that Kelly "recaptured mainstream Quaker spirituality" (1995, 10).[46] At one level, Kelly was a thorough holiness Friend, firmly planted in all four quadrants of holiness, but in a twentieth century context. His life reflects shifts and reactions to the changing religious, social, and cultural climate of Quakerism. His writings reflect those social changes, but also mirror what has always been present in Quaker spirituality. Revivalism, for example, reflected the westward migration and the changing American landscape, but also mirrored what was already present in a strong way in early Quakerism and recognized intuitively by many nineteenth century Quakers.

His immersion in the study and reading of the mystics and his broad educational and cultural background allowed Kelly to recreate a Quaker holiness that speaks across all religious traditions. Without necessarily realizing why, Friends from both liberal and evangelical backgrounds find inspiration in the writings of this spiritual descendent of seventeenth century holiness Quakerism. This legacy continues to be expressed today in the work of Richard Foster, an evangelical Friend whose writings on prayer and holiness finds a wide audience among all kinds of Quakers, liberal and evangelical, as well as far beyond Quaker circles (see 6.6).

6.5 Everett Lewis Cattell: Holiness via Evangelicalism

Another response to the splintering effects of late nineteenth century revivalism and the fundamentalist leavening of Quaker holiness came from the evangelical wing of Friends, now known as the Evangelical Friends Church. The most significant voice to speak for Quaker holiness from this sector was missionary and educator, Everett L. Cattell (1905-1981).[47] Cattell wrote the defining work on holiness as understood by evangelical Friends, *The Spirit of Holiness*. Originally published in 1963 by William B. Eerdmans, it defined holiness and a contemporary understanding of sanctification and Christian perfection for a broad evangelical audience, rather than as uniquely Quaker distinctives. Because he presented holiness in a balanced and moderate way with a healthy emphasis upon the disciplines involved in holy living, the book was reprinted in 1977 and has retained its popularity up to the present.

---

[46] Jones also warns that "present day Quakers neglect him at their peril" (1995, 10). And he wonders: "Is 'evangelical mystics' what Thomas Kelly is challenging all of us to become?" (1995, 10).

[47] Cattell and his wife Catherine were missionaries in India for twenty-one years. Upon his return, he served as superintendent of Ohio Yearly Meeting, which is now known as Evangelical Friends Church, Eastern Region. He later served as president of Malone College, an institution that developed out of the Bible Training School of J. Walter Malone, a leading holiness voice of the Quaker revival period.

Cattell's book, like Kelly's (and Harris' devotional writings earlier), was based on his preaching and thus has a sermonic, narrative quality. He explained in his preface that "It has been my happy privilege for many years, both in America and in India, to preach across the lines that divide Christians in their views of the deeper spiritual life" (1977, 6). He acknowledged that he was nurtured in the Friends Church with "its traditional emphasis on the Holy Spirit," and noted that large sections of Quakers were "deeply influenced by the Wesleyan emphasis of the National Holiness Association of America" (1977, 6).

But Cattell's book, though engaging, does not cut across the liberal-evangelical spectrum as broadly as Kelly's has done. *The Spirit of Holiness* is a simple, devotionally-oriented book of practical daily living. It does not reach, nor plumb, the mystical depths of the Christian tradition of holiness in the way that Kelly's writings have. But it does capture the spirit of holiness in an accessible, popular, contemporary evangelical format with strong Wesleyan overtones. Its message of a responsible, practical holiness would be affirmed by most evangelical Quakers (the majority of Quakers today), as well as many evangelicals in other denominations, particularly with Wesleyan and American revivalist traditions.

Cattell concluded his book with a definition of love, which, like John Wesley (whom he quoted), he identified as the essence of Christian perfection: "loving God with all our heart, mind, soul, and strength" (1977, 90). He could have quoted Barclay to reinforce his point from a Quaker source, for example, "perfection consists in loving God above all" (Barclay, 1692, 190), but he was more dependent on Wesley than Quaker sources, perhaps intentionally so, for the purpose of unifying the evangelical holiness traditions. He occasionally referred to Quakers to illustrate holiness, for example, on divine guidance, Stephen Grellet (1977, 52-53), and on the experience of sanctification, George Fox (1977, 16-27).

Cattell was known for his "passion for unity" and the active role he played in promoting spiritual renewal across the breadth of Quakerism. He tried to be a bridge to unity across Yearly Meetings. At the 1970 St. Louis Conference on the theme of the future of Friends, in which representatives were invited from all the Yearly Meetings in America, his address became a defining statement for all traditionally Christian, orthodox Quakers (Anderson, 1987, 273). In "What Future for Friends?" he formulated a basis for agreement centered on Christ, and defined what evangelicals believe is the essence of Quakerism:

> No one has a right to use the word Quaker to describe a system which is not Christocentric. What we can know intuitively has now been made crystal clear by our scholars that early Quakerism was Christ-centered and Biblically oriented. The time has come when we must stop being apologetic about our real character....May we not, in some

sense, lay aside our party banners and join hands in becoming fresh seekers after the Lordship of Christ? (Anderson, 1970, 270)

For Cattell, the substance of "the Lordship of Christ" is set forth in his irenic work, *The Spirit of Holiness*. Cattell was not concerned about the external details of how holiness appeared, such as dress or styles of worship, only that one surrendered one's self to Christ. And Christ, for Cattell and for evangelically orthodox Quakers, means the Christ as revealed in Scripture.

6.5.1   Summary and Conclusions

In comparing Kelly and Cattell to the eight essentials, we find that both maintained the emphasis on Scripture, conversion, charisma, evangelism, and perfection. Eschatology was not a major theme for either. Suffering for Christ's sake was a basic assumption for both, though neither figure made it an emphasis in their writing, nor developed a theology of suffering per se. Both men expressed deep compassion for a suffering world. Mysticism was far more pronounced in Kelly, who mined the Christian mystical tradition, including the apophatic, for its richness and inspiration, and was deeply attuned to the experience of the mystic. Cattell did not directly address mystical experience, but a sense of a holy life as mystical piety under girds his writing. His final words in *The Spirit of Holiness* convey his awareness that loving union is the essence of holiness and the mystical experience: "There is something extravagant about real love. The saints who impress us are not the devotees of sweet reasonableness, but the daring and prodigal lovers of Jesus" (1977, 101). Both Kelly and Cattell understood perfection as the goal of a fully lived, victorious Christian life.

Both figures, because they were so attuned to the "spirit of holiness," combined elements of all four Quadrants of holiness. Cattell fits most comfortably in Quadrant 2, the experiential; a strong emphasis in his writings is on the guidance of the Holy Spirit. Kelly, because of his own dramatic mid-life transformation, is one of the strongest modern Quaker representatives of Quadrant 3, the mystical.

6.6   Contemporary Trends: A Renewed Evangelical Mysticism

Cattell's work proved unifying for Quaker evangelicals searching for a core identity in the process of realignment amidst the legalistic legacy of holiness revivalism and the polarization of the modernist-fundamentalist divide. In part because Rufus Jones' interpretation of Quaker history and theology had become so thoroughly identified with modern liberalism, mysticism for evangelicals had become suspect and for some, synonymous with heresy. Thus it was not until the late twentieth century that Quaker evangelicals dared to explore the Christian mystical tradition and reclaim it as a source for *their* spirituality. Richard Foster, with his best-selling book, *Celebration of Discipline* (1978), was the first to do so in published form, continuing his pursuit through a more recent publication, *Streams of Living Water* (2000). Foster, in common with many leaders in the holiness tradition, writes devotionally and for a popular audience, rather than academically. The significance of the role of mysticism in Quaker holiness is supported by the fact that the first popular and widely-read late twentieth century work reclaiming the Christian mystical tradition for evangelicalism was penned by a Quaker. In addition to Foster's work, privately and individually some Quaker evangelical scholars are beginning to re-examine Christian mysticism.[48]

Foster is a leading voice for spiritual renewal in the Friends Church, and like Thomas Kelly, his influence extends across the Quaker spectrum and far beyond the boundaries of the Friends tradition. Foster understands both the mystical and ethical elements of holiness. In an article published in the mainstream Quaker denominational journal, *Quaker Life,* he asks "What is needed for a Quaker Renaissance today?" (1986, 10). He responds with three essentials for spiritual renewal: one, "a great new experience of God"; two, "a great new passion for purity"; and three, "a great new baptism of power." (1986, 10-13). He voices a new call to holiness:

> Quakers have always been known for being on the forefront of ethical concerns, but we need a whole new movement in this direction. We must …once again begin to pioneer in the ethical imperatives of the faith. We must call for holiness of life in new and vigorous ways in both the private and public spheres. (1986, 12)

The most public call for a renewed Quaker holiness today comes from Quaker scholar, theologian, and minister, Arthur Roberts (see 1.7.6), who has vigorously critiqued the Holiness Movement within Quakerism, outlining both its strengths and weaknesses (2003). Roberts, who understands the dynamics of renewal movements, includes holiness as ecstasy (the divine-human encounter) in his most recent message of a new call to holiness. He explains:

> Every charismatic movement since the Montanists of the Roman era has celebrated ecstatic union of the human and the divine. This has been true of monks and mystics, of Catholics and Quakers, of Baptists

---

[48] For example, Arthur Roberts, George Fox University professor-at-large, owns a nearly complete collection of the *Classics of Western Spirituality*, published by Paulist Press, modern translations of all the primary mystical texts in the Christian tradition, which he uses in devotional and scholarly writings.

and Mennonites, of Methodists and Pentecostals. God leaps through dogma and theology, transcending the limits of language....But there is no way to preserve ecstasy....But the Spirit doesn't leave us when emotion fades. Holy ecstasy is saved by losing it in servant-hood, in the name of Jesus setting captives free, binding up wounds, sharing the Good News of Christ, reconciling nations, releasing earth from sin's chains. God sends us down the mountain of ecstasy into a world yearning for deliverance, and trusts us to remember the holy ground on which in brief moments of ecstasy we stood. (2003, 23-24)

In a concluding section of his new call to holiness, Roberts describes the characteristics of a holy life, or a life of "perfection" in classic Quaker terminology, which he terms "Spirit-baptized intuition" (2003, 25). In addition to the traditional virtues of non-violence in the face of opposition, daily prayer of all types including contemplation, moral purity, the practice of spiritual disciplines, and the inward guidance of the Holy Spirit, he adds the goal of the mystic, *unus spiritus*, or union with God (2003, 26-30): "A sense of oneness with God characterizes mature spirituality. Sometimes union with the divine is experienced as fellowship, at other times as blended nature" (2003, 29). Roberts quotes from Thomas Kelly as a writer who described this union experience, and acknowledges Kelly's important "contribution to holiness theology" (2003, 29).

Roberts' new call to holiness charts a far more mystical path than traditionally articulated by Quaker evangelicals, and a theology which finds its source in the concept of *theosis* of the Eastern Orthodox tradition (2003, 30). His call harkens back to union with God as experienced and described by early Quakers and which finds its origins in New Testament teachings, especially the verse often quoted by Barclay and other early Quakers that we can "become participants in the divine nature" (II Pet. 1:4).

Roberts and Foster's writing, teaching, and preaching on holiness – Christ-centered, ethical, and mystical – is a significant recovery of the original Quaker vision for contemporary Friends. Though both men are highly regarded spiritual leaders and known for their writing and scholarship beyond evangelical circles, their perspectives are not reflected across all branches of Friends, nor widely endorsed among more conservative constituencies in the broader evangelical tradition.[49]

6.7 Chapter Summary

This chapter examined Quaker holiness at the turn of the century and traced its relationship to evangelicalism, liberalism and mysticism in the twentieth

---

[49] Some critics see "new age" or Gnostic tendencies in Foster.

century. The theology of Rufus Jones, a key American figure of tremendous influence in this period, was analyzed. Jones' historical project of a reinterpretation of Quakerism as a modern mystical movement was compared to J. Rendel Harris' holiness mysticism. In modern British Quakerism, the fervent holiness of J. Rendel Harris has been largely overlooked by historians. William Littleboy represents the more dominant trend in British liberalism toward a non-mystical and non-holiness rational Quakerism. Although Harris represents core Quaker holiness within a modernist understanding, his expressions of holiness were overshadowed and ultimately eclipsed by the approach made normative by Littleboy. Other twentieth century reactions to modernism and rationalism were also explored – firstly, the Christ-centered mystical approach of Thomas Kelly, nurtured in a Quaker holiness tradition which he discarded in pursuit of the intellectual search, only to rediscover its transformative aspects in mid-life. And secondly, I noted by way of comparison, the Christ-centered approach of Everett Cattell, an ecumenical evangelical, whose leadership in the mid-century helped the Friends Church recover their spiritual roots and modern identity through his unifying vision for Quaker holiness.

Richard Foster and Arthur Roberts are two seminal thinkers whose calls for a renewal of holiness in contemporary Quakerism have helped to recover the mystical dimension of Quaker holiness. In his most recent "new call to holiness," Roberts goes so far as to propose recovering a Christ-centered mysticism in terms of many of the themes explored in this book (2003, 26-30).

The concluding chapter summarizes the main findings of this study with a re-mapping of the standard "Quaker Tree" and argues for the relative unimportance of external forms in holiness Quakerism.

CHAPTER 7

Quaker Holiness: A New Lens

This chapter summarizes the main findings of this study and re-maps the history of Quakerism. With holiness established as the unifying theme and common link within the development of Quakerism through its history, a new model emerges which modifies previous views of historical development.

7.1   Holiness and Worship: The Unimportance of Forms

This study argues that based on the evidence shown, various external (liturgical) forms that Quakerism has adopted are incidental expressions of spirituality and are not indicative of the essential elements of Quakerism, and are therefore relatively unimportant. Forms are occasional and particular historical expressions of holiness. A significant feature of early Quakerism was its use of two contrasting forms. Both apophatic and kataphatic approaches to worship and ministry were adopted – quiet contemplative gatherings and public evangelistic meetings. This study argues for the relative unimportance of external forms (i.e., "unprogrammed" and "programmed" worship), which in the final analysis are shifts and reactions to the social and cultural climate, rather than essential elements. This conclusion challenges the received historical scholarship and traditional hardened divisions and arguments of "authenticity" over forms of worship within different branches of Quakerism.

This section first reviews the unique polarization over "forms" in Quakerism. Joel Bean, as has been shown (see. 5.2), became the most articulate voice opposing Quaker revivalism, and his negative image of the western revival movement has colored most historical studies of holiness Quakerism. Bean correctly identified many of the doctrinal excesses of the movement, though many holiness advocates themselves were also aware of the extremes sometimes proclaimed. What tended to be lost in the polemic surrounding the doctrinal debates over holiness was the goal and intent of the movement to enable individuals to participate fully in the divine life, "to be filled with the fullness of God" – the same goal and intent of the first Quakers. The revivalists taught, just as Fox did, that a person could have a direct and intimate relationship with God, and could live continually in that felt presence. The quality of life that holiness promoted, to live "in the life and power," to use Quietist terminology (see 4.3), was no different than that of early Quakers. That countless lives were transformed by holiness preaching, and hearts touched and melted by kneeling at the altar, would be hard to deny. But so much of the positive manifestations were lost in the endless polemic over doctrinal definitions, especially these three: whether the Holy Spirit indwelled both the converted and the unconverted; whether holiness was instantaneous or gradual; and whether sanctification was prior to, simultaneous with, or subsequent to justification.

This focus on precise doctrinal definitions and clarifications and attempts to map the experience and turn it into a rigid formula reduced holiness from an existential way of "being in Christ" into a spiritual artifice. Eventually holiness radicals erected this artifice, which like the tower of Babel, could only come crashing down.[1] The doctrinal polemic which raged as much internally within the revival movement as it did externally from its opponents ultimately undermined and diffused much of the real power of the movement (Peters, 1985, 174). As one Methodist theologian, looking back after the revival fires had cooled, observed, "Nearly all the controversy has been over words....Whole octavos have been wasted in refuting what nobody holds, and proving what nobody doubts" (Peters, 1985, 174).

But a significant portion of the resistance to the Holiness Movement arose over more than words; it emerged from fear and loathing of the kind of experience encouraged by evangelists. Revival meetings gave space and freedom for a much greater range of expression than a typical Quaker meeting or Protestant church service. Gifted evangelists shaped the worship experience with the new-found freedom and creativity of a liturgist no longer bound by a fixed liturgy.

In many ways the revival meetings (called "devotional meetings" by Walter Robson in his journal) had much in common with early Quaker worship – they were spontaneous, yet bounded; egalitarian – all could speak, yet gifted ministers spoke most often; emotionally expressive – tears and prayers were common, as well as singing in the Spirit. Although holiness meetings were rarely called "group mysticism" in their day, they were a form of Christ-centered group mysticism. And they were charismatic in that they gave freedom for the movement of the Spirit to arise in each individual. The most obvious *difference* between the two was in the use of silence. Whereas in early Quaker worship words arose out of the silence (thus worship moved from the apophatic to the kataphatic), in holiness gatherings the silence was filled with words, music and prayer, and so appeared to be wholly and excessively kataphatic. But I contend that the goal of holiness gatherings was to guide the worshipper to the apophatic moment of connecting with God in a vital new way, to lift the worshipper out of the realm of words, doctrines, and images, and out of themselves and their egos. The apophatic moment was the death-to-self experience. The goal of holiness gatherings was to move worshippers beyond kataphatic faith to apophatic faith ("naked faith" as the early Pietists called it),

---

[1] See Hamm, 1988, 102-111, for the most in-depth analysis of the holiness revival, but drawing conclusions somewhat different from this study.

to experience existentially and with certainty what faith, grace, and love are all about.

Holiness evangelists called this transcendence of the self "perfect love" or "baptism of the Spirit." Traditional Quietist Quakers had called it the "celestial outpouring" or the "celestial shower," which was always the goal of a gathered worship (see 4.3).[2] Granted, this is the holiness ideal and may have been rare, but for many Quakers, especially on the western frontier, truly gathered silent worship of "celestial outpourings" had become even rarer.

7.1.1   Holiness and Silence

Quaker use of silence became a key issue (in fact, it could be stated even more strongly – a pregnant symbol) which divided holiness and traditionalist. One justifiable criticism often directed at the Holiness Movement was its disregard for the practice of silence in worship as a way to experience God's presence. Most holiness evangelists (with the exception of a few who joined from other denominations) had been raised with silent worship and knew the experience well, but many had apparently found it to be inadequate, in and of itself, in the forms in which it was then practiced to bring them out of themselves and into an experience of the "fullness of God." Silent worship (group silence, particularly), had been a significant rediscovery by early Quakers of a prayer practice and personal and group discipline, long used in monasticism and the contemplative (mystical) tradition.[3]

---

[2] In the post-holiness period, it came to be stereotyped into a more individualist experience of the "Second Blessing."

[3] Robert Barclay, in his *Apology* (Sippel, 2002, 319-320), referred with high regard to a popular English monastic writer who lived just prior to the beginnings of Quakerism, Augustine Baker (1575-1641), and a work called *Santa Sophia*. Baker was a Protestant who became a Benedictine Monk and taught a form of contemplative prayer, similar to that found in the earlier fourteenth century anonymous English mystical treatise, *Cloud of Unknowing*. Baker is known for his appreciation and elevation of silence, and is perhaps a source, or at the least provides a model for, the practice of silence in early Quaker worship. Baker's writings on prayer find echoes in Barclay's *Apology* (2002, 453-454). In a work called *The Prayer of Aspirations*, Baker described this type of prayer as "naturally and without any force flowing from the soul, powerfully and immediately directed and moved by the Holy Spirit" (Qtd. in de Jaegher, 1977, 136). Baker expanded this description of aspirations in a passage that resonates with Quaker writings. The prayer of aspirations "proceed from an interior impulse, indeliberately and as if it were naturally flowing from the soul, and thereby they show that there is in the interior a secret, supernatural, directing principle, to wit God's Holy Spirit alone, teaching and moving the soul to breathe forth those aspirations....not only in set recollections, but almost continually" (Qtd. in de Jaegher, 1977, 139).

Silent worship, in the context of revolutionary England in the seventeenth century, not only created a setting for group prayer, but also provided early Quakers with a form of protest and resistance to traditional forms of liturgical worship as well as dry, interminable Puritan preaching and "singing Psalms in meter." Silent worship guided by the Spirit provided the ideal vehicle of resistance to all traditional forms of worship in the seventeenth century. By the eighteenth century, silence in Quaker Orthodoxy *was* the traditional form of worship, and had evolved into its own ritualistic patterns. By the mid-nineteenth century, it was argued, silence *became* the symbol, the absolutist form, and silent worship was no longer truly apophatic, but a ritual in itself.[4] Thus, spiritual renewal for this generation of Quakers flowed, not through silence, but through an overabundance of words, music, prayer, and praise. Renewal came through new channels, and the value of long, empty silence diminished. Silence can be filled with self, or many selves, or it can be filled with God. Perhaps this is what John Wilbur meant when he contrasted "a painful, silent meeting" with a "heavenly, solacing meeting"[5] (see 4.3).

What revivalist Quakers diminished, traditionalists elevated. What the revivalist discarded as no longer useful, the traditionalist claimed as the centerpiece of pure, spiritual religion. For Beanites and later modernists, silent worship became the *piece de resistance.* What the revivalists rejected, modernists reclaimed. Thus, for Joel Bean, for example, the true heirs of true Quakerism would be found only among the "faithful remnant" who continued to worship in silence, the highest form of worship. Silent meetings turned out to be the ideal vehicle for modernist Quaker worship because it enabled diverse

---

Barclay referred to these breath prayers in his *Apology* in proposition fifteen, where he included a section on the love of God. As is common in the mystical tradition, he compared the pure love of God to the intensely focused, passionate love of a man for a woman, in which the lover can scarcely think about anything else. He contended a person in this state will find that only a short time can pass before "the mind will let some ejaculation forth towards its beloved" (Sippel, 2002, 454). These "ejaculations" were for Barclay the natural expressions of the constant awareness of God's presence in which even in the midst of our daily routines of life are emitted as "some short aspiration and breathings" (Sippel, 2002, 453). He described this love as that which "hath taken a deep place in the heart, and possess the mind" (Sippel, 2002, 453).

[4] Hamm, though he does not share the revivalists' critique of silent worship, nevertheless notes that "silence had been the exception rather than the rule among the early Friends" (1988, 85). Barclay attested that silence almost always led to exhortation and vocal prayer in worship (Sippel, 2002, 303).

[5] Quietists understood what Barclay meant when he wrote that "this form being observed is not likely to be long kept pure without the power: for it is, of itself, so naked without it that it hath nothing in it to invite and tempt men to dote upon it, further than it is accompanied with the power" (Sippel, 2002, 343). Revivalists felt certain silent waiting was no longer accompanied with the power. Hamm notes that for revivalists, "silence and composure were almost always signs of spiritual deadness" (1988, 85).

individuals to come together in one place in apparent unity, even if they held vastly different belief systems and experienced the silence in totally different ways. In silent worship each individual can pray to a different God, or to no God at all, or they can listen attentively to their own voice. Bean, Jones, and the Quaker modernists, of course, would not have gone this far; they remained firmly Christ-centered, and in the silence they sought God's will and felt Christ's presence, but their trajectory formed the roadbed for the broad highway to a post-Christian Quakerism where silence itself became a kataphatic "form." For early Quakers, on the other hand, the silence of words led to silence of the mind, and finally to silence of the will (a distinguishing of three stages of silence found in many monastic communities).[6]

7.2 Re-Mapping Quakerism

It is impossible in the space of one book to encapsulate the embodiment of holiness in the all of the key figures representing in microcosm the evolving holiness Quaker tradition. I have argued that Fox and Barclay, with slight variations, present a homogenous understanding of holiness as a process of deepening union with God, according to the "measure" or capacity of each individual. Further, I have argued that holiness continued to be central to Quakerism through the eighteenth century. Although expressed with some variation in different types of Quietism in different cultural settings and ethos, holiness as the message of direct experience culminating in union with God did not change. Perfection remained connected to both mystical experience and core Christian doctrines in the Quietist period. Holiness played a major role in spiritual renewal and reform impulses in Anthony Benezet's (1713-1784) leadership in early Quietism and Stephen Grellet's (1773-1855) evangelical impulses in later Quietism. Both leaders combined an unusual dialectic of both inwardly mystical and radical ethical holiness.

In the breakdown, fragmentation, re-interpretation, and cultural adaptation (or non-adaptation) of American Quakerism in the nineteenth century, Elias Hicks (1748-1830), Joseph John Gurney (1788-1847), and John Wilbur (1774-1856), represent the widening, evolving, and reactionary streams of holiness which created divergent and antagonistic branches, severing the unified vision of Quaker mystical and ethical holiness held in a balanced tension within the Society of Friends for almost two hundred years. These three leaders and their separate legacies changed the shape of Quaker holiness. Hicks and Hicksism moved away from Quaker holiness and Christian orthodoxy towards a more

---

[6] Barclay described the preparation necessary for inward silence: "…before God be worshipped in the inward temple of the heart it must be purged of its own filth, and all its own thoughts and imaginations, that so it may be fit to receive the Spirit of God and to be acted by it" (Sippel, 2002, 319).

rationalist, enlightenment, and Unitarian trajectory. Gurney moved away from Quaker holiness to a Wesleyan /Anglican evangelical, but non-mystical, type, yet nevertheless helped prepare Quakerism for a renewal of holiness through revivalism. And Wilbur maintained a tradition of Quaker holiness, but in an isolationist, sectarian form.

Quaker holiness separated into modern evangelicalism and modern liberalism in the twentieth century. Two key modernist figures of this period whose ideas and visions for a new Quakerism were radically different, were Rufus Jones and J. Rendel Harris. Jones embarked on a theological and historical project of a reinterpretation of Quakerism as a modern mystical, but essentially liberal, movement. And in British Quakerism, Harris, a complex and paradoxical figure, whose fervent holiness has been generally overlooked by historians, established the capacity of a Quaker modernist to fully embrace Quaker holiness without retreating from the challenges of liberal scholarship.[7] But most modernists, such as Harris' adversary, William Littleboy, represent the more dominant trend in British liberalism toward a non-mystical and non-holiness rational Quakerism (Kennedy, 2001, 187).[8] I have argued that Harris represented core Quaker holiness within modernism.

An ecumenical, contemporary approach to holiness that also maintained core Quaker holiness within modernism is represented by Thomas Kelly. Kelly appeals to Quakers across all branches because he tapped into the mystical tradition of essential Quakerism. Everett Cattell, a contemporary of Kelly and seminal thinker from the evangelical branch of Quakerism, also took a Christ-centered ecumenical approach to holiness. He wrote a practical and balanced guide to Quaker spirituality and defined holiness for modern evangelicals.

A picture of the changing nature of holiness in Quakerism can best be summarized by a diagram of the evolution, elimination and recovery of the eight key characteristics through different time periods and movements (see Figure 4).[9]

In this chart, the eight columns represent different periods and a selection of movements of Quakerism over the centuries. The eight rows represent the key elements found in the early movement and the dynamics of change over time. The bold type indicates a basic continuation of that same element; the

---

[7] Another key figure in Quakerism whose influence on American Friends has been immense, but could not be included in this study for lack of space, is J. Walter Malone (1857-1935). His entrepreneurial spirit was central to the creation of a modern evangelical Quaker holiness movement at the turn of the century and into the first decades of the twentieth century (see Oliver, 1993).

[8] Littleboy's *The Appeal of Quakerism to the Non-mystic* (1917), his most well-known work, documents this perspective.

[9] This chart is not meant to be comprehensive. For the sake of simplicity, a number of movements, such as Wilburism and Conservatism, are not charted here. Both of these movements follow the basic pattern of Quietism.

plain type, an adaptation. For example, the first change was from a literal second coming of Christ to an internalized second coming as "realized" eschatology. Emphasis on eschatology gradually waned but reappeared in the holiness revival in a new form that was predominantly premillennialism (Hamm, 1988, 106-107).

Conversion, in the Quietist period, became primarily sanctification, or growth in grace. By the Orthodox period, conversion was wholly gradual growth in grace through membership in the community (birthright Friends). Hicksism differed from Orthodoxy in only one key element, the role of Scripture, which was gradually replaced by experience alone as a source of revelation, as in Modernism. Gurneyism, Revival Holiness, and Evangelical Holiness all reappropriated Scripture as divine revelation and the interpreter of experience.

	Radical Holiness 1646-1666	Formative Period 1667-1689	Quietism 1690-1820	Orthodoxy 1827-1858	Hicksism 1827-1900	Gurneyism 1858-1920	Revival Holiness 1870-1940	Evangelical Holiness 1940-	Modernism 1900-
Scripture	**Scripture**	**Scripture**	**Scripture**	**Scripture**	Experience	**Scripture**	**Scripture**	**Scripture**	Experience
Eschatology	Realized Eschatology	Realized Eschatology	Realized Eschatology				Premillennial Eschatology		
Conversion	**Conversion**	**Conversion**	Sanctification	Community	Community	**Conversion**	**Conversion**	**Conversion**	Community
Evangelism	**Evangelism**	**Evangelism**	Ministry	Ministry	Ministry	**Evangelism**	**Evangelism**	**Evangelism**	
Charisma	**Charisma**	**Charisma**	Leading of Spirit	Leading of Spirit	Leading of Spirit	Leading of Spirit	**Charisma**	Leading of Spirit	
Suffering	**Suffering**	**Suffering**	Quaker Testimonies	Quaker Testimonies	Quaker Testimonies	Quaker Testimonies	Christian Testimonies	Christian Testimonies	Universal Testimonies
Mysticism	**Mysticism**	**Mysticism**	Silent Worship	Silent Worship	Silent Worship	Silent Worship	Mysticism	Sense of Presence in Worship	Silent Worship
Perfection	**Perfection**	**Perfection**	**Perfection**	Obedience	Obedience	Obedience	**Perfection**	Growth in Grace	Social Action

Figure 4: The Changing Nature of Holiness in Quakerism

In the Quietist period, evangelism evolved into primarily community ministry with an emphasis on formation of the individual to the values of the community (with some exceptions). The strong community ethos continued until a concern for evangelism reappeared in Gurneyism, and was especially emphasized in Revival and Evangelical Holiness. Charisma in the Quietist period became internalized with less manifestation of the range of charismatic phenomena and intense focus on the singularity of being "Spirit-led," a *charism* which became the primary characteristic of Quaker spirituality.[10] Broader charismatic phenomena reappeared in Revival Holiness.

By the Quietist period, and the end of political persecution, suffering was replaced by the strict adherence to the testimonies and disciplines. The willingness to be identified as a "peculiar people" and to accept the marginalization of such a counter-cultural distinction became the "cross" of suffering. Testimonies as "Quaker distinctives" assumed less importance in Revival and Evangelical Holiness, and became more broadly Christian. In Modernism they were more broadly universal – "integrity, equality, simplicity, honesty."

Mysticism, by the Quietist period, found its expression primarily communally in silent (contemplative or apophatic) worship. Mysticism was reflected more widely in the spiritual experiences of Revival Holiness (worship became more kataphatically expressive). Mysticism was less predominant in Evangelical Holiness, though not totally absent. Evangelical worship became more rational and teaching-oriented, with much less space allotted for contemplative silence.

Perfection as mystical experience and ethical manifestation, the natural outcome of divine indwelling or union with God, continued to be an expectation (though not often realized) through the Quietist period. In Quaker Orthodoxy the main focus of perfection became obedience. The mystical aspect of perfection found expression again in Revival Holiness and was generally lost thereafter.

---

[10] It should be noted that Quietist ministers continued to manifest physical characteristics of "quaking" or trembling when they preached. This *charism*, considered a sign of divine unction, was believed to be the power of the Holy Spirit working within well into the nineteenth century. Hannah W. Smith (1832-1911) confirms this Quaker peculiarity in her autobiography: "I myself, even in quieter times when I was a child, would often see the preachers in our meetings [Philadelphia Yearly Meeting] trembling and quaking from head to foot, and I confess I always felt that messages delivered under this condition had a special inspiration and unction of their own, far beyond all others. In fact, unless a preacher had at least enough of this 'quaking' to make their hearts palpitate and their legs tremble, they were not considered by many to have the real 'call' to the ministry at all..." (Smith, 1903, 44). This somatic manifestation is but a variation of the tears and groanings exhibited by revival ministers when they were seen as having special unction in their preaching.

This charting of 350 years of Quaker spirituality (though drastically simplifying complex phenomena) reveals that holiness functions as a primary theme and variation in the history of the Quaker movement. Based on the criteria of the eight essentials of Quaker holiness, Revival Holiness followed most closely the original pattern of the early movement. However, this observation is not meant to imply that revival holiness as it became manifested in the nineteenth century was a truer or purer form of Quakerism. Many of its cultural expressions were quite diverse and shaped by entirely different cultural and social forces. But rather than viewing revivalism as an alien takeover, holiness theory contends that a new generation was rediscovering essential aspects of Quakerism buried within its own tradition.

Holiness theory does not contradict or devalue other important theories, based on different logic or divergent criteria, but provides a new lens to explore significant data that has been overlooked or minimized, and thus brings a more complete understanding of the Quaker path. Holiness theory circumvents many of the standard theological and doctrinal issues, as well as the unique divisions such as "programmed/unprogrammed, pastoral/nonpastoral, and use or disuse of spiritual practices that divide contemporary Quakers. The recognition of holiness as a paradigmatic theme connecting movements and branches in the evolution of Quakerism alters the standard diagrams of its growth and development and offers a fresh interpretation of the mapping of the history of the Quaker tradition (see Figure 5, p. 333). Hamm, for example, in his diagram of the evolution of American Quakerism, traces the central spine of Quakerism through the Gurneyites, emerging in the Modernists. He places holiness as a branching movement, digressing from the center (1988, 176). I argue for holiness as the central trunk of Quakerism up to the present, rather than an offshoot. Holiness is diluted today in all modern branches, yet is sprinkled throughout. Evangelicalism tends to maintain the strongest connections, but even here appreciation for Quaker holiness varies widely and misunderstandings abound.

7.3 Conclusions

Hicksites and non-holiness modernist liberals came to value silence, an essential element of holiness, above all. They overvalued one aspect of Quaker practice and gave it an exalted, absolute status, which severely restricted the range of Quaker holiness. Thus the affective experiences of revivalism could not be tolerated because they were too emotional and sensory, and too many "forms" (images) were utilized – preaching, singing, and bodily movement, for example. Because modernist liberals essentially eliminated Quadrant 1 (see Figure 3) – the kataphatic holiness of symbol, image, and doctrine, and even for many, the mediation of Christ – worshippers could interpret their own mystical (quietist) experience without any boundaries and potentially reach an apophatic moment. But as shown, more often they created their own forms and ritualized the silence. But I have argued that the apophatic emptiness of mystical experience, the losing oneself to find oneself, can be experienced in both forms of worship, quietist and revivalist, and the form is unimportant. Mystical experience often happened in the midst of boisterous revivals, just as mystical experience can happen in a post-Christian silent meeting without the mediation of Christ, even to persons not seeking or prepared for it. Anyone, in fact, in their contemplation may discover the image of God, the Light within themselves, or the divine in the human, since each human being is by nature the image of God, and this realization or discovery may be the beginning of the spiritual journey. But holiness means coming into the image and likeness of Christ, and that is a further stage.

One of the greatest of the medieval mystics, Jan van Ruusbroec, understood this kind of non-mediated quietism, analyzed it extensively and even had a cautious respect for it, which he called "natural contemplation" or contemplation "without grace" (Mommaers, 2003, 256, n8). In his own fourteenth century context, many spiritual persons used this path (one of the dangers, according to Ruusbroec, was that it led to heresy) and he summed up its limitation by saying, "However high the eagle soars, it cannot fly above itself" (Mommaers, 1995, 219). The eagle, for Ruusbroec, was the symbol for two kinds of contemplatives: the "natural contemplative" who "nests in his own essence," and the "graced contemplative" who "flies above himself in God, and that is where he rests" (Mommaers, 2003, 272). Both feel bliss and peace and an "oceanic feeling," but the source (or object) of the experience is not the same. One sinks down into his or her own essence and finds the divine in the image of God within; the other transcends beyond his or her own essence (the self is annihilated, the traditional Quaker term used) and rests in the immanent transcendence of the Father, Son, and Holy Spirit. The first is an intensified self-awareness; the second is a meeting with a Divine Other.

Quaker holiness is contemplation with grace that leads to union with God which is both transcendent and immanent, grounded in the incarnation, and a mystical participation in the divine Trinity that does not drain away personal intimacy, the felt experience of loving and desiring a Divine Other outside of self. Other kinds of Quakerism are forms of natural contemplation, sharing some elements of holiness, but not normative Quaker holiness, understood as "Christ within, the hope of glory," or "the life hid with God in Christ," or what early Quakers called perfection.

Based on the examples of major historical figures from the Quaker movement through time, the evidence supports this theory that holiness, in specifically Christian form, was the distinguishing characteristic which set Quakers apart from other movements. Quaker holiness is deeply embedded in the Christian mystical tradition, for that was the experience in which its founders were awakened to the reality of God. Holiness is always the goal of Christian mysticism. But Quakerism was never a mysticism reserved for the few who have esoteric experiences, or even a mysticism that exalted ecstatic experience. Nor was Quakerism an intellectualized, speculative mysticism, outlining steps or stages that were to be rigorously followed. Mystics are those persons who believe it is possible to be intimate with God, who have felt God's love, and who continually desire to "taste God." They are convinced that they somehow have been mysteriously reborn, and are one spirit (*unus spiritus*) with Christ.

Holiness Friends, while sharing an essence, are not all cut from the same cloth. Holiness Friends can be theologically "liberals," like Rendel Harris, Hannah Whitall Smith, and later, Thomas Kelly; or they can be conservatives, such as Thomas Story, Stephen Grellet, and John Wilbur; or they can be social radicals, like Anthony Benezet. They can worship and pray strictly in silence or in energetic and ecstatic revivals, but they are all active contemplatives. Quaker holiness tends to be socially radical and counter cultural, and always includes a reforming impulse. It is often sectarian, but also has strong ecumenical tendencies. Quaker holiness cuts across the usual doctrinal boundaries. But Quaker holiness, given the age and circumstances in which it first emerged, is intimately bound to the Christian faith, and will therefore be theocentric and Christocentric, and pneumocentric as well, which makes it functionally Trinitarian.

Holiness Quakerism is drenched in the biblical tradition, though, as with Rendel Harris, those who embrace it may not always interpret that tradition in conventional ways. But as this study has shown, the essential Christian orthodoxy of early Quakerism, while it anchored mystical experience and shaped the ethics of holiness as imitation of Christ, did not ultimately confine Quaker holiness exclusively to an orthodox Christian foundation. Elements of holiness appeared in other liberal, modernist, and non-orthodox branches beyond the original confessional framework of the faith of the first Quakers.

7.4   Summary

The language of holiness and perfection are not given much attention in academic circles, but in the spiritual world, as Rabbi Heschel writes, "holiness is the most precious word in religion" (Fox, 1997, 275). As central as holiness and perfection were to early Quakers, no historian to date has classified and examined Quakerism as a holiness movement nor oriented their research to this feature. This book is the first attempt to study the historical development of Quaker holiness. It is the first to trace the theme of holiness as the direct experience of God culminating in divine union, and to explore various interpretations of such experience through three centuries of Quaker tradition.

The generally accepted theory that Quakerism lies at the radical end of Reformation Protestantism does not fit the evidence presented. Protestantism inverted the Roman Catholic belief that union with God was the culmination of the spiritual life, and made union with God synonymous with justification by faith, the initial entry into faith. Perfection became glorification in heaven. But in Quakerism, from its inception, perfection was the culmination of growth in grace, sustained by the synergy of grace and works (loving God and neighbor), and by living obediently in the Light of Christ through divine indwelling. Thus, perfection could be experienced in this world as an inner communion with God, and not only a hope to be realized in heaven.

The holiness theory identifies Quakers more closely with the theological assumptions of the early Greek Fathers than with Protestant reformers in their concept of synergy and divinization. Their desire to create intensive contemplative communities of fully committed, spiritually awakened and aware people has more in common with the radical holiness of monastic reform movements than with the establishing of Protestant churches. Quakers, as a radical holiness movement, were determined to monasticize the people of God by creating spiritual utopias of monastic-like perfection in a post-Protestant context. Thus, they formed counter-cultural communities that were utopian-like, separated culturally, but not physically, from the world. They were to signify as a people paradise regained, because Christ had come and restored what had been lost in the fall. They created "heterotopias" – places "above the world," even though they were located in the midst of the social system (Pilgrim, 1999). This is one reason why Quakers were often called papists and Jesuits in the early period. (And like Jesuits, they were "contemplatives in action," engaged in a variety of professions in pursuit of the evangelization of the world, deeming the whole world their mission field.)

Quakers adapted a number of monastic-like principles: non-violence, practice of silence, simplicity of speech and life ("plainness," which included within a generation, a Quaker-style "habit"), egalitarianism, disuse of oaths, and an asceticism of detachment from "the spirit and vain conversation of this world" (Sippel, 2002, 429).

Quakers were a post-Reformation movement which mirrored much of its immediate Puritan context, but also drew on numerous sources within the medieval mystical tradition found in popular mystical texts that had been recently translated from the Rhineland mystics and the French Quietists. Rufus Jones' research on Quakerism as mysticism has enduring value and is not to be denied. He simply shaped his description of mysticism through modern, liberal ideals rather than accepting the evidence that Quakers were thoroughly biblical and essentially evangelical mystics. Other interpreters, such as Punshon and Gwyn, overlook the pervasive influence of mysticism and separate it from evangelicalism. Roberts in his earlier work also deemphasized mysticism, but his most recent work, the culmination of his life-long research and thinking on Quaker spirituality, moves towards a reappropriation of the mystical tradition within Quaker holiness that acknowledges and supports the validity of this theory (2003).

This study singles out holiness as the unifying and interpretive theme that integrates mysticism and evangelicalism, apophatic and kataphatic spirituality. Differing branches of Quakerism developed when external pressures from social, cultural, intellectuall, and political forces created tensions that disturbed the balance within this seamless cloth. Polarization arose, creating antagonistic branches with diverse identities born out of differing emphases on the meaning and expression of holiness.

In this study I have designed and utilized a typology of holiness as a way to best sort and classify the historical approaches to holiness and to demonstrate how Quakers drew on all of these historical types to create their own distinct forms of belief, doctrine and experience. I have examined holiness themes through their embodiment in key representative figures, primarily through the lens of their writings and practices related to holiness, critiquing them according to their relationship to the four quadrants.

This study of holiness requires all scholars of Quakerism to revisit their assumptions and research findings and look again at the central place holiness has had in the theological history of Quakerism.

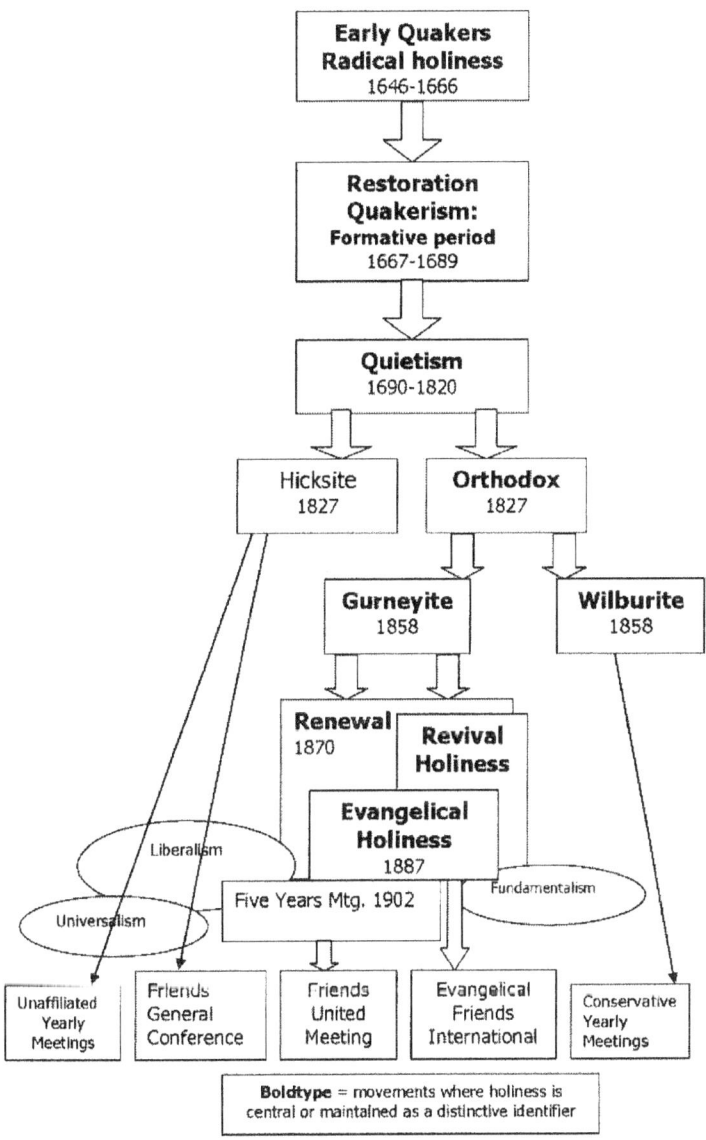

Figure 5: The Evolution of American Quakerism, 1646-2000

APPENDIX A
Sources of Early Quaker Mysticism

1. Augustinian Mysticism and Deification

Early Quakerism drew deeply on traditional sources of mystical thought and language which shaped Puritan spirituality, such as the writings of St. Augustine and medieval bridal mysticism. Augustine of Hippo's *Confessions* was the paradigmatic model for Christian conversion in the Puritan era (Hambrick-Stowe, 1986, 26). The "inward turn," an intense interiority so central in Quakerism in its theme of the inward Light, finds one early source in Augustinian spirituality, eloquently expressed in Augustine's famous prayer in his *Confessions*, "You were within, but I looked for you outside" (10.27). As McGinn points out in his study of the mysticism of Augustine, "to go within is to go above" and "the God within is the God above" (1991, 242). In Augustine is found a pattern familiar in Quaker mysticism – the *enstatic*, the movement within, which leads to the *ecstatic* – movement above, beyond self (McGinn, 1991, 242).[1]

Even though Quakers did not look to Augustine as a basis for their religious philosophy as most Western theologians did, including and especially Puritans, the pattern of Augustine's conversion as described in *Confessions* (8.8-12), seeking God in the external, then moving inward and moving beyond self is reflected in Quaker religious experience.

For example, Augustine described an experience of the withdrawing from the sensory world to be confronted by the Light within which moved him to an encounter with God:

> ....I entered into my inmost parts with you leading me on. I was able to do it because you had become my helper. I entered and saw with my soul's eye (such as it was) an unchanging Light above that same soul's eye, above my mind.... He who knows truth knows that light, and he who knows it knows eternity. Love knows it. O Eternal Truth and True Love and Beloved Eternity! You are my God, to you I sigh day and night.... And you beat back the weakness of my gaze, powerfully blazing into me, and I trembled with love and dread. And I found

---

[1] For example, Stephen Grellet, one of the most prominent nineteenth century ministers, in describing his conversion echoed Augustine when he wrote, "In the inward silent frame of mind, seeking for the divine Presence, I was favoured to find *in me*, what I had so long and with so many tears sought *without* me" [my emphasis] (Seebohm, 1862, 17) (see 3.3.1).

myself to be far from you in the land of unlikeness.... (*Confessions* 7.10.16)

For all mystics, the goal of the Christian life is to overcome sin through union with God, but unlike Quakers, Augustine was less optimistic about the possibility of perfection through divine union. For him, "the touch" of God only happened momentarily in this life and would only be fully realized after death in eternity. Augustine, unlike the majority of the early Church Fathers, used union with God language sparsely. He wrote most often of a desire for, and a fleeting, partial vision of God (*visio Dei*), glimpses which might come in this life but which would only be enjoyed in full in heaven.[2] Early Quaker mysticism had greater affinity with the concept of perfection found in Augustine's Greek contemporary, Gregory of Nyssa, than with the Latin Father himself (see 2.5.1).

Augustine, however, did stress the notion of divine sonship, which was the equivalent of the concept of divinization (McGinn, 1991, 250-1). Like the Greek Fathers, Augustine also understood the ultimate purpose of the incarnation as deification: "The Son of God was made a partaker of mortality so that mortal man might partake of divinity" (*Homily on Psalms* 52.6) [*PL* 36:646]. This notion of perfection as sonship is central to Quaker mystical perfection, so much so that George Fox occasionally overstepped the bounds of enthusiasm and called himself "the son of God." This divine sonship was experienced in the Eucharistic metaphor for Fox in much the same way that one finds in Augustine:

> The blood of Christ which satisfies the Father, which the Saints drink, and his flesh which they eat which in so doing have life is that which the world stumble at; which who drinks it, lives forever. (Fox, 1831, 3:227)

Compare this statement with McGinn, who explains Augustine's radical understanding in this way: "He can thus speak of Christ as 'transforming his own into himself' (*transfigurans in se suos*), using a metaphor of eating that calls to mind the image from the seventh book of the *Confessions*, where feeding on the divine food is said to change us into God" (1991, 252).[3] McGinn maintains with most scholars that "The Pauline notion of our joint sonship with Christ is evident throughout Augustine's works," but adds, what is not so evident is "how the bishop drew out of such scriptural texts a distinctive doctrine of deification" (1991, 251). Deification is not a natural divinity that

---

[2] Augustine's theology of perfection could best be summed up in these lines: "You will draw near to the likeness by the measure you advance in charity, and to the same degree you will begin to perceive God." *Homily on Psalms* 99.5 [*PL* 37:1274].
[3] See *Confessions* 7.10.16. and *Enarrationes in Ps.* 32.2.2 [*PL* 36:278].

needs only to be awakened, but it comes through Christ, who alone makes it possible for us to become sons of God. A much debated issue in current Quaker scholarship revolves around the question of whether or not Quakers confused or mingled the substance of God and humanity in their belief in divine indwelling, such as Richard Bailey (1992), who coined the term "celestial inhabitation" to imply a deification of absorption (which is Neoplatonic in origin) (see 1.7.5).

Early Quakers, I argue, though never precise theologians, did not make any claims to be of the same substance as God, or claim equality with God. Even in their use of "godded" they maintained a distinction between the human and God. Their claims were no more startling than that reflected in Augustinian orthodoxy, and Augustine is perhaps the most careful of the early Fathers on this key point, as a text from a *Homily on Psalm 49* demonstrates:[4]

> It is clear that because he said that humans are gods they are deified from his grace not born from his substance. . . . He who justifies also deifies, because by justification he makes sons of God. . . . If we have been made God's sons, we have also been made gods; but this is by adopting grace, not by nature giving birth. [*PL* 36:565]

Augustine's understanding of deification was not that of an individual private experience (though in *Confessions* he described one personal spiritual experience, the vision at Ostia). Perfection ultimately would be realized in the context of community. Quakers, I argue, came to the same conclusion. Union with Christ was experienced communally in silent worship, feeding spiritually on the blood and body of Christ.

In these respects Augustinan spirituality, so characteristic of Puritanism, came to be reflected in Quaker theology and experience.[5] But Quakers went a step beyond Augustine and the Puritans in that they did not see perfection as the heavenly, future goal, but a present reality.

For Augustine, union with God was always partial and fleeting in this life, and not available to all. On this point Quakerism digresses from the Augustinian Latin tradition and finds greater commonality with the Eastern Orthodox tradition of deification, found in, for example, Gregory of Nyssa and Pseudo-Macarius. Quakers probably reached their position on perfection completely independently of any direct Eastern Orthodox influence, yet the

---

[4] Augustine's sermons were preached to ordinary people in the congregation, not to an elite class of monks; thus deification was for everyone.

[5] Augustine's *Confessions* was popular reading in the seventeenth century. Fox's flaming sword experience (Nickalls, 1952, 27-28) has some parallels to Augustine's description of his mystical ascent at Ostia (see *Augustine of Hippo: Selected Writings*, trans. Mary T. Clark, 1984, 114-15). But theologically, Quakers seem to be less Augustinian than other "religion of the heart" movements. Barclay quoted him frequently to support his arguments in his *Apology*, but also took issue with him on some points.

possibility of direct contact needs further investigation. Eastern Orthodoxy provides for the possibility of union in this life through "divine energies" (*energeiai*) which transfigure human nature through God's love (Lossky, 1998, 86-87). Quakers would prefer to say union comes through the Spirit's empowerment or through the Light of Christ within, or to use Barclay's unique term, *vehiculum Dei*, which refers to this supernatural, uncreated energy (Sippel, 2002, 120, 124), a Quaker version of the same concept. "That which western theology calls by the name of the *supernatural* signifies for the East the *uncreated* – the divine energies ineffably distinct from the essence of God" (Lossky, 1998, 86).

2. Bridal Mysticism and Love Mysticism

Bernard of Clairvaux, twelfth century mystic, is another figure prominent in Puritan spirituality (Hambrick-Stowe, 1986, 28). His brand of mysticism is often called bridal mysticism, a highly Christo-centric love mysticism. Bernard wrote at length on perfection as perfect love that comes through union with Christ and is experienced as rapture. Visions are prominent in Bernard, much more so than Augustine. He was the most influential medieval figure for the Puritans, who employed his rapturous language, borrowed from the Song of Songs, to describe their religious encounters (Rupp, 1977; Hambrick-Stowe, 1986).

Moore and Damrosch, among other scholars, have observed the prevalence of the language of the Song of Songs in Quaker writings, especially in Quaker correspondence with each other (Moore, 2000, 77-78; Damrosch, 1996, 123,126). The erotic language of the Song of Songs was employed liberally by Quakers, much as it had been appropriated by medieval mystics before them, to describe mystical experience and their devotion to each other. For example, in an undated letter from Catherine Johnson to Stephen Crisp:

> ...in the life of my Father, wilt thou feel the pure love streaming forth to thee, with all the Israel of God, to whom my life is dearly united. O dear lamb! ...O what shall I say unto thee! My Father hath had me into his banqueting house, and there hath He overcome me with his love; and hath refreshed me with the wine of his kingdom. (See Song 2:4)
>
> He hath put his left hand under my head, and his right hand doth embrace me. (See Song 2:6) How can my soul but sound forth his praises, even everlasting praises and hallelujahs to the God of my life, who hath dealt so bountifully with my soul! O thou dearly beloved, my soul cannot prize any thing below Christ, so as to rest satisfied with them; for long hath been the time of my groaning, and many have been my tears, to be a possessor, yea to be married to my Beloved, that so I might be complete in him. And now is the God of tender bowels giving

me the desire of my soul, which thirsteth after Him, even as a hart for
the water, and now doth my soul feed amongst the lilies, where my life
is abundantly refreshed....(*Collectitia* 1824, 1:39-41)[6]

Similar rapturous letters written to Fox have been noted by other historians (Moore, 2000, 78). Commentaries on the Song of Songs were prolific among Puritans (Jones, 1986, 444) and erotic language including the metaphor of intercourse to describe the intensity of union with God was commonplace. Early Quakers surpassed Puritans in using such allegorical language to describe communal bonds and spiritual friendships as well.

In Fox's attempt to describe holiness as the experience of union with Christ, he used a variety of allegorical symbols, piling metaphor upon metaphor, from grafting images to marriage images:

...wait in his power and light, that ye may be children of the Light, by believing in the Light which is the life in Christ; that you may be grafted into him, the true root, and built upon him, the true foundation,...and is the rock of ages...worship him in the spirit and truth....and by this truth you may be made free, by which ye may be espoused and married to Christ Jesus, for the marriage of the Lamb is come and coming. (Fox, 1831, 8:37-38)

The language of bridal mysticism to describe divine union was not confined to the early period. In the late eighteenth century, Job Scott (1751-

---

[6] In another letter to Stephen Crisp, this one anonymous (though quite possibly from the same Catherine Johnson, the language being very similar), we find comparable lush love language. This letter also reveals how "flesh of flesh and bone of bone" could be used not only to describe union with God, but also as a metaphor of the union of saints with one another: "In that fountain of pure love which the Lord hath largely opened in me, am I drawn to write unto thee. O! how near art thou unto me with all the lambs of my Father's fold. Surely thou art even, as I may say, flesh of my flesh, and bone of my bone. I am one with thee, even a branch of the same Vine of which thou are a plant. Dear heart, how are our souls refreshed with the wine thereof; and how pleasant is the fruit unto our taste! O! praise the Lord with me, for under the shadow of this vine I am abundantly refreshed. Thou dearly beloved one, partake with me, my cup doth run over – my table is filled with abundance: therefore do thou feed with me and drink abundantly. Let us take our fill together with our Beloved: for He is altogether lovely; and there is nothing more desireable to my soul, then at all times to be filled with his love. Dear heart, I know thou art sensible how it is with me at present; for verily my heart is filled with the heavenly virtue of my Heavenly Father, beyond what words can declare; but when it meets with its own, that will find from whence this comes. O! feel me beyond what I can express; for words are too short. O! the depth, the length, and height of this incomprehensible love, which is in Jesus Christ our Lord! (letter dated 6th of 4th Month 1664) (*Collectitia* 1824, 1:70-72).

1793), a Rhode Island Quietist evangelist used it liberally to describe the born-again experience as "Divine Conception" or "celestial union," which results in perfection (see 4.1.2):

> There must be a celestial union, a real cooperation, wherein two become one [unus spiritus] Of twain the one new man is made, which is God and man in the heavenly and mystical fellowship and Union. This is the mystery of Christ... (Scott, 1831, 1:490)

Perfection as union with God in early Quakerism was described in affective, sensory language as a tangible love relationship that joins God and the human together. So strong is this transforming power that the lover and the beloved become one as in copulation. The use of bridal mysticism can be traced back to Origen and Gregory of Nyssa in the patristic period, and finds its fullest development in Bernard of Clairvaux. This language is thoroughly biblical, finding its source in the Song of Songs, and in Pauline mysticism (Eph. 5 and I Cor. 13). Union is therefore extremely personal and intimate, affective and ecstatic. The Spirit enters into and empowers the person, who becomes a totally new creature, being-at-one with God through Christ, in the Spirit. This is what Fox meant by being "renewed into the image" of Christ. Perfected persons are thus drawn into God by love and transformed, but without abolishing their distinct personhood, for they are now "sons of God." Divine sonship is another image of perfection used extensively by early Quakers, the fruit of the nuptial mystery, the merging of divine and human.

3. Monastic Perfection

Perfectionism as the guiding force of a spiritual movement first bloomed in the monasticism of the Egyptian desert in the third century. By the fourth century, monasticism had developed into the most highly organized attempt to attain Christian perfection in the history of the church. The first famous desert hermit, St. Anthony of Egypt, had his life transformed when he read Jesus' words to the rich young ruler: "If you would be perfect, go, sell what you possess and give to the poor.... and come follow me" (Mt. 19:21). Perfection for the monastic, therefore, meant imitation of Christ in pure poverty and total obedience.

For a thousand years seekers after perfection followed Anthony and others like him into monastic communities, renouncing the world, family, wealth, and material possessions, and even their own names. They took vows of poverty, chastity, and obedience to live a life of continual prayer, solitude, and inner humility. This lifestyle, if carefully followed, would lead to perfection and union with God. This radical vocation was not expected of everyone, and led to a kind of double standard of spirituality, in which perfection or holiness could only be attained by some, a special class of spiritual men and women, known as

Appendix A

the religious. Perfection was required of them, a people separated from the world, with structures created to promote prayer, contemplation, solitude, and humility, but such a state was not attainable by ordinary Christians who lived in the world amidst its distractions.

This double standard began to be challenged when the concern for spiritual simplicity and poverty began to appear among the laity in the twelfth century.[7] First in northern Italy and then in France, a few small communities began to be organized by charismatic leaders who had forsaken wealth and the world to live a simple life as artisans and craftsmen, devoting their life to meditation, almsgiving, and care for the poor. The best known of these early lay movements is the Waldensians, a movement begun by a rich merchant of Lyon, France, who became known as Peter Waldo.[8] He gave away all his wealth, choosing poverty as a way of life. The Waldensians, called the "Church of the Poor," flourished outside of the established Church for a time, but were eventually denounced as a heresy, scattered and diminished through persecution.

Waldo was a precursor to St. Francis of Assisi, who created a new lay monastic order under the authority of the church. The Franciscans, like the Dominicans begun in the same period, were new kinds of monastic orders, called Mendicants, monks who came out of the cloisters and a life of seclusion to live an itinerant, apostolic lifestyle in the world among the poor.

Theologians of the emerging Renaissance of the thirteenth century, including Thomas Aquinas, a Dominican, began to question and refute the elitist two-tier spirituality. He concluded that all of us have a natural desire to know God, and success in this quest should not be restricted to the few: "Beneficially, therefore, did the divine Mercy provide that it should instruct us…by faith….In this way, all men would easily be able to have a share in the knowledge of God, and this without uncertainty and error" (Pegis, 1955, 67-68).

In the fourteenth and fifteenth century, monks and religious continually declined in the esteem and respect of the laity. The cloister was distrusted as a place where holiness or even the most minimal spirituality could be found. Theologians who attempted to reduce spiritual experience to scholastic dogmas were also distrusted. A widening gulf between doctrine and mysticism developed. The spiritual restlessness of laity and their skepticism of the religious establishment with its abuses took shape in a new religious movement called the *Devotion Moderna*. The new devotion was subjective and

---

[7] Lay spirituality also developed around a devotion to the Eucharist, the Blessed Sacrament (Bouyer, 1968, 2:246). Some historians interpret the story of the Quest for the Holy Grail, which developed around the beginning of the thirteenth century, as a manifestation of the fervent desire to seek the Eucharist (Bouyer, 1968, 2:246). Although other interpretations abound, the Holy Grail as the desire for holiness is a compelling symbol of the quest for perfection.

[8] William Penn viewed the Waldensians as forerunners of Quakers (Endy, 1973, 120). They too, were a persecuted church and refused to take oaths (Knott, 1993, 223-4).

individualist and prepared the way for the central theme of the Reformation, justification by faith alone.

However, after the Reformation of the Church in the sixteenth century, the new Protestant wing found itself strong on "faith alone," but short on sanctification or holiness. The Protestant Reformation was a church reform, but not necessarily a renewal of spirituality. With the dissolution of the monasteries, organized holiness was lost for a time among Protestantism. Anabaptists on the continent, and subsequently, Puritans in England and Pietists in Germany, arose in the late sixteenth through seventeenth centuries to replace the mystical perfection of the monastic life with a belief that ordinary men and women could attain at least a measure of holiness and intimacy with God, even while living in families and pursuing secular vocations.

Robert Barclay clearly addressed this very issue of the democratization of spirituality – that holiness or perfection is available to everyone – by using the Quaker community as an example:

> And God hath made it manifest in this age…[and]…hath produced effectually in many that mortification and abstraction from the love and cares of this world, who daily are conversing in the world (but inwardly redeemed out of it) both in wedlock and in their lawful employments, which was judged could only be obtained by such as were shut up in cloisters and monasteries. (Sippel, 2002, 435)

The influence and model of Catholic monks and friars was far greater among Protestants than has been realized in setting ideals for the creation of radical Protestant communities and in keeping alive a vision of the mystical life in the sixteenth and seventeenth centuries.[9]

For example, a monastic work, Thomas á Kempis' *Imitation of Christ*, sometimes called "the finest flower of mysticism" (Inge, 1899, 194), was found in the library of George Fox (Nickalls, 1931). Since it is second only to the Bible in popularity in the Western Church (Egan, 1996, 399), the fact that Fox owned a copy is hardly surprising. The mysticism taught by á Kempis is the monastic orientation of perfection in literal imitation of Christ. Ascetical and apophatic, this work represents the transition from medieval monasticism to the *Devotio Moderna* movement, which became the foundation for German Pietism, a renewal movement in the Lutheran church contemporaneous with the

---

[9] A popular English monastic writer who lived just prior to the beginnings of Quakerism was Augustine Baker (1575-1641), a Protestant who became a Benedictine Monk. Barclay referred to him with high regard in his *Apology*. Baker taught a form of contemplative prayer, similar to that found in the earlier 14th century anonymous English mystical treatise, *Cloud of Unknowing*. Baker is known for his elevation of silence, and was perhaps a source for the practice of silence in early Quaker worship. Baker's writings on prayer find echoes in Barclay's *Apology* (see 7.1.1 n3).

Puritan movement in the Anglican church. *Imitation,* as with all mystical works, teaches that perfection is both grace and effort, faith and works – that grace works on human nature and transforms it. Quakers discovered that this "higher" transformed life was available to all, not just monastics.

APPENDIX B

The Relationship between Quakers and other Seventeenth Century Holiness Movements

A spiritual awakening swept across Protestant and Catholic Europe in the late sixteenth and seventeenth centuries (and found expression in Russian Orthodoxy and Judaism as well). The availability of the Bible in English, new forms of spiritual disciplines in the Counter-Reformation and an emphasis on personal experience at the dawn of the modern enlightenment age spawned new orders, new sects, and revival movements within established religious institutions (Campbell, 1991, 2). As usual with any changes to established systems, they evoked a reactionary wave of hostility, with condemnations, persecutions, and imprisonments.

The rise of Quakerism as one of many radical new non-conformist movements during the English Revolution has been carefully and thoroughly researched by a number of historians, both Quaker and non-Quaker (e.g. Geoffrey Nuttall, Christopher Hill, and Douglas Gwyn). These historians examined Quakerism in its English Puritan revolutionary cradle as a radical social and religious movement caught up in the millenarianism of those turbulent times. Quakerism arose in a very particular political and cultural context on British soil and was indelibly shaped in the womb by that social world and the religious genes it inherited and which gave it birth. But Quakerism can also be seen as part of a much broader spiritual movement all across Europe and even beyond, in which similar themes, ideas, innovations, and insights resulted in new forms of religious devotion that developed uniquely and independently in separate cultures, yet all shared one central aspect in common: all were a return to the "religion of the heart" (Campbell, 1991, 1-17; Hambrick-Stowe, 1986, 22-29). All of these new movements could accurately be called holiness movements, because all had as their ultimate goal holiness of heart and life with intentionality and zealousness.

1. Devotion to the Sacred Heart of Christ

As several recent historians have observed, the seventeenth century, both in its Protestant and Catholic forms, witnessed the emergence of the "cult of the Sacred Heart" (Hambrick-Stowe, 1986, 23; Campbell, 1991, 36-40). In the Roman Catholic Church this new devotion to the Sacred Heart of Jesus was understood as "representing the divine love for all of humankind, the human love of Jesus, and the love for God which is infused into the believer" (Campbell, 1991, 37). This form of piety was rooted in the medieval monastic tradition which had long focused on devotion to the "wounds of Christ," a sentimentalized, and even maudlin piety which became especially prominent from the thirteenth century onwards. This tradition was passed on through the *Devotio Moderna* and the mystics of the Catholic Reformation (Campbell, 1991, 37).

By the seventeenth century, devotion to the Sacred Heart had become a popular form of piety among the laity in Roman Catholicism. It eventually gained institutional acceptance when a theological explanation of its meaning and practice was formulated by Jean Eudes (1601-1680). Eudes provided a way of understanding it in harmony with Orthodox Catholic teachings (Campbell, 1991, 38). In his explication of Sacred Heart spirituality, Eudes identified the personal encounter with Christ through the affections as the goal of the Christian life: "The heart of Jesus becomes my heart, and it loves what Christ loves, including my enemies, and hates nothing but sin" (Campbell, 1991, 39). In popular iconography of the period the heart is held in the believer's hand and exudes a burning flame. (In nineteenth century iconography it is attached outside of the breast of Christ.) Devotion to the Sacred Heart is an individualized, highly affective, and deeply inward, and introspective form of spirituality. Its earliest roots can be traced to Augustine ("The heart is restless until it finds its rest in thee"). The Protestant, Calvinist equivalent to Sacred Heart spirituality is found in the Puritan "devotion of rapture." And, perhaps it could be suggested, its final evolution in the Quaker "devotion" to the inward Light of Christ.

2. Barclay and Catholicism

Two other new Catholic movements of individual affective piety which arose in seventeenth century France, Spain, and Italy and were rooted in similar impulses of devotion to the Sacred Heart were the Jansenists and the Quietists. But unlike the Sacred Heart devotion they were never assimilated into Catholic Orthodoxy and thus came into strong conflict with the Church. All three movements had their taproots in Augustinian affective spirituality (and explicitly claimed Augustine in that regard, just as Puritans and Calvinists did). Quakers also have the Augustinian inheritance, but stretch beyond it in several key areas, most importantly their view of perfection.

More directly than devotion to the Sacred Heart, the Jansenist and Quietist movements had parallels to the Quaker movement. One intriguing connection which is worth investigating more thoroughly is Robert Barclay's rather unique religious background, which on the surface seems to tie the Catholic and Protestant "religions of the heart" together. Barclay was raised as a strict Scottish Calvinist, but was sent to Scot's College in Paris to study by a zealous Catholic uncle. This Catholic College trained young priests to become missionaries to reconvert Scottish Calvinists back into the Church of Rome

(Trueblood, 1968, 26). As a youth raised a strict Calvinist, he found himself in a Catholic institution in the midst of the spiritual hothouse atmosphere of these new Catholic currents, with all their innovations and controversies swirling around him (Trueblood, 1968, 26-7). (The exact dates and length of time Barclay spent in Paris are not entirely clear from the sources – but probably as an adolescent from 1659-1663.)

Trueblood does not explore Barclay's conversion for a time to Catholicism, but only comments that Barclay's mother's dying wish was that her son be brought back to Scotland, for fear he would become a Roman Catholic if he remained in France. When his mother died, Barclay's father went to France and brought his son home, much to Barclay's uncle's chagrin (Trueblood, 1968, 27). Trueblood is inclined to minimize Barclay's Catholic interlude and any impact it might have had on his thinking by quoting Barclay's statement that all he learned there was "a little grammar" (Trueblood, 1968, 27). But these were clearly formative years, and after his return to England, Barclay, something of a prodigy, became a Quaker in 1666 at age 18, and just ten years later, at age 28, had published a full-scale systematic theological treatise, the *Apology*.

In *Truth Triumphant*, Barclay shared with his readers his own early spiritual journey, first through Scotch Calvinism:

> My first education from my infancy up fell amongst the strictest sort of Calvinists, those of our country being acknowledged as the severest of the sect, in the heart of zeal surpassing not only Geneva (from where they receive their pedigree, but all other reformed churches abroad (so called:) so that some of the French Protestants being upbraided with the fruits of this zeal, as it appeared in John Knox, Buchanan, and others so (besides what is peculiar to their principles of this kind) allege, the super-abundance thereof to precede a *fervido Scotorum Ingenio*, i.e. from the violent complexion of our countrymen. (1692, 3:186)

He then related being ensnared for a time in Catholicism when he:

> ...was cast among the Papists, and my tender years, and immature capacity not being able to withstand and resist the insinuations that were used to proselyte me to that way, I became quickly defiled with the pollutions thereof; and continued therein for a time, until it pleased God through his rich love and mercy to deliver me out of those snares.... (1692, 3:186)

He apparently converted in early adolescence to Catholicism but found love lacking:

> In both these sects the reader may easily conceive, that I had abundant occasion to receive impressions contrary to this principle of love herein treated of; seeing the straitness of several of their doctrines, as well as their practice of persecution, do abundantly declare, how opposite they are to universal love....The time that intervened betwixt my forsaking the church of Rome, and joining with those, with whom I stand now engaged, I kept myself free from joining with any sort of people, though I took liberty to hear several. (Sippel, 1692, 3:187)

He found no charity in any other spiritual group until he came upon Quakers. He admitted Quakers were accused of being uncharitable as well, and he too, had been censured for it because he engaged in dispute, but he candidly acknowledged, "how can one be drawn into disputes without something of sharpness, so that they must bear some censure or other in this respect" (1692, 188).

Whether or not Barclay had any direct contact with either the Jansenists or the Quietists is not known. Both movements developed in France at the same time as Quakerism in England. Both had much in common, yet also significant differences, and were in a kind of inverse relationship to each other. Some historians see them as two sides of the same coin, others as widely diverging. But what is most intriguing is that both represent the religion of the heart spirituality (Campbell, 1991), yet in dissimilar ways, and the Quaker movement seems to have combined dimensions of each.

3. Jansenism

Ronald Knox, in his classic but highly polemical work *Enthusiasm* (1950), lumped Quakers and Jansenists in the same heterodox and fanatical stew. Both movements, he conceded, made a "heroic frontal attack upon the forces of worldliness" (Knox, 1950, 176) and were content to rally a small following as a cost of maintaining high standards of behavior. Both were described by Knox as rigorist and antiquarian (1950, 176). Campbell concurs that "Jansenism grew out of the tradition of moral-rigorist spirituality" but with a twist: "the point of rigor was not the detail of one's confession, nor the performance of specific penitential acts, but was rather the cultivation of proper inward dispositions – true penitence, and true love for God" (1991, 18). Jansenists did not oppose the sacramental system, but they were extremely critical of its "prostitution" by those who partook of it without complete confession, sincere interior contrition, and genuine love for God (Campbell, 1991, 28). Another of their challenges to conventional religion was their insistence that no one could be ordained without an internal calling, what a leading Jansenist, Saint-Cyran, called an "interior vocation." Ordination provided credentials for authority and power within the church, but only those inwardly called and ordained by divine grace were considered true priests (Campbell, 1991, 29). The rigor and zeal of their reformist vision and the recovery and appropriation of the Augustinian tradition with an emphasis on predestination and grace alone has caused Jansenists to be viewed by some as Puritan Calvinist Catholics.

Though not all Jansenists insisted on direct personal experience of God, the theme of the heart as the center of one's will and religious affections was central, and many had dramatic mystical experiences. An outbreak of a charismatic type phenomenon known as the "Convulsionaries" erupted within the Jansenist movement in 1727. Descriptions of this dramatic religious occurrence include speaking in tongues, dancing in the Spirit, healings, miracles, and masochistic behavior (self-flagellation). There were reports of women assuming the role of prophets and priests, baptizing, giving the sacraments, and receiving confessions. Although this occurrence was considered the underside of the movement and not the mainstream, it nevertheless indicates the degree of emotional fervor contained within it (Campbell, 1991, 26). The most famous Jansenist figure is Blaise Pascal (1623-1662), who never took orders, but became the movement's strongest defender. A leading intellectual, mathematician, and scientist, he was an unlikely candidate for mystical ecstasy. But in 1654 he experienced a vivid personal encounter with God lasting for several hours, which he recorded on a scrap of paper and carried with him at all times as a kind of phylactery. He referred to it as his "night of fire."[1]

4. Quietism

Whereas Jansensism grew out of the moral rigorism of the *devotio moderna*, Quietism was a popularization of the contemplative mystical tradition, especially the Carmelite and Salesian (from Frances de Sales) spirituality. Quietism became a "mysticism of the bourgeoisie, stripped of its traditional

---

[1] Fire
"God of Abraham, God of Isaac, God of Jacob," not of
   philosophers and scholars.
Certainty, certainty, heartfelt, joy, peace.
   God of Jesus Christ.
God of Jesus Christ.
   My God and your God.
"Thy God shall be my God" (Qtd. in Campbell, 1991, 23).

Pascal discovered the God of Israel rather than the God of philosophers and scholars, experienced being caught up in the love of God, and was subsequently transformed.

setting in monastic life" (Campbell, 1991, 18) (a description which would equally apply to second and third generation Quakers).

A striking parallel to the hostility of the establishment to the Quaker movement in seventeenth century Protestant England is provided by the reactions to the Quietist and Jansenist movement in Catholic France during the same period. All were perceived to be so far from the doctrinal mainstream that they were condemned and denounced as heresies, despite the fact that doctrinal variations were actually relatively slight. Accusations of serious theological deviations were generally "trumped up" charges. The real threat of the Quietist, Jansenist, and Quaker was to the conventional basis of religious life. Quietist and Jansenist leaders were condemned by papal bull, and some of them imprisoned. The Jansenist convent in Paris was burned to the ground. Hundreds of Quakers were fined and imprisoned; four were actually martyred in the colonies, hung in Boston by the Puritan institutional establishment.

The Quietist movement is one mystical tradition in which a direct transference of ideas can be traced within the Society of Friends (see 3.2). The purpose of this comparison with other new seventeenth century religious movements is to show that Quakers in their quest for holiness were a part of a broad holiness movement, with strong mystical tendencies, sharing some similar ideas as well as divergences, but with the same motivation for deeper experience in the Christian life.

APPENDIX C

The Relationship between Quakers and Methodists in the Eighteenth Century

1. Wesley and Quakers

When John Wesley and George Whitefield defied the boundaries of conventional Anglican churchmanship by bringing worship and preaching out of the churches and into fields and marketplaces, they were derisively called "a new brand of Quakers" (Baker, 1949, 3). Open-air preaching was a practice long associated with Quakers. Wesley and Whitefield were also labeled "enthusiasts" and "ranters," terms commonly used for Quakers, Moravians, and anyone else who claimed to have a personal experience of God. The early Methodists and the Quakers had several key elements in common. They shared the belief that individuals could have knowledge of God through direct experience and could be guided by the perceptible influence of the Spirit. Both also claimed their movements were a revival of primitive (pure, true, unadulterated) Christianity (Baker, 1949, 4). Other common elements included the keeping of journals and the exaltation and recording of death-bed scenes. Doctrinally, they shared almost identical beliefs in universal atonement and perfection (Baker, 1949, 4). In behavior, both groups emphasized plain dress and speech, and a strict Puritan moralistic-rigorism that excluded common recreations, such as sports, theater, and games. In 1760 a journalist asked Wesley if he was not "a Quaker in disguise" (Baker, 1949, 4). Both groups found personal spiritual guidance and nurture in mystical writings, especially the Catholic Quietists, Madame Guyon, Fenelon, and Molinos.

Wesley claimed to have read little of Quaker literature, but he was clearly familiar with Barclay's *Apology* and Fox's *Journal*, and possibly a few other works (Hobhouse, 1972, 320). Dean Freiday, in his introduction to Barclay's *Apology in Modern English,* discusses the relatively unexplored influence of Barclay's theology upon Methodism (1980, xxxiv-xxxviii). Freiday points out that John Wesley, though publicly distancing himself from Quakerism, nevertheless borrowed portions of Barclay's *Apology* for use in his own publications. In 1741 he published an abridged version of Barclay's propositions five and six on the "Universal Redemption of Christ," resulting in a twenty-six page pamphlet entitled *Serious Considerations on Absolute Predestination, extracted from a late author* (Freiday, 1980, xxxv). Freiday claims that Wesley's pamphlet "in most places was so close to the original wording that the differences can be determined only by close comparison" (1980, xxxvi).

Yet Wesley could mockingly refer to the *Apology* in his *Journal* as "that solemn trifle" (Wesley, 1938, 3:177). Evidently the comment arose not from his true estimation of its theological value but rather from rivalry ("sheep stealing") between the two movements (Baker, 1949, 8-9). (His remark is ironic in light of the fact that Wesley himself never wrote a systematic theology.) Wesley was concerned about a number of London Methodists, including some leaders, who, having discovered Barclay's *Apology*, were being drawn into the Quaker fold (Baker, 1949, 9). Thus in 1745, Wesley felt compelled to differentiate Methodism from Quakerism and responded with mild derision towards the rival movement:

> ...finding no other way to convince some who were hugely in love with the solemn trifle, my brother and I were at the pains of reading over Robert Barclay's *Apology* with them. Being willing to receive the light, their eyes were opened. They saw his nakedness, and were ashamed. (Wesley, 1938, 3:177-178)

At least two Methodist leaders, John Webb and William Briggs, were involved in this incident (Baker, 1949, 9). Briggs apparently had his eyes opened by Wesley, but Webb, "thoroughly poisoned by Robert Barclay's *Apology*" (Wesley, 1938, 3: 232), joined with Friends and wrote a pamphlet directed to both Quakers and Methodists, *An Appeal unto the Honest and Sincere-Hearted among the People called Methodists and Quakers* (Baker, 1949, 9). In spite of the growing rivalry, controversies between the two groups remained somewhat friendly until Wesley officially critiqued Friends in a portion of his publication *Farther Appeal to Men of Reason and Religion, Part II* in 1746 (Baker, 1949, 10).[1]

Wesley's *Farther Appeal, Part I* was written to defend Methodism from his Anglican detractors, but in *Farther Appeal, Part II* (1745), he addressed the various dissenting bodies: Presbyterians, Independents, Anabaptists, and Quakers. He castigated these groups for separating over inessential points. He viewed the Presbyterians and Independents as "the smallest distance from us" ([1831] 5:128) and the Anabaptists as "one step farther from us" ([1831] 5:129). Then in addressing the Quakers he wrote, "There is still wider difference in some points between us and those people usually termed Quakers, but the difference does not reside in the same points as the former" ([1831] 5:130).[2] Wesley elsewhere pointed to the Quaker neglect of the sacraments as "a great gulf fixed" between them (Baker, 1949, 4). But in *Farther Appeal* he pointed first to their commonalities (quotation marks are Wesley's, indicating phrases lifted directly from Quaker writings):

---

[1] This essay is found in Wesley's *Works* ([1831] 5:97-142).
[2] Wesley also compared Roman Catholicism with Methodism and wrote that in her case "there was an abundantly greater difference still" ([1831] 5:134).

> You as well as we, condemn "all ungodliness and unrighteousness of men;" ...You agree, that we are all to be taught of God, and to be "led by his Spirit;" that the Spirit alone reveals all truth, and inspires holiness, that by his inspiration men attain perfect love, the love which "purifies them as he is pure;" and that, through this knowledge and love of God, they have power to "do always such things as please him;" to worship God, a Spirit, according to his own will, that is, "in spirit and in truth." Hence you infer, that formal worship is not acceptable to God, but that alone that springs from God in the heart.... ([1831] 5:130-1)

Wesley next considered whether Quakers were, in fact, consistent with their own principles, and concluded they were not: "You carry your condemnation in your own breast" ([1831] 5:131). In this pamphlet he did not focus on the content of Friends' doctrines but rather on their failure to live up to their own ethical principles. He observed that the testimonies of plain dress and speech had degenerated into a rigid and hypocritical legalism:

> What multitude of you are very jealous as to the colour and form of your apparel (the least important of all the circumstances that relate to it), which in the most important, the expense, they are without any concern at all! ([1831] 5:132)

He gave other examples of their inconsistency. For example, "They cannot bear purple; but make no scruple at all of being clothed in fine linen; yea, to such a degree, that the linen of the Quakers is grown almost into a proverb" ([1831] 5:132). He concluded with this strong indictment: "You were once what you know in your hearts you are not now" ([1831] 5:133).

Sounding more like a Quaker reformer-preacher than an outside critic, he challenged Friends, using their own idiom, to live up to the main principles they espoused: "We are all to be 'taught of God', to be inspired and 'led by His Spirit': and then we shall 'worship Him', not with dead form, but 'in spirit and in truth'" ([1831] 5:133). He acknowledged that these were "deep and weighty words," but observed that many Quakers "held fast the words, and were utterly ignorant of their meaning," turning standard Quaker criticism of their opponents back upon themselves ([1831] 5:133). Wesley affirmed that he himself acknowledged "the inward principle" and added, "I would to God every one of you acknowledged it as much" ([1831] 5:133).

Finally he confronted them on a personal level, again using their own idiom and queries:

> Doest thou experience this principle in thyself? What saith thy heart? Does God dwell therein? And doth it now echo to the voice of God? Hast thou the continual inspiration of his Spirit, filling thy heart with

His love, as with a well of water, springing up into everlasting life? Art thou acquainted with the "leading of His Spirit," not by notion only, but by living experience? ([1831] 5:133)

He concluded that Friends too often failed to measure up to their own high religious principles, principles which Wesley himself deeply respected:

I fear very many of you talk of this [leading of the Spirit], who do not so much as know what it means...Perhaps, as much as you talk of them, you do not know the difference between form and spirit...You was afraid of formality in public worship: and reason good. But was you afraid of it nowhere else? Did not you consider that formality in common life is also an abomination to the Lord? ...At all times, and in all places, worship Him "in spirit and in truth." ([1831] 5:134)

Despite some differences in the principles of these two dissenting groups, and even the great gulf in observing the sacraments between Quakers and Methodists, Wesley did not consider them significant enough to be obstacles for admission into the Methodist Societies.

Wesley's critique of Quakers in *A Farther Appeal* caused some soul-searching among Friends, as well as opposition (Baker, 1949, 11). But it was not until 1748 that Wesley threw down the doctrinal gauntlet in response to a letter written to him by a Methodist who had become a Quaker. In *Letter to a Person lately join'd with the People call'd Quakers,* Wesley tackled specific Quaker doctrines with a thorough examination of each of Barclay's propositions. This letter was quickly reprinted as a pamphlet, and became the standard Methodist refutation of Quakerism (Baker, 1949, 12, n53).

The question posed to Wesley by the letter writer was this: "Is there any difference between Quakerism and Christianity?" In response, Wesley compared his interpretation of Barclay's *Apology* to his own understanding of Christian orthodoxy. With propositions one and two, "The True Foundation of Knowledge, and Inward and Unmediated Revelation," Wesley completely agreed.[3] But proposition three, the Quaker view of Scripture, Wesley could only

---

[3] Wesley on the "Light in the conscience": Wesley's belief in prevenient grace is but a hair's breadth from the Quaker doctrine of the universal Light of Christ. Wesley, like Barclay, held to an Arminian view of free will – that a measure of free will still exists in all persons, rather than an Augustinian total depravity. However, just as in Barclay, it is not a natural free will, but a supernatural intervention: "Natural free-will, in the present state of mankind, I do not understand: I only assert, that there is a measure of free-will supernaturally restored to every man, together with that supernatural light which 'enlightens every man that cometh into the world'" (*Predestination Calmly considered*, 1872, *Works*, 10:229-230).

agree with in part. He had serious qualms about the "great impropriety of expression" used by Barclay in referring to the Spirit as the primary and principle "rule." Wesley held that only Scripture was the "rule" and the Spirit is more accurately our "guide" (1931, 3:178). On proposition four on the doctrine of the fall, and five and six on the universal redemption and the universal Light of Christ, Wesley agreed "there is no difference between Quakerism and Christianity." (Wesley, as noted above, had already reprinted a condensed version of propositions five and six.) But surprisingly, on proposition seven, "Concerning Justification," Wesley disagreed. Because Barclay did not separate sanctification from justification, Wesley contended that the Quaker understanding of justification was the Roman Catholic doctrine of "flat justification by works" (1931, 3:179). Wesley seriously misunderstood Barclay and Quakers on justification by faith, though in his letter he provided no evidence to support this challenge to Friends' doctrine of justification.

In later writings Wesley reconsidered the charge of pelagianism he leveled at Quakers and the mystics. Robert Tuttle suggests this change came through the influence of the most mystical of the early Methodists, John Fletcher (1989, 140).

Most relevant to this study, however, is Wesley's assessment of proposition eight on perfection. To this proposition, Wesley recorded, "there is no difference between Quakerism and Christianity" (1931, 3:179). Wesley's

---

Wesley's concept of prevenient grace also follows closely upon the Quaker belief of "the light in the conscience," and he is as careful as Barclay to distinguish between natural conscience which cannot save and supernatural light in the conscience which, if followed and not quenched, can draw all persons to God. This light given to all persons by grace is in the conscience and encompasses: "...all the drawings of the Father – the desires after God, which, if we yield to them, increase more and more; all that light wherewith the Son of God 'enlighteneth every one that cometh into the world' – showing every man 'to do justly, to love mercy, and to walk humbly with his God'; all the convictions which his Spirit, from time to time, works in every child of man – although it is true, the generality of men stifle them as soon as possible, and after a while forget, or at least deny, that they ever had them at all" (1755, *Notes on Rom. 2:14*).

In a "Sermon on Conscience," published in 1788, Wesley was even more explicit on his view of what the light in the conscience meant: "This faculty seems to be what is usually meant by those who speak of natural conscience; an expression frequently found in some of our best authors, but yet not strictly just. For though in one sense it may be termed natural, because it is found in all men; yet, properly speaking, it is not natural, but a supernatural gift of God, above all his natural endowments. No; it is not nature, but the Son of God, that is 'the true light, which enlighteneth every man that cometh into the world.' So that we may say to every human creature 'He,' not nature, 'hath showed thee, O man, what is good'. And it is his Spirit who giveth thee an inward check, who causeth thee to feel uneasy, when thou walkest in any instance contrary to the light which he hath given thee" (Wesley, 1872, 8: 187-188).

articulation of the doctrine of Christian perfection was in full accord with Barclay's formulation. However, he did note that the language used by Barclay, "This holy birth brought forth," was an "uncommon expression" taken from Jacob Boehme.[4] And he contended that many other Quaker expressions and sentiments were also taken from Boehme (1931, 3:179).[5]

Wesley was in full accord with proposition nine on the perseverance in the faith and the possibility of falling from grace. He disagreed in part with proposition ten on ministry and eleven on worship. He agreed with Barclay that all ministers are called and prepared by the Holy Spirit, but as an Anglican, upheld ordination, because the "Apostles themselves ordained them by 'laying on of hands'" (1931, 3:179). He also believed that ministers may be paid to cover "what may be needful to them for food and clothing" (1931, 3:180). His strongest opposition however, was elicited by Barclay's statement that women may also preach, and in traditional fashion quoted Paul's objections in both I Cor. 14: 34-5 and I Tim. 2:11-12.[6] He agreed in principle with the Quaker concept of worship in proposition eleven, that "all true worship is offered in the inward and immediate moving of his own spirit" but wrote in great depth and detail about differences in the application of this principle in the ordering of public worship. He quoted Barclay's reference to music: "We confess singing of psalms to be a part of God's worship, and very sweet and refreshful when it proceeds from a true sense of God's love, but as for formal singing, it has no foundation in Scripture" (1931, 3:183). With this statement he had no quarrel, and he admonished Friends on their neglect of singing in worship. He took strong issue with their practice of sitting in silence in worship, applying Quakers' own term for false worship – "will-worship" – to a form of public worship for which he claimed had neither precedent nor example in Scripture (1931, 3:183).

Wesley was also at odds with propositions twelve and thirteen on the sacraments, although he did not refer to it here as "the great gulf fixed between them" which he had on other occasions. At this point in his letter, he summarized the main differences between Quakerism and Christianity as being Barclay's teaching on Scriptures, justification, baptism, and the Lord's Supper (1931, 3:185).

---

[4] Boehme, a German Lutheran mystic, has been called the "Father of Protestant Mysticism" (Inge, 1899, 278).

[5] Of all the mystics, Wesley had the strongest aversion to Boehme (he uses the variant Behmen) ([1831] 5:699-705).

[6] Wesley gradually revised his objections to women's preaching, offered ways to bypass some of Paul's explicit prohibitions, and encouraged a number of Methodist women in leadership roles, but he never adopted as egalitarian a position as Barclay. He came to a justification of women's preaching as an exception for extraordinary times, but not the rule (1931, 6:257).

Appendix C 277

On proposition fourteen on civil authority and freedom of conscience, he only commented that there was no difference between Quakerism and Christianity, but proposition fifteen, the traditional Quaker "testimonies," he called essentially "superstitions" (1931, 3:186-7). Although he agreed with the principle of plain dress, he objected to the rules against titles, plain speech in the scrupulous way Quakers employed them, and their refusal to use gestures of respect and to take oaths. He did not address pacifism, but seemed to imply it was still an open question.[7] Although he had some qualms with proposition fifteen, he did not regard these differences as essential or highly significant (1931, 3:186-7). Wesley ended his letter pleading for the Friend with "an honest heart, but a weak head" not to become consumed with "having too many buttons upon your coat," and to come back to "spiritual, rational, scriptural religion" (1931, 3:187).

Frank Baker, after examining in detail the relations between Quakers and early Methodists, concluded that "with the first nine propositions, dealing with basic theology, Wesley had little quarrel, except to emphasize the importance of the Scriptures and to correct Barclay's views of justification" (Baker, 1949, 13). Wesley made some corrections to the tenth and eleventh propositions on ministry and worship, and in examining the twelfth and thirteenth on the sacraments, he did not denounce Barclay's position, but limited himself to exposing "the fallacies" on which Barclay based his arguments (Baker, 1949, 13).

The overarching mystical aspect of Quaker spirituality, which in the eighteenth century was termed Quietism, was what most separated Quakerism from Methodism, according to Baker:

> Although the two Societies had much in common in their teaching on the inner light and the witness of the Spirit, they parted company at the fork leading to quietism *via* the mystic way. Apart from a few individuals who left the ranks of Methodism, the influence of Quaker mysticism [on Methodism] does not appear to have been widespread or lasting. (Baker, 1949, 22)

2. Wesley and Mysticism

Wesley, earlier in his spiritual development, had been attracted to the mystics, most notably the sixteenth century Catholic Quietists, Guyon, Fenelon, and Molinos (Tuttle, 1989, 36-7). Though his enthusiasm for their teachings waxed and waned, he continued to value their writings enough to include them along

---

[7] Frank Baker noted that some Methodists were pacifists at that time, and the position continued to be disputed in the Conference (Baker, 1949, 13, n54).

with a number of others in edited form in his *Christian Library*. The mystical writings chosen and abridged by Wesley were also popular among Quakers in the eighteenth century (Tuttle, 1989, 18). Wesley abridged the writings of at least ten mystics and published them as devotional and instructional readings for Methodists in his *Christian Library*. All but one were Catholic Reformation mystics from the sixteenth and seventeenth centuries with deep roots in Quietism. The one exception was Macarius, an Eastern monastic of the fifth century, whose writings are thought to be dependent in part on Gregory of Nyssa (Tuttle, 1989, 22, n9).

Although Wesley eventually repudiated Quietism in its classic formulations, he published and recommended many Quietist writings. In fact, the majority of the extracts in his *Christian Library* came from the Quietists. Since this movement came under persecution during the Catholic reformation, perhaps Wesley identified with them through his own experience of opposition from the Anglican Church (Tuttle, 1989, 45, n13). Wesley borrowed from, and in certain cases, promoted, the Quietists, because they modeled a life of holiness. Wesley was attracted to the Quietists, not to affirm their doctrines, many of which he believed were contrary to Scripture and reason, but because "they expressed a growing mystical experience that relentlessly pursued the goal of Christian perfection" (Tuttle, 1989, 41). Tuttle documents how Wesley, though irresistibly drawn to mysticism, became disillusioned with it, and ultimately rejected it (1989, 43).

A similar pattern can be found in his relationship to Quakers, whose principles he recognized also promoted a life of holiness. Although Tuttle, who has written the most detailed study of Wesley and mysticism, does not specifically address Quakerism, he notes a few striking examples of this same attraction-repulsion towards Quakers. For instance, Wesley read the *Life of A. M. Shurmann* (Anna Maria Van Schurmann, a Dutch Quaker mystic, 1607-1678) and praised her in his journal (Feb. 14, 1774) for her great learning, understanding, and deep devotion to God (Tuttle, 1989, 102). He even used her writings on the atonement to counter what he considered William Law's erroneous view of the atonement (Green, 1945, 145-6).

But despite his early dependence on mystical writings, Wesley ultimately came to repudiate mysticism (and its synonym, Quietism), and thus drove a wedge between mysticism and evangelicalism. Tuttle theorizes that Methodism, though first sprouting in the soil of mysticism, was transplanted into evangelicalism. "The seeds of Methodism were then sown in the soil (however shallow) of mysticism but transplanted in time into the deep fertile soil of an evangelical faith in Jesus Christ" (1989, 100).

Wesley stated his case against the mystics in his preface to a *Collection of Hymns and Sacred Poems*, published with his brother Charles in 1739:

> Some verses, it may be observed, in the following Collection, were wrote upon the scheme of the Mystic Divines. And these, it is owned,

we had once held in great veneration, as the best explainers of the Gospel of Christ. But we are now convinced, that we therein greatly erred, not knowing the Scriptures, neither the power of God. And because this is an error which many serious minds are sooner or later exposed to, and which indeed most easily besets those who seek the Lord Jesus in sincerity, we believe ourselves indispensably obliged, in the presence of God, and angels, and men, to declare wherein we apprehend those writers not to teach "the truth as it is in Jesus." (Wesley, 1872, 14: 319)

Some time later a strong antipathy towards Jacob Boehme apparently further cooled his fervor for the mystics. In 1742, after reading Boehme, he wrote in reaction that he wished Methodists would "drop quietists and mystics" (Hobhouse, 1972, 319).

Wesley's most impassioned critique of mysticism was reserved for Jacob Boehme. Even when his opposition towards mysticism mellowed somewhat later in his life, his antagonism toward Boehme never softened. While his final verdict on Quietism was mixed (a combination of gold and dross, in which he mined the gold and rejected the dross), to Wesley, Boehme's mysticism was utterly worthless. In 1780 he produced a tract called *Thoughts upon Jacob Behmen*, which included this severe indictment:

The whole of Behmenism, including both phrase and sense, is useless. It stuns and astonishes its admirers. It fills their heads, but it does not change their hearts. It makes no eminent Christians...But it is not barely useless; it is mischievous, and that in a high degree. For it strikes at the root of both internal and external religion by sapping the foundation of justification by faith. (1831, 5:702)

Wesley, as already noted, found traces of the influence of Boehme in Quaker writings (in his comment on Barclay's language of salvation). William Law, Wesley's earlier mentor and friend, became the eighteenth century's primary theological interpreter and defender of Boehme. Law's inspiration for *The Spirit of Love* and *The Spirit of Prayer* was derived from Boehme's works (see sect. 6 on Law and Wesley).

Baker concluded that eighteenth century Quakers and Methodists, though having many similarities, "were sailing parallel courses within friendly hailing distance" (1949, 23). But by the nineteenth century, Quakers and holiness Methodists (especially in America) were often sailing on the same ship. One reason this alliance developed is that by the nineteenth century the wedge Wesley had driven between mysticism and evangelicalism was at least in part removed, as mysticism was reinterpreted in a revival context as an ecstatic experience of the baptism of the Holy Spirit, and the dark night became the penitents' struggle to overcome sin, "praying through" to the second blessing.

3. William Law and Quaker Quietism

Rufus Jones described the religious environment of eighteenth century England with this incisive summation:

> While the bloodless intellectual controversies of the eighteenth century were running their course, vital, experimental Christianity was making some very positive advances. It found its most impressive mystical interpretation for the century in the writings of William Law, and it made its greatest popular conquest since the Reformation in the Methodist Revival. (1927, 259)

But of these two most significant religious influences, the mystic William Law (1686-1761), and John Wesley, leader of the Methodist Revival, in the final analysis, Law had the closest spiritual kinship and the most profound influence on Quakers in the eighteenth century. Law, too, had a powerful impact on Wesley's spiritual development, inspiring Wesley's high ethical ideals and his quest for perfection. Wesley and Methodists were indebted to Law, and he is often referred to as "the parent of Methodism" (Hobhouse, 1972, 312). He was a mentor to Wesley at a formative stage in his life, particularly during Wesley's Oxford years (1726-1730).

Law's early life bore a certain affinity with Quakerism, despite the fact that he was a high churchman, when as a non-juror[8] he refused to take the oath of allegiance to the King and sacrificially abandoned any opportunity for a church or academic appointment. Quakers, as non-conformists, also gave up all opportunities in that regard – including the opportunity for a university education. Law received a privileged theological education at Cambridge, was ordained as a priest, but had no chance to use it in service to the Church of England. To provide himself a living he became a private tutor and chaplain in the family of Edward Gibbon, father of the famous historian.

---

[8] Nonjurors regarded themselves as the true Church of England. They were ethical rigorists on an enthusiastic quest for intensive practical piety (holiness or perfection). Their daily discipline included regular hours of prayer, frequent fasting, frequent (even daily) communion, visitation of prisoners, and care for the poor (Jones, Wainwright, Yarnold, 1986, 453). Law did not participate in other characteristic nonjuring activities such as liturgical enhancements and reuniting with the Eastern Orthodox Church. Wesley, though never becoming a nonjuror, adopted these same high ethical and devotional standards during his Oxford student days when he formed the "Holy Club" with his close friends. Extreme nonjurors departed from inherited Anglicanism and went back to primitive practices. They refused to take an oath of allegiance to the royalty then in power, thus abandoning all worldly prospects for the sake of conscience (Jones, Wainwright, Yarnold, 1986, 453).

Appendix C

Law's first two books, *Christian Perfection* (1726) and *Serious Call to a Devout and Holy Life* (1728), were reprinted by Wesley and used in the Methodist classes. Wesley wrote Law in 1738 that for two years he had used them as models in most of his preaching (Hobhouse, 1972, 313). These two early works represent Law's period of rigorous moralism, written prior to what is usually referred to as his mystical period beginning in 1732.

Some scholars see no mysticism in these stern, moralistic early works (Tuttle, 1989, 69); others see them as transitional pieces to his later more extended and profound mystical masterpieces (Rudolph, 1980, 90). Louis Dupré calls *Serious Call* a "solidly Christian but somewhat moralistic tract written in a style that holds the middle between *Pilgrim's Progress* and Francis de Sales' *Introduction to the Devout Life.*" Dupré agrees, though, that these early works are a far cry from any kind of "mystical enthusiasm" (1988, 350). *Christian Perfection,* the earlier work, is the more mystical of the two books. But Law's most consistent theme, union with God, which he developed extensively in his later works, also received treatment in his earlier writings (Rudolph, 1980, 47-48).

The Spirit of Prayer (1749, 1750) and *The Spirit of Love* (1752, 1754) were conceived after Law immersed himself in the writings of Boehme and French Quietism. While his later works could be seen, as Dupré says, as "an abrupt mystico-theological flight toward the opposite side of the spiritual horizon," both his earlier and later works must be read together as emerging from the heart, mind, and soul of the same writer – a devout non-conforming priest in the Church of England, with a strong mystical consciousness (1988, 350). Erwin Rudolph, who has produced the most recent study of Law as a devotional writer, contends for a unity in all of his writings, but with a shift of emphasis in his later works (1980, 47-48).

Law's first two works offer a solid "orthodox" support for the subsequent flight towards the mystic. As Dupré so concisely describes: "Law revealed his innermost, spiritual vision only after having built a protective wall of ascetical and moral precautions against mystical illusions" (1988, 350). This is precisely the kind of foundation and superstructure the early Quakers constructed when they created a semi-monastic hedge around their communities and established the practice of communal discernment. Similar moral and behavioral guides to holiness can be found in works such as William Penn's *No Cross, No Crown,* Barclay's final proposition "Concerning Salutations and Recreations" in the *Apology,* and other rigorous Quaker Puritan-style writings. Law's mystical-experiential holiness was built upon the same solid and necessary pillars of asceticism and moralism as in Quakerism. For Law, the way of holiness, just as in early Quakerism, began with "the spirit and practice of renunciation" and concluded with "total spiritual sacrifice" (death to self) (Dupré, 1988, 350). William Law's *Serious Call,* like Penn's and Barclay's works, was based on a "sacralization of the common life," the life of the Christian lived in and through the Spirit as he or she engaged in secular occupations and family life (Dupré,

1988, 350). But though engaged in business and trade, and all the duties of family life, the regenerated Christian did not participate in the "culture" of the world – the arts, music, sports, dancing, or entertainment.

In 1740 Law felt called to move "beyond the common life" and retreated to a contemplative monastic-style existence with Edward Gibbon's sister Hester and a wealthy widow. He spent the next eight years in a contemplative life of silence, prayer, study, and celibacy at King's Cliffe in Northhampshire (Dupré, 1988, 350-1). However, it was not a life of inactivity, aristocratic leisure, or escape from the world. It was a balanced life of contemplation and action, with outreach to the poor and disadvantaged. Law founded schools for poor children and almshouses for the homeless. All but a small portion of the community's income supported these social ministries (Law, 1978, 14).

During this time his spiritual journey intensified as he read and absorbed the writings of Jacob Boehme (Dupré, 1988, 351). Through Boehme, Law gained deeper insights into the medieval mystical tradition and the spiritual fathers of Eastern Orthodoxy.[9]

What Boehme taught, and what Quakers had taught, Law himself came to believe, that "religious revelation had not stopped with the end of the New Testament but continues even today" (Dupré, 1988, 351). (See also 6.2.4 on Harris' view of Scripture.)[10]

After an early anti-Quaker and sacramentarian period, Law's reading of Boehme and the French Quietists gradually brought him closer and closer in spirit to Quakers, until he embraced the essence of Quakerism and became a kind of ecumenical, non-sectarian Quaker in spirit, though not in affiliation (Hobhouse, 1972, 324-332). Hobhouse provides substantial evidence for Wesley's emphatic witness to Law's "essential Quakerism," and argues that the estimation of Wesley, "the greatest religious leader produced by the British Isles during the eighteenth century," carries substantial weight (1972, 312). Though Law lived and died an Anglican, every major tenet of Quakerism can be found in his writings as his mystical views expanded over his lifetime. Walker, in his biography of Law, recognizes that "it is deeply instructive to follow the path along which the High Church rigorist came to holiness"[11] (Walker, 1973, xii). This transformation occurred through his reading of the

---

[9] Hobhouse mentions the following mystical influences upon Law in addition to Boehme and the French Quietists: John of the Cross, Johannes Tauler, Henry Suso, Jan Van Ruysboeck, *Theologica Germanica*, St. Augustine, Psuedo-Dionysius, Origen, and Irenaeus. Stanwood, in his introduction to the volume on William Law in *Classics of Western Spirituality,* also identifies the Desert Fathers and *Spiritual Homilies* of Macarius as having particular attraction for Law (Law, 1978, 14-15).

[10] This is a key concept of the charismatic tradition and differentiated Quakers from non-charismatic and non-holiness evangelicals in the nineteenth and twentieth centuries.

[11] Walker says "Law is a great – if eccentric – theologian" (1973, xii).

Appendix C 283

mystical writers, and led him finally to embrace Quaker principles of mystical holiness.

4. Law's Anti-Quaker Period

In the 1730s and '40s Law wrote drafts against Quakers. During this period Law was planning a major work on the errors of Quakerism. He first became interested in the Society of Friends when he began a correspondence with a young Anglican woman named Fanny Henshaw, who was considering leaving the Church of England to join with the Quakers. Law and Henshaw never met in person, but his letters to her take a form like that of a spiritual director and directee. Despite his counsel against Quakers, she nonetheless decided to join with them, discovered her calling as a minister, and proceeded to dedicate her life and vocation to public ministry among the Friends (Hobhouse, 1927, 15). Law's opposition to Quakers reached its height in 1736-1737 when he argued passionately for the necessity of the outward sacraments. He defended an exalted, mystical view of the sacraments (Hobhouse, 1972, 216). (Non-jurors tended to be the most sacramental of all Anglicans.)

In dealing with dissenting attitudes towards the sacraments, he used the Quakers as an example of a deficient and erroneous view. Law presented an argument similar to that of one of his favorite authors, the fourteenth century German mystic Suso: "He who finds the inward in the outward goes deeper than he who only finds the inward in the inward" (Hobhouse, 1972, 216, n1).

In 1736 Law identified, as the foundation of Quakerism, the biblical text, *"God is a spirit and they who worship Him must worship Him in spirit and in truth."* This is identical with Wesley's summary statement of Quakerism's foundation (Hobhouse, 1927, 206).

Stephen Hobhouse demonstrates through long extracts of letters and major works that Law, after strongly condemning Quakerism, chiefly because of their disregard of the outward sacraments, gradually moved closer and closer toward the spirit of Quakerism, as he embraced the Christian mystical tradition (1927, 16). But in 1736 Law advised Fanny against the Quakers:

> The doctrine of the Spirit you have received from the Quakers and their books, is the tares [that] is sown amongst the good seed....The spirit that is most boisterous in you calls for a hasty, speedy throwing your self amongst a people of yesterday, that have no name or being amongst the saints of God in any age of the world since the creation. Before them there never was a saint in the world without a Church, a sanctuary, a priest and divine ordinances." (1972, 33)

Law was also certain at this point in his life that women were forbidden by Scripture to speak in church and argued against the Quaker practice of allowing women the freedom to preach publicly (Hobhouse, 1972, 71-72). Fanny Henshaw, however, had been greatly inspired when she heard a Quaker woman, May Drummond, preach at a large public meeting in Manchester around 1736. May Drummond was born into a Scotch Presbyterian family in 1710. In 1731 she joined Friends through the influence of the Quaker evangelist, Thomas Story. She was still preaching and drawing large crowds when George Whitefield and John Wesley began their open-air preaching (Hobhouse, 1972, 74).[12] Fanny, in a letter to her sister, identified with the mystical "spiritual marriage" (see Appendix A on bridal mysticism):

> The world, or even an husband to one of us, might have occasioned a separation in this life. And shall we refuse, when God condescends to wed us to Himself? Can we wish a better union, or be more happy in one another than in Him our Father, husband, and everlasting friend? O let us love Him, and He'll never leave us, nor suffer His children to be overcome by the world or its allurements. (Hobhouse, 1972, 138)

Fanny Henshaw, who was happily wedded to God, nevertheless suffered physically and emotionally with poor health for two years as she repressed her gift of preaching. When her family eventually gave her permission to join the Society of Friends and she became what was scandalously called a "she-preacher," her health was miraculously restored[13] (Hobhouse, 1972, 148, 158).

---

[12] Hobhouse writes that "the preaching of May Drummond may surely be accounted a landmark in the Women's movement. So it was at the time by...one enthusiastic feminist, who wrote in praise of her in the chief literary magazine of the day (*Gentleman's Magazine*, 1735):
   "No more, O Spain, thy Saint Teresa boast – There's one outshines her on the British coast." (Hobhouse, 1972, 74)
(It is striking that a Quaker woman preacher would be ranked even higher than the venerated St. Teresa of Avila.) Hobhouse adds that "Before the nineteenth century I doubt whether a woman speaker ever swayed audiences of the size she is said to have held" (1972, 74). Hobhouse notes that a Quaker observer who attended many of her public gathering wrote with great enthusiasm and admiration, and his only criticism of her preaching was that "her style is rather too learned... and at times she becomes too theatrical" (1972, 74).

[13] This occurred in the spring of 1737. About a year later, Law's good Friend, Dr. John Byrom, whose letters provide much of the information about Henshaw's struggle to fulfill her vocation and join the Society of Friends, became acquainted with some Quakers and began to explore their beliefs and writings. He mentioned to Law that a Quaker named Josiah Martin had written a scholarly book called *A Vindication of Women's Preaching* in 1717 (Hobhouse, 1972, 149-50). Hobhouse claims Martin is the person who introduced Quakers to French Quietism. He was the first person to translate Madam Guyon into English (1727), and his translations were the only ones available in English up to the year 1770 (Hobhouse, 1972, 137, 157). In 1738 Byrom wrote to his

In a letter to Law's friend, Dr. John Byrom, who became a third party in this literary triangle, Fanny summed up her central reason for adopting the faith and worship of the Quakers:

> My reason for professing the Quaker faith and worship is that I find it (to me at least) the most agreeable to Scripture doctrine, in perticular (*sic*) the Epistle to the Hebrews and Gallatians. (*sic*) Again I cannot find peace or satisfaction out of this way. (Hobhouse, 1972, 132)

Henshaw's revealing insight that Quakerism was the most faithful to "Scripture doctrine" challenges the usual perception of the Society of Friends in the Quietist period as being more mystical than biblical. Henshaw made this claim despite the fact that Law had written to her in a severe manner that Quakers rejected "the authority of our blessed Lord" concerning the sacraments, appointed ministers, offices, the outward church, "...and the faith and doctrine and practice of the Apostles, and all the Scriptures which contain anything relating to these things" (Hobhouse, 1972, 70).

At this stage of his life, Law was convinced that Quakers ignored clear biblical teachings on the ordering of the outward church, its offices and ministry (women were forbidden to preach), and especially the necessity of the sacraments, of which Law held a high, exalted, and mystical view. In this early period, however, Law even surpassed Quakers in his rigorist pleas for simplicity, plain dress, and proper use of money as spiritual concerns (Jones, 1921, 260-1).

5. Law Moves Toward Quakerism

Rufus Jones concluded that William Law "had no admiration for, and little real appreciation for the Quakers who were his contemporaries... but....he and they drew from the same sources" (1921, 266). Jones acknowledged their unity on the nature of salvation, direct experience of God, distrust of human learning, agreement with all the Quaker testimonies including pacifism, and the "absolute worth of the spirit of love" (1921, 265). Jones wrote that "He [Law] said, better

---

wife about a meeting with the Quaker Josiah Martin who "is a good scholar which Quakers rarely are" (Hobhouse, 1972, 149). Martin gave Byrom Fenelon's *Directions to a Holy Life* which he (Martin) had also translated from the French (Hobhouse, 1972,149). By this time Byrom had "discovered a spiritual kinship" with some of the Quakers and both he and Law were reading Boehme, who would become their "prophet of prophets" (Hobhouse, 1972, 149). In 1739 in another letter to his wife, Byrom observed that a Quaker he had met (a chemist, Joseph Clutton), was a great admirer of Boehme and lent Byrom a manuscript about him (Hobhouse, 1972, 150). According to Brazier Green, Law first encountered Boehme's writings in 1736 (1945, 60).

than they could express it, what they believed about God and man" (1921, 265), but Jones implied that Quakers better translated these values and principles into "far reaching human service" (1921, 265). Jones failed to point out their unity on Christian perfection, the way of holiness through the inward cross of Christ, and union with God. Jones stopped short of the mutual irradiation that Hobhouse deftly identifies between the Quietist Quakers and Law. Hobhouse cites many examples of Law's gradual movement, after immersing himself in Boehme and the Catholic Quietists, to a place of essential agreement with Quaker principles, including a spiritualized view of the sacraments and priesthood and a spiritual kinship with his Quaker contemporaries. Like Wesley, Law's chief criticism of Quakers as a group focused on their failure to live up their own highest principles.

Hobhouse finds in Law's *The Spirit of Prayer,* "the most essentially Quaker and at the same time splendidly eloquent passage on true worship" (1972, 295). As noted in 3.2, n7, whole portions of *The Spirit of Prayer* were reprinted by Quakers. This key work of Law is bound together in one volume with other tracts of Benezet's that deal with social issues, thoughts on war, liqueur, and slavery.

Even before writing his two greatest mystical works, *The Spirit of Prayer* and *The Spirit of Love,* Law had come to an understanding of salvation that echoed Barclay:

> Salvation wholly consists in the incarnation of the Son of God in the soul or life of man: that that which was done and born in the Virgin Mary, must be done and born in us: as our sin and death is Adam in us, so our life and salvation is Christ in us – as we are earthly, corrupt men by having the nature and life of Adam the first propagated in us, so we must become new and heavenly men, by having the life and nature of Adam the second regenerated in us. But, if we are to be like Him in nature, as we are like Adam in nature, then there is an absolute necessity that that, which was done and born in the Virgin Mary, is also by the same power of the Holy Ghost done and born in us. The mystery of Christ's birth must be the mystery of our birth, we cannot be His sons, but by having the birth of His life derived into us: the new paradisiacal man must be brought forth in the same manner in every individual person. That which brought forth this holy birth in the first Adam at his creation, and in the second Adam in the Virgin Mary, that alone can bring it forth in anyone of their offspring.[14] (Hobhouse 1972, 275)

---

[14] The original is found in *An Earnest and Serious Answer to Dr. Trapp's Discourse, 1740* (Law, 1974, vol. 2).

Hobhouse calls this a "boldly mystical passage." Yet it is no bolder mystically than Barclay, who in his *Apology* used similar language, particularly his use of "this holy birth, to wit, Jesus Christ formed within us" (2002, 167), which Law called the "incarnation of the Son of God in the soul." Barclay wrote that our justification:

> ...is the love of God manifested in the appearance of Jesus Christ in the flesh, who by his life, death, sufferings, and obedience made a way for our reconciliation....this *seed* of *grace* from which this birth arises and in which Jesus Christ is inwardly received, formed and brought forth *in* us in his own pure and holy image.... (2002, 192)

6. Law and Quaker Holiness

Quaker holiness in the eighteenth century, based on the life and writings of leaders such as Thomas Story, Anthony Benezet, John Woolman, Job Scott, Stephen Gellet,[15] and many others had more in common with the contemplative mysticism of William Law than with the Anglican evangelicalism of Wesley, though many aspects of Wesley's life and thought also appealed to Quakers.

This period of Quakerism was indelibly shaped by two forces that at first seem antithetical: the *via negativa* (the inwardness or passivity of Quietism), best exemplified in the contemplative holiness of William Law; and the emotional warmth and the heat of the activism of the Wesleyan Revival (perhaps more directly through the Moravians). Anthony Benezet's life and work, as well as the evangelistic endeavors of his contemporary, Job Scott, show strong evidence of both of these movements being integrated into a Quaker paradigm of holiness.

But Law's mystical writings, especially his inward Light terminology, and his insistence on union with God as perfection in this life, his interpretation of Scripture, his belief in continuing revelation, his emphasis on inward prayer and worship, and his opposition to war most closely conformed to Quaker holiness beliefs.

Stephen Hobhouse, a Quaker, has written the best interpretive study of William Law in *Selected Mystical Writings of William Law* and a most illuminating study of Law and his relationship to Quakers in *William Law and*

---

[15] The Quietist minister whose spiritual views most closely parallel Law's is Job Scott (see 4.1.2). Jones called him a "thorough-going mystic" and recognized a similarity with William Law (1921, 289-290). Jones ranked Scott as the foremost eighteenth century exponent of "the fundamental inner principle of Quakerism" (1921, 288).

Eighteenth Century Quakerism, the only study of its kind.[16] Hobhouse suggests that "the most obvious point of contact between William Law's teaching and Quakerism was in the doctrine of the Inner Light, which he himself puts in the forefront of his creed"[17] (1972, 324). He proceeds to demonstrate many more points of contact and Law's increasing attraction to Quakerism as his thinking, writing, and reflections on his own experience of God developed. If Hobhouse is indeed correct, it could be argued that Law is the "de facto" Quaker theologian of the eighteenth century. Since Quakers had no theologically trained leaders or teachers of their own, yet needed to develop their theological doctrines in light of a new era, Law became, in effect, the default Quaker theologian of the Enlightenment.

Like Quakers, Law was no friend of the Enlightenment's worship of reason, rather quite the opposite. Law opted for what the eighteenth century called "enthusiasm" over rationalism. Enthusiasm at the time meant "filled with God" or "filled with the Spirit." "Charismatic" or "Pentecostal" would be its equivalent modern term. For Law, enthusiasm meant being "led by the Spirit" and "the Divine Nature living and breathing in us." And "all holiness is by Divine Inspiration" (*An Address to the Clergy*, 1761, in Law 1974: 28). The Light within was the "intuition of the heart," a sixth-sense or super-rational sense (Hobhouse, 1938, 316-17). Quoting from John 15 on the vine and the branches Law concludes:

> Now from these Words let this conclusion be here drawn, *viz.*, That therefore to turn to Christ as a *Light within* us, to expect Life from nothing but his *holy Birth* raised within us, to give ourselves up wholly and solely to the *immediate continual* Influx and Operation of his Holy Spirit, depending wholly upon it for every Kind and Degree of Goodness and Holiness that we want, or can receive, is and can be Nothing else, but *proud, rank* Enthusiasm. *(An Address to Clergy*, 1974, 3:11-12) [His emphasis]

Law's concept of the "Light within" paralleled Barclay and was always equated by Law, as it was with Barclay, to something "supernatural":

> Neither can any Creature be in a better, or higher State than this [self-love, self-seeking], till something, called in Scripture, the WORD, or SPIRIT, or INSPIRATION of God, is that alone from which Man can have the first Good Thought about God, or the least Power of having

---

[16] The editors of the *Classics of Western Spirituality* agree that Hobhouse provides the best interpretation of Law. but the fact that Hobhouse is a *Quaker* scholar is not noted in the reference (Law, 1978, 27).

[17] "Inner Light" is Hobhouse's term; Law used "Light within."

more heavenly desires in his Spirit, than he has in his Flesh. (*An Address to Clergy*, 1974, 3: 9)

In dealing with deism, Law:

> ...fearlessly claimed "natural religion" and "nature" as belonging to Christ and to Christianity, but insisted that, far from conflicting with the revelation of Scripture nature could only be interpreted by the contents of that revelation as mystically understood. This understanding was by no means to be obtained by that very fallible instrument, the reason, "the idol of modern deism", but by intuition of the heart, the sixth sense of the "light within." There was indeed a true "natural religion", not at all the self-sufficient, rationalistic religion exalted by the Deists, but that nurtured by the "Light which lighteth every man," when humble, obedient attention is paid it. (Green, 1945, 105-6)

Hobhouse maintains, "in all these respects William Law is in thorough agreement with the most representative Quakerism of his day" (1972, 326). Hobhouse even suggests that Law's theology took basic Quaker understandings and experiences to new heights, particularly in "his insistence on the joys of the spiritual life and in his conviction of the immutability of God's love" (1972, 326). Hobhouse is convinced that Law's greatest contribution to Christendom is his argument for pacifism, a Christological rationale for opposition to war to which no Quaker writer had up to that time so clearly articulated:

> He links up the unlawfulness of war with the Divine Love, and proclaims to an unbelieving Christendom a God, who is indeed constantly warning His children against the terrible and inevitable consequences of sin, but who is without a spark of wrath against them, and who never punished in the ordinary human sense of the word. It is just here, I believe, that future generations will come to realize the greatness of their debt to William Law as an interpreter of the revelation of God's love in Christ Jesus. (1972, 332)

Holiness, in Law's theology, therefore, includes a testimony against war and violence as being incompatible with divine love. Anthony Benezet, as demonstrated earlier (see 3.2.1), reprinted anonymously Law's work, *The Spirit of Prayer*, and included it with his own tracts, including a tract passionately advocating against war and the use of violence. One major source of Benezet's eloquent pleas for an end to war can be found in Law's last work, *An Address to the Clergy* (1974, 3:5-103).[18] The mature holiness taught and embodied by Law was virtually identical with that of Benezet. Thus this study argues that Law became a Quaker inwardly, though he never left the Anglican Church.

In the volume on Law in *The Classics of Western Spirituality*, the editors observe that Law's appeal today is to Quakers, members of the charismatic movement, and evangelicals, but also to the spiritually minded, both within and without the church (Law, 1978, 32). In the eighteenth century his two early works were addressed to all who professed the name "Christian" and sought a deeper spiritual life. These works were among the most widely read devotional tracts of the time in England, eagerly read by Anglicans, Puritans, and Pietists alike (Law, 1978, 32). But his later works were addressed to those already "experienced" in the mystical life, and appealed to a much smaller audience. His largest and most enthusiastic audiences for these later works were the Quakers, Moravians, and Methodists.[19] But in the final analysis his mystical theology of holiness resonated most closely with Quakers to the degree that he became their de facto theologian and Quietism's greatest interpreter of the spiritual life.[20] A study of Law's legacy by an evangelical scholar, Erwin Paul Rudolph, concludes that most of Law's enduring popularity is based on his two early writings, and although his later works treat the same themes and vibrate with the same spiritual passion (i.e., holiness), their association with mysticism caused them to fall out of favor (1980, 120-1). As a result, these works are virtually unknown, even among contemporary Quakers, charismatics, and evangelicals who might otherwise appreciate them.

---

[18] This essay addressed three evils of the church:
  1. Mammon – riches. The clergy make church a business – buying and selling parsonages, cure of souls, sale of churches. Ministers are chief buyers and sellers.
  2. Swearing of oaths. Law came to the conclusion that swearing of oaths is wrong. He hoped that all Englishmen would one day follow the lead of those who refused all oaths.
  3. War: He targeted war as the evil of the anti-christ. He denounced the "Army of the Church Wolves" in the Crusades. (Law 1974, 3: 78-94)

[19] Both Moravians and Methodists had a falling out with Law; only the Quakers remained his most loyal disciples. Walker concludes that Law "approved the Quakers much more completely than the Moravians" (1973, 221).

[20] An example of Law's specific teachings on holiness is his understanding of the place of emotions. He explains that feelings have their place but they are not holiness; "they are God's *gracious Allurements*, and *Calls* to seek after Holiness and spiritual Perfection" [his emphasis] (Walker, 1973, 144).

7. Law and Wesley

In addition to his Puritan roots and his reading of the mystics during his Oxford years, four main sources of mystical influence on Wesley can be named: the Moravians, William Law, Madame Guyon, and the Quakers (Hobhouse, 1972, 319). And despite Wesley's debt to them all, he also had considerable quarrels and tensions with them. The primary influence of both the Moravians and Law are acknowledged by all Wesleyan scholars, yet Wesley ultimately separated from them both over what he considered unscriptural notions. With the Moravians he objected most strongly to their doctrine of "stillness" or passivity, variations of which were found in Quakerism and William Law, and all forms of Quietism. His extremely negative reaction to reading Boehme apparently cooled his fervour for the mystics and severed his relationship with William Law. In 1742 after reading Boehme, Wesley wrote, in reaction, that he wished Methodists would "drop quietists and mystics" (Hobhouse 1972, 319). In 1749 after reading Law's *The Spirit of Prayer*, Wesley noted rather sarcastically in his journal, "There are many masterly strokes therein, and the whole is lively and entertaining; but it is another Gospel. An excellent method of converting Deists, by giving up the very essence of Christianity" (1938, 3:422).

In 1756 an open letter by Wesley attacking Law's *The Spirit of Prayer* and *The Spirit of Love* "burst upon an astonished public" (Green, 1945, 129). Even George Whitefield, Wesley's former evangelistic colleague (with whom he also later had a doctrinal parting of ways), called Wesley's published letter, "unchristian and ungentlemanly" (Green, 1945, 130).[21] Yet despite Wesley's attack, many Methodists continued to read and admire Law, even though six men were "read out of his society for reading Jacob Behmen and Mr. Law" (Green, 1945, 317).[22]

Yet to further muddle any resolution to Wesley's final relationship to Law and the mystics (and in extension, the Quakers), we find that in 1768, Wesley published in his *Christian Library* substantial extracts (heavily edited as was his usual practice) from Law's later works, including *The Spirit of Prayer*, which he had so severely attacked. The extract even included a portion of a passage which earlier in his letter attacking Law he had "singled out as supremely obnoxious" (Hobhouse, 1972, 317). He also included Law's last work, *An*

---

[21] Wesley never reconciled with his great friend and mentor, William Law, and perhaps his later antipathy towards mysticism, which included in his mind both Moravianism and Quakerism, was a result of his disappointment that Law would embrace mysticism, and in particular the writings of Boehme.

[22] When John Byrom, a mutual friend of both Law and Wesley, confronted Wesley with this autocratic intolerance, Wesley defended the action by saying the expulsion was for *preaching* the doctrines of Boehme and Law. Byrom was bold enough to suggest to Wesley that perhaps such actions warranted his being called "Pope John" (Hobhouse, 1972, 316-7).

Address to the Clergy, which contained a substantial portion of Law's essential Quakerism, including opposition to oaths and to war (Hobhouse, 1972, 317). Hobhouse's final treatment of this paradoxical relationship is as good an explanation as can be offered:

> Indeed, when we consider the character of these volumes of extracts as a whole and the amount of mystic and Quaker teaching that has been left in them, we can only regard it as an amazing concession on Wesley's part, considering that the books were intended to be spread broadcast among his societies. Who knows what seeds they may have sown? Nevertheless I am inclined to consider this publication rather as a spontaneous act of generosity on Wesley's part – perhaps some compunction for his Letter made him a little reckless – than as an indication of any marked change of view as regards the tendency of Law's writings. (1972, 317-8)

In the final analysis, the mutual affinity between Law, Quakers, and the mystics in general to the doctrine of perfection and the pursuit of holiness ultimately overruled all other less crucial doctrinal issues. Wesley wrote just before his death about perfection: "This doctrine is the grand depositum which God has lodged with the people called Methodists; and for the sake of propagating this chiefly He appeared to have raised us up" (Wesley, 13:1872, 9). Wesley realized that when other controversies receded, William Law and the Quakers, the eighteenth century's most faithful interpreters of the Christian mystics in the Age of Reason, were in the end his greatest and most steadfast allies in promoting holiness, a passion to which Wesley had devoted his entire life and vocation.

BIBLIOGRAPHY

Abbott, Margery Post. 1997. *A Certain Kind of Perfection.* Wallingford, PA: Pendle Hill Publications.

Abbott, Margery Post, Mary Ellen Chijoike, Pink Dandelion, and John William Oliver, Jr. 2003. *Historical Dictionary of the Friends (Quakers).* Oxford and Lanham, MD: Scarecrow Press.

Anderson, Paul. 1987. 'An Ongoing Heritage': Epilogue to *The Rich Heritage of Quakerism,* Walter R. Williams, Newberg, OR: Barclay Press, 253-93.

Aquinas, Thomas. 1955. *Book One: God. On the Truth of the Catholic Faith: Summa Contra Gentiles,* ed. Anton C. Pegis. F.R.S.C, vol. I. Garden City, NY: Image Books.

Ash, James L. 1974. '"Oh No. It is not the Scriptures!": The Bible and the Spirit in George Fox.' *Quaker History* 63: 94-107.

Augustine. 1984. *Augustine of Hippo: Selected Writings,* trans. Mary T. Clark. *The Classics of Western Spirituality.* New York, NY: Paulist Press.

Ayling, Stanley. 1979. *John Wesley.* Cleveland, OH: Collins.

Bailey, Richard. 1992. *New Light on George Fox and Early Quakerism: Making and Unmaking of a God:* San Francisco, CA: Mellen Research University Press.

_____. 1993. 'The Making and Unmaking of a God: New Light on George Fox and Early Quakerism.' In *New Light on George Fox and Early Quakerism,* ed. Michael Mullet. York: Sessions.

Baker, Frank. 1949. *The Relations between the Society of Friends and Early Methodism.* London: Epworth Press.

_____. 1970. *John Wesley and the Church of England.* Nashville, TN: Abingdon Press.

Barbour, Hugh. 1964. *The Quakers in Puritan England.* New Haven, CN: Yale University Press.

_____. 1979. 'The Ethic of Movements of Awakening.' Unpublished manuscript presented at the Conference of Biblical Theologians.

_____. 1994. 'Early Quakerism as a Perfectionist Movement of Awakening.' In *Practiced in the Presence: Essays in honor of T. Canby Jones,* ed. D. Neil Snarr and Daniel L. Smith-Christopher. Richmond, IN: Friends United Press.

Barbour, Hugh and Arthur O. Roberts, eds. 1973. *Early Quaker Writings 1650-1700.* Grand Rapids, MI: William B. Eerdmans.

Barbour, Hugh and J. William Frost. 1988. *The Quakers.* New York: Greenwood Press.

Barclay, John (ed). 1841. *Letters, & c., of Early Friends; Illustrative of the History of the Society, from Nearly its Origin, to about the period of George Fox's decease; with Documents Respecting its Early*

Discipline, also Epistles of Counsel and Exhortation, & c. London: Harvey and Darton.

Barclay, Robert. 1692. *Truth Triumphant*, 3 vols. London.

———. 1692. Universal Love. In *Truth Triumphant, vol. 3*. London.

———. 1886 [1678]. *An Apology for the True Christian Divinity*. Glasgow: Dunn and Wright.

Barclay, Robert (of Reigate). 1876. *The Inner Life of the Religious Societies of the Commonwealth*. London: Hodder and Stoughton.

Barton, Stephen C., ed. 2003. *Holiness Past and Present*. London and New York, NY: T & T Clark.

Bassuk, Daniel E. 1978. 'Rufus Jones and Mysticism.' *Quaker Religious Thought* 17, no. 4 (summer): 1-26.

Bauman, Richard. 1983. *Let Your Words Be Few--Symbolism of Speaking and Silence among Seventeenth Century Quakers*. Cambridge: Cambridge University Press.

Bean, Joel. 1881. 'The Issue.' *The British Friend* 39 (March): 49-51.

———. 1883. 'Letter from Joel Bean: The Issue.' *The British Friend* 58, no. 15, (November 1): 282-84.

———. 1885. 'Letter.' *The Friend (London)* LVIII, no. 35: 286-87.

———. 1894. 'Why I am a Friend.' *The American Friend* 1, no. 23 (December 20): 1-6.

Beebe, Ralph K. 1968. *A Garden of the Lord: A History of Oregon Yearly Meeting of Friends Church*. Newberg, OR: The Barclay Press.

Benezet, Anthony. 1780. *An Extract from a Treatise on the Spirit of Prayer or The Soul rising out of the Vanity of Time into the Riches of Eternity with some Thoughts on War: Remarks on the Nature and bad effects of the use of Spirituous Liquors and Considerations on Slavery*. Philadelphia, PA: Joseph Crukshank.

———. 1831. *The Plain Path to Christian Perfection*. Philadelphia, PA: Joseph Rakestraw.

Benjamin, Philip S. 1976. *The Philadelphia Quakers in the Industrial Age 1865-1920*. Philadelphia, PA: Temple University Press.

Benson, Lewis. 1942. 'The Future of Quakerism.' Unpublished Pendle Hill lecture presented at Wallingford, PA, Woodbrooke Library, Birmingham.

———. 1943. *Prophetic Quakerism*. Published by author.

———. 1968. *Catholic Quakerism*. Philadelphia, PA: Philadelphia Yearly Meeting.

Besse, Joseph. 1753. *A Collection of Sufferings of the People called Quakers*. London.

Birkel, Michael L. and John W. Newman, eds. 1992. *The Lambs War: Quaker Essays to Honour Hugh Barbour*. Richmond, IN: Earlham College Press.

Boulding, Kenneth. 1964. *The Evolutionary Potential of Quakerism*. James Backhouse, lecture no. 136. Wallingford, PA: Pendle Hill Pamphlets.

Bouwsma, William J. 1997. 'The Spirituality of John Calvin.' In *Christian Spirituality: High Middle Ages and Reformation*, ed. Jill Raitt. New York, NY: Crossroad, 318-33.

Bouyer, Louis. 1968. *History of Christian Spirituality*, vol. III. New York, NY: Seabury.

_____. 1980. 'Mysticism: An Essay on the History of the Word.' In *Understanding Mysticism*, ed. O.P. Richard Woods. Garden City, NY: Doubleday Image Books, 42-55.

_____. 1990. *The Christian Mystery: From Pagan Myth to Christian Mysticism*. Edinburgh: T & T Clark.

Brailsford, Mabel Richmond. 1927. *A Quaker from Cromwell's Army: James Nayler*. New York, NY: Macmillan.

Braithwaite, Joseph Bevan, ed. 1855. *Memoirs of Joseph John Gurney; with selections from his journal and correspondence*. Philadelphia, PA: Lippincott, Grambo & Co.

Braithwaite, William C. 1912. *The Beginnings of Quakerism*. London: Macmillan and Co.

_____. 1919. *The Second Period of Quakerism*. London: Macmillan and Co..

Brayshaw, A. N. 1933. *The Personality of George Fox*. London: Allenson.

_____. 1946. *The Quakers: Their Story and Message*, 3rd ed. London: Allen and Unwin.

Brendlinger, Irv A. 1996. 'Anthony Benezet, the True Champion of the Slave.' In *Truth's Bright Embrace: Essays and Poems in Honor of Arthur O. Roberts*, ed. Paul N. Anderson and Howard R. Macy. Newberg, OR: George Fox University Press, 81-99.

Brinton, Howard H. 1961. 'The Revival Movement in Iowa: A Letter from Joel Bean to Rufus M. Jones.' *The Bulletin of Friends Historical Association* 50, no. 2, (autumn): 102-10.

_____. 1972. *Quaker Journals: Varieties of Religious Experience Among Friends*. Wallingford, PA: Pendle Hill Publications.

_____. 2002. *Friends for 350 Years*. Wallingford, PA: Pendle Hill Publications.

Bronner, Edwin, ed. 1970. *The Journal of Walter Robson 1877*. Philadelphia, PA: American Philosophical Society.

Brookes, George S. 1937. *Friend Anthony Benezet*. Philadelphia, PA: University of Pennsylvania Press.

Budge, Frances Anne. 1898. *Isaac Sharp: An Apostle of the Nineteenth Century*. London: Headley Brothers.

Burrough, Edward. 1659. *Epistle to the Reader, forward to George Fox's The Great Mystery of the Great Whore Unfolded*. Reprint, 1993, Bishop's Stortford: Abel Press.

_____. 1672. *The Memorable Works of a Son of Thunder and Consolation.* London.

_____. 1831. 'Epistle to the Reader.' In *Works of George Fox.* Philadelphia, PA: Marcus T.C. Gould.

Butler, Edward Cuthbert. 1923. *Western Mysticism: The Teaching of Saints Augustine, Gregory and Bernard on Contemplation and the Contemplative Life.* New York, NY: Dutton.

Cadbury, Henry J. 2000 [1948]. *George Fox's 'Book of Miracles.'* London and Philadelphia, PA: Friends General Conference and Quaker Home Service.

Campbell, Ted. 1991. *The Religion of the Heart: A Study of European Religious Life in the Seventeenth and Eighteenth Centuries.* Columbia, SC: University of South Carolina Press.

Carroll, Kenneth L. 1957. 'Sackcloth and Ashes and Other Signs and Wonders.' *Journal of the Friends Historical Society* 54: 314-25.

_____. 1972. 'Martha Simmonds, a Quaker Enigma.' *Journal of the Friends Historical Society* 53: 31-52.

_____. 1978. 'Early Quakers and "Going Naked for a Sign."' *Quaker History* 67, no. 2, (autumn 1978): 69-87.

Carter, Max L. 1999. 'Early Friends and the Alchemy of Perfection.' *Journal of Friends Historical Society* 58, no. 3: 235-50.

Cattell, Everett Lewis. 1963. *The Spirit of Holiness.* Grand Rapids, MI: Wm. B. Eerdmans.

Chadwick, Owen. 1975. 'Indifference and Morality.' In *Christian Spirituality*, ed. Peter Brooks. London: SCM Press, 205-30.

Clarkson, Thomas. 1806. *A Portraiture of Quakerism,* 3 vols. New York, NY: Samuel Stansbury.

Cole, Alan. 1955. The Quakers and Politics, 1652-1660. Ph.D. diss., Cambridge University.

Cooper, Wilmer A. 1999. *Growing Up Plain: The Journey of a Public Friend.* Wallingford, PA: Friends United Press and Pendle Hill.

_____. 1990. *A Living Faith: An Historical Study of Quaker Beliefs.* Richmond, IN: Friends United Press.

Corns, Thomas N. and David Loewenstein. 1995. *The Emergence of Quaker Writing.* London: Frank Cass and Co.

Crawford, Patricia. 1993. *Women and Religion in England 1500-1720.* London: Routledge.

Creasey, Maurice. 1956. 'Early Quaker Christology with Special Reference to the Teaching and Significance of Isaac Penington, 1616-1679.' Ph.D. diss., University of Leeds.

_____. 1962. *'Inward' and 'Outward': A Study in Early Quaker Language.* London: Friend's Historical Society.

Damiano, Kathryn. 1988. 'On Earth as it is in Heaven: Eighteenth Century Quakerism as Realized Eschatology.' Ph.D. diss., Union of Experimenting Colleges and Universities, Cincinnati, OH.

Damrosch, Leo. 1996. *The Sorrows of the Quaker Jesus: James Nayler and the Puritan Crackdown of the Free Spirit*. Cambridge, MA: Harvard University Press.

Dandelion, Ben Pink. 1996. *A Sociological Analysis of the Theology of Quakers: The Silent Revolution*. Lampeter and Lewiston, NY: Edwin Mellen Press.

Dandelion, Ben Pink. 2004. 'Implicit Conservatism in Liberal Religion: British Quakers as an "uncertain sect."' In *Journal of Contemporary Religion* 19: 219-29.

Dandelion, Ben Pink, Douglas Gwyn, and Peat, Timothy. 1998. *Heaven on Earth: Quakers and the Second Coming*. Kelso, Scotland: Curlew Productions.

Davie, Martin. 1992. 'Development of British Quaker Theology since 1895.' Unpublished Ph.D. diss., Mansfield College, Oxford University.

Davies, Adrian. 2000. *The Quakers in English Society: 1655-1725*. Oxford: Clarendon Press; New York: Oxford University Press.

Davies, Horton. 1961. *Worship and Theology in England from Watt and Wesley to Maurice, 1690-1850*. Princeton, NJ: Princeton University Press.

Davies, Oliver. 2000. 'Holiness.' In *The Oxford Companion to Christian Thought*, ed. Alistair Mason, Adrian Hastings and Hugh Pyper. Oxford: Oxford University Press: 302-3.

Davis, Robert, ed. 1953. *Woodbrooke 1903-1953: A Brief History of a Quaker Experiment in Religious Education*. London: The Bannisdale Press.

Dayton, Donald W. 1996. *Theological Roots of Pentecostalism*. Metuchen, NJ: Hendrickson Publishers and Scarecrow Press.

de Jaegher, Paul. 1977. *Anthology of Christian Mysticism*. Springfield, IL: Templegate Publishers.

Denck, Hans. 1975. *Selected Writings of Hans Denck*, ed. Walter Fellmann, trans. Edward J. Furcha with Ford Lewis Battles. Pittsburgh, PA: The Pickwick Press.

Dewick, E. C. 1938. *The Indwelling God*. Oxford: Oxford University Press.

Dewsbury, William. 1655. *The Discovery of the Great Enmity of the Serpent against the Seed of the Woman*. London: Calvert.

———. 1688. *On Regeneration*. Sermon preached at Grace Church meeting in London. Beven-Naish Collection, Woodbrooke Library, Birmingham.

DiDomizio, Daniel G. 'Spirituality and Politics in Seventeenth Century France.' In *Western Spirituality: Historical Roots, Ecumenical Routes*, ed. Matthew Fox. Santa Fe, NM: Bear & Co.

Dieter, Melvin E. 1996. *The Holiness Revival of the Nineteenth Century*. London and Landham, MD: Scarecrow Press.

Dobbs, Jack P. B. 1995. 'Authority and the Early Quakers.' Unpublished Ph.D. diss., Mansfield College, Oxford University.

Doherty, Robert W. 1967. *The Hicksite Separation: A Sociological Analysis of Religious Schism in Early Nineteenth Century America.* New Brunswick, NJ: Rutgers University Press.

Douglas, Mary. 1982. *Natural Symbols: Explorations in Cosmology.* New York, NY: Pantheon Books.

Drewery, Ben. 1975. 'Deification.' In *Christian Spirituality: Essays in Honour of Gordon Rupp,* ed. Peter Brooks. London: SCM Press, 33-62.

Dubois, Elfrieda. 1986. 'Fenelon and Quietism.' In *The Study of Spirituality,* ed. Cheslyn Jones, Geoffrey Wainwright, Edward Yarnold, SJ. Oxford and New York, NY: Oxford University Press, 408-15.

Dunn, Mary Maples. 1986. 'The Personality of William Penn.' In *The World of William Penn,* ed. Richard S. Dunn and Mary Maples Dunn. Philadelphia, PA: University of Pennsylvania Press, 3-14.

Dupré, Louis. 1996. 'Jansensim and Quietism.' In *Christian Spirituality: Post-Reformation and Modern,* ed. Louis and Don E. Saliers. New York, NY: Crossroad, 121-42.

Dupré, Louis, and James A. Wiseman, O.S.B. 1988. *Light from Light: An Anthology of Christian Mysticism.* New York, NY: Paulist Press.

Durnbaugh, Donald F. 1973. 'Baptists and Quakers – Left Wing Puritans?' *Quaker History* 62, no. 2, (autumn): 67-82.

Edwards, H. W. J. 1948. 'In Praise of Quakers.' *Blackfriars* 29, no. 342, (September): 408-17.

Eeg-Olofsson, Leif. 1954. *The Conception of the Inner Light in Robert Barclay's Theology: A Study in Quakerism.* Lund, Sweden: CWK Gleerup.

Egan, Harvey D., ed. 1996. *An Anthology of Christian Mysticism.* 2nd ed. Collegeville, MI: The Liturgical Press.

Endy, Melvin B., Jr. 1973. *William Penn and Early Quakerism.* Princeton: Princeton Univ. Press.

_____. 1981. 'The Interpretation of Quakerism: Rufus Jones and His Critics.' *Quaker History* 70, no. 1 (spring 1981): 3-21.

Evans, Jonathan, ed. 1844. *Journal of the Life, Travels, and Religious Labours, of William Savery.* London: Charles Gilpin.

Falcetta, Alessandro. 1995. James Rendel Harris, uno studioso del cristianesimo ed un uomo spirituale. Unpublished B.A. thesis, Universitai degli studi di Bologna, Corso di laurea in Lettere Classsiche.

_____. 2000. 'Testimonies: The Theory of James Rendel Harris in the Light of Subsequent Research.' Ph. D. diss., Dept. of Theology, School of Historical Studies, University of Birmingham.

Farnsworth, Richard. 1992 [1654]. *A Bunch of Grapes and An Iron Rod.* Bishop's Stortford: Abel Press.

Farnsworth, Richard and John Whitehead. 1664. *A Tender Visitation of Heavenly Love, Streaming from the Fountain of Endless Life*. York Collection, vol. 3.

Farnworth, Richard. 1653. *An Easter-Reckoning or a Free-will Offering*. London.

———. 1654a. *A Bunch of Grapes and An Iron Rod*. London.

———. 1654b. *Truth Cleared of Scandals*. London.

Finke, Roger and Rodney Stark. 1992. *The Churching of America, 1776-1990: Winners and Losers in our Religious Economy*. New Brunswick, NJ: Rutgers University Press.

Flew, R. Newton. 1934. *The Idea of Perfection in Christian Theology: An Historical Study of the Christian Ideal for the Present Life*. London: Oxford University Press.

Fogelklou, Emilia. 1931. *James Nayler: The Rebel Saint*. London: Benn.

Forbush, Bliss. 1956. *Elias Hicks: Quaker Liberal*. New York, NY: Columbia University Press.

Foster, Richard J. 1986. 'Toward a Quaker Renaissance.' *Quaker Life* (May): 10-13.

Fox, George. 1831. *Epistles II. Works of George Fox*, vol. 8. Philadelphia, PA: Marcus C. Gould.

———. 1831. *The Great Mystery. Works of George Fox*, vol. 3. Philadelphia, PA: Marcus T. C. Gould.

———. 1831. *Works*, 8 vols. Philadelphia, PA: Marcus T. C. Gould.

Fox, Matthew. 1997. *Confessions: The Making of a Postdenominational Priest*. San Francisco, CA: Harper San Francisco.

Frame, Nathan T. 1907. *Reminiscences of Nathan T. and Esther G. Frame*. Cleveland, OH: The Britton Printing Company.

Freiday, Dean, ed. 1980 [1967]. *Barclay's Apology in Modern English*. Newberg, OR: Barclay Press.

Frost, J. William. 1970. 'The Dry Bones of Quaker Theology.' *Church History* 39, no. 4 (December): 503-523.

———. 1980. *The Keithian Controversy in Early Pennsylvania*. Norwood, PA: Norwood Editions.

Galea, Kate. 1993. 'Anchored Behind the Veil: Mystical Vision as a Possible Source of Authority in the Ministry of Phoebe Palmer.' *Methodist History* 31: 243-47.

Galgano, Michael J. 1986. 'Out of the Mainstream: Catholic and Quaker Women in the Restoration Northwest.' In *The World of William Penn*, ed. Richard S. Dunn and Mary Maples Dunn. Philadelphia, PA: University of Pennsylvania Press, 117-37.

Graves, Michael P. 1993. 'Robert Barclay and the Rhetoric of the Inward Light.' *Quaker Religious Thought* 26, no. 2, (March): 17-32.

Greathouse, William. 1979. *From the Apostles to Wesley: Christian Perfection in Historical Perspective*. Kansas City, MO: Beacon Hill Press.

Green, J. Brazier. 1945. *John Wesley and William Law*. London: Epworth Press.

Grubb, Edward. 1914a. *The Historic and Inward Christ: A Study in Quaker Thought*. Bishopsgate: Headley Brothers.

_____. 1914b. *Separations, Their Causes and Effects: Studies in Nineteenth-Century Quakerism*. London: Headley Brothers.

Gurney, Joseph John. 1840. *Essay On the Habitual Exercise of Love to God Considered as a Preparation for Heaven*. Philadelphia, PA: H. Perkins.

_____. 1884. *Essay on the Doctrines, Evidences, and Practical Operation of Christianity*. Philadelphia, PA: Longstreth.

_____. 1979. *A Peculiar People*. Richmond, IN: Friends United Press.

Gwyn, Douglas. 1986. *Apocalypse of the Word: The Life and Message of George Fox*. Richmond, IN: Friends United Press.

_____. 1995. *The Covenant Crucified: Quakers and the Rise of Capitalism*. Wallingford, PA: Pendle Hill.

_____. 2000. *Seekers Found: Atonement in Early Quaker Experience*. Wallingford, PA: Pendle Hill Publications.

Hambrick-Stowe, Charles E. 1986. *The Practice of Piety: Puritan Devotional Disciplines in Seventeenth Century New England*. University of North Carolina Press.

_____. 1986. *The Practice of Piety: Puritan Devotional Disciplines in Seventeenth Century New England*. Chapel Hill, NC: University of North Carolina Press.

Hamm, Thomas D. 1987. 'Joel Bean and the Revival in Iowa.' *Quaker History* 76, no. 1, (spring): 33-49.

_____. 1988. *The Transformation of American Quakerism: Orthodox Friends, 1800-1907*. Bloomington, IN: Indiana University Press.

_____. 1993. 'George Fox and the Politics of Late Nineteenth-Century Quaker Historiography.' In *New Light on George Fox 1624-1691*, ed. Michael Mullett. York: William Sessions Ltd., 11-21.

Harris, Helen B. 1892. *The Greatest Need in the Society of Friends: The Baptism of the Holy Spirit*. London: Edward Hicks.

_____. 1896. *Heart Purity and the Atonement*. London: Marshall Brothers, Keswick House, Paternoster Row.

Harris, J. Rendel. 1892. *Memoranda Sacra*. London: Hodder and Stoughton.

_____. 1895. *Union with God*. London: n.p.

_____. 1900. 'The Influence of Quietism on the Society of Friends.' Lecture delivered at Bryn Mawr College, April 30, 1900. Philadelphia, PA: The Leeds Press.

_____. n.d. 'The Doctrine of the Inward Light.' Typescript manuscript. Harris Collection, Woodbrooke Library, Birmingham.

_____. 1914. *Three Woodbrooke Liturgies*, 2nd ed. London: Headley Brothers.

_____. 1919. *The Origin of the Doctrine of the Trinity*. Manchester: The University Press.

_____. 1925. 'A New Saint Theresa.' *The Holborn Review* (January 1925).

Hauerwas, Stanley. 1998. *Sanctify Them in the Truth: Holiness Exemplified*. Nashville: Abingdon Press.

Henry, Marie. 1984. *The Secret Life of Hannah Whitall Smith*. Grand Rapids, MI: Zondervan.

Hewison, Hope Hay. 1989. *Hedge of Wild Almonds: South Africa, the Pro-Boers & the Quaker Conscience (1890-1910)*. London: James Currey Ltd.

Hicks, Elias. 1824. *A doctrinal epistle written by Elias Hicks, of Jericho, on Long Island, in the year 1820 ; purporting to be an exposition of Christian doctrine, respecting the nature and office of Jesus Christ : With references to those texts of scripture by which its truth, or fallacy, may be readily tested.* Philadelphia, PA, New York, NY, and Baltimore, MD: S. Potter, Bliss & White, and E.J. Coale.

_____. 1825. *A Series of Extemporaneous Discourses, delivered in the Several Meetings of the Society of Friends, by Elias Hicks, taken in short hand by M. T. C. Gould.* Philadelphia, PA: Joseph & Edward Parker.

_____. 1832. *Journal of the life and religious labours of Elias Hicks*. New York, NY: I. T. Hopper.

Hill, Christopher. 1972. *The World Turned Upside Down*. London: Temple Smith.

Hinshaw, David. 1951. *Rufus Jones: Master Quaker*. New York, NY: G. P. Putnam's Sons.

Hobhouse, Stephen. 1938. *Selected Mystical Writings of William Law: Edited with Notes and Twenty-Four Studies in the Mystical Theology of William Law and Jacob Boehme*. London: The C. W. Daniel Co., Ltd.

_____. 1972. *William Law and Eighteenth Century Quakerism, including some unpublished letters and fragments of William Law and John Byrom*. New York, NY: Benjamin Blom, Inc.

Hodgkin, L. Violet, comp. 1937. *A Day-Book of Counsel and Comfort from the Epistles of George Fox*. London: Macmillan.

Hodgson, William, Jr. 1856. *An Examination of the Memoirs and Writings of Joseph John Gurney*. Phildelphia, PA: C. G. Henderson & Co.

Holden, David E. W. 1988. *Friends Divided: Conflict and Division in the Society of Friends*. Richmond, IN: Friends United Press.

Holdsworth, Christopher J. 1972. 'Mystics and Heretics in the Middle Ages: Rufus Jones Reconsidered.' *Journal of the Friends Historical Society* 53, no. 1: 9-30.

Holmes, Urban. 1984. *The History of Christian Spirituality: An Analytical Introduction*. New York, NY: Seabury Press.

Howgill, Frances. 1656. *The Inheritance of Jacob Discovered, after His Return out of Egypt*. London: Giles Calvert.

Huber, K. 2001. 'Questions of Identity Among Buddhist Quakers.' *Quaker Studies* 6: 80-105.

Huxley, Aldous. 1946. *The Perennial Philosophy*. London: Chatto & Windus.

Inge, William Ralph. 1899. *Christian Mysticism*. London: Methuen.

Ingle, H. Larry. 1986. *Quakers in Conflict: The Hicksite Reformation*. Knoxville, TN: University of Tennessee Press.

———. 1987. 'From Mysticism to Radicalism: Recent Historiography of Quaker Beginnings.' *Quaker History* 76, no. 2: 79-94.

———. 1994. *First Among Friends: George Fox and the Creation of Quakerism*. Oxford and New York, NY: Oxford University Press.

———. 1997. 'The Future of Quaker History.' *Journal of the Friends Historical Society* 58, no. 1: 1-16.

Isichei, Elizabeth. 1970. *Victorian Quakers*. Oxford: Oxford University Press.

Jones, Charles E. 1974. *Perfectionist Persuasion: The Holiness Movement and American Methodism*. Metuchen, NJ: Scarecrow Press.

Jones, Rufus M. 1901. *A Dynamic Faith*. London: Headley Bros.

———. 1904. *Social Law in the Spiritual World: Studies in human and divine inter-relationship*. Philadelphia, PA and Chicago, IL: The John Winston Co.

———. 1906. *The Double Search*. Philadelphia, PA: The John C. Winston Co.

———. 1909. *Studies in Mystical Religion*. London: Macmillan & Co.

———. 1910. *Selections form the Writings of Clement of Alexandria*. London: Headley Bros.

———. 1911. *Quakers in the American Colonies*. London: Macmillan & Co.

———. 1914. *Spiritual Reformers in the Sixteenth and Seventeenth Centuries*. London: Macmillan & Co.

———. 1916. *The Inner Life*. New York, NY: The Macmillan Co.

———. 1918. *The World Within*. New York, NY: The Macmillan Co.

———. 1921. *The Later Periods of Quakerism*, 2 vols. London: Macmillan & Co.

———. 1926. *Finding the Trail of Life*. New York, NY: The Macmillan Co.

———. 1927. *New Studies in Mystical Religion*. New York, NY: The Macmillan Co.

———. 1928. *The New Quest*. New York, NY: The Macmillan Co.

———. 1929. *The Trail of Life in College*. New York, NY: Macmillan.

———. 1930. *Some Exponents of Mystical Religion*. New York, NY: Abingdon Press.

———. 1931. *Pathways to the Reality of God*. New York, NY: The Macmillan Co.

———. 1932. *Mysticism and Democracy in the English Commonwealth*. Cambridge: Harvard University Press.

———. 1934. *The Trail of Life in the Middle Years*. New York, NY: Macmillan.

———. 1935. *Re-Thinking Religious Liberalism*. Boston, MA: Beacon Press.

———. 1939. *The Flowering of Mysticism: The Friends of God in the Fourteenth Century*. New York, NY: The Macmillan Co.

Bibliography

———. 1941. *Spirit in Man*. Stanford: Stanford University Press.
———. 1944. *The Radiant Life*. New York, NY: The Macmillan Co.
———. 1947. *The Luminous Trail*. New York, NY: The Macmillan Co.
———. 1976. 'Introduction.' In *The Journal of George Fox*, ed. Rufus M. Jones. Richmond, IN: Friends United Press, 19-49.
Jones, T. Canby. 1955. 'George Fox's Teaching on Redemption and Salvation.' Unpublished Ph.D. diss., Yale University.
———. 1959. 'George Fox's Belief in the Trinity.' *Friend's Quarterly* 13, no. 3, (July): 112-17.
———. 1962. 'The Bible: Its Authority and Dynamic in George Fox and Contemporary Quakerism.' *Quaker Religious Thought* 4: 18-36.
———. 1974. 'The Nature and Functions of the Light in the Thought of George Fox.' *Quaker Religious Thought* 16: 53-71.
———. 1995. 'Thomas Kelly: Some New Insights.' *Quaker Religious Thought* 27, no. 3: 5-10.
Jones, Cheslyn, Geoffrey Wainwright, and Edward Yarnold, SJ, eds. 1986. *The Study of Spirituality*. Oxford: Oxford University Press.
Kaiser, Geoffrey D. 1994. *The Society of Friends in North America*. Chart.
Katz, Steven. 1978. *Mysticism and Philosophical Analysis*. New York, NY: Oxford.
———. ed. 1983. *Mysticism and Religious Tradition*. New York, NY: Oxford.
Kelly, Paul M. 1986. 'Thomas Kelly Encounters Nazi Germany: His Letter from Strasbourg, 1938.' In *Seeking the Light: Essays in Quaker History in Honor of Edwin B. Bronner*, ed. J. William Frost and John M. Moore. Wallingford, PA and Haverford, PA: Pendle Hill Publications and Friends Historical Association, 183-208.
Kelly, Richard. 1966. *Thomas Kelly: A Biography*. New York, NY: Harper & Row.
———. 1995. 'New Lights and Inner Light.' *Quaker Religious Thought* 27, no. 3, (July): 43-56.
Kelly, Thomas. 1941. *Testament of Devotion*. New York, NY: Harper & Brothers.
Kendall, John, ed. 1832. *The Life of Thomas Story*, 2 vols. York: William Alexander.
Kennedy, Thomas C. 2001. *British Quakerism: 1860-1920: The Transformation of a Religious Community*. London: Oxford University Press.
Kent, Stephen A. 1987. 'Psychology and Quaker Mysticism: The Legacy of William James and Rufus Jones.' *Quaker History* 76, no. 1, (spring): 1-17.
King, Rachel Hadley. 1940. *George Fox and the Light Within*. Philadelphia, PA: Friends Book Store.
Kirk, Kenneth E. 1931. *The Vision of God: The Christian Doctrine of the Summum Bonum*. London: Longman's, Green and Co.

Knight, Rachel. 1922. *The Founder of Quakerism*. London: The Swarthmore Press.
Knott, John R. 1993. *Discourses on Martyrdom in English Literature 1563-1694*. Cambridge: Cambridge University Press.
Knox, R. Buick, ed. 1977. *Reformation, Conformity and Dissent: Essays in Honour of Geoffrey Nuttall*. London: Epworth Press.
Langton, Edward. 1956. *History of the Moravian Church: The Story of the First International Protestant Church*. London: George Allen & Unwin Ltd.
Law, William. 1974. *The Works*, 3 vols., ed. G. Moreton. Hildesheim, NY: Georg Olms Verlag.
_____. 1978. *A Serious Call to a Devout and HolyLife; The Spirit of Love*. Classics of Western Spirituality, ed. Paul G. Stanwood. New York, NY: Paulist Press.
Le Shana, David C. 1969. *Quakers in California: The Effects of 19th Century Revivalism on Western Quakerism*. Newberg, OR: The Barclay Press.
Leclercq, Jean, François Vandenbroucke and Louis Bouyer. 1968. *The Spirituality of the Middle Ages*, trans. Carlisle. The Benedictines of Holme Eden Abbey. A History of Christian Spirituality, vol. II. Kent: Burns & Oates.
Lindström, Harald. 1980. *Wesley & Sanctification*. Grand Rapids, MI: Zondervan.
Littleboy, William. 1916. *The Appeal of Quakerism to the Non-mystic*. London: Friends' Book Centre.
Lossky, Vladimir. 1976. *The Mystical Theology of the Eastern Church*. Crestwood, NY: 1976.
Louth, Andrew. 1981. *The Origins of the Christian Mystical Tradition from Plato to Denys*. Oxford: Clarendon Press.
_____. 2003. 'Holiness and the Vision of God in the Eastern Fathers.' In *Holiness: Past and Present*, ed. Stephen C. Barton. London & New York, NY: T & T Clark, 217-38.
Mack, Phyllis. 1992. *Visionary Women: Ecstatic Prophecy in Seventeenth-Century England*. Berkeley, CA: University of California Press.
Maddox, Randy L. 1994. *Responsible Grace: John Wesley's Practical Theology*. Nashville, TN: Kingswood Books.
Malherbe, Abraham J. and Everett Ferguson, trans. 1978. *Gregory of Nyssa: The Life of Moses. The Classics of Western Spirituality*. New York, NY: Paulist Press.
Maloney, George A. 1987. *Uncreated Energy: A Journey into the Authentic Sources of the Christian Faith*. Amity, NY: Amity House.
Manchester Conference, or Report of the Proceedings of the Conference of Members of the Society of Friends Held, by Direction of the Yearly Meeting in Manchester from the Eleventh to the Fifteenth of eleventh Month, 1985. 1896. London: Headley Bros.

Marietta, Jack D. 1984. *The Reformation of American Quakerism: 1748-1783*. Philadelphia, PA: University of Pennsylvania Press.

McBrien, Richard P., ed. 1995. *Harpercollins Encyclopedia of Catholicism*. San Francisco, CA: Harper San Francisco.

McGinn, Bernard C. 1991. *The Foundations of Mysticism: Origins to the Fifth Century*. New York, NY: Crossroad.

———. 1994. *The Growth of Mysticism*. New York, NY: Crossroad Publishing Co.

———. 1998. *The Flowering of Mysticism: Men and Women in the New Mysticis –1200-1350*. New York, NY: Crossroad Publishing Co.

McKay, David. 1994. '"A Better and Enduring Substance": A Typological Primer for Quaker Studies.' *Quaker Religious Thought* 26, no. 4 (April): 13-22.

Moltmann, Jurgen. 1980. *Experiences of God*. Philadelphia, PA: 1980.

Mommaers, Paul. 2003. *The Riddle of Christian Mystical Experience*. Louven, Belgium: Peeters Press and W. B. Eerdmans.

Moore, Rosemary Anne. 1993. 'The Faith of the First Quakers: The Development of their Beliefs and Practices up to the Restoration.' Ph.D. diss., Department of Theology, University of Birmingham.

———. 2000. *The Light in Their Consciences: Early Quakers in Britain*. University Park, PA: The Pennsylvania State University Press.

Mott, Edward. 1935. *The Friends Church in Light of its Recent History*. Portland, OR: Private printing.

———. 1948 (?). *Sixty Years of Gospel Ministry*. Portland, OR: E. Mott.

Mullet, Michael, ed. 1993. *New Light on George Fox and Early Quakerism*. York: William Sessions Ltd.

n.a. 1824. *Collectitia*. York: W. Alexander and Son.

n.a. 1898. 'Disownment of Joel Bean and Others.' *British Friend*, December 1898: 305.

Nayler, James. 1650. *A Salutation to the Seed of God and a Call out of Babylon and Egypt*.

———. 1653a. *The Power and Glory of the Lord*.

———. 1653b. *Saul's Errand to Damascus*.

———. 1655. *A Discovery of the Man of Sin*.

Naylor, James. 1716. *A Collection of Sundry Books, Epistles and Papers*, ed. George Whitehead. London.

Nesti, Donald S., C.S.Sp. 1978. Early Quaker Ecclesiology. *Quaker Religious Thought* 18: 4-34.

Nickalls, John L. 1931. 'George Fox's Library.' *Journal of the Friends Historical Society* 28: 3-21.

———. 1952. *The Journal of George Fox*. Cambridge: Cambridge University Press.

Niebuhr, H. Richard. 1959. *The Kingdom of God in America*. New York, NY: Harper.

Nuttall, Geoffrey. 1948. *Studies in Christian Enthusiasm, Illustrated from Early Quakerism.* Wallingford, PA: Pendle Hill.
_____. 1967. *The Puritan Spirit: Essays and Addresses.* London: Epworth Press.
_____. 1973. 'Overcoming the World: The Early Quaker Programme.' In *Sanctity and Secularity: The Church and the World (Studies in Church History, 10)*, ed. Derek Baker. Oxford: Oxford University Press, 145-64.
_____. 1975. 'Puritan and Quaker Mysticism.' *Theology*, no. 664: 518-31.
_____. 1992 [1946]. *The Holy Spirit In Puritan Faith and Experience.* Chicago, IL: University of Chicago Press.
Oliver, John. 1991. 'J Walter Malone: The American Friends and an Evangelical Quaker's Social Agenda.' *Quaker History* 80, no. 2, (fall): 63-84.
_____. ed. 1993. *J. Walter Malone: The Autobiography of an Evangelical Quaker.* Lanham: University Press of America.
Olney, James. 1972. *Metaphors of Self: The Meaning of Autobiography.* Princeton, NJ: Princeton University Press.
Ozment, Steven E. 1973. *Mysticism and Dissent: Religious Ideology and Social Protest in the Sixteenth Century.* New Haven: Yale University Press.
Packull, Werner. 1977. *Mysticism and the Early South German-Austrian Anabaptist Movement 1525-1531.* Scottdale, PA: Herald Press.
Penington, Isaac. 1681. *Works*, 2 vols. London.
Penn, William. 1682. *No Cross, No Crown*, 2nd ed. London.
_____. 1726. *No Cross, No Crown.* In *The Collected Works of William Penn*, 2 vols., ed. Joseph Besse. London.
_____. 1877 [1686]. *Primitive Christianity Revived in the faith and practice of the people called Quakers.* Philadelphia, PA: H. Longstreth.
Peters, John L. 1985. *Christian Perfection and American Methodism.* Grand Rapids, MI: Zondervan.
Pickard, I. S. 1978. *Memories of J. Rendel Harris.* Private publication.
Pickvance, Joseph. 1989. *A Reader's Companion to George Fox's Journal.* London: Quaker Home Service.
Pilgrim, Gay. 1999. Quaker Spirituality: An Oxymoron? In *Paper presented at the Quaker Stiudies Research Association Annual Conference.* Woodbrooke Quaker Study Center, Birmingham.
Punshon, John. 1984. *Portrait in Grey.* London: Quaker Home Service.
_____. 2001. *Reasons for Hope: The Faith and Future of the Friends Church.* Richmond, IN: Friends United Press.
Pyper, Hugh. 2001. 'Can There Be a Quaker Hermeneutic?' *Quaker Religious Thought* 30, no. 3 (September): 63-69.
Reay, Barry. 1985. *The Quakers and the English Revolution.* London: Temple Smith.
Ritschl, Albert. 1887. *Theologie und Metaphysik.* Bonn, Germany: Marcus.

Roberts, Arthur. O. 1951. 'Concepts of Perfection.' Unpublished B.Div. diss., Nazarene Theological Seminary.
_____. 1953. 'George Fox and Holiness.' *American Friend* XLI, no. 5, (February 26): 147-8.
_____. 1959. *Through Flaming Sword: A Spiritual Biography of George Fox*. Portland, OR: Barclay Press.
_____. 1961. 'Early Friends and the Work of Christ.' *Quaker Religious Thought* 3, no. 1: 10-20.
_____. 1967. 'Holiness and Christian Renewal.' *Quaker Religious Thought* 9, no. 1, (spring): 4-20.
_____. 1975. *The Association of Evangelical Friends: A story of Quaker Renewal in the Twentieth Century*. Newberg, OR: Barclay Press.
_____. 1981. The Kingdom of Light. *Quaker Religious Thought* 19, no. 1 (spring): 28-43.
_____. 1989. 'The Universalism of Christ in Early Quaker Understanding.' *Quaker Religious Thought* 23 (summer): 2-18.
_____. 1993. *Drawn by the Light*. Newberg, OR: Barclay Press.
_____. 1996. *Messengers of God: The Sensuous Side of Spirituality*. Newberg, OR: Barclay Press.
_____. 2003. 'Testimony to Christian Holiness within Secular Culture.' Malcolm R. Robertson Lectureship: The Haggard School of Theology, Azusa Pacific University, Oct. 20-21.
Roukema, Riemer. 1999. *Gnosis and Faith in Early Christianity*. London: SCM Press.
Royo, Antonio and Jordon Aumann. 1962. *The Theology of Christian Perfection*. Dubuque, IA: The Priory Press.
Rudolph, Erwin Paul. 1980. *William Law*. Boston: Twayne Publishers.
Rupp, Gordon. 1977. 'A Devotion of Rapture in English Puritanism.' In *Reformation Conformity and Dissent: Essays in Honour of Geoffrey Nuttall*, ed. R. Buick Knox. London: Epworth Press, 115-131.
Ryle, Canon. 1880. Religious Excitement. *The British Friend* Vol. 38, no. 7, (July 1): 182.
Schneiders, Sandra M. 1985. 'Scripture and Spirituality.' In *Christian Spirituality: Origins to the Twelfth Century*, ed. Bernard McGinn and John Meyendorff. New York, NY: Crossroad, 1-20.
_____. 1999. *Written That You May Believe: Encountering Jesus in the Fourth Gospel*. New York, NY: Crossroad Publishing Company.
Scholem, Gershom. 1965. *On the Kabbalah and its Symbolism*. New York, NY: Schocken.
Schweitzer, Albert. 1931. *The Mysticism of Paul the Apostle*. London: A & C Black, Ltd.
Scott, Job. 1831. *Works*, 2 vols. Philadelphia, PA: John Comley.
Scott, Richenda C. 1967. *Herbert G. Wood: A Memoir of His Life and Thought (1879-1963)*. London: Friends Home Service Committee.

Seebohm, Benjamin, ed. 1862. *Memoirs of the Life and Gospel Labours of Stephen Grellet*, 2 vols. London: A. W. Bennett.
Sippel, Peter D., ed. 2002 [1678]. *An Apology for the True Christian Divinity*. Glenside, PA: Quaker Heritage Press.
Sippell, Theodor. 1937. *Werdendes Quäkertum*. Stuttgart, Germany: W. Kohlhammer.
Smith, Hannah Whitall. 1888. *The Christian's Secret of a Happy Life*. New York, NY: Fleming H. Revell.
_____. 1903. *My Spiritual Autobiography or How I Discovered the Unselfishness of God*. New York, NY: Fleming H. Revel Company.
_____. 1928. *Fanaticism*. London: Faber & Gwyer.
Smith, Joseph. 1867. *A Descriptive Catalogue of Friends Books*, 2 vols. London.
Smith, Logan Pearsall, ed. 1950. *Philadelphia Quaker: The Letters of Hannah Whitall Smith*. New York, NY: Harcourt-Brace.
Smith, Nigel. 1989. *Perfection Proclaimed: Language and Literature in English Radical Religion 1640-1660*. Oxford: Clarendon Press.
_____, ed. 1998. *George Fox: The Journal*. New York, NY: Penguin.
Smith, Timothy L. 1980 [1957]. *Revivalism and Social Reform: American Protestantism on the Eve of the Civil War*. Baltimore, MD: Johns Hopkins.
Snelling, Deanne Rona May. 1997. 'Towards An Ecumenical Understanding of Christian Perfection: A Study in Deification as Taught by Clement of Alexandria.' Ph.D. diss., Faculty of Arts, University of Birmingham.
Soelle, Dorothee. 1975. *Suffering*. Minneapolis, MN: Fortress Press.
_____. 2001. *The Silent Cry: Mysticism and Resistance*. Minneapolis, MN: Fortress Press.
Spencer, Carole. 1991. 'Evangelism, Feminism, and Social Reform.' *Quaker History* 80, no. 1 (spring): 24-48.
_____. 1998. 'The American Holiness Movement: Why Did It Captivate Nineteenth Century Quakers?' *Quaker Religious Thought*, vol. 28, no. 4 (January): 19-30.
_____. 2001. 'James Nayler: Antinomian or Perfectionist?' *Quaker Studies* 6 (September). 106-117.
Swift, David F. 1962. *Joseph John Gurney: Banker, Reformer, and Quaker*. Middletown, CT: Wesleyan University Press.
Tallack, William. 1868. *George Fox, the Friends, and the Early Baptists*. London: Partridge.
Tavard, George H. 2000. 'George Fox Among Christian Mystics.' *Quaker Theology* 2, no. 1, (spring): 30-57.
Taylor, Ralph. 1992. 'Quaking: A Study of the Phenomena of Quaking, Trembling, and Shaking in Early Quakerism.' Unpublished MA thesis, University of Wales.

Tolles, Frederick. 1948. *Meetinghouse and Countinghouse: The Quaker Merchants of Colonial Philadelphia, 1682-1763*. Chapel Hill, NC: University of North Carolina Press.

Tolles, Frederick B. and E. Gordon Alderfer, eds. 1957. *The Witness of William Penn*. New York, NY: Macmillan.

Torjesen, Karen Jo. 1986. *Hermeneutical Procedure and Theological Method in Origen's Exegesis*. Berlin, Germany: De Gruyter.

Tousley, Nikki Coffey. 2003. 'The Experience of Regeneration and Erosion of Certainty in the Theology of Second Generation Quakers: No Place for Doubt?' Unpublished M.Phil. thesis, University of Birmingham.

Trevett, Christine. 1990. 'The Women around James Nayler: A Matter of Emphasis.' *Religion* 20: 249-73.

Trueblood, Elton. 1968. *Robert Barclay*. New York, NY: Harper & Row.

Turner, William, Francis Frith and William Pollard. 1884. *A Reasonable Faith – by Three Friends*. London: Macmillan & Co.

Tuttle, Robert G., Jr. 1989. *Mysticism in the Wesleyan Tradition*. Grand Rapids, MI: Zondervan.

Underwood, T. L. 1997. *Primitivism, Radicalism, and the Lamb's War: the Baptist-Quaker Conflict in Seventeenth-Century England*. New York, NY: Oxford University Press.

_____. 1970. 'Early Quaker Eschatology.' In *Puritans, the Millennium and the Future of Israel*, ed. Peter Toon. London: James Clark, 91-103.

Vann, Richard T. 1969. *The Social Development of English Quakerism 1655-1755*. Cambridge: Harvard University Press.

Vaux, Roberts. 1817. *Memoirs of the Life of Anthony Benezet*. Philadelphia, PA: W. Alexander.

Vining, Elizabeth Gray. 1959. *Friend of Life: The Biography of Rufus M. Jones*. London: Michael Joseph.

Wakefield, Gordon S. 1957. *Puritan Devotion: Its Place in the Development of Christian Piety*. London: Epworth Press.

_____. 1989. 'Anglican Spirituality.' In *Christian Spirituality: Post-Reformation and Modern*, ed. Louis Dupré and Don E. Saliers. New York, NY: Crossroad, 257-93.

Walker, A. Keith. 1973. *William Law: HisLlife and Thought*. London: S.P.C.K.

Wallace, T. H. S., ed. 1996. *None Were So Clear: Prophetic Quaker Faith and the Ministry of Lewis Benson*. Camp Hill, PA: New Foundation Publications.

Ward, Keith. 1994. *Revelation and Religion*. Oxford: Oxford University Press.

Watkins, Owen C. 1972. *The Puritan Experience: Studies in Spiritual Autobiography*. New York, NY: Schocken Books.

Watson, David Lowes. 1986. 'Methodist Spirituality.' In *Protestant Spiritual Traditions*, ed. Frank C. Senn. New York, NY, and Mahwah, NJ: Paulist Press, 217-73.

Wesley, John. [1831]. *The Works of the Rev. John Wesley, A.M.*, ed. John Emory. New York, NY: Carlton & Lanahan.
_____. 1872. *The Works of John Wesley*. Grand Rapids, MI: Zondervan.
_____. 1931. *The Letters of John Wesley*. London: Epworth Press.
_____. 1938. *The Journal of the Rev. John Wesley, A.M.* London: Epworth Press.
White, Charles Edward. 1986. *The Beauty of Holiness: Phoebe Palmer as Theologian, Revivalist, Feminist, and Humanitarian*. Grand Rapids, MI: Francis Asbury Press.
Whitehead, George, ed. 1716. *A Collection of Sundry Books, Epistles and Papers, Written by James Nayler, Some of which were never before Printed. With an Impartial Relation of the Most Remarkable Transactions Relating to His Life*. London.
Wilbur, John. 1845. *A Narrative and Exposition of the Late Proceedings of New England Yearly Meeting*. New York, NY: Piercy & Reed.
_____. 1859. *Journal of the Life of John Wilbur, A Minister of the Gospel in the Society of Friends; with Selections from His Correspondence, &c.* Providence, RI: George H. Whitney.
Wilcox, Catherine Mary. 1991. 'The Theology of the Early Friends and its Implications for the Ministry of Women in Seventeenth Century English Quakerism.' Unpublished Ph.D. diss., King's College, University of London.
Williams, Rowan. 1991. *Teresa of Avila*. Harrisburg, PA: Morehouse.
Williams, Water R. 1987. *The Rich Heritage of Quakerism*. Newberg, OR: Barclay Press.
Wilson, W. E. 1941. *Rendel Harris at Woodbrooke*. Leominster: The Orphans' Printing Press (reprinted from the *Friends Quarterly Examiner*, April, 1941).
_____. 1948. 'Quaker and Evangelical.' *Friends' Quarterly* (October): 3-15 (reprinted in pamphlet form, January 1949. Malvern: The Priory Press).
Wood, Herbert G. 1927. 'The Faiths III. The Ideals and Principles of Quakerism.' *The Free Catholic* (June): 88-90.
_____. 1930. *What Do We Mean by the Inner Light?* Selly Oak, Birmingham: Woodbrooke Extension Committee.
_____. 1945. *Rendel Harris as Letter Writer*. Selly Oak, Birmingham: Woodbrooke Extension Committee.
_____. 1951. *Theology and Prayer*. London: Central Offices, Society of Friends, Friends House.
_____. 1953. 'The First Director of Studies.' In *Woodbrooke 1903-1953*, ed. Robert Davis. London: The Bannisdale Press, 19-33.
_____. 1959. *The Guiding Hand of God*, Rendel Harris Lecture 17th October, 1959. Selly Oak, Birmingham: Woodbrooke Extension Committee.

_____. n.d. *The Quaker Message*. Selly Oak, Birmingham: Woodbrooke Extension Committee of the Society of Friends.

Wood, Herbert G. & J. Rendel Harris. 1929. *Friends and the Scriptures*. Selly Oak, Birmingham: Woodbrooke Extension Committee and Adult Section of the Central Education Committee of the Society of Friends.

Wood, Richard E. 1987. 'Evangelical Quaker Acculturation in the Upper Mississippi Valley, 1850-1875.' *Quaker History* 76, no. 2, (fall): 128-44.

Wright, Louella M. 1932. *The Literary Life of the Early Friends 1650-1725*. New York, NY: Columbia University Press.

Yarnold, Edward. 1986. 'The Theology of Christian Spirituality.' In *The Study of Spirituality*, ed. Geoffrey Wainwright, Cheslyn Jones, Edward Yarnold. Oxford: Oxford University Press, 9-17.

Yungblut, John. 1983. *Speaking as one Friend to Another on the Mystical Way Forward*. Wallingford, PA: Pendle Hill Pamphlets.

Zaehner, R. C. 1961. *Mysticism, Sacred and Profane*. New York, NY: Oxford.

INDEX

Affective 10n17, 19n35, 39, 42, 47, 84, 117, 133, 135, 227, 231, 248, 266, 290n20
Altar of Prayer 176, 179, 183
American Holiness Movement 136, 139, 161-163
Amor Ipse Intellectus Est 8
Anglicanism 2, 144n32, 174-175
Anthony of Egypt 260
Antinomian 71, 90
Anti-Revivalism under British Friends 173-183
Anti-Revivalism under Joel Bean 168-173
Apocalyptic 17, 48, 74
Apophatic 10n17, 14, 30-31, 42, 60, 91-92, 97, 102, 108, 116, 120, 124, 134, 158, 205-206, 234, 239-240, 247, 249, See also Via Negativa
Apostle Paul 49, 51, 67, 85, 87, 89, 141, 144, 213
Aquinas, Thomas 153n40, 261
Ascetic Ideals 3
Asceticism 32, 80, 90, 97, 102-103, 114-116, 155-156, 281
Atonement 35-36, 89n51, 117, 124n12, 149, 200-201
Augustine of Hippo 45, 77n37, 84, 255-258, 266

Bailey, Joshua 181
Bailey, Richard 25-26, 39, 49-53, 56-57, 67, 257
Baker, Augustine 241n3, 262n9
Baptism of the Holy Spirit 10, 12, 24, 104, 120, 144, 147, 163, 183, 216, 241, 279, See also Second Blessing
Barbour, Hugh 10-12, 16, 34, 38, 41, 43n76, 56

Barclay, Robert 4n6, 30n61, 31n62, 32, 35n66, 36, 38, 45, 60-61, 63, 75-82, 97, 105, 142, 149, 152, 153n41, 154, 202-203, 241n3, 257-258, 262, 266-268, 271-272, 274-277, 281, 287-288
Bean, Joel 164-173, 239, 242-243
Beanite Quakerism 167n7, 172-173, 242
Benezet, Anthony 92-105, 125, 243, 286-287, 289-290
Benson, Lewis 46-48, 50
Bernard of Clairvaux 258, 260
Bible, See Scripture
Black Worship 170-171
Boehme, Jacob 276, 279, 281-282, 284n13, 286, 291
Bouyer, Louis 39-40
Bridal Mysticism 258-260
Bristol, England 27, 69-72
Burrough, Edward 31, 36, 75
Byrom, John 285

Calvin, John 202-204
Calvinism 44, 202-204, 267
Cambridge Platonism 204-205
Camp Meetings 164, 171, 192n38, 240, See also Evangelism
Catholicism 3-4, 9, 25, 34n64, 39-40, 116, 202, 250-251, 262, 265-270, 277-278
Cattell, Everett Lewis 232-234, 237, 244
Charism 247
Charismatic 14-15, 23-26, 82, 104, 120, 139, 147, 158-159, 235-236, 240, 246-247, 269, 282n10, 288
Christ Within, See Inner Light
Christocentric 1n1, 28, 47, 250

Cognitio Dei Experimentalis 4
College Park Friends 167, 172
Conservative Friends 176n17, 155, 181
Conversion 8, 14, 18-22, 33, 71n26, 83-84, 107-114, 120, 128-133, 138-142, 158, 215, 245-246, 255
Convincement 19, 138-140, 209n37, See also Conversion
Cross of Christ 27, 53n91, 286

Dark Night of the Soul 85, 114, 116, 279
Deification 2, 7-8, 35, 37, 52-53, 59, 70n23, 71, 152-153, 255-258, See also Divinization, Perfection, and Union
Deism 122, 289, 291
Derby, England 65, 67
Devotio Modera 261-262, 266, 269
Devotion to the Sacred Heart of Christ 265-266, 268-269
Dewsbury, William 20
Dissenters 89, 272
Divine Indwelling 71n24, 120, 150-153, 190, 215, 247, 257, See also Union
Divine Union, See Divine Indwelling, and Union
Divinization 52, 69, 127, 151, 208, 216, 251, 256, See also Perfection, *Theosis,* and Union
Docetism 124n9-10
Drummond, May 284
Dualism 44, 124-125, 201
Dupré, Louis 281

Earlham Hall 136n23
Eastern Orthodox 52, 257-258
Ecstatic 26n50, 205, 235-236, 255, 260
Ecumenical 138, 164, 167, 173, 244
Emotions, See Affective
Endy, Melvin 43-46
Energeiai 258
Enlightenment 25, 92, 122, 134, 157, 244, 265, 288
Enstatic 255
Epektatis 79
Eschatology 14, 17-18, 48-49, 74, 120, 216-217, 245-246
Ethics 41, 226, 247
  of Jesus Christ 125, 135
Eudes, Jean 266
Evangelicalism 1n4, 56-57, 117n28, 119, 135, 136n21, 137n25, 141, 144n32, 146, 186, 217-223, 229-237, 240n7, 244, 246-248, 278
  and Arthur Roberts 54-55
  and John Punshon 55
  and Stephen Grellet 105-116
Evangelism 14, 22-23, 81, 92-93, 115n24, 117n28, 120, 158, 175, 241, 246-247
Evans, Jonathan 131
Evolution 219

Fenelon 40, 186n29
Foster, Richard 232, 235-237
Fox, George 19, 21, 23, 32, 45-53, 60-63, 63-70, 74, 199, 202, 210, 233, 243, 256-257, 259-260, 262
  and convincement 21
  and healing 25
  and journal 5, 18, 23-24
  and perfection 34-36
  and scripture 16
Frame, Esther 177
Francis of Assisi 28, 261
Franciscans 261
Freedom 22, 209-210

Gnosis 3

Index 315

Gnosticism 123-128, 134
Great Awakening 93
Great Separation 121-159
Gregory of Nyssa 8n14, 70n23, 79, 256, 260
Grellet, Stephen 105-106, 116-119, 122-123, 132-133, 243, 255n1
   and asceticism 114-116
   and conversion 107-114, 130
   and dark night 114, 116
Grubb, Edward 122n4, 124-125, 144-145
Gurney, Joseph John 123n7, 135-138, 146-147, 157-159, 192n38, 243-244
   and conversion 138-142
   and perfection 142-143
   and mysticism 143-145
   and John Wilbur 148-157
Gurneyite 137, 155, 157-159, 167, 176n17, 188n32, 246-248
Gurneyite-Wilburite Split 135-159
Gwyn, Douglas 36n69, 48-49, 57

Hagiography 4
Hagios 3-4
Hamm, Thomas 39, 55-57, 157, 161-162, 170, 191, 242n4, 247-248
Harris, J. Rendel 73, 88, 193, 195n2, 203, 207-217, 221-224, 226-228, 237, 244
   and Holiness Movement 209-211
   on holiness 213-221
   on mysticism 211-213
   on Quakerism, modernism, and holiness 217-221
Harvey, Cyrus 179-180
Henshaw, Fanny 283-285
Hicks, Elias 121-123, 133-136, 243-244
   and Gnostic theology 123-125
   and Job Scott 125-128
   and Quietist conversion narratives 128-133
Hicksites 82, 121, 132-134, 145, 151-152, 155, 157-159, 243-244, 246, 248
Hobhouse, Stephen 60n2, 95n7, 282, 283, 284nn12-13, 286-289, 292
Holiness Movement 2-4, 14, 24n45, 57, 84, 88, 93, 111n23, 119, 135-137, 138n27, 139, 146, 144n33, 162n1, 164-165, 171-172, 175-176, 183-184, 205, 222, 228, 235, 240-241, 244n7
   in America 161-163
   and J. Rendel Harris 209-211
   in comparison to others 265-270
Holiness Revival 23, 68, 110, 136, 138, 162n1, 192-194, 239-240, 246-248
   in America 161-163
   and reactions to 164-173
   and British reactions 173-183
   and Hannah Whitall Smith 183-192
Holmes, Urban 10-12
Holy Spirit 14, 15, 24, 47-48, 65, 117-118, 120, 122n6, 132, 147, 151, 168n7, 170, 204-205, 214-215, 222, 236, 240, 241n3, 246, 247n10, 249, 258-260, 274-275, See also Baptism of the Holy Spirit

Imitatio Christi/Imitation of Christ 53, 69, 70-74, 97, 104, 116, 135, 146, 157, 224, 260, 262
Imputed Righteousness 141-142
Incarnation 7, 35, 52, 76, 86, 98, 101, 105, 123-125, 128, 134, 147, 150-153, 186, 256, 286-287

Inner Light 36, 38, 66n13, 77, 132-133, 135, 148, 151-153, 158, 170, 180, 200-206, 225, 255-258, 266, 274n3, 288-289
Inward Light, See Inner Light
Iowa Yearly Meeting 164-168
"The Issue" by Joel Bean 165, 168

Jansenists 266, 268-270
Jesus Christ 4, 7, 12, 14, 17-18, 27, 31-32, 34-38, 45-46, 49, 64-65, 98, 117-118, 124-125, 127-128, 131, 145, 149, 155, 185-186, 200-201, 203, 206-207, 210-212, 214-216, 233-236, 258-260, 286-287, See also Cross of Christ, Inner Light, and Union
Jones, Rufus M. 40-48, 57, 91, 97, 105-106, 127, 128n17, 138n27, 144, 148-149, 152, 191n37, 193, 195, 205-209, 211-212, 227, 230, 237, 243-244, 251, 280, 285-286
  and mysticism 196-198
  and new Quakerism 198-200
  and inner light 200-201
  and Barclay and Calvin 202-204
  and Cambridge Platonism 204-205
Journals, Quaker 128-129
Justification 103n14, 154, 275

Kataphatic 10n17, 59, 134-135, 163, 172, 239-240, 247-249
Katz, Stephen 29n60, 45
Keith, George 95n8
Kelly, Richard 229-232
Kelly, Thomas 228-234, 237, 244
Kempis, Thomas á 262
Knox, Ronald 268

Law, William 98n11, 278-280
  and Quaker Quietism 280-283
  and Anti-Quaker period 283-285
  and moves toward Quakerism 285-287
  and Quaker holiness 287-290
  and John Wesley 291-292
Lectio Divina 120
Liberalism 1n3, 137-138, 145, 157, 209, 224, 228, 236
Light of Christ, See Inner Light
Littleboy, William 212, 224-228, 237, 244
London Yearly Meeting 136, 149, 151, 165, 166n4, 168, 182-183
Love Mysticism 258-260

Madame Guyon 61n4, 162n1, 186n29, 220, 285n13
Malone, J. Walter 198-199, 232n47, 244n7
Manchester Conference 208, 212, 217, 219
Martyrdom 12, 27-28, 71, 73-74, 270, See also Suffering
Mendicants 72, 261
Methodists 271-280, 291-292
Missionary 22-23, 115, 135-136, See also Evangelism
Modernist Movement 25, 122, 133, 135-138, 173, 198, 208-209, 211, 217-228, 234-236, 242, 244-246, 248
Monasticism 53n91, 103n14, 104, 251, 260-263, 282
Moore, Rosemary 14, 26, 37-38, 43, 50, 66, 72, 89, 91n1, 257
Moravians 93n3, 287, 290-291
Mürren, Switzerland 195
Mystical Theology 4n6, 143, 205, 290
Mysticism 14, 28-32, 37, 41-42, 45, 50, 55, 59-63, 64-69, 84-

Index 317

87, 89-90, 96-97, 105, 107-110, 116, 120, 127-129, 132, 134-135, 143-146, 150-152, 158, 162n1, 185-187, 196-201, 203-207, 211-212, 220-221, 224-237, 240-241, 243-244, 246-247, 249-251, 255-263, 265-266, 269-270, 277-279, 281-283, 286-287, 290-292
   as apophatic 30-32, 95, 157
   as kataphatic 31, 247-249
Mystikos 150n37

Nayler, James 6, 69-74
New Birth 4, 66n17, 99-101, 125-126, 141, See also Perfection and Conversion
New England Yearly Meeting 148n35, 155, 195n1
New Lights 122
Nonjurors 280n8
Nuttall, Geoffrey F. 40-43, 44-45, 265

Ordo Salutis 64, 154
Orthodox 26, 34-38, 82, 89-90, 121, 132-134, 136, 141, 155, 157-158, 164, 195, 242, 245-246, 247
Orthodox-Hicksite Split 116, 121-135

Palmer, Phoebe 162n1, 171
Parousia 18, 48
Pascal, Blaise 269
Peace Testimony 54, 81, 120, 158, 211, 289-290
Pearsall, Robert 173n13, 183n28, 210
Penitents 6n9
Penn, William 28, 53n91, 86, 90, 102-103, 281
Pennsylvania 92
Pentecostalism 22n42, 138n27, 163

Penthos 110n20
Perfectio 151, 153
Perfection 4, 7-9, 14, 32-33, 46, 49, 60-69, 69-75, 77-82, 87, 90, 97, 99-100, 103n14, 119-120, 126, 127, 133, 142-143, 146, 157, 159, 161-163, 164, 205, 228, 233, 243, 246, 251, 255-263, 275-276, 292
Philadelphia 92, 122, 176, 181, 186, 188n32, 192n38, 210, 247
Pietism 9n16, 93n2, 117, 262
Plainness of Dress 110n22, 181, 251, 271, 273, 277, See also Quaker Plainness
Plainness of Speech 110n22, 112, 251, 271, 273, 277, See also Quaker Plainness
Polhill, Edward 51n88
Post-Restoration 24, 38, 89-90
Prayer Meetings 187n30
Programmed Worship 138n26, 239
Punshon, John 19n35, 39, 55-56, 94, 139, 144n32, 192, 198, 251
Puritanism 2-3, 9n16, 12, 15, 20-22, 26n52, 33, 38, 41-43, 44-47, 57, 59-61, 90, 255-260, 266

Quaker Communion 153-154
Quaker Distinctives 145, 247, 251, See also Quaker Plainness
Quaker Plainness 110-111, 120, 247, See also Plainness of Dress, and Plainness of Speech
Quietism 12, 23-25, 42-43, 56-57, 60, 83, 119-120, 123, 134-136, 155, 163, 192, 205, 243, 246-247, 249, 266, 268-270, 277-279, 290-291
   and Anthony Benezet 91-105
   and conversion narratives

128-133
   and Stephen Grellet 105-119
   and William Law 280-283
Ranters 67, 90, 271
Rationalism 122, 124, 132, 204, 212
Recorded Ministry, Abolishment of 228
Restitution 188n33
Revivalism, See Holiness Revival and Anti-Revivalism
Richmond Declaration of Faith 137n25
Roberts, Arthur O. 2, 39, 54-57, 68, 138, 142, 235-237, 251
Robson, Walter 165n5, 171n11, 175-177, 182-183, 240
   and revivalism 177-181
Robson, William 172
Rowntree, John Wilhelm 195-196, 198, 225
Ryle, Canon 174-175

Sacraments 30, 104, 153-154, 179n20, 261n7, 269, 276-277, 283, 285
Salvation 17, 20n38, 23, 32-33, 49, 65, 98-99, 104-105, 118, 127, 130-133, 141-143, 150, 169, 286
Sanctification 10, 19n34, 64-65, 68, 77-78, 82, 93, 98, 103-104, 110, 111n23, 118, 120, 138-140, 142-143, 144n33, 147, 149, 154-156, 162-163, 189-190, 210, 240, 245, 275, See also Perfection
Savery, William 105, 112, 119, 130-132, 134-136
Schism 121-135, 136n23
Scholem, Gershom 37n70, 61nn4-5
Scott, Job 121, 125-128, 135, 287n15
Scripture 14, 15-17, 120, 137, 158, 201, 219-223, 245, 246, 274-275, 285
Second Blessing 139, 189-190, 209-211, See also Baptism of the Spirit
Sectarianism 22n41, 47-48, 93, 115n24, 119, 121, 158
Sermon on the Mount 53, 64
Silence 109, 116, 120, 163, 183, 221, 240-243, 246-248, 276
Simul Justus Et Peccator 9
Sin 61, 65, 68, 70, 72-75, 78, 84n47, 86-87, 103n15, 110n21, 118, 126, 141-142, 169, 203, 220n31, See also Perfection and Salvation
Sine Qua Non 8, 33
Social Justice 22, 93, 95-97, 120, See also John Woollman and Stephen Grellet
Soelle, Dorothee 174-175, 228n42
Sola Fides 11, 63, 82, 105
Song of Songs 258-260
Speculative 10n17, 250
Spirit-Filled/Spirit-Led, See Baptism of the Holy Spirit and Worship
Spiritus Unitas 80
Story, Thomas 58, 83-88, 284
Suffering 14, 27-28, 33, 72-74, 94, 110n22, 120, 197-198, 223n35, 247
Swearing of Oaths 251, 277, 290n18
Synergy 46-47, 126, 251

Telios 4-6, 14, 32
Testimonies 28, 111-112, 118, 156, 158, 247, 277, 285-286, See also Quaker Plainness
The Spirit of Prayer 98-103
Theologia Germanica 59
Theosis 7, 33, 51-52, 127, 147, 151, 204, 206, 236, See also

Divinization
Thomas, Mary 26n49, 178
Trinity 35, 45, 249
Triple Way 6, 20n37
Typology of Spirituality 10-12

Unio Mystica 8, 11, 35, 66, 74, 98-102, 104, See also Deification
Union 3, 43, 44, 49-53, 59, 104, 120, 126-127, 133, 151, 208, 216-217, 236, 247, 249-251, 255-260, 281, 286, See also Mysticism and Perfection
Universal Light, See Inner Light
Universalist 1n2, 36
Unprogrammed Worship 167, 239, See also Silence
Unus Spiritus 30n61, 208, 216, 224, 236, 250, 260
Updegraff, David B. 165n5, 169, 177-179, 180n23, 183n28

Van Ruusbroec, Jan 249
Van Schurmann, Anna Maria 278
Vehiculum Dei 76, 258
Via Negativa 10n17, 30, 42, 53, 97, 111, 115n24, 116, 135, 157, 197, 205, 287
Via Positiva 30, 115n24

Via Triplex 20n37, 63, 115
Visio Dei 8, 256
Von Zinzendorf, Nicholas 93n3

Waldensians 11, 28n56, 261
Waldo, Peter 261
Wesley, John 46, 53-55, 68, 78, 81-82, 87, 96, 97, 116, 118-119, 130, 139-140, 154, 163, 233, 271-283, 287, 291-292
Whitall Smith, Hannah 162n1, 172, 173n13, 178-179, 183-192, 247
Whitefield, George 93, 271, 291
Wilbur, John 148-159, 179n22, 243-243
Wilburites 154-155, 157-159, 176n17, 179-180
Women, Role of 162n1, 269, 276, 283-284
Wood, Herbert.G. 204, 206, 210-211, 213, 221n32, 224-225, 227
Woodbrooke 197, 208, 212-214, 217-218, 224-228
Woolman, John 94, 96n9
Worship 109, 167n7, 170-171, 223, 239-243, 276, See also Silence

Studies in Christian History and Thought
(All titles uniform with this volume)
Dates in bold are of projected publication

David Bebbington
Holiness in Nineteenth-Century England
David Bebbington stresses the relationship of movements of spirituality to changes in their cultural setting, especially the legacies of the Enlightenment and Romanticism. He shows that these broad shifts in ideological mood had a profound effect on the ways in which piety was conceptualized and practised. Holiness was intimately bound up with the spirit of the age.
2000 / 0-85364-981-2 / viii + 98pp

J. William Black
Reformation Pastors
Richard Baxter and the Ideal of the Reformed Pastor
This work examines Richard Baxter's *Gildas Salvianus, The Reformed Pastor* (1656) and explores each aspect of his pastoral strategy in light of his own concern for 'reformation' and in the broader context of Edwardian, Elizabethan and early Stuart pastoral ideals and practice.
2003 / 1-84227-190-3 / xxii + 308pp

James Bruce
Prophecy, Miracles, Angels, *and* Heavenly Light?
The Eschatology, Pneumatology and Missiology of Adomnán's Life of Columba
This book surveys approaches to the marvellous in hagiography, providing the first critique of Plummer's hypothesis of Irish saga origin. It then analyses the uniquely systematized phenomena in the *Life of Columba* from Adomnán's seventh-century theological perspective, identifying the coming of the eschatological Kingdom as the key to understanding.
2004 / 1-84227-227-6 / xviii + 286pp

Colin J. Bulley
The Priesthood of Some Believers
Developments from the General to the Special Priesthood in the Christian Literature of the First Three Centuries
The first in-depth treatment of early Christian texts on the priesthood of all believers shows that the developing priesthood of the ordained related closely to the division between laity and clergy and had deleterious effects on the practice of the general priesthood.
2000 / 1-84227-034-6 / xii + 336pp

Anthony R. Cross (ed.)
Ecumenism and History
Studies in Honour of John H.Y. Briggs

This collection of essays examines the inter-relationships between the two fields in which Professor Briggs has contributed so much: history—particularly Baptist and Nonconformist—and the ecumenical movement. With contributions from colleagues and former research students from Britain, Europe and North America, *Ecumenism and History* provides wide-ranging studies in important aspects of Christian history, theology and ecumenical studies.

2002 / 1-84227-135-0 / xx + 362pp

Maggi Dawn
Confessions of an Inquiring Spirit
Form as Constitutive of Meaning in S.T. Coleridge's Theological Writing

This study of Coleridge's *Confessions* focuses on its confessional, epistolary and fragmentary form, suggesting that attention to these features significantly affects its interpretation. Bringing a close study of these three literary forms, the author suggests ways in which they nuance the text with particular understandings of the Trinity, and of a kenotic christology. Some parallels are drawn between Romantic and postmodern dilemmas concerning the authority of the biblical text.

2006 / 1-84227-255-1 / approx. 224 pp

Ruth Gouldbourne
The Flesh and the Feminine
Gender and Theology in the Writings of Caspar Schwenckfeld

Caspar Schwenckfeld and his movement exemplify one of the radical communities of the sixteenth century. Challenging theological and liturgical norms, they also found themselves challenging social and particularly gender assumptions. In this book, the issues of the relationship between radical theology and the understanding of gender are considered.

2005 / 1-84227-048-6 / approx. 304pp

Crawford Gribben
Puritan Millennialism
Literature and Theology, 1550–1682

Puritan Millennialism surveys the growth, impact and eventual decline of puritan millennialism throughout England, Scotland and Ireland, arguing that it was much more diverse than has frequently been suggested. This Paternoster edition is revised and extended from the original 2000 text.

2007 / 1-84227-372-8 / approx. 320pp

Galen K. Johnson
Prisoner of Conscience
John Bunyan on Self, Community and Christian Faith
This is an interdisciplinary study of John Bunyan's understanding of conscience across his autobiographical, theological and fictional writings, investigating whether conscience always deserves fidelity, and how Bunyan's view of conscience affects his relationship both to modern Western individualism and historic Christianity.
2003 / 1-84227-223-3 / xvi + 236pp

R.T. Kendall
Calvin and English Calvinism to 1649
The author's thesis is that those who formed the Westminster Confession of Faith, which is regarded as Calvinism, in fact departed from John Calvin on two points: (1) the extent of the atonement and (2) the ground of assurance of salvation.
1997 / 0-85364-827-1 / xii + 264pp

Timothy Larsen
Friends of Religious Equality
Nonconformist Politics in Mid-Victorian England
During the middle decades of the nineteenth century the English Nonconformist community developed a coherent political philosophy of its own, of which a central tenet was the principle of religious equality (in contrast to the stereotype of Evangelical Dissenters). The Dissenting community fought for the civil rights of Roman Catholics, non-Christians and even atheists on an issue of principle which had its flowering in the enthusiastic and undivided support which Nonconformity gave to the campaign for Jewish emancipation. This reissued study examines the political efforts and ideas of English Nonconformists during the period, covering the whole range of national issues raised, from state education to the Crimean War. It offers a case study of a theologically conservative group defending religious pluralism in the civic sphere, showing that the concept of religious equality was a grand vision at the centre of the political philosophy of the Dissenters.
2007 / 1-84227-402-3 / x + 300pp

Byung-Ho Moon
Christ the Mediator of the Law
Calvin's Christological Understanding of the Law as the Rule of Living and Life-Giving

This book explores the coherence between Christology and soteriology in Calvin's theology of the law, examining its intellectual origins and his position on the concept and extent of Christ's mediation of the law. A comparative study between Calvin and contemporary Reformers—Luther, Bucer, Melancthon and Bullinger—and his opponent Michael Servetus is made for the purpose of pointing out the unique feature of Calvin's Christological understanding of the law.

2005 / 1-84227-318-3 / approx. 370pp

John Eifion Morgan-Wynne
Holy Spirit and Religious Experience in Christian Writings, c.AD 90–200

This study examines how far Christians in the third to fifth generations (c.AD 90–200) attributed their sense of encounter with the divine presence, their sense of illumination in the truth or guidance in decision-making, and their sense of ethical empowerment to the activity of the Holy Spirit in their lives.

2005 / 1-84227-319-1 / approx. 350pp

James I. Packer
The Redemption and Restoration of Man in the Thought of Richard Baxter

James I. Packer provides a full and sympathetic exposition of Richard Baxter's doctrine of humanity, created and fallen; its redemption by Christ Jesus; and its restoration in the image of God through the obedience of faith by the power of the Holy Spirit.

2002 / 1-84227-147-4 / 432pp

Andrew Partington,
Church and State
The Contribution of the Church of England Bishops to the House of Lords during the Thatcher Years

In *Church and State*, Andrew Partington argues that the contribution of the Church of England bishops to the House of Lords during the Thatcher years was overwhelmingly critical of the government; failed to have a significant influence in the public realm; was inefficient, being undertaken by a minority of those eligible to sit on the Bench of Bishops; and was insufficiently moral and spiritual in its content to be distinctive. On the basis of this, and the likely reduction of the number of places available for Church of England bishops in a fully reformed Second Chamber, the author argues for an evolution in the Church of England's approach to the service of its bishops in the House of Lords. He proposes the Church of England works to overcome the genuine obstacles which hinder busy diocesan bishops from contributing to the debates of the House of Lords and to its life more informally.

2005 / 1-84227-334-5 / approx. 324pp

Michael Pasquarello III
God's Ploughman
Hugh Latimer: A 'Preaching Life' (1490–1555)

This construction of a 'preaching life' situates Hugh Latimer within the larger religious, political and intellectual world of late medieval England. Neither biography, intellectual history, nor analysis of discrete sermon texts, this book is a work of homiletic history which draws from the details of Latimer's milieu to construct an interpretive framework for the preaching performances that formed the core of his identity as a religious reformer. Its goal is to illumine the practical wisdom embodied in the content, form and style of Latimer's preaching, and to recapture a sense of its overarching purpose, movement, and transforming force during the reform of sixteenth-century England.

2006 / 1-84227-336-1 / approx. 250pp

Alan P.F. Sell
Enlightenment, Ecumenism, Evangel
Theological Themes and Thinkers 1550–2000

This book consists of papers in which such interlocking topics as the Enlightenment, the problem of authority, the development of doctrine, spirituality, ecumenism, theological method and the heart of the gospel are discussed. Issues of significance to the church at large are explored with special reference to writers from the Reformed and Dissenting traditions.

2005 / 1-84227-330-2 / xviii + 422pp

Alan P.F. Sell
Hinterland Theology
Some Reformed and Dissenting Adjustments

Many books have been written on theology's 'giants' and significant trends, but what of those lesser-known writers who adjusted to them? In this book some hinterland theologians of the British Reformed and Dissenting traditions, who followed in the wake of toleration, the Evangelical Revival, the rise of modern biblical criticism and Karl Barth, are allowed to have their say. They include Thomas Ridgley, Ralph Wardlaw, T.V. Tymms and N.H.G. Robinson.

2006 / 1-84227-331-0 / approx. 350pp

Alan P.F. Sell and Anthony R. Cross (eds)
Protestant Nonconformity in the Twentieth Century

In this collection of essays scholars representative of a number of Nonconformist traditions reflect thematically on Nonconformists' life and witness during the twentieth century. Among the subjects reviewed are biblical studies, theology, worship, evangelism and spirituality, and ecumenism. Over and above its immediate interest, this collection provides a marker to future scholars and others wishing to know how some of their forebears assessed Nonconformity's contribution to a variety of fields during the century leading up to Christianity's third millennium.

2003 / 1-84227-221-7 / x + 398pp

Mark Smith
Religion in Industrial Society
Oldham and Saddleworth 1740–1865

This book analyses the way British churches sought to meet the challenge of industrialization and urbanization during the period 1740–1865. Working from a case-study of Oldham and Saddleworth, Mark Smith challenges the received view that the Anglican Church in the eighteenth century was characterized by complacency and inertia, and reveals Anglicanism's vigorous and creative response to the new conditions. He reassesses the significance of the centrally directed church reforms of the mid-nineteenth century, and emphasizes the importance of local energy and enthusiasm. Charting the growth of denominational pluralism in Oldham and Saddleworth, Dr Smith compares the strengths and weaknesses of the various Anglican and Nonconformist approaches to promoting church growth. He also demonstrates the extent to which all the churches participated in a common culture shaped by the influence of evangelicalism, and shows that active co-operation between the churches rather than denominational conflict dominated. This revised and updated edition of Dr Smith's challenging and original study makes an important contribution both to the social history of religion and to urban studies.

2006 / 1-84227-335-3 / approx. 300pp

Martin Sutherland
Peace, Toleration and Decay
The Ecclesiology of Later Stuart Dissent

This fresh analysis brings to light the complexity and fragility of the later Stuart Nonconformist consensus. Recent findings on wider seventeenth-century thought are incorporated into a new picture of the dynamics of Dissent and the roots of evangelicalism.

2003 / 1-84227-152-0 / xxii + 216pp

G. Michael Thomas
The Extent of the Atonement
A Dilemma for Reformed Theology from Calvin to the Consensus

A study of the way Reformed theology addressed the question, 'Did Christ die for all, or for the elect only?', commencing with John Calvin, and including debates with Lutheranism, the Synod of Dort and the teaching of Moïse Amyraut.

1997 / 0-85364-828-X / x + 278pp

David M. Thompson
Baptism, Church and Society in Britain from the Evangelical Revival to *Baptism, Eucharist and Ministry*

The theology and practice of baptism have not received the attention they deserve. How important is faith? What does baptismal regeneration mean? Is baptism a bond of unity between Christians? This book discusses the theology of baptism and popular belief and practice in England and Wales from the Evangelical Revival to the publication of the World Council of Churches' consensus statement on *Baptism, Eucharist and Ministry* (1982).

2005 / 1-84227-393-0 / approx. 224pp

Mark D. Thompson
A Sure Ground on Which to Stand
The Relation of Authority and Interpretive Method of Luther's Approach to Scripture

The best interpreter of Luther is Luther himself. Unfortunately many modern studies have superimposed contemporary agendas upon this sixteenth-century Reformer's writings. This fresh study examines Luther's own words to find an explanation for his robust confidence in the Scriptures, a confidence that generated the famous 'stand' at Worms in 1521.

2004 / 1-84227-145-8 / xvi + 322pp

Carl R. Trueman and R.S. Clark (eds)
Protestant Scholasticism
Essays in Reassessment

Traditionally Protestant theology, between Luther's early reforming career and the dawn of the Enlightenment, has been seen in terms of decline and fall into the wastelands of rationalism and scholastic speculation. In this volume a number of scholars question such an interpretation. The editors argue that the development of post-Reformation Protestantism can only be understood when a proper historical model of doctrinal change is adopted. This historical concern underlies the subsequent studies of theologians such as Calvin, Beza, Olevian, Baxter, and the two Turrentini. The result is a significantly different reading of the development of Protestant Orthodoxy, one which both challenges the older scholarly interpretations and clichés about the relationship of Protestantism to, among other things, scholasticism and rationalism, and which demonstrates the fruitfulness of the new, historical approach.

1999 / 0-85364-853-0 / xx + 344pp

Shawn D. Wright
Our Sovereign Refuge
The Pastoral Theology of Theodore Beza

Our Sovereign Refuge is a study of the pastoral theology of the Protestant reformer who inherited the mantle of leadership in the Reformed church from John Calvin. Countering a common view of Beza as supremely a 'scholastic' theologian who deviated from Calvin's biblical focus, Wright uncovers a new portrait. He was not a cold and rigid academic theologian obsessed with probing the eternal decrees of God. Rather, by placing him in his pastoral context and by noting his concerns in his pastoral and biblical treatises, Wright shows that Beza was fundamentally a committed Christian who was troubled by the vicissitudes of life in the second half of the sixteenth century. He believed that the biblical truth of the supreme sovereignty of God alone could support Christians on their earthly pilgrimage to heaven. This pastoral and personal portrait forms the heart of Wright's argument.

2004 / 1-84227-252-7 / xviii + 308pp

Paternoster
9 Holdom Avenue,
Bletchley,
Milton Keynes MK1 1QR,
United Kingdom
Web: www.authenticmedia.co.uk/paternoster

www.ingramcontent.com/pod-product-compliance
Lightning Source LLC
Chambersburg PA
CBHW071152300426
44113CB00009B/1181